OUT
OF
THE
SHADOWS
The Life of Millicent Baxter

Penny Griffith

Out of the Shadows - The Life of Millicent Baxter

Copyright © 2015 Penny Griffith 2015

First Published: October 2015 by
PenPublishing - http://www.penpublishing.co.nz
Wellington, New Zealand
Reprinted November 2015

ISBN 978-0-473-33510-6

Designed and typeset by PenPublishing

Printed by: Printing.Com Wellington, New Zealand

Publication of this book was assisted by a grant from The Peace and Disarmament Education Trust, Department of Internal Affairs Te Tari Taiwhenua, Wellington.

Cover design by Torsten Sohrmann - www.buch-gewand.de

Contents

Acknowledgements

The list is far too long to mention all the people who have been involved over these six long years from conception of this biography to its birth. Then towards the end of the gestation period I made the decision to have a home birth and produce my baby myself - so my dependence on people to help me learn the necessary new programmes became increasing large as deadlines approached.

But my heartfelt thanks go to those tireless academics who helped me in my research: to Paul Millar, Bruce Harding and John Newtown at the University of Canterbury; Lydia Wevers and Steven Loveridge at the University of Victoria; Kevin Clements and Lawrence Jones at the University of Otago; staff at the Hocken Library in Dunedin, the Macmillan Brown Library, the Beckenham Library in Christchurch and the Alexander Turnbull Library. And to the staff at the Central Library in Wellington (where I occupied a desk every weekday for two years); the National Library in London and the Newnham College Library at the University of Cambridge. Thanks also to Wellington historians David Grant, Ray Grover, Michael Kelly, and Margaret Lovell-Smith, the excellent biographer of Helen Connon.

Many thanks to all the people I interviewed, particularly including: the publisher of The Memoirs of Millicent Baxter, the inimitable Dame Christine Cole Catley (now deceased); Elsie Gill's granddaughter Rosamund McCreadie and her step-father Don Lawson; Millicent and Archie's neighbour at Kuri Bush, George McIntosh; Millicent and Archie's close Catholic friends and advisors, Frances Mulrennan and Shirley McLeod, Cecily McNeill Jim Neilan and Stuart Sellar; Toni Wilson of the Dunedin Naturalists Field Club where Millicent virtually ruled the roost until she died; Dunedin Librarian Mary Ronnie, Wynn Greeves (ninety-three when I interviewed her, the only woman I met who had known Millicent as a fairly young woman}. My very grateful thanks also to all others I interviewed including Max Broadbent, Paul Donovan, Ray Edwards, Pamela Gordon, Jan Kelly, Richard Hatherly, Megan Hutching, Peter Low, Pauline Mahalski, Paul Oestreicher, Sally Page, Mary Ronnie and Redmar Yska.

I give very special thanks to the Baxter and Macmillan Brown families: Archie and Millicent's son Terence Baxter, his wife Lenore (now deceased), his daughters Katherine and Helen and his son Kenneth; James K. Baxter's son John; Archie's nieces Diane Dore, Clarice Holland and Margaret Gibson; Archie's great-nephew Barry Baxter and great-niece Linda MacKenzie, and to Millicent's niece Antonietta Baldacchino. I'm indebted to Bob Kerr who allowed me to use some of his masterly paintings he prepared for an exhibition on Archie Baxter and Mark Briggs. Also to Paul Donovan and Gary Blackman, two professional photographers who so generously donated their photographs, and to Jo Hickey who managed to

Acknowledgements

photograph me for the back cover one windy Wellington day. And a special thank you to Torsten Sohrmann who designed the book cover so skillfully, and to Sara and Mark Hearne for the website.

Also, my gratitude goes to the Peace and Disarmament Education Trust, Department of Internal Affairs Te Tari Taiwhenua for two grants.

Finally, but of course not least, there are my dear friends and family who never failed to ask how the book was going and to those who even foolishly offered to proofread draft chapters of the book: Felicity Cuzens, Steven Loveridge, Bill Griffith, Cecily McNeill and Geoff Walker. And to those who offered very sound, and very necessary, technical advice: Peter Farrell, Suzie Griffith, Phillip Griffith, Geoff Palmer, Torsten Sohrmann and Stephen Stocks.

I am also hugely grateful to my proof reader and copy-editor Georgina Christensen for her eagle eye and for her valuable suggestions, many of which have been incorporated into this book. I take full responsibility for any errors that might remain.

But… my greatest thanks are to Millicent Baxter.

Introduction

This book began life six years ago when I decided to write a biography of Annie Mary Anne Henley Rogers, the first woman to graduate from Oxford University.[1] I was about to begin my research when a friend in Dunedin asked rather haughtily 'And why aren't you writing a biography of the first woman to attend a New Zealand University?' A much better idea, I thought, and discovered Helen Connon. But an excellent biography had just been written about Helen Connon, so I found her daughter, Millicent Macmillan Brown, instead.

Throughout her ninety-six years of life, Millicent Baxter was surrounded by fame, or at least by figures of great prominence in New Zealand. Her mother was the first woman in the British Empire to earn a degree with honours. Her father was John Macmillan Brown, one of the founding professors of the University of Canterbury and Chancellor of the University of New Zealand, an irascible and difficult man with boundless enthusiasm who expected nothing less from his family and students. Much of my research in Christchurch was done in the Macmillan Brown Library at the University of Canterbury beneath stern and lofty stares from the portraits of John Macmillan Brown and Helen Connon.

Millicent's husband, Archibald Baxter, is New Zealand's most renowned World War One conscientious objector. He endured shocking brutality during the war years in New Zealand, England and at the Front. Her son, James K. Baxter, is arguably the country's most celebrated poet and was a pacifist himself until his premature death at forty-six in 1972. Terence, the older son, still alive at ninety-three at the time of writing, shares his mother's lack of fame. He is known because of his father and brother but also has a story to tell as a man transformed by his experiences of being imprisoned as a 'conchie' in World War Two.

Far from being overwhelmed by the fame of her parents, husband and son, Millicent was a forceful and sometimes daunting character with a crushing wit, lucid intellect and sharp political mind. She was offered an MA honours degree at the University of Cambridge and became a leading promoter of pacifism in New Zealand at a time when women just did not do such things. A strongly independent young woman, she defied her controlling father and turned her back on a life of privilege and prosperity to live with a poor rabbiter from the backblocks of Otago, a remote part of New Zealand's South Island, a man who had been ostracised by society for his pacifist beliefs. How she and Archie Baxter met is an extraordinary love story. Millicent became the pivot and driving force of her husband and sons' lives, and in some ways they lived in *her* shadow.

Some literature has been written about Archie and a vast amount about James K., but apart from her own selective memoirs, little has been published about Millicent and most of that only as an adjunct to James and Archie. Her memoirs are reserved and incomplete. Even her family was disappointed by them, feeling that the real Millicent didn't emerge.

In 2008 under the unfaltering eye of Paul Millar, today's rock of knowledge on James K. Baxter, I wrote a paper on the poet's mother, Millicent Baxter, for my BA Honours degree at the University of Canterbury in Christchurch. The suggestion was then made that I should make pacifism and the Baxter family the subject of an MA at the University of Victoria in Wellington. Sadly, the Christchurch earthquakes and eventual destruction of my home made this too difficult a task for me to continue. But good usually emerges from bad, and rather than finishing the degree, I started writing a book on this remarkable woman.

My initial idea for this book was a biography of Millicent to give more prominence to this remarkable New Zealander. But Archie, Terence and James loom too large to be mere appendages to Millicent, and pacifism is a strong link between the four of them. So, while Millicent firmly holds pride of place, Archie, James and Terence feature strongly. As there is a wealth of material written about James, this book includes only a precis of his extraordinary life while bringing to the fore his complicated relationship with his mother. Similarly, because Archie's war story is well-known to many people from his own book *We will not cease*, the recent film *Field Punishment No 1* (2014) and the proposed memorial in Dunedin to him and other New Zealand conscientious objectors, I include only a brief outline of his atrocious experiences in the army, focusing instead on what the book and film omitted: his personal background and his marriage to Millicent. Because little has been penned about Terence, I have given a lot of attention to this unusual and self-effacing man. I have also given weight to Millicent and Archie's pacifism and the effect it had on their two sons and many other members of the Baxter family.

There have been problems, as there are for all biographers. Millicent, Archie and James died in decades past, and I met none of them. Neither are there friends or relatives remaining who knew Millicent and Archie in their early years. Millicent and Archie are now beginning to fade from memory into history. Of the four subjects of this book, Terence is the only one I have personally interviewed and is, therefore, extremely important. This is reflected in the text that includes extracts from the large numbers of interviews made with him in 1995 by Paul Millar and by myself from 2010 onwards. He is now in his nineties and was swimming and riding his bike until very recently, but his recollections of his parents and brother are diminishing. James's wife, Jacquie Baxter, died before I could meet her, and I had only one interview with Terence's ex-wife, Lenore Baxter, for two hours. She passed away the following week. Of course there are Millicent's and Archie's memoirs and they have become my bibles. But Archie's memoir, *We will not cease*[2], is a blow-by-shocking-blow of his army experiences and tells nothing of his life before or after. Millicent's memoirs are almost all about the people around her, little about her and almost nothing about war or politics. For both of them, I can only speculate on their views of what they *don't* write about. At times, the writing of this book has been like staring into the blank of the past, but through a myriad of papers and books and interviews with people who knew her, I believe I have found the real Millicent, not just the loquacious, daunting, unemotional Millicent. Archie was easier to discover and it is difficult not to love this quiet and humble man with his unswerving conviction in his beliefs combined with his total absence of bitterness. I have often found myself longing to sit down at a dinner table with him and ask, 'If everyone in Britain and New Zealand had been a pacifist like you, how would the outcomes have been different?' And I would ask, 'What *really* made you become a pacifist, Archie?' What was it about the speech from a pacifist on his soapbox that day in Dunedin in 1899?

There are some clues, but clues are not answers. Often, I surmise and speculate, and I have endeavoured to make it plain when I do so. I have shared many cups of coffee with Terence and thoroughly enjoyed the company of this beautifully spoken, genuine and gentlemanly man. Often we would talk on the phone; the most reliable time to catch him was after midnight: he rarely went to bed before 3am! When we met, we always had to go to a cafe; he would never let me inside his house where I thought I might have discovered little bits of forgotten evidence of his parents – as with his mother, housekeeping is not a priority. So to 'find' Archie, Millicent and James K., I have undertaken over a hundred interviews with present members of the Baxter family and friends who knew them well, and this has aided me greatly to piece together the fragments of the puzzle. There have, however, been biographies written on Helen Connon and James K., and for much of the biographical material on the family background, I have drawn frequently on Frank McKay's The Life of James K. Baxter; Paul Millar's Spark to a Waiting Fuse: James K. Baxter's Correspondence with Noel Ginn, 1942-46; Margaret Lovell-Smith's Easily the Best – The life of Helen Connon, 1857– 1903 and of course Millicent's The Memoirs of Millicent Baxter.

Lastly I would like to say what a privilege it has been for me to tell this story. I'm far from being a patient person, but throughout the six years of research and writing never has there been a single day when I have thought 'Oh no, not the Baxters!' It truly has been an honour to unearth the story of this exceptional woman, her family, and the effects they had on one another, on New Zealand and, in some ways, the world.

Penny Griffith
Wellington, New Zealand
October 2015.

Foreword –
by Professor Kevin Clements

In the Dictionary of New Zealand Biography there is a single-word entry under the heading of Baxter, Millicent Amiel 1888 –1984. Not 'daughter of the famous Helen Connon' or 'daughter of the revered John Macmillan Brown', not 'the mother of two sons' (one, the most famous poet in the country), simply 'Pacifist.' In writing this foreword, I will focus on the passion in Millicent Baxter's adult life – pacifism in New Zealand.

New Zealand is one of five white-settler societies, the others being Australia, Canada, South Africa and the United States. It was colonised and settled during the heyday of British colonialism in the mid-nineteenth century. Modern New Zealand therefore has been profoundly influenced by British interests, persuasion and force. For example, the New Zealand wars of the late nineteenth century resulted in the forced expropriation of land from Maori to the British Crown, the negative legacy of which continues to blight Maori–Pakeha relations today.

From 1840 onwards, British settlers developed the small colony economically, politically and militarily. During this period the New Zealand government managed its own domestic affairs, but foreign and defence policies were the preserve of the British government. Where Britain went, New Zealand went. It was taken for granted that New Zealand was an antipodean outpost of Britain and that there was a convergence of defence and security interests between both countries. So when Britain got embroiled in the Boer wars in the late 1890s, it was expected that New Zealand troops would join imperial forces in fighting the Boers, and we did. This later led to the introduction in 1909 of compulsory military training for all boys and men over the age of eleven. Then in the First World War, New Zealand was asked by the United Kingdom to support the imperial war effort whenever necessary by developing a military force to supplement that of the UK itself. Once again New Zealand fell into line and we agreed to provide a quota of troops to be incorporated into the imperial war machine.

Because of the vagaries of the international date line, New Zealand declared war on Germany before the United Kingdom, on 3 September 1939, with the New Zealand Prime Minister Michael Savage saying 'both with gratitude for the past and with confidence in the future, New Zealand joins Britain in declaring war against Germany. Where she goes, we go; where she stands, we stand.' This mindset of serving King and Country was taken for granted by most New Zealanders. Historians studying First World War diaries of New Zealand soldiers do not find evidence of them fighting for freedom or democracy. They fought to demonstrate that 'colonials' could pull their weight with the 'mother country' in defending the British Empire.

Throughout its history, however, what the New Zealand government could not guarantee was a free flow of volunteers to fight in all these wars, even in the first phase of British colonisation and the New Zealand wars. This meant that it had to introduce conscription to ensure white recruits to the Crown. The Militia Ordinance Act of 1845, for example, required able-bodied non-Māori men who were British subjects aged between eighteen and sixty to make themselves available for training or service near their own settlements. This was the first indication in New Zealand that in order to achieve and maintain a 'monopoly of force and coercive capacity' the state had the right to recruit young men into the military. This policy was reiterated in the Militia Act 1858, which re-introduced conscription during the New Zealand wars. These Acts were the first pieces of legislation in NZ that confirmed the New Zealand government's right and capacity to coerce individuals into military training and military service.

Because of the conflation between British and imperial patriotic interests there was little questioning of these acts and regulations. It was assumed that the price of citizenship was a willingness to serve for God, King/Queen and Country. As John Stuart Mill put it 'War is an ugly thing, but not the ugliest of things. The decayed and degraded state of moral and patriotic feeling which thinks that nothing is worth war is much worse. The person who has nothing for which he is willing to fight, nothing which is more important than his own personal safety, is a miserable creature and has no chance of being free unless made and kept so by the exertions of better men than himself.'[3] It was in response to this kind of attitude that courageous individuals in New Zealand and other parts of the Empire started wondering about where to draw the line in relation to the rights of the individual and the rights of the state. They contemplated whether there were things that the state might request which were offensive to individual conscience and therefore had to be resisted.

In relation to killing on behalf of the state, the traditional peace churches – the Quakers, Mennonites and Church of the Brethren for example – had long argued that the Old and New Testament injunctions not to kill should apply to states as well as individuals. George Fox, for example, in his Quaker Peace Testimony to King Charles II in 1660 said 'We utterly deny all outward wars and strife and fightings with outward weapons, for any end or under any pretense whatsoever. And this is our testimony to the whole world. The spirit of Christ... which leads us into all Truth, will never move us to fight and war against any man with outward weapons, neither for the kingdom of Christ nor for the kingdoms of this world.'[4]
It was this Testimony that fuelled what some think of as the first resistance to militarism in New Zealand. Thomas Mason and his sons from Taita, near Wellington, were Quakers with a religious commitment to pacifism and nonviolence. They

objected to enlisting in the militia in 1864 and, indeed, any efforts to forcibly conscript individual citizens into the military. Their logic was simple: if there is a biblical injunction against violence and killing then that had to take priority over state demands for obedience to military authority. This position has powered the peace testimonies of all the so-called historic peace churches. This is why members of these churches have been given some privileges in relation to their conscientious objection to military service. Those who are not members of these churches, however, have had to argue the case for why personal conscience should prevail against state authority. These individuals have been forced to argue their personal conscientious objection to military service on religious, political or humanitarian grounds.

The first systematic assault on militarism in New Zealand was resistance to the CMT legislation of 1909. This was opposed by pacifist religious leaders, socialists, feminist and humanistic pacifist groups who claimed that the legislation denied civil liberties and would lead to the militarization of the nation's youth. The emerging New Zealand Labour Party opposed the legislation on both political and humanitarian grounds. Irish New Zealanders, for example, could see no reason why they should fight for a British Crown overseas when they were under British occupation at home. Little by little, a significant minority of New Zealanders chose to resist recruitment into what they saw as the 'sharp end' of British imperialism. It was into this environment that Archibald Baxter and other New Zealand pacifists took their stand in refusing military service and refused to put on the uniform when drafted into the First World War.

There was little political oxygen available for those who opposed the call to arms. Conscientious objectors were ostracized and dismissed as dangerous 'cranks', unpatriotic and subversive. They had little support in a community that was dedicated to beating war drums, activating patriotic and xenophobic propaganda and which felt that there was some divine right in being British and colonizing the world. But as the First World War ground on, the situation became particularly problematic in relation to the industrial-scale slaughter that occurred. This war consumed youth from all across the British Empire. It was clear that the New Zealand government could not meet its commitment to the imperial war effort, and it had to introduce conscription to ensure enough soldiers for the front lines. The Military Service Act of 1916 required the registration of non-Māori men aged between twenty and forty-six. These groups were sorted into two divisions – the unmarried or recently married, and everyone else. In 1917 the act was extended to include Māori – though conscription was only imposed on Tainui Māori. No Māori conscripts served overseas. A total of about 135,000 men were conscripted during the First World War and about 32,000 of these eventually served in the war, compared to almost 70,000 who volunteered. This conscription campaign aroused strong opposition and two large anti-conscription conferences were held during 1916, representing the radical-labour movement, Irish republicans and pacifist groups. Māori who had opposed the Crown during the land wars of the nineteenth century, such as the Waikato and Tuhoe tribes, also resisted conscription and about a hundred were arrested. Only Quakers, Christadelphinians and, later, Seventh-day Adventists were automatically exempted from military service. Most other conscientious objectors were imprisoned for up to two years with hard labour and sometimes were returned to prison if they still refused to go to war.

Fourteen especially determined conscientious objectors were forcibly shipped overseas and faced severe punishments on the front lines in Belgium and France – this was the group that included Archibald Baxter. Archie Baxter was undoubtedly affected by the political ferment occurring all around him but was convinced by a Marxist lawyer that all war was morally untenable and the First World War was a graphic illustration of imperial rivalry for power, possessions and colonies. As you will see from his story in this book, however, the New Zealand government wanted total submission from its able-bodied male population and dissenters such as Baxter and the others were considered huge patriotic nuisances. As Penny highlights, the Government's treatment of conscientious objectors during the First World War would now be considered cruel and inhuman punishment. They lost their civil rights, were tortured and punished beyond belief on the front lines of the war, and socially and political harassed on their return home. Baxter's stand was well captured by his son and poet James K Baxter who said:

> When I was only semen in a gland
> Or less than that, my father hung
> From a torture post at Mud Farm
> Because he would not kill. The guards
> Fried sausages, and as the snow came darkly
> I feared a death by cold in the cold groin
> And plotted revolution. His black and swollen thumbs
> Explained the brotherhood of man,
> But he is old now in his apple garden
> And we have seen our strong Antaeus die
> In the glass castle of the bureaucracies
> Robbing our bread of salt. Shall Marx and Christ
> Share beds this side of Jordan? I set now
> Unwillingly these words down:
> Political action in its source is pure,
> Human, direct, but in its civil function
> Becomes the jail it laboured to destroy.[5]

This book reflects on mobilisation, war and resistance to war through the lens of Millicent Macmillan Brown and Archie Baxter. Theirs is a love story but it's also a story about the ways in which ordinary individuals make courageous decisions and do courageous things in order that the rest of us do not have to fight their battles all over again. This is not meant to imply that Archie and Millicent garnered enough popular support before and during the Second World War to make conscription impossible. On the contrary, the second Labour Government passed the National Service Emergency Regulations in 1940 to re-introduce conscription. What these two people and others did manage to do, however, was to ensure that the treatment of Second World War conscientious objectors was a little more humane than those who resisted the First World War. None were taken to the front lines, and none were tortured and broken as happened during the First War. So the treatment meted out to Baxter and the other thirteen 'hard core' resisters was widely recognized as unacceptable even though it took another thirty to forty years to generate a greater sensibility in New Zealand to the unacceptability of war as a means of resolving conflict.

Opposition to the Vietnam War, the development of a national anti-nuclear policy and growing resistance to foreign adventures indicate just how far New Zealand has come since the nineteenth century. But we would not have got where we are without the quiet and determined positions of people like Archibald and Millicent Baxter. It was Margaret Mead who said 'Never doubt that a small group of thoughtful, committed people can change the world. Indeed, it is the only thing that ever has.'

This book is about two such thoughtful and committed people who did change the world through profoundly heroic acts at a time when heroism was seen as the preserve of the military. Archie and Millicent's story reminds us that political power depends on the willing compliance of the people. When this compliance is not forthcoming the state can see its coercive capacity disappearing, which is why it has always reacted so negatively to those who conscientiously object to war or who resist state authority.

But as Penny so eloquently argues, people can only take such bold and unpopular stands when they are in a loving relationship; when they have the support of family and close friends; when there are groups, organisations and parties who understand that our freedom does not rest on unquestioning obedience to authority but a willingness to radically resist, especially where the demands of the state and personal conscience are at odds with each other.

This is a book that must be read by many so that we understand what is needed to be fully human in a world that is often hostile to realising common humanity. Out of love stories come political stories and out of these come political and social change. There is a lovely poem by William Stafford that sums this up very clearly:

Objector

In line at lunch I cross my fork and spoon
to ward off complicity–the ordered life
our leaders have offered us.
Thin as a knife,

our chance to live depends on such a sign
while others talk and The Pentagon from the moon
is bouncing exact commands: "Forget your faith;
be ready for whatever it takes to win: we face
annihilation unless all citizens get in line."

I bow and cross my fork and spoon: somewhere
other citizens more fearfully bow
in a place terrorized by their kind of oppressive state.
Our signs both mean, "You hostages over there
will never be slaughtered by my act."
Our vows cross: never to kill and call it fate.[6]

Kevin Clements, Director
National Centre for Peace and Conflict Studies
University of Otago
Dunedin, New Zealand (July 2015)

Prologue – The Letter

On a clear crisp day in the middle of the winter of 1918, life changes suddenly and completely for Millicent Macmillan Brown. A knock on the door interrupts her daydreaming in the lounge of her father's huge house that overlooks the sprawling plains from Christchurch to the Southern Alps.

She is handed a typewritten copy of a letter from Archibald Baxter to his parents in a remote part of Otago in New Zealand. The letter has taken nearly four months to travel from the battlefront at Ypres. She skims over the sheet of paper, but soon she is riveted. The words of rage tempered with charity fly from the page: 'I have suffered to the limit of my endurance, but I will never in my sane senses surrender to the evil power that has fixed its roots like a cancer on the world… But you will be glad to know that I have met with a great many men who have shown me the greatest kindness.' The letter is an epiphany for Millicent. This man Archie Baxter instantly captivates her and she must meet him. The destiny of the professor's daughter and the poor rabbiter is sealed.

PART ONE
Child to Woman

CHAPTER 1

The College Idol and the God Professor

Millicent's life began on 8 January 1888 in Christchurch and ended ninety-six years later in a hospital bed in Dunedin.

Millicent's parents, Helen Connon and John Macmillan Brown, ensured her start in life was one of privilege. Helen's excellent salary as principal of Christchurch Girls' High School paid most of the household expenses, allowing John Macmillan Brown to amass a small fortune by investing the money he made from the students who swamped his lecture theatres.[7] Both parents had outstanding academic careers. Helen held the extraordinary position of being the first woman in the British Empire to gain an honours degree, while John was Professor of English and Classics at Canterbury College and is renowned for navigating the fledgling College to the forefront of higher education in New Zealand.

Helen Connon's short but brilliant life started on 16 January 1857, or so we think. There is no surviving official record of her birth. There are also no recorded accounts of her early life.[8] Her daughter Millicent, always a pedant for accuracy, says in her memoirs that Helen was born in 1860,[9] but she also told Bruce Harding that her mother always took two years off her age.[10] Helen was remarkably silent about her background, which leaves us to wonder if her silence was due to the family's shame of their humble beginnings, or if the Connons were simply a reticent family. Consequently, much has to be construed, not necessarily very reliably, from family stories and from an impassioned biography written about Helen by a friend Edith Searle, later Edith Searle Grossmann, who used information gained from Helen's sisters and mother.[11] [12] It is widely accepted that Grossmann's biography of Helen is somewhat gushing and tends towards exaggeration in the descriptions of her subject. For example, she describes Helen as 'Dea certe' – a phrase which means 'assuredly a goddess.'[13] However, that tended to be the writing style of the day, and Grossmann does give a rare first-hand account of Helen Connon. In the absence of very much information on Helen's history, Margaret Lovell-Smith's 2004 biography of Helen has quoted Grossmann many times while pointing out the unreliability of some of Grossmann's claims.

Although all known records list Helen's Welsh-born father, George Connon, as either a carpenter or a builder, according to Millicent in her memoirs, he seems to have had a colourful start in life. Helen's father was born in India. His father was an officer in the East India Company, risen from the ranks. According to Millicent 'He died and his widow came home bringing the child [George]. The unfortunate woman died on the wharf at Liverpool and the child was brought up by an uncle.'[14] This story may be a fiction; Millicent's 93 year-old memory wasn't always accurate, and Margaret Lovell-Smith in her biography on Helen Connon maintains that George's father was a gardener.[15]

George eventually became a carpenter and took opportunities when he saw them. One of his decisions was to marry Edinburgh-born Helen Hart, which he did in July 1854. If George's past was colourful, his wife's was vivid – if we can believe the compelling family legend that Millicent relates that Helen Hart was the love-child of Lord William Murray Nairne, the son of Lady Nairne of Perthshire. Nairne was an Oxford graduate who seduced one of his mother's maids then insisted on marrying her, a very unusual thing to do for those times. As a result he was disinherited and earned his living by tutoring. He educated his sons but not his daughter Helen, who became maid companion to her grandmother, Lady Nairne.[16]

It's not known how Helen Hart and George Connon met, but shortly after

Collins Street, Melbourne in the 1850s, etching by unidentified artist Ref: State Library of Victoria,H92.301/128

their wedding in 1854 the couple joined the multitudes bound for the goldfields in Australia. They travelled 107 days on board the Constant as assisted migrants, arriving in Melbourne in February 1855. The first flush of gold fever had abated, but there was still plenty of work for a carpenter. A year later their first son, George, was

born and family records indicate that their first daughter, Helen, was born on 16 January 1857.[17] Young Helen spent her first three years in the Melbourne suburb of Fitzroy. Melbourne's huge growth at that time had resulted in overpopulation and unemployment. After the birth of John in 1861, the family moved a hundred and twenty kilometres inland and joined the 31,000 gold prospectors who had found 131 tons of gold at the imposing town of Castlemaine.[18] Many churches and schools, a substantial brick railway station, gracious residences and ornate hotels were being built, and George would have been fully occupied. But it was his wife who was the driving force of the family – a restless woman and a devoted Presbyterian. A photograph shows a long, strong and intelligent face.[19] The Scots laid great store by learning, and Helen Connon senior believed vehemently in education for females. If Millicent's story about the Lord Nairne connection is true, perhaps Helen Hart was getting back at her grandfather for not educating his daughters. In any event, it was her obsession for education for females that would place young Helen on the stepladder to her academic career.

After nearly nine years in Australia, the Connon family found themselves clustered together on a crowded Melbourne wharf anxiously venturing into another life in yet another country. The family now numbered seven, including one-year-old Martha and grandmother Ellen Hart who had joined them from Scotland. They had decided to follow the flood of gold-seekers to Otago, New Zealand, at the peak of the gold rush there. Whale and seal products, flax as well as kauri timber and gum had all been highly successful exports, but gold had surged to the top of the list in the middle of the century. As they waited to board the Lawrence Brown, five-year-old Helen's teacher came down to the wharf to farewell the family. He had so much faith in his pupil's potential he urgently told her mother to 'Never grudge any trouble that is taken for that child's education; she will repay everything that is done for her.'[20] He turned out to be so very right.

The tall sailing ship landed in Port Chalmers, the port of Dunedin, in November 1863. In that year alone 37,000 people had swarmed into the town, and industrially and commercially Dunedin had now become the first city in the new colony. The family settled close to the corner of Albany and George Streets. New Zealand's first university was founded in that area six years later with the wealth that had poured in from the goldfields. Dunedin was starting to develop the infrastructure of what would become an impressive city but, despite its grandiose appearance, it

Princes Street, Dunedin.
Ref: Alexander Turnbull Library 1/4-002689.

had an underbelly of poor sanitation and ill health. The poorest people were living in tents and child mortality was higher than in England. The Connons lived in a low-lying damp area and they were heartbroken when baby Martha died of scarlet fever in 1864. A year and a half later, six year-old John died of croup. Both are buried in the Southern Cemetery. It was an awful few years with more family deaths leaving George and Helen with only their two eldest children – their namesakes.

During their time in Dunedin, young Helen went to North Dunedin School, 'the old stone school' in Union Street, and her parents paid four shillings a quarter for her classes in reading and writing. Since she was clearly such a bright student, they may also have paid six shillings per quarter for additional subjects such as geography.[21] This together with brother George's fees would have fully stretched the Connon finances. Although Helen was the eldest girl and her help was much needed at home, her mother was prepared to make that sacrifice for her daughter's education.[22] It seems that Helen was a model child. In the eyes of her sister Maria, she was 'the recognised flower of our flock'[23], and she made an impression on any adults she met. Her father was especially attached to Helen. A young, enthusiastic and dedicated teacher called Robert Stout, who appears in this story several times, taught Helen at this time. A Scotsman from the Shetland Islands, Robert would often play with the children at lunchtimes and place a sweet on each pupil's desk; with 80 pupils, that was a generous act. He taught for two hours in the evenings at night-school during the winter and Latin in the mornings. In December 1865, during her time with Robert, Helen was awarded a volume of Longfellow's poems, for best general marks in the girls' first class, division two.[24] Helen would keep in touch with Robert Stout all her life. Later, he was knighted as Chief Justice and also became Premier of New Zealand.

The gold rush in Dunedin peaked in 1864 with 10,000 gold miners but plunged to fewer than 6000 by 1867. The Connon family was on the move yet again, probably in early 1866. This time it was to Hokitika on the West Coast where gold had been discovered in late 1864[25].

Hokitika c 1869
Ref: Alexander Turnbull Library A-104-025

The family stayed here for about eleven years and this became young Helen's most settled period. Hokitika was a rough mining town with 102 hotels to entertain the 37,000 inhabitants who had come from all corners of the world chasing 'the colour.' The pubs were permitted to remain open twenty-four hours a day. Horseracing, ice-skating and cricket were popular and vaudeville entertainers, gymnastic troupes and ventriloquists performed at the newly opened Prince of Wales Opera House. By 1867 there were a variety of churches: Wesleyan, Roman Catholic, Anglican and Presbyterian as well as a Jewish synagogue.[26]

The Connons lived in Tancred Street where George had a workshop as well as a house. It was just one block away from the hectic high street that was sandwiched between ocean and river. The mighty Southern Alps provided a stunning backdrop. For nine-year-old Helen it must have been a beautiful, exciting but very forbidding place to live. The river constantly flooded the town, and she would probably have been among the crowds that gathered to watch the ships negotiate the infamous sandbar. Five ships were wrecked there the year they arrived. Despite that, 50 coastal vessels arrived every month in 1867 and, for a brief time, Hokitika was the busiest port in the colony.[27]

Helen was able to attend a school run by Archdeacon Henry Harper who arrived in Hokitika at the same time as the Connon family. She was soon at the top of the girls' class and was winning prizes. It is likely that in 1871 she was being taught in the boys' classes. James Scott, a Scotsman from Aberdeen University, accepted Helen into his newly established Hokitika Academy, a Presbyterian Church school.

Again Helen excelled. In 1872 she walked off with the girls' arithmetic and grammar prizes and also came first in geography, dictation, Latin and Euclid. Outshining the boys, she became dux of the school then in 1873 won the most coveted prize for being the best scholar of the school, Facile Princeps: 'Easily the Best.' This would become the title of Margaret Lovell's biography of Helen Connon about 140 years later. By now there were seventy-nine boys and sixty-four girls at the Academy[28], and Helen had started to assist Scott by teaching a separate class for girls.[29] Helen was clearly such an extraordinary young woman that Scott began the process of arranging for her to start her own girls' school,[30] but before this could take effect the family shifted yet again, in 1874, this time to Christchurch. The move was probably to improve George's income. With little Hester Connon having being born around 1866 and Maria in October 1871,[31] there were now four children again – two more mouths to feed.[32]

The small city of Christchurch had been founded only twenty-six years before

the Connons settled there by the Canterbury Association, formed in 1848 by John Robert Godley and Edward Gibbon Wakefield. Their mission was to establish a Church of England colony in New Zealand made up of selected Anglican families. It was decided to name the city Christchurch after the college John Godley had attended at Oxford University. The Association hoped to establish a colony of 15,000 people,

Port Lyttelton, showing the first four ships and emigrants landing from the Cressy, 28 December 1850
Ref: Christchurch City Libraries CCL PhotoCD 10, IMG0017

and land was bought from the New Zealand Company to be sold to the settlers to raise money for the building of schools, roads, and churches.[33] The first four shiploads of settlers – they came to be known as the Canterbury Pilgrims – arrived in Lyttelton in December 1850. The Rhodes brothers at Purau and the Deans brothers at Riccarton who had arrived in 1839 and 1843 respectively, supplied them with vegetables, dairy produce and mutton. Gradually the new arrivals moved their families and possessions over the tortuous Port Hills road to Christchurch where the town had been established.[34] One of the immigrants was Walpole Cheshyre Fendall who would form the suburb Fendall's Town, which by the late nineteenth century had become known as Fendalton. It was here that Helen Connon and John Macmillan Brown bought their first house.[35]

Helen was just fifteen years old when her family moved to this fledgling city. It was the first move the Connons had made to a town that hadn't been created to serve a gold rush. When the Connon family arrived, the 'damp-ridden swamp' that was Christchurch had the worst record in the country for sanitation, and the following year recorded a mortality rate twice the country's average. But a sewerage system installed six months after their arrival began to transform the health of its inhabitants, and the Connons must have breathed sighs of relief when they saw the improvements. Having previously lost two children to sickness, their surviving children now had far better chances for survival. The little city was also thriving owing to increased wool and wheat prices and a new railway link through a tunnel to the port of Lyttelton. The country's immigration policies had led to an influx of 20,000 people into Christchurch between 1871 and 1876. The temporary wooden buildings erected by the early settlers were being replaced by impressive stone edifices. There were churches and banks, a hospital, a museum, gentlemen's clubs and two daily newspaper offices. In mid-1874 there was also the establishment and subsequent construction of Canterbury College which was affiliated to the fledgling University of New Zealand. All this meant better work prospects for George.

According to Millicent's memoirs, the family initially settled in Avonside, the city's second oldest suburb. The little cob church, the Holy Trinity Church, had been built in 1857 and consecrated by the much-loved pioneer, Bishop Harper, the father of Archdeacon Harper who had taught Helen Connon in Hokitika. Around the time the Connons arrived in Avonside, additions were made to the church of a stone chancel and transepts designed by the famous architect Benjamin Mountfort. Mountfort also designed Canterbury College and Christ Church Cathedral.[36] Following the series of disastrous earthquakes in Christchurch in 2010 and 2011, Avonside Church was demolished and a considerable part of the large suburb of Avonside was deemed to be in the 'red zone' for demolition.

Although Helen, as the oldest girl, was much needed to help in the home, her

Helen Connon aged about 21
Ref: Macmillan Brown Library 1991-1-6746

mother decided to make another attempt to further her gifted daughter's education. Just after Christmas 1974, she mustered all of her considerable courage and met Professor John Macmillan Brown at Canterbury College, established only six months before. She pleaded with him to enrol her daughter, who was only sixteen. He had hardly stepped off the boat from England and got over the Christmas celebrations, and now he was being asked to do the unheard of – admit a female to the College.

He was born on 5 May 1845 in the Ayrshire town of Irvine, Scotland and christened John Brown. Ann Brown was his strict, evangelical Calvinist mother, a strong believer in education particularly for women – this educational fervour seems to run through all of Millicent's forbears. Ann made sure that her daughters attended ladies' schools and her sons, the excellent Irvine Academy. His father, also John, was a rotund, jovial man, a sea captain and ship owner. He left his large family in the Firth of Clyde for long periods while he traded in the South Seas including China and South America. He would bring home 'great jars of tamarind and ginger and baskets of dried litchi and persimmon from China and candied seaweed from Japan... carved ivory and feathers of the birds of paradise and a tortoise to live for years on the hearth or in the garden and a cockatoo to learn to swear.'[37] His son John, the sixth child of the family, would inherit his father's insatiable curiosity and great love for travel.

John's boyhood was a happy one with plenty of outdoor exercise: fishing for 'pickies' with his younger brother, getting into scrapes with his friends bird-nesting, scrumping for apples and turnips and playing his favourite game of conkers. To stop himself falling asleep during the many sermons he had to endure, he decided to learn the shorthand recently invented by Pitman. He practised by taking down, word for word, the sermons he attended. It proved to be a masterstroke, giving him 'one of the most valuable arts in [his] long life of reading and hearing and observation.[38] He would use Pitman's shorthand throughout his life: in lectures as a student, in preparation for examinations, to jot down his thoughts, and eventually in his groundwork for his own lectures. Unlike many of his school friends who went to sea, John was a high achiever at his co-educational school. When his father's uninsured ship and cargo sank in Belfast Lough leaving him unable to support his son, John financed himself through Edinburgh and Glasgow Universities by giving private lessons.

He then won a scholarship to Balliol College, Oxford University in 1869 and was taken under the wing of Benjamin Jowett, the dynamic Master of the college. He became one of Jowett's favourites[39] and was included in his Sunday salons. As one of Jowett's best students, he mingled with the intelligentsia of Victorian England, and this had a lasting impact on him. However, due to a health breakdown and insomnia, something that would affect him all his life, John was unable to complete his final examinations. He went down from Oxford,

John Macmillan Brown, c 1875
Ref: Macmillan Brown Library MB1991-1-6762

obtaining a second-class degree, but this came with Jowett's assurance that he nevertheless was 'as a student and a man, in the first class.'[40]

After regaining his health while working in Scotland for the Geological Survey of Great Britain, John decided that his best prospect was a chair at a university outside Britain, and in 1873 his chance came. Jowett selected John to take the position of Professor of English and Classics, one of three foundation chairs at the Canterbury

College in Christchurch in the young colony of New Zealand. Two others were also chosen: Alexander Bickerton as Professor of, initially, Chemistry, then Physics; and Charles Cook as Professor of Mathematics and Natural Philosophy. John's salary would be £600 a year plus his students' fees. W. J. Gardner, in his history of the College, tells us that John arrived in Christchurch on Christmas Day 1874 and was taken to the site of the new Canterbury College, which although edged by the elegant Botanic Gardens and Hagley Park was just a bleak section of land around Worcester Street. It had 'an old wooden house crowning a natural mound of sand. It was a symbol of his situation; the real work hadn't begun, useless material had to be cleared away, and the task of putting down the barest foundations of a university would be a wearisome one.'[41]

This ambitious, zealous young Scots scholar was up to all of that. As his grandson, James K Baxter, wrote in his introduction to John's memoirs, John 'licked the English and Classics departments into shape at Canterbury College before the turn of the century.'[42] Grossmann says he became the 'father of the College.'[43] Immensely energetic, he threw himself into his work, toiling sixteen hours a day even during vacations, and he expected his students to do the same. The indomitable John Macmillan Brown had a forceful, often extremely dominating, personality. Gardner describes him: 'Macmillan Brown's youthfulness, his dark handsome features and his easy self-assurance were bound to make a good impression on students. Yet, the normal seriousness of his face and the intensity of his gaze made him a formidable person to confront.'[44] He was a short man who held himself stiffly upright at all times; he had a barrel chest and thick dark hair and wore a moustache, and a beard which varied in length at different times of his life. Although his memoirs show he had a good, sharp sense of humour and was even a lot of fun, his outward appearance and supercilious manner gave the impression of being unapproachable – exactly the same image that Millicent would inadvertently present as an adult. His mastery of English literature was legendary and he eventually gained a reputation as the most outstanding university teacher in New Zealand prior to 1900.[45]

At Canterbury College, John upheld the Scottish ideal of a higher education being

Canterbury College - the Clock Tower designed by Benjamin Mountfort, prior to the East Wing and Great Hall additions, c.1877.

made available to all deserving young people regardless of their class and the Oxford values of free intellectual enquiry. He rapidly placed Canterbury College at the forefront of higher education in New Zealand. His first objective was to teach graduates who would staff the country's growing number of secondary schools, and he was so successful that Canterbury College earned a reputation as

24

a nursery of headmasters and headmistresses.[46] Unfortunately for John Brown, there were four Professor Browns in New Zealand at that time, so he assumed his maternal grandmother's name of Macmillan and became John Macmillan Brown.[47] [48] Ostensibly, this was to avoid confusion, but the decision seems to smack of his distinctive sense of self-importance and it is more likely he did it to add distinction to his otherwise couldn't-be-more-ordinary name.

So early in 1875, at the meeting with young Helen's dauntless mother, the pivotal decision was made. John, always an advocate for female education, in fact later referred to as the 'first practical promoter of higher education for women in Australasia'[49], accepted her plea and admitted Helen Connon as the college's first female student.[50] Grossmann, in her biography of Helen, explains what an extraordinary leap this was for the times and what prejudices Helen had ahead of her:

> Girls who inherited their fathers' literacy or scholastic tastes were mercilessly ridiculed, and their inclinations and ambitions were crushed as being contrary to the law of nature. The most meagre and superficial education was enough for them: French, the rules of English grammar, letter-writing, a very small dose of arithmetic, the recitation of poetry, fancy work, and the accomplishments of in-different piano-playing and drawing– all taught without the least regard to the girls' various natural talents. The change was made to some extent all over the British dominions, and under various leaders. But nowhere was it so thorough as in New Zealand. And within that colony it was the work of the first women pioneers of education, and especially of one who, from her childhood upward, was marked out for something beyond the narrow routine of the ordinary woman's life.[51]

Having just turned seventeen, Helen launched herself into a daunting timetable of study and matriculated the following year. These were embryonic days in the lifespan of university education in Christchurch. Lectures were held in all sorts of places in the little city, often in freezing cold, dusty rooms in Oddfellows Hall in Lichfield Street or in the wooden annex to the public library on the corner of Hereford Street and Cambridge Terrace, where John taught classics, history and English literature.[52] Grossmann recollects the wide variety of students who ranged in age from fourteen to forty, from the well-educated elite to those with no high-school education at all, all thirsty for new knowledge:

> One was a sailor, one a farmer, another a schoolmaster, another an elderly clergyman, another a schoolboy. The parents of some had themselves been cultured scholars. The parents of others

couldn't do much more than read and write. They had not the least idea of what was expected of them or what university work implied. Fortunately both lecturers and students were animated by the enthusiastic zeal that only pioneers can share.[53]

While we have no record of Helen's feelings for John at that time, it is likely she shared the virtual hero-worship of him with her friends Kate and Lilian Edger and Edith Grossmann. A decade later when he was visiting Nelson, Kate Edger wrote to him to persuade him to visit on a night when there would be no other visitors. She and her sister Lilian wanted him all to themselves. She wrote 'If you only knew what a treat it is to us to see and hear you – we could have stayed last night for hours only we knew it wouldn't do.'

By this time, 1876–1878, (although there are no electoral rolls to attest to this) it seems George Connon leased or perhaps owned a quarter-acre section with a house and workshop in Hereford Street near the corner with Colombo Street. George by this time was already under financial strain, and paying Helen's fees proved too much. In 1875 the fees were ten shillings and sixpence a term for lectures delivered twice a week[54]. George became bankrupt in 1877. It is probably for this reason that Helen began teaching at the newly opened Christchurch Girls' High School, on the corner of Rolleston Avenue and Antigua Street (today Hereford Street)[55] in the same group of buildings as the Canterbury College.

Christchurch Girls' High School,
Latimer Square. 1913.

William Rolleston, the Superintendent of Canterbury's Provincial Government, had provided £3000 for the Board of Governors of Canterbury College to establish the school, demonstrating a significant wish to improve education for females.[56] In 1977 there were five teachers including the principal Mrs Georgina Ingle and Helen's friend Kate Edger as first assistant.[57] When Helen joined the staff early in 1878, the school buildings were completed, but there was still no staffroom, and the girls had to eat their lunch in a rat-infested cottage in the grounds. According to the enthusiastic Grossmann, the school became 'the best in the colonies,'[58] and certainly it received very good reports from its examiners and inspectors.[59]

Initially Helen taught English literature and was immediately popular. Even though she taught in 'the sleepy time of afternoon school', the girls loved her as a teacher and for her beauty. One student Margaret Lorimer wrote, 'She was not a teacher in the modern sense. She seldom used the blackboard or made any attempt at demonstrating. She merely talked quietly and interestingly, often assuming in us a knowledge which we did not possess and thereby stimulating us to remedy any deficiencies.'[60] Helen was earning a salary of £160 a year, was independent of her parents and able to contribute towards the family's keep. Her working day ran from 9 am to 4 pm, but somehow she still managed to study eight subjects a term at Canterbury College, a phenomenal workload.[61] Many of the men resented clever women. To them, women students were 'bluestockings' or 'hyenas in petticoats'[62]. Helen became very disillusioned when debating in the Dialectic Society on the subject of higher education for women. The young male students won the debate after much derision and advice to the women to keep to cooking and nursing. She was very upset and never again took part in debates on women's rights.[63] Despite this emotional setback, Helen Connon proved herself to be an international groundbreaker in her seven years at Canterbury College. She became New Zealand's top woman scholar[64] and began to achieve her list of other extraordinary 'firsts': the first woman to enter a New Zealand university and the first woman to combine secondary school teaching with undergraduate study.

She was not the first woman to graduate from a New Zealand University – or from a university in the British Empire – as is often quoted. Kate Edger had graduated BA in Auckland in July 1877,[65] three years before Helen gained her BA degree in Christchurch in July 1880. Grossmann was at Helen's graduation and later wrote 'I can well remember the scene, the Provincial Chamber, with its stained glass windows and early colonial imitation of English Gothic architecture, crowded with spectators, the professors in coloured hoods on the dais, the men gradually coming up one by one and passing down the steps, then a beautiful young girl, white as marble while the professor [Macmillan Brown] presented her for the degree and the aged chancellor made a speech in her honour.'[66] Kate Edger and her sister Lilian joined Helen at Canterbury College to study for their MAs. One of Helen's admirers, James Reeve Wilkinson, wrote about those days: 'The chief attraction for me was the quiet beauty of the College, Helen Connon...and the two Miss Edgers of Auckland had almost a world-wide reputation as the first women graduates.'[67] In the same year Canterbury

Helen Connon in BA graduation robes July 1880. The white camellias indicate 'excellence in women'.
Ref: Macmillan Brown Library 118-13429.

College had become so successful that it had more students than all the other New Zealand universities combined.[68]

In the following year Helen gained an MA with first class honours in English and Latin, topping all of her firsts by becoming the first woman in the British

Empire to gain an honours degree. At that ceremony, held in Christchurch's Provincial Council Chamber[69] in front of the cheering crowd, Helen was presented with a bouquet of white camellias, the flower that would become the symbol of New Zealand women's right to vote ten years later. While there is no record of her parents attending these celebrations, it is easy to imagine the immense pride of George Connon, an obscure carpenter, and wife Helen, whose dreams for her daughter had been realised.

Young Helen was now a renowned beauty with Grecian good looks: serene and statuesque. Contrary to the fashion of long hair or chignons, Helen wore hers cropped.[70] She became known as 'the Idol of the College'[71] and had many male admirers. Grossmann would see her 'walking, book in hand along the avenue under the blossoming chestnut trees and limes... sitting on a garden seat absorbed in the histories of Tacitus.'[72] She seemed the ideal of womanhood to everyone who knew her. Quiet and reserved, Helen nevertheless had a force of character hidden beneath the surface. The position of Principal at Girls' High School became vacant after the first headmistress, Mrs Georgina Ingle left after five years, and with her unique honours degree and her first-class teaching certificate Helen was the perfect candidate for this pioneering role in the education of New Zealand's young women. At only twenty-five, Helen became the principal in October 1882, an extraordinary accomplishment. At that time, senior pupils were paying fees of £4 4s per term. Helen received a salary of £300 plus £1 for each of the eighty pupils per year,[73] a substantial income for a woman in those days. However, her male counterpart at Boys' High School received almost three times as much.[74]

The following year, Kate Edger was appointed principal at Nelson College with her sister Lilian as Assistant[75]. This left Helen with a huge workload. However, with her modern curriculum and teaching methods the school progressed. It became widely known and achieved an excellent reputation for a high examination pass rate. But Helen realised that education should be also tempered with relaxed classes such as singing, drawing, sewing and lawn tennis, as well as exercise and gymnastics.[76] Proper gymnastics dress had to be worn – scratchy navy-blue serge knickers and tunics trimmed with white braid – as well as overcoats 'to spare the blushes of passers-by.'[77]The teachers of course also wore very correct dress; even the female caretaker wore a crinoline.[78] Helen was strong about what she wanted from and for her girls but was a gentle disciplinarian. Morale among students and staff was high. One new entrant, Janet Prosser – she subsequently became a key figure in Millicent's life – wrote with a passion similar to Grossmann's: 'It is sweet to recall all the traits we loved her for; how gravely and yet how gently she would rebuke our youthful exuberance of spirits, and set before us the duty of bringing out the best that was in us!'[79]

During her early years as principal, Helen had her two sisters at her school as pupils. Being ten years older than Hester and fourteen years older than Maria, she also took on the mothering role, making a home for them at 80 Lichfield Street in about 1882.[80][81] Both sisters did extremely well and Hester joined Canterbury College in 1884 when she was eighteen. This was during the start of the 'long depression' that lasted into the 1890s. Despite a brief boom in wheat and the first successful shipment of frozen meat to England in 1882, prices for farm products sagged and the market for land dried up. The country lost people through emigration, mostly to Australia. Sadly Helen's parents were casualties; George was made bankrupt again in 1880 and doesn't appear in any New Zealand electoral rolls or directories after that year. Either that year or sometime soon thereafter, George and his wife, Helen, left Christchurch and settled in Sydney.[82]

John Macmillan Brown c 1920s
Ref: Macmillan Brown Library 118-13089

Meanwhile, John continued to make a deep impression on students and colleagues at Canterbury College. He had reached iconic status as a lecturer in English and he is said to have once declared, egotistically to say the least, 'I am Canterbury College.'[83] Charles Brasch called him 'one of the intellectual dynamos and steam-rollers of his time'[84] and the founding editor of The Listener, Oliver Duff, once said 'I knew him in his terrifying prime.'[85] Alexander Bickerton was also a very popular, if unconventional, lecturer and he became John's closest friend.[86][87] John's reputation reached Britain and Australia and, extraordinarily, he turned down two Chairs, one at Melbourne University and the other at Merton College, Oxford.[88]

Now in his late thirties and tired of living the bachelor life in the Christchurch Club in Latimer Square where he lodged, John had for some time contemplated, what he called, a private, domestic life. This was partly because he couldn't invite any students to the club to offer them hospitality.[89] Furthermore, his 'eye had long rested' on Helen, the young girl student he had taken the gamble on all those years ago. John lectured in science at Girls' High School every Thursday afternoon. He had been watching Helen while she was teaching and had noticed the powerful influence she had over the girls. He writes of this in his memoirs. 'Their attitude was little short of worship... I have never seen anything in all my experience of teachers to compare with her serene power.'[90] He knew that she had refused several offers of marriage – according to Grossmann 'from young students and from grey-haired scholastic dignitaries'[91] – but he found her very beautiful and finally proposed to her.

Initially Helen refused him, wanting to prove that young women could progress in life on their own without the help of men. She was also very keen to finish educating her two sisters before she married. It is not known when she accepted John's proposal but Millicent maintains that Helen refused to marry him for seven years.[92] This seems unlikely as that would have meant Helen would still have been John's student at the time of his proposal. Society would have thoroughly disapproved of such a proposal. It is possible that the couple kept the engagement secret. John says in his memoirs that when he proposed to her 'She granted my petition on condition that I should allow her to remain for two or three years in the school she had come to like so much.'[93] He makes no commentary on a seven-year engagement. To the contrary, John indicates in a letter to his great friend Julius Von Haast, the famous explorer, geologist and creator of the Canterbury Museum,[94] that their engagement was very brief indeed. Dated April 1886, the letter says he is going to marry Helen Connon in December. He refers to their last conversation just four months previously: 'I remember that going down in the train you were sentimental over what might occur in our lives before you returned, and as a shot in the dark one of the impossibilities that might occur you said "Perhaps you will be married." At that time it was simmering in my mind.'[95]

Whether the engagement was seven months or seven years, certainly, John was very proud of having won the prize that had eluded so many suitors. Millicent recalls her father often telling her about men they knew, saying 'He wanted to marry your mother.'[96] Grossmann writes effusively of the couple's relationship:

> From their first meeting dated the beginning of what was to develop into a rare union of mind with mind. With her it remained for many years purely intellectual and came near the true ideal of Plato. She told me once that she thought friendship was the highest form of love …[The professor] found in the girl, whose mind was open and eager for knowledge, his ideal scholar, and before long his ideal woman. The regard between her and her former master, was a foreshadowing of the mutual devotion of each for the other…his thoughts filled her mind and grew with her, and his influence, as she herself said, moulded her life and character. There were never two natures more perfect complements of each other, hers the receptive and his the imaginative. Yet hers was too strong a character not to influence him in turn, and it was no doubt owing to her that he became the champion of women, especially in the matter of education.[97]

On 9 December 1886, twelve years after John accepted Helen into the college, the 'God Professor' and the 'College Idol' married.[98] Helen was twenty-nine and John, forty-one. The wedding was a private affair at Helen's home in Lichfield Street, with two witnesses: her sister Hester and the man who would become Hester's husband the following year, architect Samuel Hurst Seager. They honeymooned in Sydney with John's youngest sister Mrs Gordon Craig, or Aunt Pata as she became known. Helen's somewhat feminist proviso to the marriage that she continue as principal of Christchurch Girls' High School, saw her hold that position for another eight years. A married woman heading a high school would have been unique in those days. Up until the beginning of World War Two it was rare for married women to work outside the home at all.

Certainly the marriage agitated the ever class-conscious Christchurch community. John had married his student, someone twelve years younger, but above all, there was a vast class difference between a professor and a carpenter's daughter. Decades later, Millicent would tell Christine Cole Catley, the publisher of her memoirs, that some academic women in Christchurch would have nothing to do with her mother after she got married.[99] Christine suspected that these women might have hoped to win John for themselves, but perhaps it was due to the age difference between Helen and John or, even more likely, sheer snobbery.[100]

Grossmann writes of this marriage as a loving one. They certainly exchanged copious letters when they were apart, expressing how much they missed one another. When Helen died, John was distraught. In his memoirs, John writes of her beauty and her attributes as a teacher, a companion and a mother. There is no record of Helen expressing her feelings about John. She never was one to express her emotions, and her daughter Millicent would inherit the trait. The marriage brought John some obvious advantages: Helen was beautiful and sought-after Helen was beautiful and that would have made him happy to display her as his wife. Being married was socially advantageous: they had bought a house together and he could now entertain guests and bring his students there. For Helen, despite the disapproval of some society ladies, marrying John meant a social position, security, an intellectual companion and the possibility of children.

After their honeymoon in Sydney, the couple moved into Holmbank, a house in what is now called Wairarapa Terrace: a tree-lined street in fashionable Fendalton, close to what is today's University of Canterbury campus.[101] The house had been built by Ted Cox on land owned by his father-in-law, Robert Wilkins,[102] a Scottish pastoralist and landowner who lived on Holmwood Road nearby.[103] The house is no longer standing. It was demolished in the early 1980s, but from electoral rolls and from John and Millicent's descriptions, it appears to have occupied the northwest side of the junction of Garden Road and Wairarapa Terrace where today there are several substantial houses. The earthquakes in 2010 and 2011 badly damaged some of this area. At the time of John's purchase of Holmbank and the land surrounding it, Wairarapa Terrace wasn't yet a road but simply a track from Garden Road running through their property. It was used for droving cattle from the farming regions surrounding Christchurch to the Addington stock and sale yards.[104] Holmbank was located in an area that was, and still is, considered fashionable. From the 1880s, sales plans in many Christchurch suburbs often mentioned if a subdivision lay next to the residence of a notable citizen; location played a vital role in defining one's social position. The high-status housing of this area extended from Merivale, where the influential Rhodes family had settled, into Lower Fendalton including the subdivision along Holmwood Road and Wairarapa Terrace.[105]

John had taken Helen to see the house before they married and both were delighted with its situation on the bend of the Wairarapa Stream which rippled its way to the Avon River.'[106] Despite its proximity to the centre of Christchurch, the area was still very rural. Set in two and a quarter acres of land close to the source of the Avon River, the Holmbank grounds almost doubled in size as John bought more and more land over the next few years.[107] It was a wonderfully secluded spot. It would have taken about thirty-five minutes for John to walk the two and a half kilometres through the beautifully landscaped Hagley Park to Canterbury College, or for Helen to walk to Christchurch Girls' High School, which by now had moved from the university site to Cranmer Square. Millicent notes that her father walked twice a day, there and back[108]– perhaps he returned home to lunch – which would have meant twelve kilometres a day. But to someone who was used to walking fifteen to twenty-five kilometres a day as a young man, he would have thought nothing of it, possibly using the time to think of something new to interest his students.

Initially, Holmbank was an unpretentious, box-like, two-storey house built of kauri with four main rooms both upstairs and down. John had arranged for his brother-in-law, Samuel Hurst Seager, to adapt the house to his and Helen's liking before they moved in after their honeymoon in Sydney. At some stage, a double-storey porch and a conservatory were added. The garden ran down beside the Wairarapa Stream and around the full perimeter of the property.[109] One of John's passions was tending the

John Macmillan Brown and nursemaid with pram. Holmbank, Fendalton, probably taken just after Millicent was born, in early 1888. Ref: Macmillan Brown Library 12939

garden at Holmbank. He would get up early every morning and set to with his spade and hoe, feeling invigorated and healthy as he worked, free from the effects of his insomnia. It was the first time he had gardened since he was a boy, and he loved it. He planted trees for shelter but mainly for ornamentation to soften the rather stark house. A favourite native tree was the ribbonwood; he enjoyed viewing a row he had planted as he sat at the splendid mahogany desk his students had bought him as a wedding present. He wheel-barrowed shingle from around his land to fill in swampy areas that edged the stream and eventually created a shingle walkway along the whole boundary with the stream, lining it with trees to provide shade.[110] In time, he built rustic bridges and garden seats and developed a native fernery with rare and exotic plants from Australia, California and Japan. The lawns from the house swept down to the stream where a boatshed and bathing place were especially built for Helen. Grossmann spent time walking with Helen through a rose walk he created, and declared Holmbank to be one of the loveliest of all New Zealand homes.[111]

Helen and John spent much time buying elegant possessions, and the inside of the house was richly furnished with antiques and paintings. The house was, however, dominated by John's vast library which he had transported from the college to Holmbank. 15,000 books that took up half a kilometre of shelves lined the walls of not only his study but the hall and staircase as well.[112] Grossmann maintained it was the finest private collection in New Zealand,[113] a collection he was willing to share with his students. The couple grew their own fruit trees and vegetables and kept horses, dairy cows, pigs and hens.[114] John chose the cows from cattle droves passing along the road to the Addington sale yards,[115] buying direct from the drover rather than bidding against other buyers at the sale yards. He employed a young English groom called Tomlinson to help. It was a lot of work for only one man, to tend the huge garden and vegetable plot, milk the cows, feed the pigs and to take care of the horses.[116] John was particularly proud of his cows, an Ayrshire-Jersey cross, which produced high volumes of both milk and cream. He delighted in finding that one cow could produce enough milk for at least eighteen pounds of butter.[117]

The couple entertained at Holmbank regularly on Sundays when John followed Benjamin Jowett's custom of inviting several students – each group according to their friends or similarities – to breakfast on Sunday mornings and others in the afternoon. He considered this custom to be one of the most important methods of education.[118] There is no doubt that John did this for educational reasons rather than to make himself popular. He tried as far as possible to foster acquaintanceships amongst his students and to help students to overcome any shyness that they might have expressing their point of view. He found it very strenuous: 'I often found this Sunday morning's work exhausting as I had to lead the conversation into lines that would draw out their best... to pilot the talk so that everyone should feel that he or she had shown the best side and taken full share in the give and take of conversation.'[119] But although his door was always open to his students, he was also autocratic and very demanding. Millicent comments drily, he was 'rather a strain on his womenfolk and rather a strain, perhaps, on his students.' [120] Helen had to organise all the catering and those Sunday events took up the only day in the week that she or John need not have worked. Life had become even more demanding than before they were married, and now both had very public profiles. John's headaches and insomnia worsened and his class numbers increased – he had up to 150 in his essay class – but still he had infinite energy.

Then, three weeks before the new school and university year started, conveniently for their work, committee and social life schedules, came the birth of their first child, Millicent.

CHAPTER 2
A Solitary Childhood

Millicent Amiel Macmillan Brown made her entry into her privileged world on Sunday 8 January 1888, a little over a year after John and Helen married. Before we look at how this baby grew into such an intriguing and complex woman, it is time to consider what was going on in Christchurch and New Zealand at the time she was born.

James Belich gives a flamboyant account of colonial New Zealand that was flourishing at around this time:

> Five hundred thousand people from a standing start in 50 years, 1,200 miles from anywhere and 12,000 miles from the somewhere…Four cities, dirty and ramshackle, with orphans and derelicts tucked under shabby carpets of deficient charity, but vibrant with the hum of getting on. Camps, towns and stations sprouting like crazy mushrooms, bloating and bursting, desiccating, hanging on or taking off. Whores, housemaids, ladies and yeowomen levering old world against new to prise out some space for themselves…Publicans, gentry, carpenters; aspiring, conspiring, expiring…More gold than the Inca ever possessed, sifted, washed and crushed from whole hills. Thousand-year-old trees mown like grass, made into heat, shacks, railway sleepers and the largest wooden building in the southern hemisphere [Government buildings, Wellington]. Hundred-year-old whales carved into giant lumps of lard and melted in the pot into lamp oil for London streets and drunken Cossacks…Violence in bulk, from the casual fist, husband to wife, mate to mate, stranger to stranger; through the bloody horrors of the Musket Wars to the most 'modern' conflict people had yet died in [Boer War]. Horses and bullocks, men and women, steam machines and (London) money pushing the whole amazing edifice onward and upward…Slaving, fighting, fornicating, lying, striving, changing, transforming, converting…A booming, burgeoning neo-Britain, growing hysterically, tamed only historically. Love it, loathe it, or both;

this was colonial New Zealand, and boring was the one thing it was not.[121]

Christchurch was one of those dirty and ramshackle four cities Belich so colourfully describes. But Millicent had also been born into a climate of great change. Health conditions in the city were improving dramatically. A sewerage system was completed in 1882, and pressurised water mains and flush toilets were in operation by 1909, making a great contribution to the fall in the death rate from 30 per 1000 to the national average of 10 per 1000 by 1911.[122] In the fifty years prior to her birth, half a million white settlers, or Pākehā as they had

Illustrated Australian news :Landing immigrants at Lyttelton. Ref: Alexander Turnbull Library ID: PUBL-0119-1878-13

come to be known, had arrived in New Zealand. The aftermath was the demise of thousands of Māori because of newly introduced diseases.

The production of gold began to diminish, and in 1872 was replaced by wool as the leading export. But the bubble of the economic boom burst with the 'long depression' of the 1880s and 1890s. Things could have been a lot worse if it hadn't been for the continuation of industrial and railway development which included the introduction of refrigerated meat exports. The country's trade balance had achieved a modest, regular surplus by the time of Millicent's birth.[123] Over this period, Christchurch and Dunedin had become the two largest cities in the country.[124] Christchurch landowners were amongst the privileged class of sheep farmers, merchants, officials, financiers and professionals – nose-to-the-grindstone people. Social class was mostly 'loose' rather than 'tight,' and as Belich comments 'In New Zealand, there was no-one above them.'[125] Amongst that "gentry" were John and Helen Macmillan Brown, professionals whose landowning assets would swell substantially over the next twenty years.

So Millicent Amiel Macmillan Brown was born into this advantaged environment. Her middle name was, according to Grossmann, after the nineteenth century protagonist in the philosophical Amiel's Journal written by Swiss philosopher, poet and critic Henri-Frédéric Amiel,[126] which both Helen and John had been reading. Aware of how she was expected to fit into the plans of her parents, Millicent states in her memoirs that even her birth had been carefully planned: 'I was born on 8 January 1888, in time to give my mother three weeks' respite before term began.'[127] John's memoirs are mainly about his career and include only a few pages on his family life, tucked away at the end of his book, with little about Millicent. But he does record her arrival in an affectionate way as 'a new attraction.'[128] He admits to

35

finding her one of the most good-tempered babies and a ray of sunshine in the house. They never heard her cry, not even in the middle of the night when an earthquake (large enough that it broke off the upper part of the cathedral spire) struck.[129] Helen and John rushed into the nursery to find the terrified nursemaid holding a totally placid nine-month-old Millicent, upside down. It seems she was destined to cope with drama while showing little outward emotion.[130]

Millicent Amiel Macmillan Brown aged 2 to 6 years.
Ref: Macmillan Brown Library MB1991-1-6718, MB1991-1-6731 and MB1991-1-6791

There are few records of Millicent's early months, but she certainly fitted in very cooperatively with her parents' lifestyles. She was a regular sleeper, she cooed, she smiled and seemed the perfect baby. We can assume she was bottle-fed because when she was about six weeks old she developed some ailment due to Molly the cow jumping the fences to get to the river and consequently spoiling her milk. Millicent was instantly better when she was fed milk from a neighbour's cow.[131] The nursemaid appears to have taken full charge of Millicent in her early months, and Helen, despite her obvious love for her daughter, had little to do with her day-to-day care. This was very common in these social circles, but Helen and John didn't employ the nursemaid in order to enjoy their social life, rather, it was to enable Helen to continue working every day at the Girls' High School.

John's initial admiration for his first-born appears to have waned fairly promptly; a record of Millicent's first twenty months was kept in the form of a diary, presumably by the nursemaid. In a rare mention of John, she reports him 'getting rather annoyed at being kept a very few minutes outside Stranges[132] whilst three bonnets were being selected to be sent home for the baby's approval.' When she was a little older, Millicent's 'short clothes', leggings, dress and jackets to replace her long nightgowns, required at least three more people to help with the sewing, but they all had to wait until John was away at the University of New Zealand Senate meeting. Nevertheless, as a young child, Millicent seemed very fond of John and loved to imitate his actions. Maria Connon, Helen's sister, who temporarily lived with Helen and John, had a lot of contact with Millicent when she was an infant. Years later when she had her own baby she wrote 'When I look at our little grub, I often think what a marvel of cleanliness Millicent was; why, she never needed bibs at all...'[133]

Even though Helen and John had little to do with Millicent's day to day care, they certainly ensured that the nursemaids they employed were educated and literate, a rarity in those days. It was crucial to both of them that Millicent had all the mental stimulation she could possibly have. Millicent was clearly a rapid developer; at eighteen months she was able to say her letters and had an outstanding ability to repeat rhymes. By this time she was being fed Nestlé milk and bread, sago, and oatmeal porridge and still had the occasional bottle before going to sleep.[134] At an early age, she was clearly already aware of her father's attachment to work; when Helen sang nursery rhymes to her, 'Baby, baby, bunting, father's gone...gone where?' little Millicent would shout, 'Gone to lecture!'[135]

Photographs of Millicent at around this time show a chubby, rather plain and serious-looking little girl engulfed in lace and frills. Her expression is always relaxed and she gazes placidly but confidently into the camera. Somehow, she always looks older than her age. As she reaches her teens she looks remarkably like her mother, full-faced, composed and quite plump; Molly the cow clearly did her job well. Millicent remembers 'the delight of watching [her] mother skim the rich yellow cream from the pans, and being able to scrape off the little rim of cream left behind. We had cream with our porridge and cream with our pudding... Perhaps that's why I had gall bladder trouble in later life.'[136]

Typical of their social class at the time, little mention is made of the names and lives of their employees, apart from Gertrude Boulton, an ex-pupil of Helen's, and Tomlinson the groom/gardener. Millicent tells us that Tomlinson worked 'for a wage that wouldn't have kept him, much less his family, in meat nowadays' – nowadays being the 1960s.'[137] She was clearly very fond of Tomlinson. He would drive her home in the dog-cart on the rare occasions she went to children's parties: 'I hope he received overtime rates. I enjoyed it all immensely. I used to tell him the names of the children I had met and he would give me potted histories of their parents, sometimes scandalous, not sexually of course, but financially', she adds hastily. She remembers being embarrassed at these parties when she was faced with the difficulty of replying to 'When do you go to bed?' Like children today, she knew if she told them her normal time was seven o'clock, she would go down hopelessly in her friends' estimation, so she would say eight o'clock. When they replied nine or ten, it never struck Millicent that they were probably lying too. 'One's prestige depended on how late one went to bed, or said one did.'[138]

Helen had always been an advocate of physical exercise and loved walking, rowing along the Avon River in a canoe and riding her beloved horse, Scimitar. Millicent remembers countless journeys with her parents in the dog-cart, which had two seats in front and two foldable seats behind, facing to the rear. They ventured into the bush-clad foothills of Canterbury and Kowai Bush in search of native ferns for John's fernery at Holmbank.[139] Her father insisted on driving, not very well it seems; he didn't understand horses, and it was nothing to him to career onto the pavement as he turned corners in town. But of course, for him not to have driven would not have been manly.[140] Conversely, Helen had always been a bold and competent horsewoman and would ride among the steep passes and roads of the Port Hills and Banks Peninsula.[141] Scimitar, however, terrified Millicent, particularly when she had to hold him while Helen made calls. He went lame once and it amazed her to see her mother casually lift his hind legs one at a time to extract stones with a hoof-pick.[142]

Helen and John loved travel, and they holidayed whenever time permitted: tramping in the Kaikoura mountains, climbing in the Southern Alps and exploring the Hauraki Gulf. When Millicent was old enough, she went too.[143] She remembers being very frightened by the turkeys during a stay at the Castle Hill homestead in the mountains. She remembers being fearful of the seemingly bottomless bath at Hanmer Springs[144] – but forgot it all very soon, happily eating queen pudding for dinner that night. These were the days when the ferry sailed from the Christchurch port at Lyttelton, up the east coast and across Cook Strait to Wellington in the North Island. The family once took a ferry to Kaikoura on a day trip. There was a storm on the journey back, and as there were no cabins the sick passengers lay in bunks around the saloon, the females in the bottom level, the males above. But John and the captain were unaffected and calmly ate their meals in the midst of it all. Like her mother, Millicent always suffered from seasickness on rough voyages and felt her father's good seamanship was a quality more than any other she would liked to have inherited.[145]

For the first seven years of Millicent's life, not only John but also Helen worked full time. A working mother was unheard of in that class of society, but Helen wanted to prove that it was possible for a woman to have an independent career and to fulfill all the duties of wife, mother and household manager. This was still the time when women in New Zealand, as in Britain, had little or no say in major household decisions, but Helen made sure she did. Their hectic social life and manic work regime affected the health of both of them. Chronic insomnia was with them their entire lives. Millicent remembers her father being plagued by recurrent nightmares: 'He would be discovered shouting and standing on his bed attacking imaginary rats. When a noise broke out next door, my mother would bang on the wall and the noise would subside.'[146]

In 1891, it seems that Helen had an abortion, or as John put it in his memoirs 'the baby's life had to be sacrificed for that of the mother.'[147] [148] Helen also had a serious bout of influenza. Additional stress from work brought her to a state of exhaustion and the couple were forced to take a break. They travelled in England, Scotland – the land of their forebears – and continental Europe for several months in the second half of 1892; hardly a way for an exhausted person to recuperate. They left four-year-old Millicent behind in New Zealand. She remembers howling when she saw the cab drive her parents away. She was left in the care of Helen's sister

Maria, then twenty, who was a student at Canterbury College. Gertrude Boulton, who lived in Avonside close to where Helen's parents had settled,[149] gave Millicent her lessons.

Their trip took place during a period central to women's rights which were being fought for in Britain and her colonies. In New Zealand, Britain's farthest, newest and final colony, feminism was producing radical changes for women. Women were now taking up public employment and being admitted to all university degrees and to all professions.[150] In 1891 and 1893 there were more female Arts graduates than men.[151] Despite that, to support husbands, bear children and keep house was still the role of the vast majority of women in Victorian and Edwardian societies. Women's suffrage became a dominant cause in the women's rights movement. In New Zealand, it was university-educated women from the newly established Canterbury Women's Institute (CWI) in Christchurch, and above all the Women's Christian Temperance Union (WCTU) led by Kate Sheppard, that led the fight for women's suffrage. Interestingly, another campaigner was the feminist and social reformer Anna Paterson Stout, wife of Robert Stout that influential teacher of young Helen Connon in Dunedin nearly thirty years earlier who had risen to be New Zealand's Prime Minister from 1884 to 1887.

Millicent was five in September 1893 when, after many women had experienced discouragement, derision and even abuse, New Zealand became the first country in the world to extend the right to vote to all adult women. Not surprisingly, although she did not belong to any official women's group, Helen's name appears on the WCTU's second petition for women's suffrage.[152] John maintained that Canterbury College played a large part in the granting of women's suffrage as a consequence of the university admitting and granting degrees to women. Many of these women had led and supported the campaign, Helen being one of them. Also, some of his colleagues had been behind the formation of the CWI, which had been so instrumental in winning women's suffrage. In fact, James Reeve Wilkinson, who had been an ardent admirer of Helen at university, was a convener of the meeting that eventuated in its formation. The CWI was also a strong supporter of pacifism, which would later become a passion in Millicent's life. In April 1896, the National Council of Women of New Zealand (NCW) was established in Christchurch and it is still New Zealand's leading women's organisation.

It was into this innovative environment that Helen and John returned to New Zealand the following February. They had both spent time trying to cure their health problems during their visit to Britain. John had consulted a well-known London oculist about his on-going eye troubles and was issued with glasses which initially gave him complete relief. In Edinburgh, they also consulted with the man considered to be the most famous obstetrician of the day to discuss as John writes 'the sacrifice of the last baby and [we] received sound advice which ultimately added a second girl to the family.'[153] Of course, John doesn't record what that sound advice was. Typically, upon returning home, they immediately plunged back into their hectic lifestyle, and despite the trip proving to be a good break for them and the fact that John's constant headaches seemed to have been cured by the glasses, the couple still suffered from persistent sleeplessness. Something had to give, and Helen finally resigned from Christchurch Girls' High School in September 1894 at the age of thirty-seven. It seems that Helen's resignation might have been to reduce stress to increase the chances of a successful pregnancy, but Millicent says that in the year following her mother leaving Girls' High School 'a sister arrived but unfortunately born dead. Nowadays that would most likely not have happened.'[154] It would be another two years before Helen and John had their second child.

Helen had been the principal at Girls' High School for nearly twelve years. She left having proved herself to be a nineteenth-century feminist who was successful as an academic, a professional, a much-loved teacher, a wife and mother. She had done an enormous amount for female education in Christchurch. Some years later, Miss Eileen Fairbairn, another teacher at the school, spoke about Helen at a school assembly: 'Her dignity and beauty were answers to those who feared and said that educating girls was freeing them to ape men, making them hard and unfitted to be wives and mothers. By sheer personality, she achieved for women a place in scholastic life which was unique at that time in the world and put all her energy into building up this school of ours into one where learning was held in respect.'[155]

John also had always been a great advocate of education for women, but their views on education for their own children didn't follow the conventional belief that children should be taught in groups. It is highly possible that they were influenced by Rousseau's educational theories – we know that Gertrude Boulton gave Helen a copy of Rousseau's La Nouvelle Héloïse – with its emphasis on individual attention and not starting lessons at too early an age[156]. Millicent, and later her sister Viola, never received any school education in New Zealand. Instead, Gertrude Boulton became their governess, teaching lessons at the home.[157] When Helen resigned from her job, she became Millicent's tutor. They would take a walk together in the morning before their classes began. Every day there were two hours of French, spelling and Latin. Helen briefly attempted to teach Millicent music but, as Millicent admitted, she didn't have a musical ear, and Helen would get irritated. Helen and John also employed another ex-pupil of Helen's as a governess. This was Janet Prosser, the girl whose exam paper Helen had scrutinized so carefully on her wedding day. Janet also taught Millicent additional subjects including music, but it is not known if she was any more successful than Helen at this vexatious task. Both Gertrude Boulton and Janet Prosser became family friends, and Janet would later play a vital role in the meeting of Millicent and Archie Baxter and Millicent's resulting lifelong zeal for pacifism.

John's extensive library of books became the source for Millicent's education for many years. The consequence of being the offspring of two such brilliant academic parents was beginning to have its effect. By the age of seven, Millicent was reading 'all the fairy tales that were extant at the time, the classical and Scandinavian mythologies.'[158] She recalls overcoming her fear of lighting wax matches – wooden ones were fine – the time she sat up nearly all night reading Wuthering Heights by candlelight. Afterwards, she hid the candle under the mattress so no one would find out how far down she had burnt it.[159]

Bereft of young company until her sister Viola was born when she was nearly ten, Millicent had a lonely childhood. Helen and John clearly loved their daughter but they were, more often than not, wrapped up in one another or in their own interests. She became a rather serious, learned little girl. She could have been described as her father is in the Dictionary of New Zealand Biography: 'Rather short in stature with dark hair, a serious expression and piercing eyes'.[160] To ease her loneliness, Millicent used her rich imagination to invent her own 'companions' and tell herself stories: 'I wished to be a heroine, Joan of Arc and people like that. In my stories I flew continuously with a wonderful boy. I called him Boy and he could fly better than I could – we used to fly all over the place. He could do things that I couldn't and I came trailing behind, a very secondary person. He was the wonderful one.'[161] This is a rare example of Millicent allowing frank, personal feelings to shine through. Her perception of herself often seems to imply that she felt herself to be unimportant, not necessarily depicting low self-esteem but feeling that she wasn't a central figure in relationships. This attitude is also obvious in her memoirs when she refers to her time at university and her life alongside Archie Baxter.

But, suddenly, Boy could be forgotten because 'the great event' of her childhood happened; the Dendy family arrived.[162] In 1893, Arthur Dendy was appointed Professor of Biology at Canterbury College.[163] Vera and Margaret, two and four years younger than Millicent respectively, were two of Arthur Dendy's daughters. At last Millicent had someone to have fun and adventures with and to be a normal, mischievous child. She led the younger girls into endless scrapes: 'I induced them to climb naked into the greenhouse tank when they were living on the Cashmere Hills and to career round the garden in the same state when surprised by the gardener.'[164] Through her new friends she made more, among them the three sons of Charles Bevan Brown, the headmaster of Boys' High School in Christchurch.

Life in the small provincial city of Christchurch towards the end of the nineteenth century must have been a fascinating place to live; Christchurch led the country in many fields: women's suffrage and temperance movements, sanitation reforms, education and sport, and it had more than its fair share of reformers, eccentrics, freethinkers and radicals. Prospering from the exports of Canterbury farmers while many other centres were still suffering from the 'long depression' of the 1880s, the city sprawled even further into the plains of Canterbury with the gaggle of boroughs increasing by the year. Though there were areas of poverty,

Christchurch Press Co Limited and Whitcombe & Tombs next door.
The Weekly Press, 15 Dec. 1900, p. 57.

the city was a bustle of bicycles, steam-trams and a host of coaches and carriages: dog-carts to broughams, landaus to buggies, phaetons to hansom cabs. Mark Twain visited Christchurch in 1895 and joked that half the population rode cycles and kept the other half busy, dodging them.[165] It had a plethora of churches serving over two-dozen different religious denominations, a fine museum and beautiful botanic gardens, a public library, a university college and a pier in Brighton. Robert Falcon Scott's first Antarctic expedition, departing in 1901 from the port of Lyttelton, marked the start of the city's continuing association with Antarctic exploration. The physicist Ernest Rutherford, who won the Nobel Prize for Chemistry in 1908, began his university career at Canterbury College from 1890 for five years under Professor Bickerton before moving to Cambridge University. He was a good friend of John and Helen. After a time at Cambridge, Rutherford returned to Christchurch briefly in 1900 to marry Georgina Newton, his landlady's daughter.

In 1895, two years after Helen's resignation, John's ongoing problems with his eyesight, headaches and insomnia along with mental exhaustion led him to resign his chair at Canterbury College. A year later he was farewelled at the college by a very large group of present and past students. He gave an emotional reply to the praise they gave him, admitting that he was suffering from mental exhaustion; something that today we would describe as a nervous breakdown, or perhaps a midlife crisis. His former arrogance seemed to have left him; he conceded that he had made mistakes and even suggested that his students should cultivate idleness. Most surprisingly of all, he said he now considered science to be a more important subject than English Literature.[166] According to Millicent, her father had never got on with many of his colleagues, and she always felt that he would have been happier in Dunedin at the University of Otago where many of the professors were Scots; at Canterbury College he was the only one.[167]

John was only fifty when he resigned, but ceasing to earn a salary caused no financial hardship to the Macmillan Browns. With their joint salaries and John's shrewd ability in investing money in property and shares, the couple had accrued a good deal of money and they were able to travel regularly to Europe with Millicent.

Millicent's first trip to Europe was in March of the year of John's resignation; she was eight. They took the New Zealand Shipping Company steamer Rimutaka to London via the Straits of Magellan on a voyage plagued with rough weather, which Millicent survived on a diet of port and lemonade![168] They spent time in Devon and Cornwall then went on to the Continent: France, Switzerland, Italy and Austria. They were inveterate walkers, with John, of course, always in the lead. Often they travelled by horse and coach, choosing not to travel in the body of the coach but perching themselves on the outside seats at the back, with hoods and leather aprons to protect themselves from the weather. This gave them a wonderful view, and the pace was slow enough for Millicent to identify the alpine plants which became a lifelong interest.[169] The one trait Helen had that infuriated her husband and marred what Millicent construed as her parents' happy relationship, was Helen's complete lack of punctuality. She would catch trams, trains and ferries by the skin of her teeth. Perhaps this was Helen's way of fighting John's dominance, but as John was a very punctual man, it drove him wild and he did nothing to conceal his anger: 'He was unrestrained in showing his feelings', comments Millicent, 'Like many little men he was rather fierce.'[170]

They continued journeying through Czechoslovakia, Germany, Belgium and Holland then travelled across to Harwich in a storm. As always, Millicent was seasick: 'My father escorted me to the lavatory walking backwards before me like the guards in Papillon, with a basin in his hands.'[171] They had a brief trip to Scotland – one of many in Millicent's life – then towards the end of the year the family returned to New Zealand on board the Ionic of the Shaw Savill and Albion Line.[172]

The following year, in November 1897, Millicent came home from a day spent playing with the Dendy sisters and found that a baby sister had arrived.[173] Helen had obviously concealed her pregnancy convincingly. Viola Helen was born on 16 November and was nicknamed 'Baby Bunting' by the nurses; Millicent's version for her new sister was 'Bunty' and it stuck. John records in his memoirs that 'the addition added new vitality and happiness to the household' then adds a rare mention of Millicent: 'The elder sister delighted in the new plaything whom we called Viola.'[174] Gertrude Boulton came to live at Holmbank to look after the new arrival. One of Viola's first memories was of trotting alongside her mother, flourishing a small white parasol and 'looking enchanting in pale cream with a turquoise-blue velvet belt.'[175]

Although they were clearly loved by their parents, both sisters felt remote from them. They ate their meals separately from their parents and employees always ran the household. Even Millicent's hair was brushed by a servant rather than by her mother.[176] Viola later admitted something that Millicent probably would have

At Holmbank, Fendalton Millicent and baby Viola and the gardener Tomlinson
Ref: Macmillan Brown Library 118-12947, MB118-12954, and on the right with George Connon. c 1900. By knd permission of Antonietta Baldacchino)

echoed: 'My mother I liked, but she was a shadowy figure and belonged to my father's world more than mine whereas Gertie [Boulton] was mine, always there, always comfortable and never impatient.'[177] Both sisters felt this emotional detachment from their parents keenly, and John's grandchildren would later talk about his parental reserve. Neither sister was brought up to follow any religious

43

faith, but Millicent always said her prayers, taught to her by her nursemaid, who had been very shocked by her not saying them.[178]

A photograph taken around 1899 outside the porch at Holmbank, shows the family of four. John stands stiffly, holding Viola in his arms and looking straight into the camera. Helen, dressed neatly in a white dress with matching hat, is seated on a wicker chair looking sideways at the photographer. Millicent sits on the ground with legs outstretched reading a book. It is a sunny day. Ivy almost covers a stained-glass window set in the weatherboard walls of the house. A man with a bowler hat hovers in the background and stares up at the camera; perhaps he is Tomlinson, the gardener. A woman in an apron,

Old Holmbank, Fendalton. Millicent, Helen, John, Viola, maid on the balcony, a gardener, c 1999.
Macmillan Brown Library Ref: 118-12940

again probably a servant, looks down on the scene from the balcony above. Possibly it's Gertrude Boulton; although a friend, she was also a servant, so it wouldn't have been seemly to have her join the family group in the photograph. Studio photographs of Millicent at this period show her looking remarkably like Helen and dressed in starched blouses with puffed sleeves and Peter Pan collars. In one shot, she is in a wicker chair cuddling little, wide-eyed Viola. Viola made all the difference to Millicent's life, although there was almost ten years between them. When Viola was very young, Millicent sometimes became frustrated with her, but the sisters were good friends for life.

During this time, John was preparing his most popular lectures for publication

The boatshed at Holmbank, with John, Helen and Viola in a boat on the Wararapa Stream. Possibly Millicent on the bridge. 1890s

and building a cottage on a large piece of land that he had bought in 1897. It was on volcanic rock in the triangle between what later would become Dyers Pass Road, Hackthorne Road and Macmillan Avenue. This was the third house he had built in the Cashmere Hills. This time, he employed his brother-in-law, the renowned architect Samuel Hurst Seager, who had married John's sister Hester in 1882, to design a New Zealand version of a log cabin modelled on a Tyrolean villa that

44

he and Helen had seen and loved on their travels.

Helen and John named the house Matatea, meaning open and free, fair of weather.[179] The thick outside walls and the ceilings were made of solid wood, and the views of the Southern Alps and Canterbury Plains were magnificent.[180] Hurst Seager's designs were very modern and distinctive for the time, influenced by the English Arts and Craft movement. The rooms were light and airy, letting the sunshine stream in, and the exposed wooden panels, coved ceilings, curved archways and built-in bookcases were all hallmarks of Seager's architectural style.[181] His design of Matatea introduced the bungalow style to New Zealand.[182]

Matatea, 2 Whisby Road
Christchurch, 1990s.

John's decision to build this house was motivated partly by his hope to cure his and Helen's ongoing insomnia by providing a residence that would enable the family to escape from the fog that smothered Christchurch particularly in the winter. This wild, windswept tussock area of the Cashmere Hills was a great contrast to where Holmbank lay in flat, damp Fendalton, which John believed caused 'low fever and depression'.[183] Millicent recalls how her ankles became chapped in those cold winters and how she had to wear heavy woollen underclothing: 'combinations, back and legs in one piece'. She was delighted with the idea of a winter residence in the hills, particularly as her great friends the Dendys were now living in that area.

Every day, the gardener brought the things they needed: meat, fruit and produce from town and from Holmbank.[184] [185] John left the family for four months in 1899 to go to Canada and the United States, partly to try to relieve his own insomnia but also to seek publication of his first work of fiction, a satirical fantasy called Riallaro.[186] His letters to Helen show how much he missed his wife and family. One from New York says:

> I wish I were with you and the little ones. It is utterly miserable being away from you. And I am as resolved as you that I shall never go away again without you again. This life isn't good for much except to be with those you like most. And nothing impresses this on me so much as the solitude of living in a big, bustling city. And to think I have to go off so much further from you too. Won't I be glad when I shall be able to take my return passage and feel on my way back to you.[187]

The couple were missing one another acutely. Helen's responses were in the same vein:

'I have been longing and longing for the Frisco mail, a whole month without news of you seems endless ... How nice it will be to have you back again and you will never go away again without us ... I miss you very much and I do wish you were home again. I hope you don't have to go to England and that you will be home in September when the garden and everything will be looking nice.'[188]

Nevertheless, while John was away, Gertrude and Helen continued enjoying a happy family lifestyle with Millicent – whom Helen often refers to as 'the party' – and little Viola. Helen writes to John, 'Bunty looks so happy when we go out driving [in the cart] sitting between Millicent and me. The party is very good and very busy, much interested in her 'calisthenics.' She doesn't go to the Domestic School after all as I thought it would be rather much for her – she has to practise at home instead. We still read our French at night and we have not finished reading Woodstock [a Walter Scott novel].'[189] Millicent wrote directly to her father that she was using the microscope every day under the guidance of Janet Prosser.[190] Helen, the two children and Gertrude went to Sydney to meet John on his way home to New Zealand. They visited Helen's parents at Turramurra, her sister Maria as well as John's sister, Bessie Craig, and her husband and children at Neutral Bay. Helen wrote to John about how little 'Bunt' thrived everywhere she went but how the rather rough and precocious eleven-year-old Millicent was 'very funny with these [Craig] boys, holds her own with them, and gives them little drubbings all round. I can see they are young enough not to be altogether amused sometimes.'

Despite his previous longing for home, John's lust for travel still persisted after his return. The next year, with Helen, both children and Gertrude Boulton in tow, he left Christchurch to travel around Europe for two years. It would turn out to be the last overseas trip John and Helen did together.

The family took lodgings in Upper Norwood, close to the Crystal Palace, London. Now twelve, Millicent went to school for the first time but only briefly. It was a school run by the Girls' High School Day Company which Millicent attended while her parents travelled in Scandinavia and the Continent. The issue of Millicent's education is an interesting one. John wanted his two girls to be as brilliant as their parents. Millicent's education in New Zealand had always been conducted at home. Perhaps they felt that they could do a better job of educating their girls at home than could the school. Now, they may have considered that Millicent was lacking the benefits of an array of tutors and the company of other schoolchildren. Certainly, at the London school, Millicent became aware that her level of achievement for the different subjects differed considerably from those of the London students. 'For English, history and geography I was in the class normal for my years. For arithmetic and French, in both of which I was poor, I went down one class. For Latin I went up amongst girls of fifteen and sixteen who seemed to me practically grown up.'[191]

The family went to Garlieston in the southwest of Scotland where Millicent learned to swim. They then travelled on to Paris. John parted from his family again, travelling to Wiesbaden, east of Frankfurt, for five to six months' treatment at the famous eye clinic of Dr Hermann Pagenstecher, who recommended that he 'should not read or indulge in any close work.'[192] He walked for miles in the surrounding mountains and went to numerous concerts, rousing in him a love of Mozart, Bach, Beethoven, Saint-Saens, Gounod and Thomas.[193] Whatever the treatment was at the clinic, it had no long-term effect on his eyesight or his insomnia. Meanwhile, Helen, Gertrude, Viola and Millicent journeyed through the spectacular autumn colours to Montreux on Lake Geneva and stayed in the Pension Depallens, which had a splendid view of the lake and mountains.

Millicent attended the local high school to learn French, her mother realising she

would have far more chance of learning the language there than in any of the private schools 'swarming with English girls.'[194] She gained a very good command of the language and would never forget it. Helen, Gertrude and Millicent also loved receiving private French lessons from a Mademoiselle Röring, which involved little Bunty who would learn her lessons from a phrase book and teach her favourite doll.[195]

Helen and John were always preoccupied with their health, and for Helen, at least, this concern also extended to an anxiety about Millicent's physical well-being. Helen felt Millicent needed a great deal of open air to keep her well, so mother and daughter would take walks in the surrounding hills and mountains between lessons at school. Following John's advice,

Millicent (about 13, and Viola, probably in Switzerland.
(By kind permission of Antonietta Baldacchino)

Millicent was given a dose of Parrish's Food, a red syrup of iron phosphate, and a bottle of white wine at dinner every night. In no time at all, Millicent showed great improvement![196] Almost every day, Helen and Millicent would write to John on small, lined notebook paper, frugally using every inch of both sides, sometimes curling last minute words around the edges of the paper. Millicent's letters, sometimes in French, would start with 'Dear Daddie' and Helen's with 'My Dear Daddie' ending with 'love from Mammie, H. Macmillan Brown.' John's return letter would be waiting for Helen every morning at her breakfast table. There was no doubt about Helen's feelings for him at that time; she missed him terribly and constantly urged his return. Much of their writing was to do with their health: John's eyes and Helen's insomnia. Helen sometimes found a few nights' relief by taking Sulphonal.

John returned from Wiesbaden in time for Christmas, and Millicent went luge-riding with her parents on the hills nearby, John on one luge and she and Helen on a larger one.[197] The family stayed on together at Montreux until the end of the first school term in 1901. This happy period was marred by Viola contracting pleurisy. She recovered rapidly despite a specialist in Lausanne misdiagnosing the problem as a stomach complaint. He prescribed a purgative, calomel, and a play in the snow to which the infuriated John responded by flinging the calomel out of the window. He thought he had probably saved Viola's life by simply keeping her warm.[198] Helen had another miscarriage which she felt had been caused by running down a hill to be in time for lunch with the Consul's wife. She never fully recovered. After the miscarriage, Helen was ill in bed for the several weeks they spent in the Rhone Valley. Millicent took frequent walks in the valley with her father, further kindling her love of plants and flowers. The flowers delighted her. The way was 'carpeted with primroses and enormous cowslips... grape hyacinths and Solomon's seal, and in the woods... hepaticas, blue, pink and white.'[199]

When Helen felt well enough, the family travelled through Europe and back to Scotland. John had the idea of settling in Britain permanently but, as with so many expatriates, the pull of New Zealand proved too strong.[200] They sailed home via Sydney, and on the last leg of the journey Helen's father, George Connon, came down to the wharf to see them off. He was very upset at parting from his daughter saying he would never see her again. He was right, but not as he imagined. It was not he who died, but Helen. Helen's mother felt the separation from her daughters keenly and always maintained a very caring correspondence with Helen: 'My dear Helen... haven't had a letter this week... Anything the matter with you seems hard for us to bear. I feel I could suffer any pain if it were to save you from it... We are both keeping well. Father thinks Millicent is forgetting him altogether.'[201]

Their arrival back in Christchurch in January 1902 was noted in the Canterbury Times.[202] Back at Holmbank changes took place, not always for the better. The Dendy family had departed for England so Millicent's best friends had disappeared. Tomlinson left because John wouldn't give him a raise, and Millicent maintained they never had satisfactory gardeners from that time on.[203] After a while, Millicent did make new friends: Kate and Joan Fulton who lived close by on Wairarapa Terrace, but they were never as close as the Dendys had been. Helen returned to her normal way of life: paying calls, taking people out for drives, garden parties (with strawberries and cream presented on tables around the garden) and such things. But her health wasn't good, in fact, it was deteriorating. Although she was stoical, a trait Millicent inherited in full, she still had frequent bouts of sleeplessness. John would become impatient and irritable with Helen's permanent state of poor health, and this made her worse.[204] It was ironic because he, himself, was in a chronic state of ill health: sleeplessness, eye problems and stress. Millicent talked very candidly to Christine Cole Catley about her parents' relationship – a passage that didn't make it into the memoirs reads

> She was inclined to weep at the least thing. She used not to
> be like that but she was. That irritated him terribly. He was

frightfully irritated by her. I think it was because she withdrew from their physical contact. He was a very strongly sexed man and I think that was the cause of his trouble. She wouldn't have wanted contact... I now think that was the cause of all the trouble. He would completely agree that that was alright but at the same time it irritated him. He never went elsewhere. Never.'[205]

The ongoing health conditions of both Helen and John affected the lives of all the family. The situation worsened when five-year-old Viola fell victim to pleurisy for a second time, and although she fully recovered once more, the worry greatly affected Helen. As Helen's insomnia worsened, it came to dominate their lives. John had a cottage built in Sumner where Helen could enjoy the sea air, and there she did start to sleep better. They saw a lot of her sister Hester (Hetty) and her husband Samuel, who lived close by. While Helen was away in Sumner, John coached fourteen-year-old Millicent for the Junior and Senior Scholarships for the University of Sydney, but often father and daughter were at odds, which in turn caused tension between Helen and John.

One evening around that time, Millicent was returning home from a cooking class when a young man followed her along Wairarapa Terrace and accosted her near the gate at Holmbank. She tells the tale in her typically straightforward way: 'He walked beside me producing his penis and making remarks about it and other things. I pressed on, got to the gate, and rushed through.' Helen wasn't at home, so she told John who immediately sent for the police. Life became a nightmare for the household; the constables kept bringing young men to the house for identification until Millicent finally recognised the perpetrator through his birthmark. Millicent hated the fuss that was made over the incident and always regretted telling her father, believing that her mother would have played down the whole affair. Millicent ends the story phlegmatically: 'From then on I took an interest in sex. I hadn't before.'[206]

The fuss that John tended to make in times of stress may have partly contributed to Helen's death. In February 1903, Helen and fifteen-year-old Millicent went with John's sister Bessie and her husband Robert to Rotorua, a renowned destination for international visitors to view its geothermal activity: the geysers and boiling mudpools. It was common for people to visit Rotorua for the curative powers of the mineral waters. Helen was still unwell but confided in Millicent, not her husband. Millicent says '[She] had shown me the ulcers that lined her mouth, but strangely enough she didn't show them to my father, nor did she go to a doctor. If she had, possibly our lives would have been different.' Perhaps Helen didn't tell John because she thought he might get impatient. The decision turned out to be disastrous. When they reached Rotorua her health deteriorated drastically: the ulcers had spread to her throat and she could barely swallow. She did then go to a doctor who sent her to an isolation ward where she was treated for diphtheria. For some reason, Millicent always maintained that the diagnosis was wrong,[207] but the symptoms certainly do not rule out diphtheria. Millicent went with John twice a day to see Helen, talking to her behind glass. Helen was given the diphtheria antitoxin, the only known remedy in those days, but it was too late. She grew steadily worse and was finally given morphia. John writes that 'She was gently patient and did her best to still our fears. It was the saddest vigil I had ever kept and doubtless I showed my anxiety on my face, for she constantly did her best to soothe my fears and assured me she was sleeping well under the influence of morphia and that her throat was improving.'[208]

She died in her sleep on 22 February 1903. She was forty-six. John was bereft: 'At last her heart gave way and news came that she, the best friend I ever had, had died. Nothing will ever obliterate the memory of that sad day.'[209] Millicent was also distraught. She records being very angry when her father put a broken column over her grave in the Rotorua cemetery, symbolising Helen's severed life. 'I remember thinking how completely inappropriate it was. At fifteen, everyone over forty is old.'[210] On the broken column, the inscription includes the words 'leaving her husband and children desolate. A noble life nobly but too soon spent.' John also planted a favourite Australian shrub and a native ribbonwood from Holmbank to cover the grave. Probably the reason the body wasn't brought back from Rotorua to Christchurch was the infectious nature of diphtheria.[211]

The effect Helen Connon's death had on the city of Christchurch was dramatic. Flags at half-mast hung from schools and the university, and the University Senate awarded accolades for her remarkable academic journey. John commissioned James White, an Australian sculptor, to carve a white marble bust, which was presented to the university in 1904 and for many years graced the south-eastern

corner of the hall, perched high on a carved limestone ledge. The bust has been removed to the present site at the university in Ilam where she continues to provide an inspiration to university women.[212] A copy was made to sit in what is now the Great Hall of the Arts Centre. Despite extensive damage by the earthquakes in 2010 and 2011, the Great Hall has been repaired and the bust remains there today. Also in 1904, a beaten-copper memorial plaque was unveiled at the Girls' High School in Helen's memory.[213] In 1918, the first residential hall was opened by the university and called the Helen Connon Hall. This closed in 1974. The Helen Macmillan Brown Memorial Prize, set up by Christchurch Girls' High School in 1903, is still being granted today, and in 1920, John established the Helen Macmillan Brown Bursaries. Helen is remembered for her remarkable academic and professional achievements and her contribution

Bust of Helen Connon
(taken by Christine Toner in 2015)

to the feminist cause. John never remarried. Whilst he undoubtedly shared many happy periods with Helen, their marriage was marred by insomnia and other ailments. It was a complex relationship. He once told Millicent 'Your mother's mind was a closed book to me. I never could tell what she was thinking.'[214] The loss of Helen was so great that when he and Millicent returned to Holmbank after Helen's death he found that his grand house had 'lost its greatest ornament and attraction; it was like finding a body without a spirit.'[215]

CHAPTER 3
Getting an Education

In her memoirs eighty years later, Millicent conceals her deep emotion about her mother's untimely death but she did admit this to Christine Cole Catley: 'I was just desolated, completely… One can't tell when one's grief died out…'[216] At the same time, she had little sympathy for her father, with whom she felt little connection, and during the four months following Helen's death there was further deterioration in their relationship. In his anguished state, left alone to bring up a teenager and a five-year-old daughter, John became extremely irritable and often incapable of controlling his temper. He was still coaching Millicent. He was an overbearing disciplinarian and a stickler for getting his own way, and one wonders if a son might have challenged this aspect of his character. Throughout Millicent's life, she and her father had ambivalent feelings towards each other. She writes 'I look back on it now with considerable sympathy for my father. I had none then, only resentment and I think even hatred…. I wasn't the brilliant student he had expected... I was, I think, just ordinary average and I had too much to do.'[217] While Millicent was no shrinking violet, this again illustrates her tendency towards self-effacement. In fact, this 'ordinary average' young woman would prove capable of achieving academic heights rarely attained by women of her time.

Now with no mother, this was a very emotional time in her life. In his biography of her son James, Frank McKay mentions that in a rare moment of personal revelation, Millicent admitted to a close friend that she had received little emotional warmth even from her mother and how much she had regretted it. [218] McKay has his own insight into Millicent's reticence and reserve: 'With no mother and a father who was a martinet, she was deprived at a determining period in her development of the emotional warmth and encouragement adolescents need.'[219] John displayed much more affection towards little Viola, whom he called a 'beautiful little replica' of his wife.[220] While there is no indication that, as a child, Millicent was ever jealous of Viola, absence of evidence is not evidence of absence. She does say in the introduction to her father's memoirs that when her mother died 'It is possible that if she had lived, I would have become very jealous of my sister.'[221] We do learn later from Terence that, despite the fact that Millicent loved her sister dearly, she did become envious of Viola's looks and popularity as a young woman. When asked by Christine Cole Catley if she ever recalled feeling jealous of Viola, Millicent replied

Never never never. But if my mother had lived I would have been jealous, I know that. I was passionately fond of my mother. She would have shown affection for the youngest, and naturally I would have been jealous. I didn't care enough of my father to bother about him being fonder of my sister than myself. It didn't worry me in the least. I didn't love him enough I am sorry to say… the trouble was that when he undertook to teach me. I hated him…He and my mother didn't get on awfully well… she told me. She confided in me. Why I don't know. It upset me. She felt she had to. She was quite wise not to confide in her sister and there was nobody else so she confided in me.[222]

John's expectation was always that Millicent and Viola would not only follow in their mother's academic footsteps but that they would also obtain degrees at Oxford or Cambridge. He didn't want either of his daughters to marry and expected that at least one would look after him domestically and accompany him on his frequent travels both at home in New Zealand and abroad. Both girls had to read to him regularly. He would fall asleep, but as soon as they stopped reading he would wake up and insist they went back and read it all over again.[223]

But despite the difficulties with her father, Millicent toiled with him through French, German, Latin, English, Greek and Roman History and Modern History 1790-1815. With another tutor she studied maths, arithmetic, geometry, algebra and trigonometry. But father and daughter still argued to such an extent that Millicent's Aunt Pata, in Sydney, heard of their quarrels and was alarmed enough to invite them both for a complete break from study over the winter. The arrangement did them both a great deal of good, restoring their spirits and ridding John, for the time being anyway, of his excessive tetchiness.[224]

Millicent fell in love for the first time, with a cousin in Sydney. He was a medical student with Spanish ancestry. It turned out to be a one-sided affair, and Millicent likens it to a crush that a schoolgirl feels for her teacher. However, her feelings for him lasted with varying intensity for the next six years. John and Millicent returned to New Zealand and for a while their relationship was much better. But Millicent still felt she was overburdened with work and her *bête noir* was mathematics, particularly algebra, a subject she loathed and was never good at. At sixteen, she returned to Sydney and sat the senior scholarship gaining an A in French, a B in Latin and a C in English but failing in mathematics and history. Back at Holmbank and facing the junior exams with the dreaded algebra she knew she was incapable of passing, she went out on the lawn in her nightgown in a southwest gale and got completely soaked in the hope of getting pneumonia to avoid the algebra exam, but it was all to no avail. She failed so outstandingly in mathematics that her father couldn't believe she had sat the exam. But Millicent loyally concedes that he bore the news manfully and never reproached her.[225]

Still with no matriculation either in Sydney or New Zealand, she returned to Sydney in February 1905 aged seventeen and spent a year at the Presbyterian Ladies' College in the suburb of Croydon, the longest period she had ever spent at school. She enjoyed herself. The work was well within her capabilities and she made a lot of friends, something she was always good at.[226] At the end of the year, she sat the matriculation examination and passed. She was overjoyed: 'I don't think all the other exams I afterwards passed ever brought me the extreme unalloyed delight of that first passing. My aunt with whom I lived took me to the theatre in celebration.'[227]

Study for a BA in Latin, French and German followed at the University of Sydney. In Latin they learned *The Georgics*: a poem in four books, one of the many works by the Latin poet Virgil that they examined. She recalls them as being easy but many years later discovered that her husband, Archie Baxter, a mere rabbiter with a far less cerebral pedigree, knew far more about *The Georgics* than she ever did. Millicent thoroughly enjoyed her time at university; the feeling of being liberated at last from a dominating and unhappy father must have been bliss. Furthermore, during the vacations when she returned to Holmbank in Christchurch, Millicent found that she was treated far more as an adult. People of note often visited her father, including Heinrich von Haast, the son of geology surveyor Julius Haast, himself a friend of John's; Michael Myers, who was later Chief Justice and Arthur Rhodes, ex MP and Mayor of Christchurch. To Millicent's chagrin, she had to accompany her father when he, in turn, paid calls to his friends and acquaintances. This formidable array of such lofty men was daunting, and paying calls always dismayed her, even when she returned from overseas eight years later with a lot more poise and maturity.[228]

In her memoirs, Millicent skims through her three years at the University of Sydney in just three lines: 'The three years at Sydney University were very pleasant – plenty of gaiety, dancing, swimming, sailing and expeditions into the countryside. Every year I went back home across the Tasman in early December and returned to Sydney in early March.'[229] In contrast, she writes fifty lines to tell of a riding and tramping visit to the Lakes in Central Otago when she was nineteen. She was never a natural academic, and it's easy to see where her heart lay. That journey with Heinrich von Haast, his wife and Michael Myers gave Millicent the sense of adventure she loved: sleeping on a stretcher over the bath at the one hotel in Wanaka, swimming in the lake surrounded by magnificent mountains, clinging onto a bolting mare through streams and fords in the Matukituki Valley, crossing and re-crossing the Rees River on horseback, seeing the waterfalls rushing down Mt Earnslaw and delighting in a garden of flowers on the banks around Lake Harris.[230] Travel, adventure and flowers, they were her loves.

She completed her BA in Sydney in 1908 achieving third class Honours. She knew she hadn't worked hard enough so was satisfied with that result whereas John was unhappy, expecting more. In April 1909, John and 21-year-old Millicent set out for England in the South American luxury liner *Asturias* which had 'lifts and suites and all sorts of luxuries.' On reaching England, they stayed together in London until John went up to Glasgow to have the degree of Doctor of Laws in English conferred on him by his old university. Millicent stayed in Weybridge, Surrey with her old friends the Dendys. Dr Dendy was now Professor of Zoology at King's College, London. She travelled with her father to the University of Cambridge for the Darwin centenary. Millicent was struck by the magnificence of the University ceremonial apparel: 'Our dresses, pale pastel shades mostly, were completely eclipsed by the gorgeous robes of the men. Sir Robert Stout was in black and gold. My father was magnificent in the scarlet of the LL.D. of Glasgow…Two Portuguese delegates had what looked like lampshades on their heads. Altogether, a magnificent show.' Millicent was clearly now feeling far more comfortable in social situations, and she and John went to several receptions, garden parties and dinners. [231]

In accordance with their mutual passion for travel, Millicent and John toured England, Scotland and the Continent, mainly Portugal and Spain. Millicent had been accepted into the University of Cambridge, and in October 1909 she took up residence at Newnham College, run by the vice-principal Joan Pernel Strachey, the sister of Lytton Strachey the biographer and member of the legendary Bloomsbury Set. Newnham had been established in 1871 as a house in which young women could reside while attending lectures at Cambridge. This was long before women were allowed to become full members of the university and receive

Peile Hall, Newnham College, Cambridge
(taken by Penny Griffith in 2014)

degrees. Millicent lived at Melrose Hall for the first year then for her second and third years she resided in Peile Hall, a magnificent construction completed the year she moved in. It was surrounded by beautiful grounds, flanked on one side by the older Sidgewick Hall. Miss Strachey was head of both halls and in 1923 became principal of Newnham College. She was well known for encouraging equality for women and the entry of women into new fields of employment.[232] Millicent liked her very much once she saw past the 'austere figure in pince-nez… tall, thin and reserved.' She coached her students in Old French, a language that Millicent loved.[233]

Millicent's father pressed upon her how fortunate she was to attend an Oxbridge university and made her account for every penny she spent.[234] She rapidly made good friends, and canoeing on the River Cam became a favourite pastime. Canoes were easier to handle than punts and Millicent and her friends would take their

Millicent Macmillan Brown about 22
Ref: Hocken Library MS-975-228 S15-596

lunch far up the river. Margaret Dendy came to stay one weekend and two South African male students took the two girls punting and to the theatre – chaperoned. Of course they had to be back at Peile Hall by 11pm or suffer the consequences. The male students often used the river to swim in and frequently stood naked drying themselves, 'Quite naked, oh yes' she remarks to Christine Cole Catley.[235] When canoeing, Millicent would want to hurry past the men as often they shouted remarks to the girls. One day Maurice Bevan-Brown ran down to meet the girls wearing only a towel. This horrified Millicent, or so she says. [236] Millicent often walked in the surrounding fen country but, apart from primroses, cowslips and violets, she couldn't identify the flowers there. She wouldn't have envisaged then that she would later become an expert on plants, able to identify a great many by their Latin names. She started to take an interest in her clothes, and a cousin in Sydney remarked later 'You were so chic. You seemed to us the last word in fashion and we admired you immensely.'[237] But judging by photographs taken of Millicent throughout her adult life, it's hard to imagine her being the last word in fashion. Albeit always well dressed, she usually appears in an unadorned dress or a blouse tucked into a very plain skirt, more often than not with a large, plain hat rammed down on her head – black for winter, white for summer. Her appearance wasn't of huge importance to her; she was too sensible and down-to-earth for that, though she always dressed appropriately for the occasion. She wouldn't have spent hours in front of a mirror. On one of her overseas trips with Archie, Terence and James she relates 'At Adelaide I had my hair washed and set while Archie and the boys wandered indignantly about, waiting for me. They weren't accustomed to my spending time on my hair, and I never did again.'[238]

Millicent had been brought up without any formal religious instruction, and although she always believed in God, religion had never been of any great importance to her. At Newnham College it was acceptable to have no religious beliefs, but if one did it had to be Anglican. Anything else was socially beyond the pale. This horrified Millicent: 'It roused extreme antagonism in me, so after some consideration I proceeded to join the Presbyterian Church... it was a gesture of defiance.'[239] She would display this characteristic bluntness and rebellion in later life when she encountered prejudices against pacifism.

During the long hot summer of 1912, she went to her beloved Scotland again. 'As I crossed the border a freshness and freedom seemed to breathe in through the windows. Scotland always attracted me far more than England: the moors, the stone walls, the lack of prettiness.' At the end of that summer, she went to Belgium with a Newnham College friend, Irene Wall. They proved to be a pragmatic pair. Finding that the country sold only sour bread and butter with the coffee, not rolls or jam, they found a mass of ripe wild blackberries at the side of the road. The locals never ate them and told the girls they were poisonous, but they ignored that and at the delightful old walled town of Bouillon bought 'a saucepan, a pound of sugar, a bottle of methylated spirits and a spirit lamp, also a jar to put the jam in.' They set up their apparatus in some woods in the Ardennes, borrowed some matches from a peasant ploughing nearby and made enough jam to have for breakfast for the rest of their trip.[240]

Millicent in her early 20s
Ref: Hocken Library E1074/12 S15-599

Millicent loved dancing and went to balls. During one vacation, she went to the St John's College Ball at the University of Oxford. She danced till dawn. Finally, later in 1912, the fun was replaced by feverish activity for about three weeks before the dreaded examinations. She gained a second-class honours in the Tripos, the final honours examination for a BA degree at Cambridge University. The Tripos is divided into two parts, the first part is broad-based, but the second part allows specialisation within the student's chosen field. Millicent's specialisation was French and Old French. A disappointed Miss Strachey wrote to her: 'I am not going to congratulate you. You know you ought to have got a first, if you had worked.' But Millicent was always phlegmatic about academia: 'That was my trouble. I had slacked; I was born lazy.'[241] As usual, she was being self-critical, yet to get a degree of any kind, let alone an MA from Cambridge, was rare indeed for a woman of that time. Although their names appeared in the Tripos and honours lists, women had no degrees conferred on them at that time, and it wasn't until 1948 that Millicent could have had her Cambridge degree conferred.[242] [243] Characteristically, when she was given the opportunity by Cambridge, she couldn't be bothered to make the effort to do so.[244]

In a hansom cab, Millicent felt very sad as she was driven down Cambridge's Silver Street for the last time. 70 years later she reflects with great affection on that period in her life: 'That easy, pleasant life, unlike any other in the world, with its interesting work and delightful companions, was moving irrevocably into the past. And so was all the life of the middle class in England as I had known it, soon forever to be destroyed in the war.' But she also saw the other side of that English way of life: 'Perhaps it was right that it should go. We were so comfortable, so self-satisfied and around us were evils everywhere in the world which we never saw nor thought of. We see them now. But sometimes I feel a nostalgia for those times.'[245]

After Cambridge, Millicent elected to go to Germany to the Halle University for eighteen months where Old French was extensively taught and where she was also able to learn the German language. She boarded in the house of Professor Gutzeit and his wife, both from East Prussia. The plan was for her get a PhD in French, and she enjoyed herself there, particularly socially of course: 'I had a very good time there, plenty of society, balls, parties and evenings. Anna Pavlova gave a performance at Halle, and well-known actors would often come down and give some Shakespeare plays, always so popular in Germany.' It seems that, as usual, the social life interrupted her study time, and her endeavouring to learn an unknown language as well as her main subject was all too much. She failed to get her degree, but, characteristically, she had no regrets about that and simply valued learning the new language.

It was 1914, and John was anxious for her to leave Germany because of the increasing speculation of war, although there was no sign of it in Halle. He also wanted her back to play hostess at Holmbank to the many academic visitors he still entertained. She had several farewell parties, and her friends saw her off with bottles of liqueur, chocolates and flowers. Millicent writes 'I didn't mind pulling up my roots. They hadn't gone very deep. A lot of people I hadn't liked at all. And a lot of people I had liked. But I had had a very interesting time.' Back in England, Millicent considered whether to follow John's wishes or, with her qualifications in languages, get an interesting secretarial job. She was reluctant to return to New Zealand. She had become accustomed to her free and independent life on the other side of the world. She also realised that teaching was the only appropriate job for her in New Zealand, and she didn't like teaching. Finally, however, the dutiful Millicent agreed; her father had paid for her education and she felt duty-bound to do what he wanted.[246]

But, she had to have one last fling. She went with Vera Dendy to Paris. Vera had never seen Paris. Millicent knew Paris well and was able to show off all the sights. They had a wonderful time and Millicent tells a story in which one can just picture these two girls shocked and nervous but giggling together afterwards at what happened, as any two girls in their twenties would do irrespective of their generation – though Millicent relates it in her usual serious way:

[Vera] was pretty and somewhat provocative in appearance. She was always getting accosted in the street – just exuberance and fun on the part of the accoster. 'It's your own fault' I said. 'It's the way you look and the way you behave. I don't get accosted.' Such remarks were never wise. A few days later we were returning from Versailles on top of a double-decker tram with long seats running down the length of the tram. A man sat down beside me and started pushing his knee under mine. I told Vera. She said 'Change with me and I'll kick him.' But I had no faith in this kicking business. How could one possibly kick accurately on top of a swaying tram? So I refused. When he began to push his hand under, we got off at the next stop. He followed us but we went into the metro and he didn't go there. Vera simply remarked, 'Well, your man was pretty unpleasant looking.' And he was.[247]

Her carefree life was now at an end. The Holt liner *Ascanius* set sail from Liverpool with Millicent on board, and on 28 July 1914, just before the ship reached Freemantle in Australia, the news reached them that Austria had declared war on Serbia, a declaration that eventuated in bringing the great powers of Europe to war. Like most young people, Millicent was very excited about it and had no thought of likely consequences: 'I didn't think clearly about it at all, but just accepted what was said in the papers.' Nevertheless, she was very disturbed to hear of the persecution of people with German names who had come to New Zealand to avoid conscription.[248]

The journey was made more fun by the presence of her great friend Margaret Dendy who was going with her father to the British Association annual convention in New Zealand. With the news of the war, members of the Association disembarked in Adelaide with the intention of getting the first boat they could back to England, but Millicent went on to Sydney. She found very little had altered in the five years she had been away, and the war had as yet made little impact on Australia and New Zealand. She became aware of her now very English accent when she noticed a difference between her pronunciation of certain vowels and that of her relatives. With that youthful desire to conform and her natural lack of pretention, Millicent tried to pronounce her vowels as they did. In fact, she never lost her upper class Cambridge society accent; recordings made in the 1980s have her speaking with what would be considered today a very refined English accent. She arrived back in Christchurch to find that her father and Viola had moved from Holmbank to a newly constructed house, which they also called Holmbank, in Macmillan Avenue,[249] a few minutes' walk from their cottage, *Matatea*. He had chosen a section of land for the new house on land that he had previously owned. It was in the Cashmere Hills. He had sold the land in 1908, '60 beautiful hillside sections... in beyond doubt the very finest hillside sites that have ever been offered to the public of New Zealand.... Macmillan Avenue, running through the centre of the subdivision, will have concrete channels and asphalt paths and will be the finest thoroughfare to be found anywhere on the Port Hills.'[250] With such persuasive writing, it is small wonder that he had become such a successful entrepreneur.

Since his retirement, John had been busy with his many interests in history, art, native flora and particularly the anthropology of the Pacific countries. He had inherited his father's passion for travelling the high seas and spent increasing amounts of time researching in the South Pacific. For periods of up to six-month at a time, he collected plants and artefacts to further the study of the regions cultures. His investigations into flora, history, art and anthropology would result in articles and books on the Dutch East Indies (Indonesia) and the origins and ethnology of the Polynesians.[251] The new Holmbank was on a raw hillside, and John spent a huge amount of money creating, with the help of Viola, a striking and glamourous garden and fernery with hundreds of exotic plants he had brought back from his journeys to the Pacific. His grandson Kenneth says that it was considered at the time to be one of the best gardens in Christchurch.[252]

The second Holmbank on a new section in Cashmere, Christchurch, c 1915
Ref: Macmillan Brown Library 118-12918)

The relationship between Millicent and her father had not improved with absence. Millicent had revelled in five years of independence and she found it very difficult to adjust to his patriarchal attitude and his directions: 'We had many clashes... In some ways I think I was very like him and it came out more then than at any other time.'[253] Millicent spent time cataloguing John's library and read entire sections of the collection. Her passion became biography; she told Frank McKay

The second Holmbank, in Cashmere, Christchurch, 1980s. (Taken by Bruce Harding)

that she was always was far more interested in people than in ideas.[254] Viola was now nearly seventeen and the two sisters had become very good friends and remained so for the rest of their lives. Millicent found Viola 'a most delightful companion and friend. How lucky I was! Lots of people don't get on with their sisters. I did, and we have remained close friends for the rest of our lives. Miss Boulton's sister, Miss Emily Boulton, had come to be housekeeper, and the two Miss Boultons and Viola and I made a harmonious quartet. I don't say that we didn't sometimes have dissensions – everyone does. But on the whole we got on very nicely.'[255]

Since their mother died, Viola, like Millicent, had essentially been brought up by Gertrude, and Viola didn't go to school until she was fourteen. Unlike her sister, Viola got on very well with her father, perhaps because she had always been his favourite and he didn't seem to dominate her as he did Millicent. Viola was happiest with him when they read stories to one another in the evenings. She felt his character had two sides to it: 'one inherited from his puritan and anxious mother, the other from his gay and companionable father.'[256] Viola now had the run of her father's huge library as Millicent had. John had been tutoring her in classics and English, but she couldn't keep up to his expectations of sixteen hours study a day and felt she let him down with her results. Instead of meeting his desire for her to follow her sister to Cambridge, she pursued her love of art and went to the Canterbury School of Art.

It was at the art school that Viola befriended writer Ngaio Marsh, who would later become famous as one of the 'Queens of Crime.' Ngaio lived a few minutes' drive away in Sherwood Lane on the lower slopes of Cashmere, and Viola would often borrow John's old Packard, a luxury American car, and drive Ngaio and herself to the school. There was a relationship by marriage between Ngaio Marsh and the Macmillan Browns: Ngaio's mother was the cousin of Samuel Hurst Seager, Helen's sister's husband. Viola's portrait of Ngaio still hangs today in the lounge of Ngaio Marsh House, now a heritage building. During that mid-war period, there were few entirely fit young men for these life-loving girls to have fun with, but Ngaio and Viola still went to many parties, and glamorous parties they were. John always insisted that Viola was home by nine, and she highly resented having to leave before her friends. Millicent's son, Terence, remembers from his childhood his aunt Viola being a lot prettier than Millicent and recalls l suitors arriving with sports cars to take her out. He told Paul Millar in an interview in 1995 that 'When I used to go up there when I was young, in holiday time, all those beautiful sports cars used to come round. I thought they were coming to see my grandfather, but it wasn't him, it was her. One of them would be top dog, and he'd be able to take her away in the car.'[257]

Millicent rarely mentions the war. This is in contrast to her later interest in politics. Perhaps she felt that such matters were sufficiently well-known by the time she published her memoirs in 1984 and that she had nothing to add to what her average reader would already know, oblivious that readers would be interested in the opinion of this intelligent and politically knowledgeable woman. What she does tell us is

> For the first nine months things were very ordinary. The war hadn't yet made much impact. One saw soldiers in the streets…
> A lot of us went down to Lyttelton to see the First Expeditionary Force set out. Men were hanging on to every part of the rigging

and the bulwarks. I remember Archie Burns (I didn't know him but the people with me did) being particularly jolly and vociferous. He came home very changed. Sitting in a car between his brother-in-law and another man, he pulled out a revolver and shot himself. That has stayed in my mind for sixty years.[258]

Even in 1915 when Viola and Millicent went to Sydney for the winter and stayed with their aunt and uncle, the Gordon Craigs, and New Zealand's participation in the war in Gallipoli was reaching its height, she writes only of social activities in Sydney and having measles, rather than comment on war and politics. She does later include the characteristically succinct statement 'The war went on. Atrocity stories circulated everywhere. People became more and more embittered.'[259] The impact of World War One on Christchurch was as devastating as in other cities and towns in New Zealand. 24,000 men enlisted in that city during the war, and 2,739 of them were killed.[260] The home-front war effort was very successful; those who had helped to make the 1906–07 New Zealand International Exhibition such a triumph starting organising fund-raising for the war on a large scale, and Christchurch women responded prodigiously, knitting balaclavas and socks and the like, rolling bandages, and packing 'trench comforts' for the troops.[261]

Ever the pragmatist, Millicent just got on with things and clearly did her fair share in the war effort albeit seeming almost dismissive of her contribution: 'In the spring of 1915, I started on the usual war work, rolling bandages at Dorothy Bennett's on the hills, working at the Red Cross Central Depot[262], making up parcels at the Lady Liverpool [Fund] Depot, the usual sorts of things that girls did then.'[263] The Lady Liverpool Fund had been established two days after the start of the war by the wife of Lord Liverpool, the Governor of New Zealand and later the country's first Governor-General. Each year the Fund sent several parcels to every soldier overseas, especially around Christmas. The basic parcel contained two pairs of socks, one handkerchief, soap and a pencil. Often they included 'home comforts' such as shortbread and cigarettes, which were designed to remind the soldiers of New Zealand and impress upon them that they remained in the public's mind.[264]

Millicent becomes more animated when she talks of later working with an Anglican clergyman, the Reverend L. Hard, in the Enquiry Bureau of the Red Cross, obtaining from Army Base Records the names of all the men posted missing and believed killed and sending the information on to the relatives. She briefly leaves aside her distant way of writing when she comments 'It was interesting work and Mr Hard and I got on very well. We talked on many, many subjects besides our official business.'[265] Whether or not there was some romantic interest in Mr Hard is not known. If so, is Millicent in her memoirs showing herself to be a replica of her mother in her remoteness and inability to express her emotions? Or is it due to the contemporary distaste of imposing one's emotions on others? Certainly her dislike or disinclination to show emotion would last all her life. Without doubt, she wasn't as quiet and reserved as her mother was. Everyone who met her remarks on her loquacious personality, but at the same time she almost always kept her deeper sentiments to herself.

Having scrupulously mentioned just about every year of her life in her memoirs, Millicent omits mentioning much of the remaining period of the war. Her story recommences in mid-1918 when she first hears of the man who will change her life.

CHAPTER 4
The Leap to Pacifism

It was probably July 1918 when Janet Prosser, Millicent's ex-governess and long-time family friend, came to see Millicent at Holmbank in the Cashmere Hills. She handed Millicent a sheet of typewritten paper. It was a copy of that crucial letter that had been written by Archie Baxter from the battlefront in Ypres four months earlier in March 1918 and subsequently published in N.Z. Truth:

Somewhere in France
March 5, 1918

My Dear Father and Mother

I have just time to send you this brief note. I am being sent up the lines tomorrow. I have not heard where Jack and Sandy are. As far as military service goes, I am of the same mind as ever. It is impossible for me to serve in the Army. I would a thousand times rather be put to death and I am sure you all believe that the stand I take is right. I have never told you since I left New Zealand of the things I have passed through, for I knew how it would hurt you. I only tell you now, so that, if anything happens to me, you will know.

I have suffered to the limit of my endurance, but I will never in my sane senses surrender to the evil power that has fixed its roots like a cancer on the world. I have been treated as a soldier who disobeys (Number 1 Field Punishment). That is hard enough at this time of the year, but what made it worse for me was that I was bound to refuse military work, even as a prisoner. It is not possible for me to tell you in words what I have suffered. But you will be glad to know that I have met with a great many men who have shown me the greatest kindness.

I know that your prayers for me are not in vain. I will

pray for you all to the last. It is all I can do for you now. If you hear that I have served in the Army, or that I have taken my own life, do not believe that I did it in my sound mind, no matter what anyone says. I never will.

We are all standing together, although we are not far apart. I have not much more time, but I will write again as soon as I can.

Your loving son,

Archie Baxter (Passed by Censor)

Copy
Base Records Branch. NZ Military Forces.[266]

Reading the letter was a seminal moment, an epiphany, for Millicent. She writes 'my whole life changed… from then on I began to look at things quite differently. It altered my whole outlook on politics and everything in life. I keep it in my handbag to this day.'[267] And indeed she did; it was transferred from handbag to handbag. The letter stayed with her until she died. It is interesting to ponder why Archie's letter altered her 'whole outlook on politics and everything in life.' Was this so, or was it a retrospective claim? It's difficult to find clues in her text. She certainly writes effusively in her memoirs about her marriage to Archie but otherwise rarely expresses such emotion. When her memoirs were published she was quoted in the *Otago Daily Times* as saying she became a pacifist on impulse. 'It's peculiar, but sometimes these things just happen. It was just an emotional impulse. You can't explain it.'[268] In any event, it was several months after reading Archie's letter that she visited him. She had not anticipated she would visit him nor even expected that he would survive the war, but the letter certainly did set her life on a new course.

Millicent tells us that it was Blanche Baughan, the well-known Christchurch poet and writer, who had copied Archie's letter and sent it to *N.Z. Truth*, the popular socialist tabloid newspaper which in those days was pacifist. *N.Z. Truth* hadn't published the letter immediately upon receipt of it because government regulations dictated that all war-related stories had to be passed by the censor for publication, particularly if they alleged brutality to men in military custody. In June 1918 the censor finally allowed publication of the letter and *Truth* used it to illustrate the use of 'crucifixion' on New Zealanders at the front[269]. They also printed a copy of a telegram that had been sent to John Baxter on 14 May 1918, telling him that Archie had been admitted to a mental hospital in the UK.[270]

We don't know how the letter got from Archie's parents to *Truth*, but we do know how it ended up in Millicent's hands. In March 1918, having made no efforts to monitor the progress in Europe of 'The Fourteen' – the name by which they would come to be known – the Defence Department was nevertheless aware of substantiated evidence of brutality, to both 'defiant' and 'genuine' objectors overseas and also in the Wanganui Detention Barracks, and the public were beginning to hear about such cases. The commander of the Wanganui Detention Barracks was Lieutenant J. L. Crampton, a brutal man who believed violence would achieve submission. One prisoner in Wanganui, Thomas Moynihan, reported that he was handed a rifle after 48 hours' bread and water punishment and was forcibly dressed: 'The sergeant banged the barrel of it against the side of my face saying "Will you hold it," I did not answer. He banged me several times till the blood was streaming down the uniform.' The rifle was then tied to Moynihan's wrist and inserted through his shoulder lapel. 'Then somebody suggested that Crampton take my photo. He said "damned good idea" and went away to get his camera.' Then Moynihan, still refusing, was pushed... kicked, punched, pulled by the hair and had his head pushed against the wall.[271]

Baughan was deeply interested in social welfare and an outspoken opponent of capital punishment. Her main concern at this time was for more humane and effective care of prisoners and 'society's misfits.'[272] She and another Christchurch activist Sarah Page supported the war but abhorred cruelty. They had learned of the treatment being meted out at Wanganui, now they knew about Archie Baxter. Baughan, Jessie Mackay and Mary Johnson widely circulated copies of the Archie's letter and the telegram regarding the mental hospital. They attached a covering note concluding that Archie Baxter had been 'driven, through repeated punishment as a disobedient soldier, into mental illness'. They asked 'What have the Germans done that is worse than gradually torturing into mental instability a fellow countryman – and that for his conscience's sake?'[273]

Janet Prosser as the go-between was quite possibly a pacifist at the time; certainly in her memoirs Millicent mentions Prosser's attendance at the War Resisters International Conference in Copenhagen in 1937.[274] Perhaps she thought Millicent might be influenced by the letters, or simply would be interested as an intelligent bystander.

The letter has now become famous and is pivotal to the story of Archie and Millicent as well as pacifism in New Zealand. Millicent writes that the letter 'moved me, right out of my shell into the open; and in the open I have remained, looking into things, questioning them.'[275] Apart from the highly emotive element of a 'soldier' writing to his parents about the brutal treatment he was receiving, the effect it had on Millicent was profound. She exhibited no evidence of pacifist leanings prior to this point; in fact, no evidence of any political opinions. John appears to have been a militarist and imperialist along with most of his friends. In The Press in 1917, under the heading of Red Feds and Prussianism is an account of John's address at the Overseas Club on 'Some Aspects of Peace and the Future' where he drew attention to some rather startling resemblances between Prussian ideas and those underlying the Industrial Workers of the World and the New Zealand Federation of Labour (the Red Feds):

Now if you look at [the IWW's] acts you will find that they intend to destroy the industry of Australasia. They are almost all idle vagabonds who live upon the fellows who work. Those that arrogate certain virtues clearly show that they do not possess them. So it is with the pacifists – they claim to be the true friends of peace; but the peace that the pacifist wants is exactly the same kind of peace that the Kaiser wants – a breathing space in order to gather force for another attack on freedom and civilisation.[276]

But while we will never know why Archie' letter struck such a chord in Millicent, what we do know is that she wasn't brow-beaten by her dominant father – that her political views weren't simply a thoughtless copying of her father's. The letter became a key in her life, and from that occasion on she became a pacifist.

At that time, the pacifist movement in New Zealand had made only a minor dent in the barrage of patriotism that overwhelmed the country. Before charting the narrative of Millicent and Archie's individual paths to pacifism it is time to look very briefly at the overall story of pacifism in New Zealand. It goes back much further than most people realise. The Moriori people of Rēkohu (Chatham Islands), New Zealand's most easterly region, about 800km east of Christchurch, are said to have practised pacifism hundreds of years ago when they introduced a regime of no cannibalism, no war and no killing of any kind. They symbolised their non-violence beliefs by wearing white feathers in their hair.[277] The white feather later became an enduring international symbol of peace. Ironically it is also a symbol of cowardice.

On the mainland by the mid-1880s the new Pākehā settlers had control of the colonial frontier. But in 1881, a month before Archibald Baxter was born, an incident occurred at Parihaka that made it the symbolic birthplace of pacifism in New Zealand. Two years earlier the people of this Māori settlement, which lies close to the foothills of Mt Taranaki, began a programme of passive resistance to

land acquisition by the Pākehā. They erected fences across roads, ploughed up paddocks of Pākehā farmers and pulled out survey pegs that had been positioned for a proposed road. Many were arrested and held without trial.

Arrest of ploughmen at Parihaka, 1881.

The government decided to take military action. Just after dawn on 5 November 1881, 1589 volunteers and armed police, many on horseback, charged down the surrounding hills and invaded the village. They were met with complete passivity;

several hundred unarmed Māori were seated in the marae quietly awaiting the coming of the troops. An 'army' of 200 little girls chanting songs and spinning tops

met the first onslaught of charging horses. The leaders, Te Whiti o Rongomai and Tohu Kakahi, were arrested and jailed for seven years. Over the next few weeks most of Parihaka's inhabitants were evicted. Dick Scott, in his book Ask That Mountain – The Story of Parihaka, writes that the women were raped, and their houses, animals and land destroyed.[278] This event is one of the most shameful episodes in colonial New Zealand history.

Volunteer soldiers ready to invade Parihaka, 5 November, 1881 (taken by William Andrews Collis)

Twenty years after the siege of Parihaka, pacifism did not sit well with the patriotic fervour that flourished in New Zealand during the second Boer War (1899–1902). New Zealand was still attached 'umbilically' to the 'mother country' with its principal reliance being trade, particularly for meat and dairy exports. Eager to display the country's commitment to the British Empire, New Zealand sent 6500 troops and 8000 horses to Africa. Archie Baxter very nearly became one of them. Millicent was about twelve when, in 1900, against this backdrop of nationalism, the president of the CWI, Wilhelmina Sherriff Bain, delivered a speech on peace and arbitration at the National Council of Women (NCW) conference in Dunedin, enraging local newspaper editors and patriotic residents. Like Kate Sheppard, Bain was a Christian Socialist and a promoter of women's rights, but she had also become a staunch pacifist.[279]

Pacifism was on the increase. The Peace and Humanity Society was founded in Wellington in 1902 and it was the forerunner of many peace groups, both political and religious.[280] But pacifists in New Zealand, as with the rest of the world, were mainly women. They were a small but vocal minority of the population whose campaigning was prevalent during the South African War, at the introduction of compulsory military training (CMT) in 1909, and during World War I. Voluntary organisations such as the Women's Christian Temperance Union (WCTU), the NCW and the CWI, started to voice their opinions on women's rights and reforms, and the Religious Society of Friends, known as the Quakers, actively expressed their abhorrence of war. In 1906 the idea of CMT was debated with the idea that young men and boys should boost New Zealand's national defence. After much contention, the Defence Act was passed in December 1909, forming a universal obligation for boys and young men from twelve to thirty to be militarily trained.[281] In 1912, William Massey of the pro-compulsionist Reform Party became Prime Minister, resulting in more pacifist and anti-militarist societies springing up in retaliation. In addition to the Quakers there were new religious organisations: The Passive Resisters' Union, the Freedom League, the Anti-Militarist League and the National Peace and Antimilitarist Council of New Zealand. There were new secular groups such as the National Peace Council and the New Zealand Freedom League (NZFL).[282] Finally the pacifist voice was being heard and, later in the year, the Defence Act was amended to exclude boys twelve to fourteen years of age from compulsory military training.[283] The Fabian Society, a socialist organization founded in 1884 in London, closely affiliated itself with pacifism, and two founding members of the UK Fabian Society visited New Zealand in 1898, Beatrice and Sydney Webb. Thirty years later, another Fabian Society member visited New Zealand, George Bernard Shaw.

Despite the rise of pacifist societies throughout New Zealand and Britain, on 5 August 1914 the Governor of New Zealand, Lord Liverpool, stood on the steps of parliament in the country's capital of Wellington and announced to a 15,000-strong crowd that as a dominion of the British Empire, New Zealand was in a state of war with Germany. Within a week 14,000 young men, overcome with patriotic fervour had volunteered.[284] One young man ran a bayonet through his mother's piano and threatened to shoot her when she denied him permission to sign up.[285] The Minister of Defence, Sir James Allen, arranged to send an expeditionary force of 8000 men with a promise that the unit would be maintained at full strength throughout the war.[286]

As the war became one of attrition, particularly after the huge losses at Gallipoli in 1915, further reinforcements were required. But visible evidence of the reality of war in the form of coffins and mutilated bodies had begun to change people's minds about enlisting. When Lord Kitchener's accusatory finger in Your Country Needs YOU! posters ceased to bring forth sufficient volunteers, the government set up the National Register towards the end of 1915 to discover how many of the eligible men would be prepared to enlist. About one-sixth indicated that they wouldn't be prepared to undertake war service either at home or abroad.[287] Backed by public support, the government decided there were too many 'shirkers' and that compulsion must be used.

But conscription in New Zealand was hugely controversial. The Labour Party, pacifists and anti-militarists were against it. Christchurch had always been known for non-conformity, and anti-militarism thrived there. Two-thirds of the country's objectors to CMT were from Christchurch.[288] The Military Service Act 1916 became law in August that year. It allowed the conscription of males between twenty and forty-six years to form the Expeditionary Force Reserve. From this reserve all future troops were selected by a monthly ballot system which James Belich likens to a game of Lotto: 'In a room in Wellington sat 233 drawers, containing 116,500 cards with numbers and names on them. The marbles rolled here, too, and thousands won first prize, a one-way trip to France.'[289] Of the troops New Zealand sent to war 91,941 were volunteers and 32,270 were conscripted – the conscription ratio was roughly one in four.[290] There was a political storm after the Act was passed. In December 1916, Labour Party member and future Prime Minister Peter Fraser, who would later become a friend of Archie and Millicent, was convicted of sedition for advocating the repeal of the Act and served twelve months' imprisonment for the offence. Bob Semple, Tim Armstrong, Jim O'Brien and Paddy Webb, all future Labour cabinet ministers, also went to prison for their opposition to the war or conscription.[291]   Most women supported the war at the start, and many shared the prevalent hatred of things German. Anna Paterson Stout, wife of Robert Stout (later Sir Robert), founded an Anti-German League which in three months had acquired1500 members. It has been said she was triumphant when a German teacher from Nelson committed suicide.[292] Feminists were prominent in the White Feather League which 'awarded' a white feather as a symbol of cowardice and unfulfilled duty to one's country to any healthy young man who hadn't volunteered. Some soldiers' mothers, and, no doubt, daughters, sisters, wives and girlfriends, wanted all other mothers' sons to share the same risk of death and mutilation as their own.[293] Women of the Christchurch White Feather League out for a day's shirker-hunting were chased off the streets by other women.[294]

The majority of eligible men who objected to military service were religious or were conscientious objectors, 'conchies' as the latter came to be called. There were five main groupings of conscientious objectors: The religious objectors belonged to religious denominations that declared military service to be 'contrary to divine revelation'. Of these, the government deemed exempt only Quakers, Christadelphinians and Seventh-day Adventists. The Māori objectors were primarily political and pacifist with no desire to be involved in what they saw as a white settler war. The Irish objectors belonged to the Sinn Féin, the republican political party in Ireland, viewed Britain as the enemy. The socialist objectors were militants who were more against capitalism and the use of workers in the army than they were against Germany. Pacifist objectors were people who refused to enlist simply because personally they didn't believe in war. Of course there was often an overlap between these categories. For example, many socialist conscientious objectors were also religious objectors.[295]

It was into the pacifist conscientious objector category that Archie Baxter firmly planted himself. He was a rabbiter from a remote corner of Otago who had his own passionate conviction that all war was wrong and was prepared to go to any lengths to never be part of it.

After reading Archie's letter, Millicent felt at odds with the people she mixed with: 'Most of the people I knew were still solidly war-like, that's to say, normally patriotic. There was terrible hostility to any pacifist opinion.'[296] So, like Archie, she found herself alone in her new views. She found it a very painful experience. Only her sister gave her any sympathy, although Viola never became a pacifist herself.[297] Millicent gradually got to know people of like mind, not many, but enough to give her some support. But unlike Archie, Millicent didn't yet have the courage to broadcast her newly formed pacifist views to everyone and she felt she was a coward for that lack of courage. Seeing the ferocity of the feelings pacifism inspired in non-pacifists, she couldn't bring herself to reveal her change of views, particularly to her father. In the 1919 election she felt that morally she couldn't vote for the Conservatives, but neither could she be disloyal to her father by voting Labour 'So I recorded an invalid vote. I wish I hadn't been such a coward, but there it was.' Her morality and honesty, especially about herself, would be evident throughout her life. She continues: 'And to belong, for a considerable part of the rest of my life, to an unpopular minority, I found very hard.'[298]

But these thoughts about pacifism or anything else were halted by the arrival of the shocking influenza pandemic, or Spanish Flu' as it was called, that swept through New Zealand in the last three months of 1918. It spread out of control as soldiers returned from Europe at the end of World War One and as large numbers of people met together to celebrate. People showing influenza symptoms sometimes collapsed within a matter of hours after their onset and even died on the same day. There were of course no influenza vaccinations available and no antibiotics for those who fell ill. During World War One nearly 18,000 New Zealand soldiers died in four years of fighting, and about half that number died from the influenza epidemic in just two months.[299] At its height, in November, ordinary life was impossible. Shops, offices and factories shut down through lack of staff and schools, hotels and theatres were closed by order of the government.[300]

Millicent was asked if she would help operate a special telephone enquiry line at the hospital. She worked on the telephone from 2 pm till 10 pm with a brief meal break. She would receive an enquiry about a patient, put them on hold while she rang or visited the ward concerned and then update the enquirer. All too frequently she had to summon relatives to a dying patient or tell people their loved one had died. It was chaos in the wards and mistakes were made: 'Sometimes summoned relatives would be crossing the courtyard when a porter would come rushing in to say "It's the wrong people. I gave you the wrong name!" and I would hurry out to stop them; but almost always their turn would come in time.' The wards were shocking places to be in and Millicent constantly heard patients cry 'Get me out of here! I can't bear it.' At the end of one of the wards where the private rooms were she could hear one of the house surgeons vomiting continuously.[301]

It is clear she was profoundly affected by the whole experience and in a rare show of emotion she writes 'There were of course no antibiotics then and they died, died, died.' In retrospect, Millicent realised the whole experience had been a great strain on her nerves, already badly affected by her new pacifist concerns: 'I don't think I had a nervous breakdown but I was inclined to burst into tears if I was contradicted, and other ridiculous symptoms' she writes impatiently. She went for a break to friends at New Brighton, but the ring of the telephone which was on a party line shared with the grocer disturbed her so much they had to take it off the hook. For the rest of her life she hated hearing a telephone ring and disliked ever having to use them.[302]

In the middle of 1919 the family went to Sydney in a converted German vessel, the Prinzessin. She was a solid ship and Millicent declares that for the first and only time in her twenty-eight crossings of the Tasman she wasn't seasick. Viola enrolled at The Sydney Art School. Whilst Millicent was visiting friends, she had a curious meeting with Mary Gilmore (later Dame Mary Gilmore), the prominent Australian socialist, poet and journalist who had been a pacifist during the war. They clearly had a disagreement and Millicent recalls 'She had views on the colour question which didn't seem to me to accord at all with her pacifism. She was very firm. She said to us "You ladies are unmarried and likely to remain so." By this time she was really angry. "You have no right as single women to express an opinion on this matter." '[303]

Back in New Zealand in January 1920, Millicent decided it was time she did something about the shortage of teachers in New Zealand. She felt strongly that she needed to make her mark in the world. Convinced that she didn't want to teach in the Canterbury district, probably because she would be under the vigilant and critical eye of her father, she travelled third class to Wellington in the old ferry Rotomahana to see the Secretary of the Education Board. Millicent's granddaughter, Katherine Baxter, feels that Millicent was actually more interested in positioning herself in politics and being part of the political scene in the capital and possibly went to Wellington with the intention of starting as the secretary of an MP.[304]

Expecting to be greeted with open arms by the Education Board, Millicent was told that she wasn't qualified for primary school teaching. Nevertheless, she had excellent qualifications as a secondary teacher and was later offered a post as teacher of modern languages at Wellington Girls' College. She felt thrilled to have been offered the job and was looking forward to her new life in Wellington, but it was not to be.

An opportunity had suddenly presented itself to John. He learned that the Professor of English, Professor Gilroy, had died during the jubilee celebrations of Otago of University. Although John was now seventy-four and had retired from Canterbury College twenty-four years beforehand, he had been Vice-Chancellor of the University of New Zealand since 1916. He agreed to temporarily fill the post. His reputation obviously went before him, and the university accepted him, 'no doubt in fear and trembling' remarks Millicent.[305] Typically, he insisted that he couldn't manage without his older daughter – Viola was still at Sydney Art School. Millicent would have to go with him. For an independent woman like Millicent, the decision to put her dominating father first must have been an extremely difficult one, but she finally agreed and turned down the Wellington teaching position. She felt very resentful about it. However, John's selfishness and Millicent's dutiful deference proved to be a turning point in her life.

They moved to Dunedin around March 1920, staying in comfortable lodgings in Onslow Home, a boarding house close to the beach at St Kilda. From his first year in Dunedin, John's closest friend became Sir Robert Stout. By this time, John had made great deal of money. Millicent says that by his judicious speculation in shares he became the only professor in New Zealand to make such wealth: 'He had flair. It was said he was the best gambler in New Zealand, but he didn't really gamble.

He knew what he was doing, and would keep on till the last moment and sell out at the last moment, in time. Other people didn't. People often asked him for tips. He cheerfully gave them but I used to think, "You silly people, he won't tell you when to sell out," which was what he had always managed so wonderfully.'[306]

Millicent bought a typewriter and started attending classes to learn shorthand – just as her father had done as a boy. But the teacher was a little too inclined to confide his marital troubles to her, so she left. On Sundays she took to going out for long walks, sometimes with her old childhood friend Robin Bevan-Brown, who was studying at the Medical School. John obviously approved of the relationship and began to give Robin tips for investment. Millicent and Robin laughed together over this, knowing where his hopes lay. She started to get to know people involved in politics and befriended Creta Milligan, the wife of Roy Milligan, a lecturer at the Medical School who was interested in pacifism.[307] She was introduced to members of the Labour party but tended to find them boring and one-sided. She was shocked at the Victorian attitude of the wife of one of them who said to her 'Don't go bothering about politics. Mr Right's waiting for you!'[308]

At the end of the winter term, John decided he had done enough for Otago University for the time being and went away on yet another of his trips abroad, leaving Millicent with his lecture notes to help one of his assistants, Bertha Clement, to manage and teach his classes and to supervise examinations. Bearing in mind that she had never been a teacher and for twelve years hadn't touched the subject of English, it is not clear if Millicent gave lectures, but she certainly supervised examinations.[309] Charles Brasch, who would become the founding editor of the literary journal Landfall, says that around this time she used to visit his uncle, noting a 'strong independent inquiring mind',[310] as one of her chief characteristics.

Then, in the spring of 1920, she went in search of this Archibald Baxter she had heard so much about.

PART TWO
The Husband's Story

CHAPTER 5
The Rabbiter

New Zealand's best-known pacifist, Archibald Baxter, was born five weeks after the siege at Parihaka and three months after Helen Connon became the first woman in the British Empire to gain an honours degree. Had she lived, she would have been his mother-in-law. While Millicent's background was almost entirely Scottish, Archie's was completely so. His paternal grandfather, John Baxter, was a farm labourer from Rothesay on the Isle of Bute in the region of the West Highlands. He married Janet McKellar, but she died in 1857 after their fifth child was born.[311] John then joined the throng of Scots escaping poverty by migrating to the goldfields of Otago, New Zealand.

Mary Baxter nee McColl b 1858
(By kind permission of Jan Kelly)

He boarded the Lady Egida in Greenock on 18 October 1860 with four of his children. It was the ship's maiden voyage and she was proclaimed as the largest vessel with the greatest number of passengers to have ever landed in Otago.[312] Among the four Baxter children was seven-year-old John, who would become Archie's father.

They arrived in Port Chalmers, the port of Dunedin, on 28 January 1861 and after the usual stint in the immigration barracks settled in Brighton, a little seaside town about eighteen kilometres south-west of Dunedin. It is believed that John Baxter, like many Scottish immigrants at that time, spoke only Gaelic. He had a passion for playing the bagpipes, a pastime that he would pass on to his son John and great-grandson

John Baxter, born 1852.
(By kind permission of Diane Dore)

James. He was an austere, strong, hard-working man but didn't have enough capital to buy a farm. He tried his luck at the goldfields and struck gold at Dunstan, now Clyde, in Central Otago. Little is known of his domestic life. Frank McKay points out that 'The silences in the early family history reflect the patriarchal society to which Baxter's ancestors belonged.'[313]

Archie's maternal grandfather, Archibald McColl, came from another family of Scottish Highlanders, the McColls. They came from Ballachulish in Argyllshire on the shores of Loch Leven, also in the West Highlands but a hundred and sixty kilometres from the Isle of Bute where the Baxters lived. Their ancestors had fought in the Battle of Culloden in 1746. Archie Baxter's ancestry shows no trace of the pacifism that he would become involved in from his teenage years. The Baxter family tree has several Baxters marrying McColls, resulting in a number of Archibalds and Johns for both surnames. This particular Archibald McColl, the maternal grandfather, left Glasgow with his wife, Margaret Learmond,[314] and family on board the Alpine and after the ninety-three-day passage they arrived in Port Chalmers in September 1859, a year before the Baxter family. He never spoke English fluently during his forty-seven years in New Zealand. Their five sons and two daughters ranged in age from one to twenty-four. The baby, Mary, would later marry the younger John Baxter.

Archibald and Margaret McColl built a sod cottage on a property in a remote area below Saddle Hill in Creamery Road, Ocean View, three kilometres northeast of Brighton, which they farmed. In 1879, nearly twenty years after the Baxter and McColl families reached Dunedin, their son John Baxter now aged twenty-eight and Mary McColl aged twenty-one married and the new branch of the Baxter clan began. The Baxters would have eight children in seventeen years. The birth rate of settlers in New Zealand between 1840 and 1880 was among the highest in the world, almost nine children per married woman, so the Baxters were certainly not considered an unusually large family.[315] Following the birth of their first son John (Jack) in 1880, Archibald McColl Learmond Baxter was born on 13 December 1881 in his McColl grandfather's sod cottage on the farm on Creamery Road, below Saddle Hill. A new child arrived every two to three years: Mark, Hugh (Hughie), William (Billie), Donald, Alexander (Sandy) and lastly, in 1897, Margaret (Maggie or Peggie). Unusually for the time, Archie's parents managed to bring up their family without the death of a child.[316]

The early 1880s was the time of the long depression, and while Helen Connon (now Mrs Helen Macmillan Brown) was enjoying the position of principal at the Girls' High School in Christchurch and enjoying Holmbank with its servants, young Archie and his siblings were being brought up in a very humble and poor household. John Baxter, like his father, was a hard worker. He was an emotional but fearless man who travelled away from home to where he could find work as a casual farm worker and seasonal shearer. But he was also a spendthrift, so the family was always poor. A lot of his money went on alcohol; all his adult life he had been a hardened drinker and was probably an alcoholic, a weakness that his grandson James would inherit and eventually recognise in himself. Mary Baxter often had to depend on a very generous Brighton storekeeper, Barney Wasserbrenner, for credit.[317] John would frequently take Archie to Dunedin with him when he went to sort out his financial affairs, and at the end of the day Archie would have to search the pubs to find his inebriated father and take him home. Interestingly, none of John Baxter's sons turned to drink. John did manage to give up alcohol for thirteen years. He hung religious texts around the house as a reminder to keep sober, but his extravagances remained, and the family lived from hand to mouth. John was also a deeply religious man although he seems not to have imposed his strict church-going habits on his children.[318]

Mary Baxter was a short, sturdy but feminine woman who, to a large extent, brought up their eight children on her own as John was so often away working or spending their money in the pub. But she took no nonsense from him and thought nothing of throwing him and his bagpipe-playing friends out of the house when she had had enough. She was strong and resilient, the decision-maker of the family. She had a broad-minded attitude to life, and perhaps she instilled this into Archie, teaching him to think outside the square of the accepted and conservative opinions of the time. By all accounts, she was an innovative woman and somehow found time for hobbies in taxidermy and painting in oils and watercolours.[319] Her great sense of fun and humour shows in the few photographs of her that survive. One photograph shows her sitting on the ground at their Creamery Road farm on a sunny day. John Baxter is there, sporting a white moustache and dressed in a casual suit, white band-collar shirt and trilby hat. Mary's hair is pulled severely back and parted in the middle. She has chubby cheeks and a broad smile and nestles a kitten in her lap.

One family story tells of Mary going down to the beach and praying for food, hoping that they might be able to get a fish, when one came up out of the water, right to her feet.[320] Mary was typical of the stoic hard-working women of the times. Her grandson James later wrote of her taking trips to Dunedin for provisions: 'She carried a sack of oatmeal on her back / Twelve miles, walking beside the breakers / From the town to her own gate.'[321]

Both Archie's parents were long-lived: Mary died in 1932 aged eighty-four, and John Baxter, when he was eighty-six in 1939. Just before John died, Archie experienced a vision of an old man beside his bed-ridden father. This he took to be an ancestor who had come to help his father over.[322] Millicent would later give many examples of Archie seeing apparitions or presences, making the assumption that he had extra-sensory perception.[323]

The Baxter children were lucky in one regard at least: they went to school. The Education Act of 1877 had established free, compulsory primary education for all New Zealand children. Up until then, not many children received an education as only the well-off could afford school fees. In the Saddle Hill area, three schools were opened in the early 1860s: Kuri Bush School, Saddle Hill School and Brighton School.[324] However, in 1888 – the year Millicent was born – Jack Baxter was suffering from bullying at Saddle Hill School, so John and Mary decided to send eight year-old Archie there early, in order to give support to his older brother. Young though he was, Archie was more articulate than Jack and more able to talk their way out of trouble, an ability that would stand him in good stead in the future.

Apart from its educational role, the school was a social centre and many concerts and dances were enjoyed there by people of all ages. They came from miles around, despite the road often being a sea of mud in wet weather, and all around the hill, the light of lanterns could be seen heading towards the school when there was an evening of entertainment. The sole teacher in Archie's four years there was Mr McBryde, who taught at the school for thirty-one years. He must have been an extraordinarily busy man; in addition to teaching seventy children every day, he had to bring in wood for the fires, clean the school once a week, clean the chimneys three times a year and keep the fences in good repair.[325]

Two years later, Archie moved to Brighton school where he stayed until a day after his twelfth birthday in December 1893. John was still not making enough money to provide for the family, so he and Mary decided that, with his innovative capabilities, Archie should leave school and start working. He took a variety of jobs on other peoples' farms: he shot rabbits, thinned turnips, minded cows and sheared sheep. Some years later he did fencing and carted coal and became a roading contractor. Within a few years of leaving school, he had accrued enough money to buy a cow, which provided Mary with ample milk, cream, and butter for the large family. By the time he was twenty-one he had become a good horseman and was made head ploughman at Gladbrook Station near Middlemarch, seventy-two kilometres from Brighton.

Archie eventually became the most successful of all the Baxters and McColls, and around 1898 he also had a piece of luck when he won a small block of land in a lottery. The land was part of one of the larger estates taken from the Maori by the colonists in the Land Wars. These estates were beginning to be split up into smaller plots of land to provide for poorer settler farmers. Archie's land was on Scroggs Hill, about five kilometres inland from Brighton. Archie stocked the farm with sheep, pigs and chickens then handed

Archie, Jack and Hughie Baxter 1906. Family Collection

it over to his father who had always felt that having his own farm would be the end to all his troubles. But soon John Baxter was in debt again. Bailiffs were brought in and the land was sold. Archie returned from Central Otago where he had been rabbiting, bought back the farm and made it profitable.[326] Later, he sold the farm to finance a horse and dray to use in the coal-carting business and to enable him to take up a contract with the local council to cart gravel for road construction, employing his brothers as a ready-made work gang.[327]

Archie was a quiet and dignified person who always expressed his opinions in a reasoned way. He was an avid reader and acquired a great deal of knowledge by his own effort. He was passionate about poetry, particularly that of Robbie Burns and the English romantic poets including Keats, Shelley and Byron, as well as the very popular Australian poet, Henry Lawson. This was a passion that he would pass on to his son James. Archie had an excellent memory and would entertain his family and social gatherings by reciting his favourite poems, often by heart, in his soft West Highland accent.[328] There were constant family discussions about poetry, and he recited poetry to himself as he laboured in the open air. He wrote his own verse in the Romantic tradition, and some ballads of his were published in the Taieri Advocate. Some of these can be found in the Hocken Library in Dunedin. He also wrote an untitled novel about his Gaelic-speaking forebears who prospected for gold at Gabriel's Gully. It was never published; the text is unsophisticated and unpolished but it nevertheless illustrates how this man, with little formal education, was able to develop his use of language to become a fairly accomplished writer. This capacity to express his views and his ability to tell his story convincingly, along with a tenacity to back convictions with action, all served in the creation of his iconic pacifist memoir We will not cease.

It is believed that in 1899 (when eleven-year-old Millicent was occupied at home at Holmbank with Helen and baby Viola) Archie was thinking of enlisting for service in the Second Anglo-Boer War, also known as the South African War. Like most young men, he thought that going to war to fight for the Mother Country would be 'an awfully big adventure', an idea that widely existed until the middle of World War One when the reality of war became apparent. But at that point, Archie heard a plea for pacifism that proved to be all-important in his life.

Archie was seventeen. In 'We will not cease' he does not name the speaker but it is believed that he was the Dunedin lawyer and MP Alfred Barclay[329] who gave an address on 11 April, 1899, at Roslyn in Dunedin. It was entitled The Origin of Wealth, being The Theory of Karl Marx in Simple Form.[330] Forty years later, Archie describes Barclay in his memoir as 'a brave and upright man, whose voice was as of one crying in the wilderness, so unlikely did it seem that his point of view would ever be accepted by more than the very few.'[331] [332] It is difficult to know exactly what Archie was referring to here, whether it was pacifism or anti-capitalism. Or if it was the socialist objection to workers being compelled to fight for a capitalist war.

It is not known how Archie came to attend Barclay's speech but he and his brothers were keen readers and it is possible they read the notice publicising the event in the local newspaper. There is a copy of Barclay's speech in the National Library in Wellington but there is no mention of pacifism. Instead, as the title suggests, the speech was a simplified version of Karl Marx's theories on the origin of wealth. It explained the production and distribution of wealth and that the two prime factors of wealth were land and labour. Barclay claimed that in the modern capitalist system in New Zealand, workers were receiving one fifth of the value of what they produced.

Perhaps the subject of pacifism arose during question time? If so, Barclay's impassioned address appears to have compelled Archie towards pacifism overnight. Archie's conversion took place well over a century ago and his memoir gives us no clue as to why he made this abrupt about-turn from being on the brink of volunteering to fight in a war, to pacifism. The question is echoed with Millicent's sudden switch to pacifism nearly twenty years later, although in her case it seems to have been more a political awakening from unthinkingly accepting the view of her father and her father's circle that surrounded her. What we do know is that Archie at Archie at the young and impressionable age of seventeen was won over by Barclay's arguments and became an ardent pacifist for the rest of his life. He scrutinised every pacifist and socialist journal he could lay his hands on and his convictions steadily strengthened into a passion that would last for the rest of his life.

For a very long time, Archie felt alone with his views: 'I ploughed a lonely furrow and for a long time did not even get the support of my own family.'[333] His opinions were considered extreme in the parochial and conservative farming community of Brighton. In pacifist terms, he was an absolutist from the beginning. He opposed any war for any reason, 'war – all war – was wrong, futile and destructive alike to victor and vanquished.'[334] But Archie's personal brand of pacifism related to abhorrence of war, rather than of violence per se. Indeed, it would be wrong to assume that Archie was wholly peaceful; he was rough and tough and for years both before and after hearing Barclay speak, he would get into fights and never hesitate to use a gun daily to shoot rabbits – in fact he later taught his sons Terence and James to shoot.[335] As his younger brothers started to attend school, Archie became the de facto leader of the 'Baxter Gang', a name that the Baxter brothers used later as a work gang.[336] Terence recalls his father telling him that they took on other gangs of boys using matagouri branches stripped to form a sort of spiked club like a medieval weapon.[337] Archie later became a reputable boxer and marksman, was strong and wiry, and a force to be reckoned with.

Initially his family teased him for his new outlandish views. They soon began to hear the same sort of discussions from some of the members of what would become the Labour Party. Through his quiet but passionate persuasion, all his brothers eventually became pacifists and in Otago the name of Baxter came to be equated with pacifism. In 1912 James Keir Hardie visited New Zealand and Archie was so impressed by this Scottish left-wing labour leader that he would later name his second son after him – James Keir Baxter. Archie became very interested in the principles of the Workers' Party in Britain and felt socialism was a necessary part of pacifism.[338] Although it would be another four years before the New Zealand Labour Party was established, there were an increasing number of socialists in New Zealand in the years leading up to World War One. Not all socialists were pacifists, but many believed that this was a war between capitalist nations using workers as soldiers. New Zealand workers, they argued, had no quarrel with German workers.[339]

Archie Baxter was thirty-three when World War One broke out in 1914 and his pacifist convictions became even more fervent. Most people in Brighton were caught up in the patriotic zeal, but when the National Register of all males between the ages of seventeen and sixty was taken in 1915, Archie refused to agree to undertake any service in the army, either at home or abroad. He believed that if enough men refused to fight, governments would be forced to resolve conflict peacefully. When conscription was introduced in 1916, the only possibility for exemption was on narrow religious grounds: only Quakers, Christadelphinians and Seventh-day Adventists were exempt, and while Archie was a Quaker at heart, he had never joined their Religious Society of Friends. He could easily have pressed the point but he declared 'I would never have gone before an Appeal Board to plead my case, for I did not consider that any Board had the right to be judge of a man's sincerity.'[340] Paul Oestreicher, a renowned Quaker pacifist, whose parents were good friends with Archie and Millicent Baxter and who knew the couple himself as a boy, has his own views about how Archie would probably have felt about these principles:

> I think there was a sort of almost proud independence in the way Archie saw life... you don't have to join anything to be genuinely yourself... I suppose in classical, philosophic terms he was a humanist, although he was not an intellectual and he didn't need to prove anything. It was just in his bones. But he was a humanist who had no specific belief in God... the Quakers are called the Religious Society of Friends; they're not just a group of pacifists. They are a group of people with a long religious tradition and I think Archie would have too much integrity to join a religious society when he did not feel religious.[341] [342]

The number of conscientious dissenters (as opposed to religious objectors) was increasing, and while fathers, sons and brothers were being maimed or losing their lives fighting to save the Mother Country, conchies were considered to be shirkers: men who lay around doing nothing, not even undertaking work away from the front. Under Section 5 of what some deridingly called the 'Family Shirkers Clause' of the Military Service Act 1916, men in families in which no male had volunteered could be called up without being balloted.[343] Archie was fully aware this could happen to him and any of his brothers, except Mark who was married with children and therefore exempt. Animosity towards the conchie Baxter family was growing. Reverend Joan Pascoe recalls having played at Brighton primary school with the Baxter children at that time. The close friendship between the two families ended when Archie became a conscientious objector. Because Joan's father and uncles had fought in the war and were all wounded, a rift developed between the two fathers. The attitudes of the parents were in turn reflected by their children.[344]

By this time, Archie was working on the McColl farm in Creamery Road and also took on shearing during that summer to accumulate as much money as possible for the family. He knew he would have only three weeks' notice if he was required to serve in the army. He knew that if he refused conscription, he would be offering himself up to harassment from the community and official punishment by the government.

CHAPTER 6
The Conchie's War against War

It is the end of February 1917.[345] Archie is at the Creamery Road farm in his shirtsleeves, washing his face and getting ready to go into the sale yard. His horse is feeding in the yard outside.[346] A local policeman Archie knows well appears suddenly and another springs out from behind the hedge. Together, they seize him and with no time for farewells to his family they force him into a cart and he is taken to Dunedin. A guard of four men with fixed bayonets ensure maximum public exposure by marching him down the centre of the main street to the St Kilda Battery, a mortifying experience. He writes 'The future held many worse experiences in store for me, worse from every point of view, but nothing ever cut me again like that first, deliberately inflicted, public humiliation.'[347] He and his older brother Jack, who has also been arrested, are taken by train and ferry to a detention camp attached to Trentham Military Camp north of Wellington. Their youngest brother, Sandy, arrives shortly afterwards. At Trentham, the three Baxter brothers refuse to put on uniforms and they are sentenced to twenty-eight days detention in the Alexandra Barracks in Buckle Street, Wellington. Archie is subjected to days of a diet of bread and water. There is no mattress, so he sleeps on the bare floor. [348]

This is the start of what proves to be a stream of abusive actions committed against Archie by the army and police for the next thirteen months. His argument in court was that neither having taken the oath nor having agreed to serve in the army he wasn't a soldier and couldn't, therefore, be charged with disobeying the lawful command of a superior officer.[349] He was to hold fast to this simple rationale throughout his dealings with his interrogators over the coming months, and while the response was almost always rage and the infliction of punishment, they were nonplussed by his argument. He would have made a good lawyer. As Peter O'Connor says in The Awkward Ones: dealing with conscience, 1916-1918 'A handful of men could by their passive resistance drive the military authorities almost to distraction.'[350] All three Baxter brothers were found guilty, and each was sentenced to eighty-four days' hard labour, initially in the Terrace Jail in what was formerly known as Woolcombe St in Wellington[351] then later in Mt Cook prison.[352] They were fingerprinted, given prison clothes patterned with the broad arrow and locked in isolation in cells three paces long which were narrow and dank. Inside were foul-smelling blankets, a stool, a tin basin and a chamber pot. The entire absence of fat in the meagre prison diet resulted in some inmates resorting to eating the mixture meant for greasing boots. This was the start of Archie's long road of starvation and the loss of a third of his bodyweight.

When their sentence was at last over the Baxters were returned to Trentham Camp, but on being offered their kits they refused them again and were immediately sentenced to another twenty-eight days' detention. Each time he was sent to the barracks for detention Archie found there were several more objectors: 'teachers, clerks, workers of all shades of opinion.'[353] To his delight it wasn't long before he found two more of his brothers at the barracks: Hughie and Donald had also stood up for the cause. The Baxter family was to become even more besieged; a few months later Billie was arrested. Mark was married and away from the farm, so John and Mary Baxter now only had Maggie at home.

James Allen as Minister of Defence was becoming progressively concerned at the increasing number of conscientious objectors and felt that an example had to be made; imprisonment in New Zealand could hardly be comparable to fighting in France. In mid-1917 it was decided that the more defiant objectors would be transported to the battlefields of Europe with no training, and if they continued to resist they would be open to punishment like regular soldiers. This decision was made despite common knowledge of the failure of Britain's transportation policy in 1916 when seventy absolutists were forced to the front line in France, given Field Punishment, court-martialled and sentenced to death. Not one of the seventy gave in, and they were eventually returned to Britain.[354] Trentham Camp Commander Colonel R.H. Potter, made an independent decision to action the policy ahead of time and chose to send fourteen of his most uncooperative objectors to Britain.

What happened to Archie for the next twenty-three months is recorded in detail in his 1939 memoir 'We will not cease' and shown in the 2014 film Field Punishment No 1,[355] so what follows here is a brief description of Archie's extraordinary story of his enforced time in the army, with supporting information from other sources.

Early in the morning of 14 July 1917, the three Baxter brothers and another objector, William Little, were silently marched down the streets of Wellington to the transport ship Waitemata which was berthed in the harbour. The ship's commanding officer had no idea they were coming on the voyage. They were manhandled down a gangway into the depths of the old ship to the 'clink', which measured about six by three metres and had two tiers of bunks. Here they met ten

The Waitemata (Painting and permission by Bob Kerr)

other objectors: Mark Briggs, Garth Ballantyne, Henry Patton, Frederick Adin, Thomas Harland, Albert Sanderson, Lewis Penwright, Daniel Maguire, Lawrence Kirwan and David Gray. Some of the earlier arrivals had thrown letters onto the wharf and one of the letters, from Garth Ballantyne to his mother, listed the names of the objectors.[356][357] Initially it was barely recorded in the daily press[358], but when the news finally became known it caused an outcry amongst Labour Party circles. Once on board the Waitemata, The Fourteen 'intractables' were hauled up on the poop deck in front of the hundreds of troops who had been ordered to watch indignities performed on them. Mark Briggs had to be dragged up the stairs; he would prove to be the most uncompromising of The Fourteen. They were all stripped naked and forcibly dressed in uniform to the derision of hundreds of troops who watched. This occurred regularly over the duration of the voyage. Most of the time, they all remained shut up in the depths of the ship except for short periods of exercise on deck. In contrast, the ship's cook and others poked such things as chocolate, cigarettes, fruit and, once, a 'beautifully cooked' steak down the ventilator shaft for the objectors to devour.[359] Throughout his life, Archie would experience great divergence in the responses to his pacifist beliefs – from brutality to acts of great kindness that put the good doer at risk. Awareness that not everyone opposed him was of great solace to Archie.

It was a rough journey to Cape Town, and twelve out of the fourteen prisoners were very seasick, Archie among them.[360] The state of 'the clink', that had no basins, can only be imagined. In the Indian Ocean, Archie, Jack Baxter and Albert Sanderson contracted measles – a serious condition in those days. They reached Cape Town on 22 August, and those suffering from measles were offloaded to the Maitland Hospital in the town. The period of convalescence in Cape Town was a holiday to Archie compared to his experience on board the Waitemata and to what would later befall him in England and France. In November, they boarded the Llanstephan Castle, and within a few weeks the ship had sailed from the tropics to the snow-laden harbour of Plymouth where it arrived on Boxing Day 1917.

Postcard of Sling Camp, Bulford, England.1918 the chalk Kiwi was carved after Archie left – see note 361

The prisoners were immediately transported by train to Sling Camp in the middle of the vast Salisbury Plains in Wiltshire, just eight kilometres from Stonehenge and eighteen kilometres from the medieval city of Salisbury.[361] When the commanding officer learned of Archie's unshakeable views against serving in the army he said to him 'You realise, of course, that you will not have an easy time. How far are you prepared to go?' And Archie replied 'To answer honestly, I am prepared to stand to the utmost limit.'[362] Archie would cling to this simple principle throughout the remainder of the war, indeed for the rest of his life. All the objectors were offered non-combatant service such as driving ambulances, stretcher bearing or becoming medical orderlies – brave and noble services – but to do this still meant wearing a uniform which, at this stage, none of them was prepared to do. The punishments inflicted on them during the next few weeks were accompanied by threats of greater reprisals. Penwright, Adin and Sanderson submitted. Frederick Adin wrote to his sister: 'A few weeks more of imprisonment would have killed me. I was nothing but skin and bone when I came out of the hospital, and I couldn't have stood it if I had gone back to prison.'[363]

With Archie, the officers used everything from calm reasoning to full-scale violence. In their eyes, he provided no satisfying defence for his rejection of war. To them 'I am against all war' was incomprehensible. He was beaten, isolated, put in leg-irons and threatened with court-martial. His hands were continually handcuffed behind his back during the day to prevent him removing his uniform and his cell was often freezing. Brigadier General George Richardson, commander of the New Zealand Expeditionary Force in Britain, had decided that the objectors should be separated, given detention, field punishment and sent with their units to the trenches, even if they had to be carried on stretchers.[364] Others of the objectors had been sent in stages to the trenches over the previous five months, with the exception of Gray who had been deported to Britain in error.[365] Now it was Archie's turn for the Front.

In February 1918, Archie was emotionally moved by a great cheer from his sympathisers amongst the soldiers as he left Sling Camp.[366] He was taken to Étaples, the principal depot and transit camp for the British Expeditionary Force.[367] There, the base commander Lieutenant Colonel George Mitchell was determined to break the spirits of these objectors once and for all and warned that they would be shot if they continued to refuse to submit, even though that would run the risk of martyring them. Harland, Ballantyne, Little, Jack and Sandy Baxter finally succumbed and became stretcher-bearers or medical orderlies,[368] and Maguire agreed to become a soldier: his objections were to do with Irish political concerns rather than with war in general.[369] After persistent refusal to obey orders, the remaining four objectors were sent to the Abeele military camp just over the Belgian border about sixteen kilometres from Ypres, and handed over to the military police. Archie's further refusals to serve in the army now resulted in sentences of twenty-eight days of Army Field Punishment No 1 or 'crucifixion' as it was colloquially called.

Army Field Punishment No 1 was used in the British Army and other armies of the British Empire. It was introduced in 1881 following the abolition of flogging as a common punishment. The man being punished by this method was restrained by fetters on his hands and feet attaching him to a fixed object such as a gun carriage wheel for up to two hours per day. During the early part of World War One, the punishment was often applied with the arms stretched out and the legs tied together, reminiscent of a victim hanging on a cross thus giving rise to the nickname 'crucifixion.' The punishment was intended to humiliate and cause discomfort and to act as a visible deterrent, but after the death of a British soldier receiving it in 1916 as punishment for losing his gas helmet, new regulations in January 1917 stipulated that the soldier should be attached to an upright pole so as to 'be standing firmly on his feet... which must not be more than twelve inches apart and it must be possible for him to move each foot at least three inches... If his arms or wrists are tied, there must be six inches of play between them and the fixed object... for no more than two hours a day, three out of every four days and 21 days in all'.[370] The term 'crucifixion' never went out of use until Army Field Punishment No 1 was finally abolished in 1923.[371]

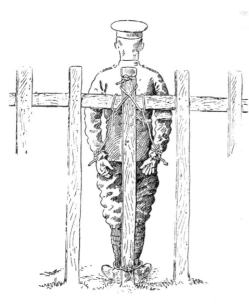

Correct methodology of
Army Field Punishment No 1

The New Zealand Division field punishment camp known as Mud Farm was a half-acre compound surrounded by an abundance of barbed wire. In We will not cease, Archie gives a searing account of the brutality he endured there:

> He took me over to the poles, which were willow stumps, six to eight inches in diameter and twice the height of a man and placed me against one of them. It was inclined forward out of perpendicular. Almost always afterwards he picked the same one for me. I stood with my back to it and he tied me to it by the ankles, knees and wrists. He was an expert at the job and he knew how to pull and strain at the ropes till they cut into the flesh and completely stopped the circulation. When I was taken off my hands were always black with congested blood. My hands were taken round behind the pole, tied together and pulled well up it, straining and cramping the muscles and forcing them into an unnatural position. Most knots will slacken a little after a time. His never did. The slope of the post brought me into a hanging position, causing a large part of my weight to

come on my arms and I could get no proper grip with my feet on the ground, as it was worn away round the pole and my toes were consequently much lower than my heels. I was strained so tightly up against the post that I was unable to move body or limbs a fraction of an inch.[372]

Archie Baxter undergoing Army Field Punishment No 1 at Mud Farm, 1918.
(Painting and permission by Bob Kerr)

Almost all the rules laid down in the Manual of Military Law were broken: the post was not upright, his hands and feet were bound tightly with his arms stretched high behind him and his heels were not allowed to touch the ground. All this was done to ensure maximum pain in an effort to break Archie's resolve. In addition, he was subjected to the punishment for as many as four hours, instead of the maximum of two hours laid down in the regulations. Strung up on his pole and left totally alone, Archie suffered increasing pain until it seemed unendurable:

> Between my set teeth I said: 'Oh God, this is too much. I can't bear it.'…The mental effect was almost as frightful as the physical. I felt I was going mad. But I couldn't allow myself the relief of groaning as I did not want to give the guards the satisfaction of hearing me. At the very worst strength came to me and I knew I wouldn't surrender. The battle was won and though the suffering increased rather than decreased as the days wore on, I never had to fight it again.[373]

This was Archie's moment of epiphany. The scene conjures up the image of the crucifixion of Christ; a tenacious and undaunted man alone on the 'cross' who, filled with unbearable pain, is suddenly attacked by doubt. But Archie's doubt is not about God but about himself and humanity – questioning whether his resolve will hold up against the agony. But he then seems to hit the pain barrier, force himself through it and win the fight against the suffering, the authorities and, above all, against war.

Archie and Kirwan were hung on poles like human scarecrows most afternoons – for two, sometimes four hours every day. Afterwards, offenders were almost always put on shot drill to 'loosen their joints', actually just another form of shocking punishment for already weakened men. The prisoner would have to stand with a 28lb bag of sand (made heavier by wetting) balanced on his hands held out in front of him. Then, to blasts of the warder's whistle, walk, place the bag on the ground, pick it up, walk, place the bag on the ground again, pick it up and so on for up to an hour at a time. Punishments like this, in addition to inadequate diet, lice-ridden clothing and having to bathe and shave in icy water, caused the prisoners to become sick and weak.[374] Archie felt empathy for the German prisoners who arrived at the camp 'with sand-bags on their heads, looking about as war-like as a pen of hoggets. They were only little boys, fair-haired and blue-eyed, without a man among them, and they were in terror of death.'[375]

When the weather became cold and rough, all the prisoners other than Archie and Kirwan were taken off the punishment. These two hardly spoke to one another as they endured hanging on their poles hour after hour in the freezing cold. They began to suffer mentally and physically, further exhausted by sleeplessness, fever and lack of food, but they refused to give in. One day they were left hanging on the poles in sub-zero temperatures in a blizzard, covered with snow. Archie was without a coat. Asking for one risked a refusal and Kirwan being forced to relinquish his. Archie could have died, but a visiting New Zealand sergeant happened to see them and insisted on them being taken down. Although that was the last time they had to endure Field Punishment No 1,[376] [377] worse was to follow.

Patton finally relented under the strain of the punishment and became a stretcher-bearer. Archie, Briggs and Kirwan were sent back to the base at Étaples where Mitchell ordered them to be sent to the trenches. Now knowing that he was to be sent to the front line the next day and that his life was in imminent danger, Archie wrote to his parents back home in New Zealand describing what had happened to him and how his attitude to serving in the war was unchanged. This was the letter that would change the course of his life and of Millicent's when she read it in that grand house in the Cashmere hills. Archie never imagined that such a letter would get through the censor, but somehow it passed through unaltered. Two or three months later, it reached John and Mary Baxter in Saddle Hill, New Zealand and would be published in the sensationalist Truth newspaper in June 1918.

Archie, Kirwan and Briggs were sent to the camp at Belgian Chateau, two and a half kilometres from the shell-ruined town of Ypres. The military police gave Archie a steel helmet, dressed him in full uniform, put on him a box respirator[378] and subjected him to a gas test. When they forced a rifle with a fixed bayonet on him, he refused it by thrusting the bayonet into the floor.[379] The prisoners were handed over into the charge of the provost-sergeant who Archie names in his book as Booth who despite using extreme violence had no effect on Archie. Archie, so weary now from constant interrogation, was questioned by the Captain in charge:

'You want your nation to win the war?'

'I don't want any nation to win. A decisive victory on either side will mean sowing the seeds of future wars.'

'Is that the way you look at it?... You are an obstructionist and I'd rather see you with your skull knocked in against the parapet than let you get back to New Zealand.'

'I'm sorry you have such feelings about me.... I don't feel that way about you. And if I am broken, what good should I be to the authorities or anyone else?'

'That doesn't concern us. It's your submission we want, Baxter, not your services.'[380]

This last sentence says it all. Archie's refusal to submit was his invisible power. His determination had always been greater than the effect of their punishment. This in turn intensified the army's resolve to break his spirit. His submission would be a triumph to the army and he could be held up as an example to others considering refusal to serve. It is important to note, however, that although he received undeniably brutal treatment, these punishments were meted out to soldiers who refused to obey orders. As the army historian Ray Grover points out, from the army point of view, objectors were soldiers and the army punished them to appropriate degrees when they refused to follow an order. In Archie's case, he was an absolutist and obeyed no orders at all, so he was continually punished throughout the twenty-one months he was in the army. [381]

The unwavering Booth tried yet another tack and informed Archie that he was to have no food until he obeyed orders. On the fourth day without food Archie was desperate with hunger and the cook slipped a large, freshly cooked rissole for him onto a ledge in the wall of the cookhouse. Small kindnesses like this went some way to compensating for the brutality. And his luck was in when he found an emergency food ration in an old disused hut. A little fox terrier he had befriended sat hopefully at his side, knowing that if Archie had a bit of food he would have his share.[382]

Every day, Archie, Briggs and Kirwan were ordered to walk the

Duckboards at the Front.
(Painting and permission by Bob Kerr)

kilometre distance to where the Otago Battalion was based at the front line, but on one occasion Briggs refused. Booth hauled him outside by the wrists, tied cable wire around his body under his arms and, with the assistance of three redcaps, dragged him on his back for two kilometres on the duck boards to the trenches. The nails of the battens ripped off clothing and his back was torn to shreds. They came to a large shell-hole filled with freezing water. Briggs was thrown into it, pulled through it by the wire, then tipped backwards into the hole again. When Briggs managed to get his head above water, Booth threw a handful of muck into his mouth. "Drown yourself, you bastard", he yelled. But the redcaps hauled him out and got him back to the camp. He had a flesh wound over half a metre wide on his right back hip and thigh. Instead of being taken to hospital, he was treated in the medical hut. Somehow he survived the ordeal. Booth forced Archie to look at the wound, snarling 'That's the way you'll be tomorrow.'[383] [384]

Fifty years later, in the foreword to the 1968 edition of We will not cease, Archie writes of his moment of self-realisation when he sees the state his extraordinarily courageous collaborator is in:

> To oppose the military machine means to accept the possibility that one may be physically destroyed by it. In my own experience, the moment when I recognised this clearly was when the military police showed me Briggs with the enormous wound on his back, and said 'That's the way you'll be tomorrow.' I did not think that Briggs would survive their deliberate violence, or that I would survive it either. And I was able to accept this with a calm mind. I slept and woke again. Once I had accepted the ultimate fact, the military machine had no power at all over me. In fact the blow did not fall as it had on Briggs, but came more slowly in another way, by starvation. But I had already made my decision at the time when I saw Briggs.[385]

So even on the morning after that horrendous incident, Archie still refused any order. Booth got out his revolver and threatened to shoot him, then struck him on the face and body continuously. Failing yet again, he then took Archie some distance away to an ammunition dump that was under heavy German fire and left him there, calling out 'I hope a shell gets you and blows you to your Maker.' Archie found himself in the midst of a storm of spouting, belching mud, fire and flying fragments, and he waited for what seemed inevitable, death. But the shells struck everywhere except where he was and he had a strange and ethereal experience, another example of the mystical side of Archie's character: 'The normal instinct of self-preservation seemed for the time being to leave me entirely. I felt quite calm and peaceful and saw everything round about bathed in a bright white radiance.'[386]

It was from this point that the army officials seem to have given up on their attempts to force Archie to obey orders. But Archie was exhausted and demoralized by what was now a year of persistent resistance met by severe physical and mental violence. He and Kirwan had been unnerved by Briggs's experience. Kirwan had reached the limit of his endurance, submitted and became a stretcher-bearer.[387] Archie never condemned those who 'gave in' and became ambulance drivers, medical orderlies or stretcher-bearers, but neither does he express his reasons for not doing the same. It seems likely that it was because those tasks, while helping wounded soldiers, would necessitate wearing a uniform and working for the army – the war machine – and would contribute to the killing of people. Archie was often asked how he would reply if a future son questioned him about not serving in the war. His reply: 'My answer would be "I did my best to stop it." '[388]

There were now only two of the original fourteen objectors left. For some time, Archie was sent up to the front line every day. He was in the trenches under heavy shellfire alongside the soldiers. Most of them ignored him, but others showed him respect and even admiration and gave him cigarettes as a sign of friendship. A number of the soldiers he was with were hit by shells and died. At one point, he too was almost killed when his box respirator failed to work properly during a gas attack. For weeks he 'coughed up black stuff.'[389]

At the beginning of March, 1918, Archie was moved back to Abeele, and knowing that he was destined for the Somme, he became conscious of, 'an intense weariness, an unspeakable longing to rest and be done with it all in this never-ending struggle.' One morning, Captain Stevenson came into the hut followed by four men and, when Archie as usual refused his order to go on parade, Stevenson became enraged. He struck him in the face, knocking him down time and again and kicked him. Finally, he ordered several men to bring him outside onto the duck boards, to lift him up as high as they could and to drop him on his back onto the boards. The soldiers lifted Archie high but lowered him to the ground very gently, keeping hold of him all the time. Cursing, Stevenson issued the order three times and three times they lowered him in the same gentle way to the ground.[390]

Archie was crammed into a train wagon with the platoon for the first stage of the journey to the German offensive at the Somme. They overnighted with no substantial food at a station then marched through the country along winding roads. Archie was starving and knew he was unlikely to survive, but again the absolutist character of this man comes to the fore:

> I realised that it was now a fight to a finish and there could be only one end to it, but I made my decision, to fight it out to the end. It was now a very bitter fight. I find it hard to write of it even now. Sometimes – quite often – I was sunk in despair, seeing nothing but utter hopelessness in my fight, in any effort to overcome the forces of destruction. The world would just go on for a thousand years and the effort of man to progress beyond mutual destruction was futile. At times I didn't bother to think about it at all, but just kept on.[391]

At first, hunger drove him to hunt for odd scraps of food and the dregs of tea, but after that, as his body adjusted to hunger, he ate nothing. His health, both mental and physical, finally gave way. He had lost one third of his body weight, dropping from seventy-three kilograms to a little over fifty.[392] He lagged so far behind during the march that he became detached from the platoon. He lost consciousness then woke the next morning in just his underclothes. He had no recollection of taking off his uniform or boots but presumably had done so as a final act of rebellion: he wouldn't have wanted his body to be found in uniform. He was now completely alone and he knew that to survive he had to catch up with the other men. With shells bursting close by, he crawled on hands and knees and came to a large shell-hole full of water. At that point he could go no further. Lice-ridden and covered in mud, he collapsed semi-conscious on the edge of the crater.[393]

He was found there, near Marieux, by two Canadian soldiers.[394] Archie maintains in his book that they were British soldiers, 'Tommies,'[395] but it appears he was in no state to know who anyone was at that stage. They led him on a horse to an English dressing station and on 1 April he was put on a train to a stationary hospital in Wimereux near Boulogne.[396] He was unconscious on arrival. He was diagnosed with mental weakness and confusional insanity then classified as 'insane and not fit for trial or punishment.'[397] A Medical Board examined him and he was furious with himself when he found that he was trembling uncontrollably and the perspiration was running off his hands. His voice was just a hollow whisper.[398] The Medical Board confirmed the diagnosis of insanity, adding that this was the reason for his 'desertion.' One of the doctors intimated to Archie that they had exaggerated the diagnosis to safeguard him from execution or from court-martial as the New Zealand Army could not court-martial an insane person.[399] There was certainly no evidence that Archie was ever mentally deranged, although he certainly showed signs of shell shock.

On 5 May 1918, Archie was taken to The Royal Victoria Hospital, a large military hospital at Netley near Southampton,[400] and placed in 'D Block,' the psychiatric section for mentally disturbed soldiers – another house of horrors. Then he was transferred by train to Middlesex Hospital in Napsbury, then known as the Napsbury Asylum.[401] There he learned that his brother Sandy was in hospital in England with rheumatic fever, and sometime later he read a heading in a newspaper 'Last Member of Notorious Baxter Family Sent to Jail.' That would have been Billie Baxter, who was court-martialled in March 1918 and sentenced to eleven months of hard labour.[402] By this time, Archie had become so depressed and apathetic that he could find no energy to write home to his parents. Eventually, a New Zealand colonel came to the hospital and told the inmates they were being sent back home, but Archie and many others had lost interest; New Zealand seemed dim and vague and so far away. To his surprise, the Colonel shook Archie's hand warmly and told him he knew all about Archie's objections to war and could imagine something of what he would have suffered: 'I only want to assure you that you have my very best wishes. I hope you soon get back to your own people and make a speedy recovery.' Archie was completely nonplussed and couldn't trust himself to speak: 'It takes time to get used to being treated as a human being, just as it takes time to become accustomed to harsh treatment.' In August, they went by train to Southampton and by boat across the channel.[403]

For five days they travelled by train through France to Marseilles and then boarded the hospital ship Marama.[404] Finally, on 21 September 1918, they docked in Auckland harbour. Archie was the first conscientious objector to be returned to New Zealand,[405] and his homecoming was a harsh one. So that Archie wouldn't be able to say that he had won in his stand against military service, a military doctor told him it was solely on account of his health that he had been returned home. In Wellington, Minister of Defence James Allen, having little knowledge of what had happened to The Fourteen objectors apart from what had been published in N.Z. Truth, decided to go on board and meet Archie, aware that Archie's return could reignite controversy. The doctor who interviewed Archie in Auckland had reported him as dull and apathetic and of slow cerebration but that these were congenital defects and that he would need no further care.[406] This looked promising to Allen and, without any preliminaries, he plunged into questioning him. Was he still of the same mind with regard to military service? Had he been badly treated in the army? Was it true he had been subjected to Field Punishment No 1? Describe Field Punishment No 1! Archie answered all these questions mechanically and, standing against the cabin wall, described the punishment, demonstrating the torture inflicted on him with no word of protest. Some of the conversation was recalled by Archie:

> Allen asked 'Are you a conscientious objector?'
> 'I was...' I was beginning when he broke in: 'You were. Are you not one now?' But I had to dash his hopes. 'I was called one in the army, but I don't call myself by any name.' [407]

At the end of the interview, Allen made no comment but shortly after Archie had returned home, the Otago Daily Times published an article with a statement from Allen discrediting Archie by saying that he was of a 'surly and morose disposition,' that it was Archie's arrogance that caused all his hardships and that he had opposed the will of the community.[408] To be fair, Allen knew little about the situation of The Fourteen. Evidently, he had made frequent attempts to gain information but accurate details were difficult to receive particularly as communication was slow, making it virtually impossible to keep close and continuous track of the men. No one knew the details of what happened to Archie, Mark Briggs and the others until the Labour Party Leader Harry Holland, the most outspoken Labour critic of conscription and advocate for objectors, compiled the experiences of some of The Fourteen in his self-published and hard-hitting book Armageddon or Calvary: The Conscientious Objectors of New Zealand and The Process of Their Conversion.[409] In it, Holland vehemently protested against Allen's allegation, but few people read it. In the environment of euphoric patriotism following the celebrations of the end of the war, the article let the Defence department off the hook and was hugely damaging to Archie's reputation, particularly in Brighton; his standing in the village was tarnished for a long time to come.[410]

The Marama continued its journey via Lyttelton to Dunedin on 21 September,[411] and when Archie went to claim his landing pass he was ordered to report to Dunedin Hospital for an appointment. When he protested, he was told harshly that he would obey orders and report in uniform or be arrested. Archie wondered if he would ever be free of the army. But Archie was reunited with his family, an event he recorded with his usual restraint: 'My people were waiting for me.'[412] His people must have been shocked at the sight of this gaunt and now very taciturn man. Shortly afterwards, his brother Donald, who was still incarcerated in the Waikeria Reformatory near Hamilton, wrote to Archie saying how delighted he was that the day was coming when he would be released and home again, 'when ink on paper will not be needed between us, the day when I will again grip the clean hand that refrained to be stained with the blood of its fellow man.'[413] But it would be well over a year before Donald was released: he finally returned home in 1920, having been imprisoned for almost three years.

Like so many others around them, John and Mary Baxter had suffered with the absence of their sons. John, now seventy-four and crippled with arthritis, and Mary, sixty-eight, had farmed the property on their own until Hughie and then Billie returned home. Supporting Archie's pacifist views had isolated them from local society, but they were resilient people and their belief in what their sons had been fighting for had helped to maintain them. Sadly, Hughie, always a favourite with the family and popular at dances and everyone around him, died in November 1918 in the influenza epidemic[414], only two months after Archie returned.

After Archie's initial joy at seeing his family, he became aware of a wide gulf now existing between himself and them. To him, they all appeared to be exactly what they had always been whereas Archie had changed forever. Everything seemed to touch a raw nerve with him. When the policeman who had originally arrested him came to see him about some business, anger rose inside him: 'I thought violently, spoke violently and had difficulty in refraining from acting violently.' And now his only chance of complete freedom from the army lay in doing everything the authorities wanted: report in uniform to the hospital when they said, accept the pay they sent him and be discharged like any other soldier. So he reported in uniform to the hospital every few days for many weeks as ordered, not for any treatment. He was regularly kept waiting for hours by the sergeant in charge: 'If I protested, I was treated by the sergeant as a creature without sense or human feeling. People wondered, seeing me going in day after day always in uniform. I could not explain.'[415]

Finally he was presented to the Medical Board, who greeted him with undisguised hostility. Nevertheless, the recommendation for his discharge went through. Irony resides in his discharge papers, dated 5 December 1918. They bear the words 'Disch. being no longer physically fit for war service.'[416] How did he become physically unfit? Furthermore, the army was so determined to make him a soldier that the discharge report states he had served every day that he had been in the army from the time he was arrested to the date of his discharge.[417]

'And so my experiences in the army ended' writes Archie flatly at the end of his book. Perhaps to him, his victory over the army was at too great a cost. He sounds exhausted. Nevertheless, his extraordinary dignity and absence of rancour about the treatment he had received remained and was probably the key to his survival. Throughout his time at war, Archie experienced the contrasting behaviour of the brutality shown him by some of the officers in command and the extraordinary generosity and support given him by some of the ordinary soldiers.

The torture that was inflicted on Archie was to affect him for the rest of his life, but he emerged at the end of the war as a man who knew that he had never given up nor gone against his personal principles of pacifism. He had been a man fighting his own war within a war. After his return, the vilification against the Baxter family increased more than before he was arrested. Those who had not experienced the war had very little understanding of what it had been like for those in the trenches and there was no understanding of what conscientious objectors had suffered. Some in Brighton didn't believe Archie's account of his experiences.[418] One conversation with a relative over a cup of tea is revealing:

> 'And you were in France?'
> 'Yes, I was in France.'
> 'How lovely for you to get a chance to see all those places. I believe France is a very beautiful country.'
> 'Yes, it was lovely for me.' [419]

CHAPTER 7
The Princess and the Pauper

Shortly after Archie's return home, the government decided it wasn't going to let conscientious objectors off the hook. In December 1918, the Expeditionary Forces Amendment Bill was passed, which amongst other provisions deprived military defaulters of their civil rights for ten years and refusing them employment in the government or local authorities. This seems extraordinary; in effect, objectors – and there were more than 2000 – were punished twice.[420] Through the oversight of an army official, the military law pursued Archie's brother Hughie beyond the grave; his name appeared in the New Zealand Gazette as a defaulter to be deprived of all civil rights for ten years.[421] [422]

Archie was now a marked man. Millicent maintains that the government tried to stop him earning a living by threatening the people who employed him,[423] and some farmers did refuse to employ him. Instead, he made his base at his parents' farm and returned to rabbiting and labouring in the outlying areas such as Clyde, saving to buy his own farm. As in the rest of New Zealand, many people in Brighton openly abhorred the conchies and hostility and ostracism continued for a long time. In many ways it was hardly surprising; 1,545 men from Dunedin alone were killed in military action in World War I.[424] Belinda Cumming, who researched the social repercussions experienced by Otago families who espoused pacifism, including the Baxters, writes 'sharing their pacifist views also meant sharing the notoriety they inevitably gained and made them hugely unpopular within wider society.' Young Maggie Baxter, twenty-one when the war ended, suffered because young men wanted nothing to do with the sister of the infamous Baxter brothers.[425]

The brothers re-formed the 'Baxter Gang', which had a work ethic that was different to that of other locals, who viewed them not only as pacifists but also as radical independents. Uninterested in becoming wealthy or owning smart houses, they simply earned as much as they needed for the moment. They were happy-go-lucky young men and wouldn't think twice about downing tools to fish or hunt. None of them drank. All of them except Archie were keen race-goers. They all believed in God,[426] but none of them went to church.

So while Archie sought to carve out his life again in Otago, Millicent regularly caught sight of the copy of that letter by Archie for well over a year whenever she opened her handbag. Many years later in 1981 in an interview with Radio New Zealand, Millicent commented that, in the letter, Archie had said he was unlikely to survive, so she didn't expect to ever meet him. Nevertheless, she had kept the letter.[427] In the spring of 1920, she was still living in Dunedin. She knew a good deal about Archie Baxter because he was, after all, New Zealand's most notorious conscientious objector. One day, she plucked up courage and made an audacious decision. She would travel to Brighton to meet this Archibald Baxter. She had no idea if he was still at his parents' house or even in the region, but down she went by bus, clutching her handbag with the precious letter. She found the house and knocked on the door. Archie's parents and his siblings Donald, Sandy and Maggie were there but not Archie. He was away rabbiting in Central Otago.[428]

Unabashed, she made the journey several times, but each time Archie was away. During these visits she came to know the family and got on well with them. What a contrast between this small woman with her refined Cambridge accent and the rumbustious family of rabbiters. Barriers of class and education were apparently ignored, extraordinary for those days. She even had a 'mild flirtation' with Donald Baxter, he was very good-looking and twenty-eight, eleven years younger than Archie. But no, Archie's letter had changed her life and she had to meet him. Typically, in her memoirs, Millicent doesn't expand on her feelings at the time, but she had idolised the idea of this man, and at thirty-two, she may have had hopes for a romantic relationship. This may explain her extraordinary gumption to seek him out.

Meanwhile, Archie Baxter kept hearing about this little Miss Brown, 'five foot one and three-quarter inches in stockinged feet'. He was intrigued when he heard about this forthright young woman with penetrating blue eyes who had been turning up on the family doorstep.[429] His friends told him that her beauty was genuine and not out of a bottle.[430]

It would be six months before Archie came back from his stint at rabbiting that winter in Central Otago. One day in September 1920, Millicent visited yet again and at last he was there. Archie wasn't good-looking and was unimpressive compared with Donald. His harrowing time in the army still affected him. He had grown a straggly moustache to hide his dreadful teeth which had decayed irreparably during his time overseas. He also had protruding eyes: 'They stuck right out like a crayfish's', writes Millicent, 'This was caused by the strain, the extreme strain, of what had been done to him in the war. His eyes went back to normal in time. He must have had pretty solid nerves for them to recover.'[431]

Despite his appearance, Millicent fell in love. 'Archie was everything I had hoped for; someone with something I had not really believed I should ever find; the perfect understanding I had imagined and never found.' It seems Archie felt the same; he later told Millicent that the moment he saw her he knew that she was the woman he had dreamed of all his life.[432] Faced with such statements, it is tempting to reach for the cliché and say they were destined for one another.

They were very much in love, but Millicent had one doubt. She loved him in every way except she lacked a real physical attraction for him, and sensuality was important to her. She was so concerned about this that she confided in a friend 'I like him immensely and I admire him enormously, but I have no physical feeling for him. Is it right to marry without it?' The friend replied 'Wait till you embrace!' And embrace they obviously did. 'She was right' writes Millicent still with joy fifty years later, 'after that there was no question about it. I knew what I was doing was right.' The jigsaw puzzle was complete. Millicent had found everything she wanted in her Archie, and it seems Archie's feelings equalled hers. He was two months short of his fortieth birthday when he met Millicent, and he told her he would never have married if he hadn't met her.[433] Millicent also told Christine Cole Catley 'He always said that being with me helped him live a lot longer... He'd got the one he wanted. For him it was fulfillment as well as for me.'[434]

That November, Archie invited her up to Middlemarch in Central Otago for the weekend where his brother Mark and his wife were living. Archie's sister Maggie was also staying there with her young Scotsman fiancé, Jock Fowler. The foursome climbed the Rock and Pillar Range. They all wrote their names on a scrap of paper and left it inside a tobacco tin in a crevice in the summit rock. Archie now had an even greater incentive to save money. Millicent went back to Christchurch and he went shearing. The couple wrote to each other constantly. They were both extremely anxious when Archie came up to Christchurch to meet Millicent's father, and they were right to be.

John was aghast at his elder daughter marrying a rabbiter. He tried very hard to persuade Archie that the marriage would be a huge mistake as Millicent was used to a way of life that Archie could never give her. Archie stood his ground, so John worked to persuade Millicent out of the relationship, telling her that in a few months her feeling for Archie would have gone and she would realise the error of her ways. Millicent replied courageously 'I am not a young girl. I'm a grown woman and my feeling for him is not just sex.'[435] While she could understand how her father felt, she knew that he couldn't understand that what she and Archie had would last forever.

Another matter on Millicent's conscience was that she hadn't told her father that Archie was a notorious conchie. Archie wanted to tell him everything but knew Millicent couldn't face the inevitable confrontation. Honesty was paramount to both of them, and Millicent felt she was a coward for not telling the whole truth and always regretted it. However, it didn't take long for John to find out: 'People were only too anxious to tell him what a scoundrel my husband was... it would have been better if we had told him. Today, of course, I would.' reflects Millicent, 'I no longer belong to a persecuted minority. Things have changed from those days and changed enormously.'[436] It is easy to understand John's reaction; he had had such hopes for his daughter. He had given her the best of education and had dreams of her following in her mother's footsteps – excelling in her work and marrying a top academic. Instead, she was marrying an uneducated farmer, one with no realistic hopes of bettering himself, and he was an infamous conscientious objector. But John might also have had other reasons to disapprove of his daughter's choice of husband. Max Broadbent, who later became the manager of the Macmillan Brown

Library at the University of Canterbury, gives his views:

> There was quite a lot of charisma in the Baxter family, and I imagine lots of native ability which had never previously surfaced because they arrived in Otago as very poor Highlanders presumably without education or opportunities in their native Scotland. The wider family would have been regarded with serious misgivings by Professor Brown and by most people in the establishment, as not good marriage and career material. I think that the most interesting thing about Millicent was the independence of mind and heart that found the Baxter connection magnetically attractive when all prudence should have steered her away from the danger. Marrying Archibald was a decisive break with the comfortable life of conventional success that was what she got from her father's influence, which had formed her. This presumably is what her father thought and why there was such trouble when she married Archibald.[437]

Broadbent goes on to expand on Millicent's extraordinary choice:

> I think myself that there would have been quite a lot of the wayward Highlander in the Brown genes too – the Macmillan element – which is probably what surfaced when Millicent threw in her lot with the small farmer from coastal Otago with a record of rebellion against established opinion…I think the original, rebellious and charismatic element in Archibald and his wider Highland family needs to be taken into account. They seem to have been attractive and gifted, with the ability to capture the attention and loyalty of others. They probably had all the vitality and fatal attraction that the desiccated world of scholarship familiar to Millicent from childhood, lacked, without a mother's influence to soften things and make them bearable. It is hard to know, without personal knowledge, but one can speculate.[438]

Both Millicent and Archie had very liberal ideas on marriage, and they agreed that if they had been married to other people when they met, they would have recognised their marriages were wrong, would have broken them and lived together no matter what people thought. She told Christine Cole Catley 'we were of such absolutely different backgrounds that under normal circumstances we would never have met… it didn't matter if we were married, or if I were 30 years older than he was. We would have lived together no matter what. Archie's people were just as opposed to the marriage as my family. They saw quite wisely that we were of absolutely different backgrounds – but we loved each other.'[439]

Millicent and Archie went back to Dunedin and Millicent spent the three days of residence necessary to obtain a marriage licence. Archie's notoriety even affected their wedding; the couple had difficulty persuading anyone to be a witness. One friend said she was too afraid to agree. Finally they had their two witnesses: a teacher at the high school, Mrs Kerr, who had been a pupil of Millicent's mother, and a primary school teacher, Miss Gow, whom Millicent had come to know and like. On a mild summer's day on 12 February 1921, only four or five months after they met, Archie and Millicent were married at a registrar's office in Dunedin. The registrar was shocked at the flippancy of this fairly mature couple during the ceremony and said to her 'Mrs Baxter, this is a serious matter.' Clearly some giggling and nudging had gone on to cover up what Millicent calls their 'deeper feelings.'[440] Presumably she means their love for one another – these weren't times when people, even those in love, showed overt affection – but it was likely the result of nervousness about her future with Archie; she was joining her life with an infamous conscientious objector, still seen by some as a 'shirker', and he was a rabbiter with very little money, to boot.

The couple were so absorbed in each other that they left the registry office ceremony, bade farewell to their two witnesses and never even thought of a wedding breakfast.[441] What a contrast between this wedding and the one Millicent would have had if her father had had his way and she had married a leading Christchurch academic. Millicent makes no mention in her memoirs of why they didn't have a traditional wedding, but it would be hard to imagine her asking her father to pay for the wedding, and who would they have invited? Who would come? Would it invite trouble? It seems the couple simply decided to marry with no one knowing the date and face the consequences later.

The newly-weds spent the rest of the day at the Ross Creek Reservoir[442], a beautiful bush area in Glenleith in north east Dunedin, and for their honeymoon they had a simple but idyllic week in Brighton in a cottage lent to them by one of Archie's uncles. Nearly every day they went up the Brighton River and bathed and picnicked. The freedom of being with one another away from prejudice and critics, and the excitement of starting their new lives together made them feel like a teenage couple rather than a woman of thirty-three and a man of forty.

Archie then took Millicent inland to Middlemarch in Central Otago to stay with brother Mark and his wife while he returned to rabbiting with his brothers at Hyde, a hundred and ninety kilometres away. Hyde was a small country town where there was less bad feeling against him than in larger towns and on the coast. Archie now poisoned the rabbits with strychnine, a cruel occupation for this mild man who loved animals, but he was making good money, and now Archie had the added incentive of saving to buy a farm for himself and his new bride. [443]

Millicent and Archie were anxious to have children as soon as possible so were bitterly disappointed when Millicent had a miscarriage. She recovered rapidly, so different from her mother. After some months, she went from Middlemarch to

Christchurch for a few days to see friends. Her father was away on another of his archaeological trips and she probably chose this as a good time to visit. These were early days of the marriage and her father hadn't yet accepted it. In one of her chats to Christine Cole Catley, she says 'My father didn't say ever that he really liked Archie – he said he was a good man and that he didn't want to hear any more about it. All the same, my sister said he used to rage and storm about it. Later he became quite friendly and he would come and visit us and he was interested in his grandchildren. We used to stay up there in Christchurch sometimes and he was quite nice to us. To his mind Archie was not an academic and therefore he couldn't enter into the things he wanted to talk about. He would have preferred me to marry an academic.'[444]

As soon as Millicent got to Christchurch, she sensed that local opinion considered that she herself was now tarnished by marrying a conchie. Her good friends

Gertrude and Emily Boulton didn't want her to return to her old home; they said 'it would cause talk'. But Millicent defied them: 'I didn't care… I didn't visit anyone. People could talk if they liked. It didn't matter to me.'[445] She was rapidly developing a stoic disregard for contrary opinion and it became a principle she was always prepared to follow in order to maintain her integrity and the relationships she valued. Despite not being a pacifist, her sister Viola continued to support Millicent unwaveringly; they had always been very close. Like Millicent, Viola had an independent spirit and would remain sympathetic to Archie and Millicent's views and concerned about their welfare all her life.

Archie Baxter just after his marriage to Millicent, at his brother Mark's home in Middlemarch
Ref: Hocken Library MS-975/226

After a few weeks, Millicent returned from Christchurch to Dunedin. Archie met her at the station and together they started hunting for a farm – and a home.

102

CHAPTER 8
From Mansion to Shack

One beautiful spring day in 1921 Archie and Millicent visited a farm at Kuri Bush, a tiny settlement eleven kilometres south of Brighton on a stunning coastline. They fell instantly in love with it and, as Archie had made enough money rabbiting, they decided to buy it. Considering his disapproval of their marriage, John Macmillan Brown was generous in giving the pair some money towards their purchase. According to Archie and Millicent's elder son Terence, John could by this time 'see a very happy marriage going on. He softened to it a little, and he saw that she had a pretty good man.'[446]

The site of Millicent and Archie's house in Kuri Bush
(taken in 1983 by Gary Blackman)

From being the daughter of two wealthy intellectuals and living in a city mansion where she had never learned to cook or housekeep, the professor's daughter made her new home in a remote four-roomed cottage with no running water or electricity. As Christine Cole Catley remarked 'Christchurch University society would have been scandalised! Someone from the very cream of Christchurch society – something that no other city in New Zealand had – marrying a poor farmer![447]

Their farm was at the top of a small hill in sight of the Kuri Bush beach just across the road. The beach, with its blindingly white sand and Pacific rollers pounding the shore, looks as it did in Archie and Millicent's time. Moturata Island appears like a massive submarine rising from the ocean. It is a million-dollar view, but even today there are hardly any houses around. Colourful ice plants, flaxes and marram grass cover the sand near the road that snakes its way down the coast from Dunedin to Taieri Mouth where the Taieri River, the fourth longest river in the country, flows out to the sea. The road itself, tarmacked a long time after the Baxters left, is lined on both sides by bracken, cabbage trees, ngaio and the occasional massive old macrocarpa tree

103

grown for shelter. An old two-storey barn stands on the inland side of the road. It looks reasonably intact until you walk around its side to find the notorious New Zealand southerlies have whipped away a good portion of the battered iron roof, and broken weatherboards struggle to keep the barn standing. At the time of writing, the old barn is the only relic of the Baxter farm, and it won't be long before the elements will wear this away as well.

Archie built that barn, which also served as their dairy. They never got around to

View today from Millicent and Archie's farm in Kuri Bush (taken by Penny Griffith)

Brighton. Bedford Parade is on the top of hill, top right of the picture. (taken by Penny Griffith)

Millicent and Archie's barn in Kuri Bush (taken in 1983 by Gary Blackman)

The Baxter's grandson and son, Kenneth and Terence Baxter at the Kuri Bush barn, 2010 (taken by Penny Griffith)

Knarston's General Store, Taieri Mouth
c 1920s

Taieri Mouth today
(taken by Penny Griffith 2010)

giving the farm an official name; they simply called it Kuri Bush.[448] The property covered about 150 acres. A mixed farm of that size was hard for one man to run but not large enough to warrant two. Archie and Millicent first had to clear the manuka around the place, and then they farmed sheep and cows and kept a few horses for ploughing. Pigs, hens and calves roamed the yards, and often a calf would pull Millicent's washing off the line. Just below the house was a tidal pond with pukeko and paradise ducks.[449] Local Māori still owned much of the land further inland from their farm, and a lot of feral cattle roamed free there, offspring of animals that had escaped from the neighbouring farms. Local Māori would occasionally round up some of them and take them to the sale yards. Sometimes these animals would invade the Baxters' and neighbouring farms: 'They were a fearful nuisance', claims Millicent. The farmhouse had a sitting room, kitchen and two bedrooms, and there was a shed at the back. There were no modern conveniences of course. There were brass kerosene lamps and a wood range which Archie kept well stocked with manuka from the bush at the back of the property.[450] Millicent maintains that she did better cooking in that wood range than she ever did in any electric range. An outside toilet was in one corner of the section: 'We called it a lavatory not a dunny,' she emphasises primly.[451]

At thirty-three, far from being a young bride with no life experience, she was a mature, well-travelled young woman, and it is extraordinary how easily she made the transition to this humble and unsophisticated situation. A fence enclosed the area around the house, and Millicent delighted in planting trees and tending a garden, her lifelong passion for plants finding an outlet at last.[452] Rainwater was collected in a tank by the chimney, and she did the washing in zinc tubs on a bench outside in water heated on the wood range. Later in life, Millicent told Frank McKay that she recalled people saying 'look at what he's brought her to.' With a twinkle in her eye, she drew out the long vowel in brought. 'If only they had known how happy I was.'[453] Later, her son Terence confirms this: 'She was a very, very happy woman, absolutely happy with her whole life.'[454] He also remembers her walking out the back to get water from the big brass tank with a tap, using a kerosene tin as a bucket and tapping her thigh as she sang some song while she waited until it filled. At lunchtime she would cooee to Archie, her voice carrying into the hills where he would be working.[455]

Millicent had had servants in Christchurch to do everything for her, and in her memoirs she admits to her lack of training in the household arts. She had never kept house before nor cooked anything except scrambled eggs and shortbread. But she learned from the French, Italian and German cookbooks she bought and used New Zealand wine for cooking. Archie must have been shocked at this change in diet, but Millicent writes confidently that 'Archie ate my meals quite cheerfully.'[456] But there are stories among the Baxter grandchildren that when they moved to Brighton, Archie would often leave the house on some excuse after eating Millicent's exotic dinners, walk around the corner to one of his brothers' homes and eat the 'proper' tucker of meat and two veg that he had been used to all of his farming life. Another story is that Maggie's daughter Margaret always noticed 'the Millicent smell' whenever she visited her, and it was only years later when she went to her first restaurant that she realised what it was – garlic![457]

By trial and error, Millicent quickly learnt to make stews, roasts and 'marvellous puddings... éclairs and wonderful biscuits with meringue topping with nuts. They looked elegant and tasted elegant too.'[458] She became extremely proud of her cooking and baking skills. Every Christmas she used to make fudge, coconut ice and lollies and put them into little baskets she had made. She would then decorate them with crepe-paper frills and tie bows to the handles. These, she would personally deliver to all the nieces and nephews in Brighton.[459]

They grew oats for the plough horses, which they bagged into sacks and stored in the barn loft. Terence remembers seeing a horde of mice leaping out of the sacks, fat from eating the oats. It was the only time he heard his father curse.[460] The cows were milked in the dairy. With no electric light, Archie would carry a kerosene lamp that Millicent had lit after first warming the bulb to prevent it cracking.[461] Eventually they acquired a generator and installed one of the first electric milking machines in the area.[462] They sold their milk to the Knarstons, a large family of Swedish origin who ran the store at Taieri Mouth, the nearest township to Kuri Bush. Millicent would walk the ten kilometres there then back (later with two children in a pram) to buy her provisions and meet up with others. Millicent remembers 'One would occasionally meet a boar returning from giving his services at a farm, trotting purposefully along the road to his home.'[463] The Knarstons also provided a daily van-delivery service for the bulk supplies Millicent or Archie needed. The driver took orders for the following day. They would also transport the Baxters' produce: cream and wool.[464] The van also operated as the bus to Dunedin, travelling several times a week with passengers sitting beside the driver or on the floor. Mail was delivered two or three days a week by Tom Palmer, and the Baxters' barn used to be a stopping post to feed the horses that pulled his dray.[465] The Baxters themselves had a gig, and they often drove over to the Taieri for picnics. On a day-to-day basis, Millicent and Archie were self-sufficient. They had butter made from their own milk, eggs from their hens and bacon from their pigs. Without electricity for a refridgerator, they weren't in a position to slaughter their own sheep and cows. In time, with hard work, the farm became a success.

Millicent was in her element in this new style of life: 'The lack of conveniences didn't trouble me in the least. Life was delightful. People have said that the change in my way of living must have been rather like the fairy tale of the princess and the peasant. What they didn't know was that Archie was the prince. What had been done to him in the war had only strengthened his nobility of character.'[466] For someone who rarely expressed her emotions, Millicent never repressed her feelings for Archie. But their personalities and characters contrasted strongly. Millicent was gregarious, loquacious and assertive. Archie was resilient and practical. He was also quiet and reserved, but alone with his wife he would open up: 'Archie and I used to talk and talk, early in bed in the morning, before work began. That's where we did our main talking.'[467] Later in her memoirs, Millicent reveals her views on marriage: 'I think one of the most necessary ingredients of a happy marriage is to share the same sense of humour, private jokes known only to husband and wife, ridiculous nicknames, absurd situations... That is one of the things one misses when one's partner dies. One doesn't find it again on earth. I believe also that monogamy is essential for the perfect marriage. If it's a good marriage, money, everything, is shared perfectly naturally.[468]

Despite their obvious happiness together, life in the early years was sometimes difficult. There was considerable hostility from the community towards Archie and the couple were often ostracised. The local authorities continually harassed them. In running their farm the couple had to keep strictly to petty government official regulations that were enforced on them but not on their neighbours, and often Archie would be fined for petty offences. Once, he decided to pre-empt the situation by applying for a licence to run his milk separator, but the officials in Dunedin laughed at him, saying that nobody in Otago had such a thing, to which Archie replied 'Oh yes, but my situation's different' and insisted on being given the licence.[469] Although they didn't have much gorse (a noxious weed) on their land, they constantly had notices to remove the little they had and were frequently fined for infringements of regulations that they and everyone else knew nothing about.[470]

Immediate neighbours were friendly and helpful, but others could be confrontational. Millicent believed that someone deliberately broke the leg of Archie's favourite horse. That was a great shock to them both, but they could never prove who it was.[471] On another occasion, two men arrived at the house and tried to sell them a bolt of cloth. The Baxters refused and always suspected that it was an attempt to prove Archie was guilty of receiving stolen goods.[472] George McIntosh, a grandson of the Baxters' good friends and neighbours Hugh McIntosh and his wife, says that Archie would never go to the police and complain; '...when people got to know about this, they would actually prey upon them [the Baxters], and there would be real damage done around the place. Dad would say "Get the police out." Archie would say "No!" '[473] Probably his mistrust of the police was due to the treatment he received from them during the war. And he was probably right in thinking he would get no help from the police; believing him to be a communist, police in Dunedin would follow him when he visited there to see if he went to the communist headquarters. This victimisation continued even after they sold the Kuri Bush farm nine years later in 1930 and moved to Brighton.[474] Interestingly, McIntosh claims that Archie was adamant that New Zealand didn't need a police force, and all that was needed was for everyone to follow the law[475] – more evidence of his absolutism.

The saving grace was that Millicent and Archie had the support of one another. There is no mention, at least throughout Millicent's memoirs, of any dissent between herself and Archie, although at times both must have found the other difficult to live with. For years Archie suffered physically and mentally from the effects of his wartime experiences. Millicent phlegmatically took these concerns in her stride:

'When we first went to live on the farm, Archie had what I think used to be called night sweats. He would wake in the morning with his pyjamas soaking. But that passed just as his protruding eyes gradually went back to normal.'[476] Millicent also maintained that Archie's circulation was ruined by weeks of hanging off a post during Field Punishment No 1 in 1917. Even in the middle of summer he wore heavy woollen underclothes but still his legs would feel ice cold. She also thought that his later heart problems and angina were a consequence of his treatment during the war.[477] It is difficult to conceive that after the inhumane treatment this man had suffered for so long he could return to a normal way of life and become accustomed to being treated like a human being again.

Millicent stood out in her new environment: 'an exotic in that simple rural scene.'[478] She was an intellectual and a modern sophisticated woman who spoke with a very posh voice, and although she seems to have been liked and accepted among most of the Baxter family, there were some in her community who found her daunting and others who viewed her as a snob. Her Cambridge accent wouldn't have helped, though she tried hard to change it. She also had the mannerism of closing her eyes as she spoke. Frances Mulrennan, who later became a close friend, remembers this mannerism very well: 'She would be talking and her eyes would be... closed. You were always looking at her eyelids.'[479] It was no affectation, and it happened with everyone she spoke with. Millicent was an unquenchable talker and clearly sorted her thoughts out as she spoke, but her closed eyes and lifted chin may well have suggested a supercilious air to those who didn't know her well. Some people have said that James had the same mannerism of closing his eyes as he spoke. 'Her deportment was so marvellous', Frances continues, 'She knew how to behave in public... People used to say "Oh! She's so aristocratic", and she said "I'm not, I'm not – I'm a middle class Scot." '[480]

Millicent was well aware of her position in her new life and adapted herself from her lofty environs in Christchurch to her new surroundings. 'When I was a child, one didn't know one's tradespeople socially. The butcher commiserated with my aunt and me regarding the death of my mother. My aunt stiffened – the butcher was [acting] out of his class – even though she prided herself on not being a snob. When I married, I immediately came to the level of my butcher and grocer.'[481] She used to tell the McIntoshes that if only people knew how false the upper crust were, they wouldn't want to be like them.[482] George McIntosh also recalls discussions between Archie and his father Hugh: 'They used to have great arguments about the League of Nations and Dad always said it would never work... because as soon as it's tested, it'll fail. And he was right. The Japanese went into Manchuria and the Nations did nothing about it. And of course the Baxters could never see a military solution – but that didn't stop Japan, did it? Or Hitler. So I think they were very disappointed. They had a lot of disappointments I think, the Baxters, in regards to the peace movement in those days.'[483]

At harvest-time, Millicent and Archie would often provide accommodation for two workers in the shed at the back, and they would also sleep visitors there.

Millicent recalls one rather problematic guest, the aunt of a local man Arthur McCarthy. Arthur had been on the run from conscription and Archie had taken some risk helping him. This rather eccentric aunt was an ardent pacifist and she decided she wanted a holiday in the country at Easter. This coincided with harvest time when the Baxters already had two men sleeping in the shed. Millicent said to Archie 'What on earth am I going to do with the woman? How am I going to get blankets?' He said "I'll give you four clean sacks. You can stitch them together into a bag sheet. The weather's quite warm and we can have that. She can have our blanket." So she did. Miss McCarthy stayed for two months!'[484]

Within a few months of arriving in Kuri Bush, Millicent became pregnant and the couple were thrilled. She became elephantine and everyone suspected twins, at least. Of course she continued her daily routines and was cooking meals for the harvesters up until a few weeks before she was due to give birth. Harvesting and chaff cutting in the area was done communally with all the neighbouring farmers lending a hand. Millicent would often have to cook dinner for eight or ten men, but the mill-owner was temperamental and she rarely knew whether he was going to finish and have the meal at the McIntosh place or have the meal at the Baxters. The result was that both Mrs McIntosh and Millicent had to have a full meal ready for him. The McIntosh's daughter would often come over and help Millicent[485] 'Mrs McIntosh was very kind always to me, very, very nice', Millicent told Christine Cole Catley. Then adds as an aside: 'very conservative, a woman of her generation, a woman who believed that her daughters never knew about sexual relations until they were married.'[486]

However, George McIntosh has some comments to make on Millicent's cooking that are interesting in the face of Millicent's claims that her cooking was excellent:

> Yes well, there was another wee side to that story. She was such a rotten cook the mill man didn't want to stay there for dinner, and if he could work it out, he would make bloody sure he got down to the McIntoshes… Of course mill men can be pretty bloomin' critical. In those days it was a threshing mill with a steam engine, traction engine and everything, and it would have a set crew – it was Jim Brown's mill, I'm pretty sure – Jim and Jack Brown. They were hard old cases. I remember them very well, and they wouldn't be put about by a rotten cook, don't you worry about that. They'd be coming down to where they knew they'd get a real good feed, and Mrs Baxter was not a good cook… My mother was a marvellous cook and very noted for it. She was a cook to the Primate of New Zealand, Bishop Neville, in Dunedin for quite a long time. Bishop Neville said she was the best cook in the world. He said, "Maggie's a better cook than the King of England's got, and I know because I've tasted the cooking of both." Mum could cook rabbits and ducks

and pheasants and things like that absolutely wonderfully well, and make good meals. Mrs Baxter wouldn't have much idea of cooking for a big swag of men – it was a big, big thing.[487]

Millicent would be mortified to hear that. She was so proud of her cooking skills.

Shortly before Millicent had the baby, Archie became seriously ill with bladder trouble. They were loath to get a doctor because it cost so much, but Archie was passing blood in his urine and was vomiting continually. His sister Maggie was staying with them at the time, but she was terrified of meeting bulls on the road and refused to go for help, so off went Millicent despite her condition: 'my husband's life was more to me than fear of bulls.' She set off on the kilometre-and-a-half walk to the schoolhouse, the only place with a telephone, but it was shut. Archie was furious that Maggie had allowed her to go. He recovered, just as he had to do in prison, without a doctor.[488]

Finally, fifteen months after they were married, on a mild winter's day on 23 May 1922, Millicent gave birth to their first son, Terence. The 36-hour labour had been extremely difficult, and Millicent puts this down partly to her small size and older age, she was thirty-four, and partly because the baby was in a posterior presentation. She was badly torn and lost a great deal of blood.[489] They named their boy Terence John MacSwiney after Terence MacSwiney the famous Irish Republican who, two years before, had been elected Sinn Féin Lord Mayor of Cork during the Irish War of Independence.[490] Terence was a beautiful, contented baby who would become a good-looking boy then a handsome man. As the first child, he was fretted over by overly conscientious parents. Millicent and Archie believed in the world-famous child-rearing techniques of Frederic Truby King including feeding by the clock. His book, Feeding and care of baby[491], became their daily child-rearing bible.[492] [493] This rigid, no-nonsense approach had Millicent and Archie ignoring

Terence Baxter aged about 8 years
Ref: Hocken Library c/nE1070/22 S15-599c a50

the baby's cries all day and sitting up until 11.30 each night to bring up his wind after his 10 o'clock feed. The regime proved too much for both parents and child. The local Plunket nurse was indignant: 'People like them should never read Feeding and Care. Just go ahead with what you are doing instinctively and leave the book alone!' They reverted to usual baby-care techniques and everybody was happy.[494]

The publication of Archie's letter in Truth back in 1918 had created a political storm, and Archie Baxter was now well-known throughout much of the country. While reviled by many in the community, this modest and unobtrusive man was now revered by such well-known Labour politicians as Peter Fraser, Paddy Webb and Michael Joseph Savage, all of whom visited the Kuri Bush house to talk with him. Archie seldom saw anyone he had met or seen overseas, but soon after they were married, Archie chanced upon one: 'Why, there's...' He crossed the street to where some students were walking. He immediately came back and said sadly 'He doesn't want to know me.'[495] The man had become friendly with him in South Africa and they had discussed poetry, literature and politics together. Archie was deeply saddened by this. He felt that if the young man had been alone, he would have acted differently; it wasn't the done thing to mix with an ex-conchie. This man wasn't the only one who made it plain he no longer wanted to know Archie. In the mid-1920s, the secretary of a Labour Party branch in Dunedin organised a visit to the farm by Peter Fraser, Labour Party member of parliament and later, Prime Minister. Millicent writes 'Fraser made it obvious he wished he weren't there with us – he was looking ahead at his political career.'[496] He was indeed. Much of his previous pacifist ideology was gone.[497]

Millicent was thirty-eight and Archie forty-four when James Keir was born five weeks premature on the cold winter's day of 29 June 1926. They named him in honour of Keir Hardie, the Scottish left-wing labour leader Archie had heard speak in 1912. James would write a poem in his later sardonic style about his own birth in The Man on a Horse:

> Not too far from the Leith water
> My mother saw a mandrake grow
> And pulled it. A professor's daughter,
> She told me some time after how
> She had been frightened by a cow
> So that the birth-sac broke too soon
> And on the twenty-ninth of June
> Prematurely I looked at the walls
> And yelled...[498]

After the struggle giving birth to Terence, Millicent remembers this birth as being sublimely easy. She makes no mention of frightening the cows or birth-sacs breaking in her memoirs, but she does describe James' premature entry into the world with reflective elation as 'a very easy birth. I could feel his head pushing through the bones with rhythmic jerks and I felt myself caught up in some marvellous cosmic experience.' James was only a little over five pounds and this resulted in the family nickname of Jumbo the Elephant, shortened to 'Jum', by which the family call him to this day.[499] [500] Millicent and Archie called Terence 'Ten'. Terence was initially resentful of James and was once found prodding him so hard with a straw broom that it broke the baby's skin,[501] but the two boys grew to get on well. Millicent admits she really wanted two boys and two girls but that it wasn't to be. She had, nevertheless, a happy acceptance of 'what will be, will be'; her attitude was very much to make the best of things. She adds later in her characteristically honest and matter-of-fact way 'I don't think I am naturally fond of children, Archie was, but of my own children I was.'[502]

She fell happily into a routine of looking after the boys, Archie, the house and the farm. In the mornings, Archie would get up first, take Millicent a cup of tea and bring in Terence and James for nappy changes and cuddles. She got up at 7.30, made breakfast, bathed and dressed the children, then did her house chores.[503] Most days, she would do the washing in the zinc tub outside, and in the evening after a hard day's work, often helping Archie with farmwork, she would mend, sew and make clothes. She never did learn to use a sewing machine, so made all the boys' shirts out of old clothes by hand.[504] There is no mention in her memoirs of Millicent and Archie listening to music, nor does Terence remember any music being played. They had no radio, but both she and Archie would read books keenly. Terence tells of his mother's zest for reading that continued all her life: 'She used to bring about six books home with her from the library; she was always reading, and that was her life.'[505] Although he wasn't a deeply religious man, Archie read the Bible aloud to the family on Sundays, and at Easter he would read the narrative of Christ's passion.[506] Terence also remembers Millicent reading the Bible and singing hymns around the home during his childhood:[507] He was always puzzled how they managed to read in the evenings with just a kerosene table lamp. After they moved to Brighton they had electric light. Although they were amongst the first to get a car, Terence thinks they were probably the last house in the area to have a radio: 'I used to visit other peoples' houses to listen to their radio and even when my parents did acquire a set they rarely used it except to listen to the overseas news. Our parents didn't approve of us using it.' [508] Even when she moved to Kinsman Street, she was still not keen on radio and she never possessed a television.

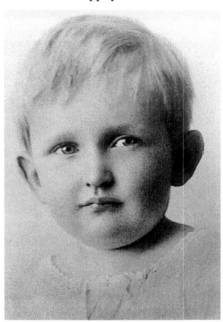
James K Baxter agedabout 2
Family collection

Terence also told Paul Millar

> My father only had a limited education – he sort of educated
> himself. He did a lot of reading – he read completely differently

to my mother. I used to watch them when we'd be sitting around the fire in the wintertime. She'd move through a book no trouble at all – finish one in an evening sometimes – so much so that I could hardly believe that she'd got it all in. Once or twice I'd ask her something about it and she'd know exactly what she'd read, absolutely accurately. She didn't like people saying things that were inaccurate; she'd go and write a letter to the paper if she knew something was wrong. But it took my father a long time to work through a book, and quite often I'd see him turn back a page, and look it over and think about it and 'Oh yes,' and then go on again.[509] He read on the lives of famous men of the day or in the past, particularly the poets and writers of the U.K. He was also an admirer of Tolstoy.[510]

While Terence was quiet and watchful as a boy, James's golden hair and deep blue eyes belied the fact that at four years old he was a bit of a larrikin and had a propensity for pyromania. He was constantly setting fire to gorse bushes and then running to his parents in horror when the fires got out of control. Millicent would punish the boys when needed: 'I smacked my children when necessary, but not often. Children need loving discipline and guidance.'[511] Childhood at Kuri Bush seems to have been a paradise for both children – scrub, river and trees to play in near the farmhouse and miles of 'playground' across the road on that wild white coastline. James remembered his father taking him outside at night:

> Holding me up to look at
> the gigantic rotating wheel of the stars
> Whose time isn't ours.[512]

It all became fodder for James's future prose and poetry:

> rocks, beaches, flax bushes, rivers, cattle flats, hawks, rabbits, eels, old man manuka trees . . . provided me with a great store of images that could later enter my poems. Among the books at home were one or two of Norse and Greek mythology. I became the companion of Odin and Thor and Jason and Ulysses. That was an indispensable education.[513]

But James seems also to have felt compelled to create words to destroy the image of that happy childhood; he would never admit to it being joyful or blissful: 'From an old house shaded with macrocarpas / Rises my malady.'[514]

Long before he went to school, James came under the influence of his parents' interest in literature and particularly poetry. He learned by heart the works of Robbie Burns and the romantic English poets introduced to him by Archie. Terence recalls Archie lifting James onto his knee and reciting one of Burns' poems: 'My brother would take it all in, and like most children, want it over and over again. So he'd get the poem again the next night and get to know it himself and he got the feeling for poetry that way.... He started writing poetry very, very young. From then on of course, he was at it all the time. He was never without some sort of little notebook. Anything at all around him seemed to just move him to write poetry.'[515] James himself says, 'Before I was six years old, I knew "Tom O' Shanter" by heart and parts of other poems by Burns, having received them orally from my father, without whom I would never have come to a knowledge or practice of poetry.'[516]

When Terence was six he went to the Kuri Bush School, a kilometre and a half from the farm, for just one year, 1929. The little wooden school had a roll of sixteen that year and the teacher, Mr M J O'Connor, was reported as being 'industrious and attentive to duty, and the instruction is very fair.' He clearly had plenty to do. The Inspector, Mr H D Pritchard reports, 'The school is well organised and is under very fair management. Order, discipline and tone are good.... The interior of the school needs painting, and the picket fence between the residence and the school requires repairing. Due provision exists for ventilation. The supply of firewood should be fully maintained. The seat of the boys' out-office needs scrubbing. The appearance of the school-room would be much improved if a few framed pictures could be procured.'[517] But however good the school was, it couldn't stop its pupils bullying young Terence. His accent together with his parents and their strange beliefs made him good bait, and McKay says he was roughly initiated into the facts of life by the local kids.[518]

Archie and Millicent decided to send him to Brighton School, and that made them think about making a move thirteen kilometres north to the township itself. In addition, the destructive sea wind had blighted their wheat for too long, and the climate was getting Archie down. Arthritis affected his shoulders so badly he couldn't put on his coat without help. Millicent was convinced that much of this was due to his hanging on a pole for days in shocking weather eleven years earlier. The decision to move was made, and early in 1930 after almost ten happy years in Kuri Bush, they sold the farm and the family moved to Brighton.[519]

PART THREE
The Family

CHAPTER 9
Roving and Writing

Number 15 Bedford Parade, Brighton was the Baxter's new address. Unlike their home in Kuri Bush where just the shed and a few macrocarpa trees remain, this house still stands – tall, sturdy and well maintained. When the Baxter family moved there in 1930, it was a rather imposing, high-quality home: a four-bedroomed two-storey house, set on a hill on a road running parallel to the sea.[520] What luxury after their tiny Kuri Bush property which had no running water or electricity. Having sold the farm, the Baxters could afford to buy such a home. The stairs led up from the galley kitchen to what would famously become known as James's 'fuggy room at the top of the stairs.'[521] The

15 Bedford Parade in 1983. (Taken by Gary Blackman)

family already knew the area well; the original Baxter house was at 32 Bath Street where Archie's parents lived with their daughter Peggie and, later, her husband, Jock Fowler. Archie's parents and most of his brothers[522] lived in Brighton, so Archie, Millicent and the boys saw them often. Two of the brothers lived in Bedford Parade itself: Sandy and his wife, Eileen, at number 9 and Donald, his wife, Myrtle, and their family at number 11. Bedford Parade was a twin road with trees in between that the boys loved to climb.

Inevitably, poetry would be recited when the Baxters got together. Donald told his daughter Diane how they would usually start: 'One would have a line... then another one would come in, and then they'd all recite the poem together.'[523] There wasn't much drinking done; the Baxters generally weren't drinkers. Diane remembers Millicent having a faint disapproval of alcohol: 'Archie wouldn't like to do something that she wouldn't like him to do, and probably vice versa. I don't think she would be bossy, but I just don't think she liked alcohol, and he respected her dislike of it. She possibly knew he had a beer, but they weren't drinkers as such. They weren't boozers.'[524]

There were about three hundred residents in Brighton, and many in the close-knit community together with holiday-makers would swim off the sandy beach around the picturesque cove. Until a year before his death at ninety-four Archie's arthritic father, John, took a daily bathe in the sea there, even throughout those notoriously freezing-cold Otago winters. Brighton proved to be a much better climate than Kuri Bush for Archie, and he soon found work shearing in the Maniototo and the Strath Taieri at Hyde with its surrounding rugged hill ranges to the north and west of Otago Harbour. Millicent settled in to make the family home as she wanted it and started creating an alpine garden which she described as '… a magical garden, a fairy-tale garden with an archway leading through to the main lawn'[525]. She was outgoing, a renowned conversationalist and notoriously untidy. Everyone who remembers her, without fail, remarks how chaotic the house was. Terence recalls 'There's a few things he [Archie] wasn't happy about. Every time there were visitors there'd be things lying about… he didn't help very much but he'd be concerned about it. Probably, if he had set to and tried to tidy up she would have done it with him… but he didn't do it. He just complained about it. He'd say "I don't know what these people are going to think."'[526]

Lawrence Jones, now Emeritus Professor of the University of Otago, a pacifist and a Quaker, remembers Millicent from the years they spent as near neighbours – they lived diagonally across the road: 'She was a great talker and a voracious reader. They had lots of friends and when one dropped by Archie or she would find the place in a state of disarray with great piles of books and magazines. "Oh just move those books out of the way", she would say, waving her hand at the nearest chair, and the visitor would have to do so in order to sit down.'[527] Max Broadbent confirms this trait. He knew the Baxters' friends, the Gills, and their daughter Patricia Lawson[528]. 'They used sometimes to get into Millicent's kitchen to tidy up…. Patricia told me that Millicent cooked well but couldn't be bothered with domestic routines. On one of their clean-up expeditions, Patricia, or her mother, found thirty-two opened bags of icing sugar in different cupboards!'[529] Clearly, Millicent found it easier to buy another bag rather than rummage through endless provisions to find what she wanted. She preferred to spend her time on what really mattered to her: her family, her garden, her books, her alpine plants and her passion for pacifism.

Unlike Millicent, Archie was a quiet, contemplative and private person. He liked nothing better than busying himself in the garden: improving the soil by mixing compost, peat and gravel with the underlying clay and tending his vegetables. Also, he was a regular attender of Labour Party conferences and once attempted local politics by standing for the Taieri County Council. He was unsuccessful. His anti-militarist past would not have helped. Undaunted, he petitioned the neighbourhood for the abolition of schoolboy conscription that forced boys fourteen to eighteen years of age into cadet training. In that endeavour, Millicent found that Archie's charm overrode her probably rather clinical approach: 'On one petition in South Dunedin, I went with him. I took one side of the street, he the other. I got five signatures, he got twenty-five. I must say that I frankly hoped that no one would answer the door when I rang.' As a member of the Women's International League for Peace and Freedom, Millicent also petitioned for disarmament. In 1931, Archie and Millicent founded the Dunedin branch of the No More War Movement, which held meetings regularly in the Harrop Street Hall, behind the cathedral.[530] Today, Millicent

Archie Baxter in his garden
Ref: Hocken Library MS-975-226 S15-596

as well as Archie may well have been politicians.

Millicent joined the Country Women's Institute, and for a time she was president. She started folk dancing classes there, all the rage at the time, and her sister Viola came down to give a hand. Millicent invited lecturers from Dunedin to speak at the meetings but retrospectively felt that she tried to be too highbrow. Probably she was so for the little town of Brighton at that time. Apart from the enduring legacy of his past, Archie seems to have been a popular, much-loved person, but Millicent ran into a lot of trouble with

Millicent and Aunt Viola 1937. Hill above Salisbury,
Ref: Hocken Library MS:229 S15-599b MS-975-229

the community in Brighton. One of those interviewed for this book was ninety-two-year-old Wynn Geeves, who was about fifteen when she first met Millicent in about 1933. Even at that age she was able to see how the locals were strongly divided in their opinion of this woman who was so dissimilar to them. Other than Terence, Lenore Baxter and George McIntosh, Wynn was my only interviewee who knew Millicent as a relatively young woman (when she was about forty-five). Wynn was married to Russell Geeves, who had been at Kuri Bush School with Terence and who had fought in World War Two, been captured by the Germans on Crete and made to work in several concentration camps including Auschwitz. Although Russell liked Archie as a person, he disagreed with his pacifism, so Wynn was astonishingly open-minded in being interviewed for a book on a local pacifist family. She was worried about revealing the divisions in the community regarding Archie and Millicent yet wanted to do so. Her interview has been invaluable in painting a picture of those early times in Brighton and the controversy that Millicent, Archie and the other Baxters caused:

> I've always been keen that somebody would record what Millicent did there; she was just a walking history book… I used to work milking cows, housework etc. with people who were eight, ten, fifteen years older than me and I used to hear all the gossip. They used to say Millicent knew too much, she was an old know-all because she had a good sort of historic mind. No I did not think she was a snob. The whole trouble was a great number of people had not had any education, so therefore it was a jealousy thing, I'm quite sure. There was quite a wee wall of pettiness. It's not around now like it was, the pettiness is not nearly the same…
>
> And Archie stood out different as well. A lot of what he learnt was out of books that the other ones had never read or heard about, so there was a kind of a jealousy. But he, and the other Baxters too, had to find it and learn it themselves. But some people pooh-poohed Archie… it was the horrible, horrible thing in the district between people who went to War and people who didn't. And the Baxters, and Archie, well it was 'keep away from them.'…
>
> I might have only been 15 when I knew [Millicent] first. There were about fifteen of us and most of us were keen on learning, and Millicent, she thought that was great and she made us all join the Country Women's Institute. Then she hooked us into all sorts of things. And some of the old ladies in the district more or less tried to make her educate us younger ones. And she certainly did lift us up quite a bit…She should have been a teacher. She wanted to make us to be more use than what we

were. She was wonderful.

Then she wrote several plays; she wrote this one good play that had a part for everybody. It was fun in that it made the whole group of young people more or less much more loving and friendly and it made the district very, very different. Millicent was a leader...I owe her quite a lot because of the knowledge that she poked into me and it was appreciated... I liked her and enjoyed her company. And enjoyed her family.

Yes, they had friends; they were likeable people. But Archie had the anti-war thing... and well there were those little walls that were brought into the kids, which was mean. Oh that was horrible, there were walls between different families. A lot of that should have been stopped by the older people, but I don't know whether they knew what to do.'[531]

Wynn Geeves's comments about Millicent contrast strongly with those of a cousin of Archie, and her husband, who lived two or three doors away from Millicent and Archie. They liked Archie very much but vehemently disliked Millicent. The husband thought she was an 'upper-class, toffee-nosed snob' who sought out Archie because he wasn't mainstream because it was a trendy thing to do. They felt she never communicated well with them and would greet them at her half-opened front door with her head down, saying 'What do you want'?

Perhaps Millicent was ashamed of her untidy house. Perhaps she knew she was disliked and didn't know what to do about it. But what is important is that some people felt put off by Millicent's educated and academic manner. George McIntosh maintains that this sort of attitude was pure prejudice: 'Some people say anything if they're prejudiced. Just trying to pull down a tall poppy'[532] Don Lawson, who was married to Elsie and Jim Gills' daughter Patricia, maintains that Brighton at that time was 'a hotbed-of-rednecks sort of rural community.'[533] So it is small wonder that the few people who disagreed with war, like the Baxters, the Oestreichers, the Jones's, the Gills and the Lawsons, were very much drawn towards one another into a fairly tightly-packed group, thereby unintentionally excluding themselves from the many in the village.

I agree with George McIntosh. Even in 'egalitarian' New Zealand with its long-held value of supporting the underdog, Millicent suffered from the tall poppy syndrome. She was often disparaged by people who were themselves inverted snobs who perceived her to be above them. Lenore Baxter, who would later become Terence's wife, had her theory on how Brighton folk viewed Millicent: 'It must have been very hard for them to have Millicent so different, and Millicent might sometimes have been misunderstood. She was very, very kind and very generous, and during the depression she did a lot of good work, like going around to poor people with blankets and things, which might have seemed a little patronising. But to her it was the right thing to do.'[534] Although it's impossible to know how conscious Millicent herself was of the extent of her unpopularity among some Brighton people, she was certainly aware of at least one incident – involving another cousin of Archie – about which she would forever feel ashamed:

> As the war went on, feeling in Brighton became more hostile. It unfortunately produced hostility in me. On one occasion, the husband of Archie's cousin came across the road as we were waiting for a bus and attacked him – verbally, of course. I don't suppose his wife approved of his action, but from that time on until she died years afterwards, I cut her. After the war was over and feelings had died down, I very much regretted my action, but there I was, landed with it.
>
> It was a source of embarrassment every time I saw her – a severe retribution for a silly action. I didn't have the courage of the man in the township who had abused Archie and, before he died, admitted that he deeply regretted what he had done. Now all these passions have died away and we don't have controversies on these issues.[535]

How curious that this otherwise strong and intensely honest woman couldn't bring herself to apologise to the woman.

James, Millicent and Terence Baxter c 1931
Ref: Hocken Library S04-333

Terence, Millicent and James
Ref: Hocken Library S15-596

The Baxters imbued their sons with their love for travel. They bought a little two-seater Ford and for six years the four of them went away for three weeks in the summer, touring much of the South Island. Terence would sit on the seat between his parents, and little James sat on his mother's knees:[536] Their favourite areas were Ohau as a base for exploring the Southern Lakes area and Wanaka from which they visited Haast Pass and Queenstown. The mountains were higher than Archie had previously experienced. Once, they ventured up the Matukituki Valley where they all experienced an overwhelming sense of the menace of the mountains. Later, when he was 16, James wrote 'The mountains crouch like tigers / They are but stone yet the seeking eyes grow blind.'[537] They would rarely stay in campgrounds, preferring to freedom-camp in places where larger vehicles couldn't go. The little Ford had a high clearance so they were able to travel to places where others couldn't. Once on a visit to Queenstown over the Crown Range, the Cardrona River wasn't yet bridged and they crossed it twenty-three times.[538]

Archie would set up a tent constructed of waterproof sheets spread over branches of dried manuka. He also caught rabbits and cooked them in billies slung on an iron bar over an open fire. Fresh vegetables, honey, milk, cream and butter were delivered in a van that would do the rounds of campers.[539] There is a photograph in the Hocken Library of Millicent and the two boys, probably aged about six and ten, sitting in a clearing in the sunshine. The billie is boiling away on the open fire. Terence is sitting upright, looking intently into the camera and Millicent is leaning back stiffly, legs stretched out in front of her, the ubiquitous hat rammed down on her head and, yes, she is clutching her large handbag. On her lap lolls young James, basking in the sunshine.

Terence remembers Archie having a passion for lighting fires, perhaps that is where James got it from: 'He was always very keen to get a fire lit. Nothing my father liked better than to be burning rubbish out in the garden or lighting a fire somewhere. And of course it suited him down to the ground when we could go camping. In those days we just had an open fire of driftwood.' Once, in the Queenstown camping ground, there was a plague of earwigs and they streamed down the insides of the tent. They collected in the hollow handle of the frying-pan and poured out over the Archie's hands. [540]

Terence had started at Brighton School where the headmaster and his assistant taught the fifty pupils in two classrooms.[541] Archie had been a pupil there forty years before. Although Terence was happier there than at Kuri Bush School, he gradually became the slightly withdrawn person he is today. Millicent remarks that he 'so outgoing and friendly as a small child, seemed to have altered. A cloud seemed

Brighton School 1934. Terence 2nd row 6th from right, James 1st row, 4th from right. (By kind permission of June Wilson)

to come down on him at times, and impatience and anger on the part of teacher or parent increased it.'[542] She and Archie felt they had obviated any sense of resentment that Terence might have had when James was born and he had ceased to be the only preoccupation of his parents, but Millicent did sometimes wonder whether there was some subconscious reaction to his brother which deeply affected Terence's nature. She always wished she had been able to have James earlier so that there wouldn't have been a four-year gap between her sons.[543] McKay analyses Terence as being the stereotype of the sensitive, introspective first child and James, that of the relaxed, more outgoing younger brother: 'They were different physically; Terence was rather tense and tended to be moody. James was thickset and used to lumber along. He was easy-going and for the most part good-tempered.'[544] With her

Blackman Brighton Boatsheds about 1983
(Taken by Gary Blackman)

customary honesty, Millicent sums up her boys' characters: 'Both boys were generous but Terence was the one who was conscientious and dutiful, caring about peoples' feelings.... Terence had a natural sense of propriety, which Jim had not.'[545] Despite their wide differences in nature and interests 'Ten' and 'Jum' got on well as brothers, but Terence found that James didn't want to play the games he played: 'For instance, I wanted to go and sail boats in the pond and he'd come down and give me a hand. I'd want him to get over the other side and turn the boat around. Well that was all right for a while, he'd help. But after a while he wanted me to help him. So we didn't do a lot together.'[546]

James's first experience of school was not a good one: 'On that first grim day I sidled into the room and went straight to the fat black stove and put my hand on it. It was hot, not red hot, but black hot. So I hid behind the teacher's dress... I remember her as a vague, kind, middle-aged woman... Some time later, when I stole her strap and took it home and hid it in a rusty can under a macrocarpa tree she did not punish me for this infantile protest.'[547] Perhaps his charm on women was already working. He sailed through the lessons although he took little interest in what he was taught so scored low marks. The headmaster mistook these results for low intelligence.[548]

Referring to this lifelong disdain for formal education, Frank McKay maintains 'James always felt closer to the rugged, uneducated, working-class Baxters. His grandfather, Macmillan Brown, represented for him a system of education with a puritan devotion to hard work and a goal of material advancement, conformity and respectability. Against these values he was increasingly to rebel.'[549] He was also uncoordinated and was poor at sports throughout his time at school. It wasn't long before James acquired what Millicent calls 'a rather bawdy attitude to sex, which prevailed in most primary schools. I can remember him trying desperately to catch Terence's eye as Archie and I discussed the English 'No More War Movement' [with] the secretary, Lucy Cox. Her name amused Jim. Terence, always discreet, kept his eyes down.'[550]

At the age of seven, James started composing poetry. Lenore Baxter told Frank McKay 'It was [Archie's] encouragement that both boys tried their hand at writing verse from a very early age – and that habit took root in one of them! One cannot help but wonder what sort of gifts Jum would have developed if he had been reared away from his father!' Nevertheless, Millicent read many books and poems to James, and he could read quite well before he went to school. He also became immersed in a favourite subject of Millicent's, the mythology of Scandinavia and Ancient Greece.[551] Millicent told Michael King, in an interview arranged by Christine Cole Catley for the publication of Millicent's memoirs, that she thought it was a mistake that James knew so much before he went to school because he was far in advance of the others 'And in those days they didn't push them on and he became frightfully lazy because he

James aged 10

didn't need to work... he had a tendency to laziness in doing school or academic work and it pursued him all his life.'[552]

The grandparents played only a small part in the boys' childhood. Mary Baxter died when Terence was ten and James was six, but the few memories Terence has of her are fond ones. He remembers Archie telling him that their house burned down once, and Mary became so alarmed about her children playing with fire that when she caught one of the boys doing so, she heated up the poker in the fire and spanked him with it so he would never do it again.[553] Terence has memories of being frightened when John Baxter played the bagpipes very loudly in the house. Terence always felt at his happiest when he was outside in nature and felt uneasy inside his grandparents' house: 'I didn't like being left there while my parents went to town because I felt I was locked in – on a wet day anyway... it affected me.'[554] This gives us forewarning of how his subsequent imprisonment affected him. Being with John Macmillan Brown in Christchurch was no better. Macmillan Brown was in his eighties when the boys were young so they had to be on their best behaviour. Terence says 'To be honest, I never really liked him. He was a severe old gentleman, like a general, and they all respected him and everybody had to be quiet when he was about. My mother and the two women that did the cooking called him 'the professor'... It's a pity because many children remember their grandfathers and grandmothers with great pleasure, don't they?'[555]

Millicent was usually the family decision-maker. She was a stricter parent than Archie, who was softer and more pliable and would talk things through with the boys. But neither son had any doubt of the love from both their parents. Millicent made absolutely sure that the boys had excellent manners, and both inherited her Anglicised accent. Terence recalls being teased by wider members of the Baxter family and at school for his pronunciation of 'cows' instead of the more acceptable 'keows'.[556] James's voice would become famous as he recited his poetry around the country, and it was much remarked on because of its beautifully articulated, resonant tone. His mother said that listening to his speaking voice was like listening to music.[557]

As James's poetry evolved away from his early Romantic style and became more earthy, Millicent ceased to appreciate it. Terence maintains she didn't approve of James's poetry despite her natural loyalty to him.[558] Terence's wife, Lenore, got to know and like her mother-in-law very well, they were both intellectuals. She comments that Millicent's lack of appreciation of James's poetry was because her interests lay elsewhere; they were in history, international affairs and politics. While she enjoyed novels and was especially fond of biographies, she never read poetry for pleasure.[559] Archie on the other hand always supported James's poetry. Terence remembers that his father was more broad-minded:

> My father... would give a little bit of a grin about it, or note that he might be sailing a bit close to the wind now and again. Of course he admired practically anything that my brother wrote. I think it was quite a good thing for my brother in a way. He had the support of his father all the way through, right until the day [my father] died. He always had this feeling behind him that his father approved of him.[560]

Terence acknowledges that he didn't always approve of James's poetry or, sometimes, his behaviour, but he always speaks warmly of him. Kenneth remembers 'there was certainly no animosity between the two brothers, but not necessarily a lot of bonhomie and back-slapping either. I think Jum was more demonstrative, so if he was introducing his brother to somebody he might give them a bit of a slap on the back, but my dad wouldn't do that. [561] James later became famous for his bear hugs, but Terence of course would never dream of doing the same, and according to her grandchildren, neither would Millicent.

By this time, Millicent and Archie had become very good friends with Elsie and Jim Gill. The Gills were pacifists and Jim had been a conscientious objector in World War One. Like the Baxters, the Gills also suffered the contempt of the Brighton community. Don Lawson, who married their daughter Patricia, gives an example of some of the abuse the Gill's endured: 'Jim Gill's pacifist beliefs were in the days when Brighton had drop-and-carry toilets, and people emptied their shit cans onto his garden.'[562] Elsie Gill, who had been brought up at Kuri Bush,[563] qualified at Trinity College of Music London and was a piano teacher. Although she was seventeen years younger than Millicent, the two women became the closest of friends; they walked and talked and read together every day. Their upbringing, with its emphasis on following social protocol, never left either of them, and they referred to each other in public as 'Mrs Baxter' and 'Mrs Gill' and probably would have thought that to do otherwise would have been a sign of great disrespect.[564] Millicent told Christine Cole Catley that she didn't like the informal Christian name usage in public one bit. She didn't like her name, she would have preferred the name Margaret and hated being called Millicent by people who were young enough to be her grandchildren.[565]

Elsie Gill and Millicent Baxter
Ref: Hocken Brown Library MS-975-231 S15-596

Even to her cherished friends, Millicent could be forbidding. She could upset some people without even knowing it. Elsie's daughter Rosamund McCreadie says 'Millicent could stand her ground and very quietly, just sort of not move. You would know by the look on her face that she'd said what she was going to say and that was it. My grandmother would be devastated when it happened with her... Millicent didn't mince words. I think if she wanted to say something, she said it, whereas my grandmother would have gone two feet the other way.'[566] We begin to see the picture of this tiny, tough, indomitable woman around whom some people were a little uneasy. Rosamund McCreadie continues: 'I always remember her being quite an outspoken person but was quite, what I would call, acidic. She wasn't nasty but she certainly had a bite to her tongue.'[567] While Millicent herself did wonder if she was a little 'highbrow' for some, she would have been distressed if she had known the effect that she had on some people.

The family was on their summer holiday in Waikaia and Curio Bay in the Catlins in January 1935 when Millicent received a telegram from her sister Viola to say their father was ill. They left immediately, but water had got into the little Ford's fuel tank, and it gave out in a remote area near Gore. A farmer put them up for the night, and when Millicent telephoned Viola in Christchurch she heard that John had died peacefully in his chair on 18 January 1935. No doubt he died satisfied that he had been, in the words of his grandson James, 'one of the servants of the cause of intellectual progress.'[568] He was eighty-nine. Millicent went to Christchurch by train and attended the memorial service in Canterbury College Hall. Because there was no crematorium in Christchurch at that time, she and Viola travelled to Dunedin where John was cremated at Andersons Bay. They returned to Christchurch to settle the estate. Their father had been chancellor of the University of New

Zealand from 1923 until his death, and for several days afterwards the Christchurch newspapers applauded his extraordinary achievements in the world of education and the study of cultures of the Pacific region. Millicent had always had a volatile relationship with her father, and her reaction to his death took her aback. She remembers bursting into tears at one stage, an act that was very uncharacteristic of her.[569] John had had an enormous influence on both his daughters but Viola had spent most of her life living with her father. For her, his death was the end of an era.

Viola's story is an interesting one. At the end of 1920, her father made it clear that, with Millicent fleeing the nest to marry Archie Baxter, his younger daughter should now stay to look after him. He even added it would kill him if she left.[570] Nevertheless, fond though she was of her father, around 1921 Viola moved to London to study at the Slade School of Fine Art then spent a year in Florence living with an Italian family learning the language. She returned to New Zealand in 1923 and lived again with her father. That same year, Dame Nellie Melba was on her second concert tour of New Zealand and was with the up-and-coming Italian tenor Angelo Notariello. After the Christchurch

John Macmillan Brown at Holmbank, Cashmere, probably taken around the early 1920s.

Ref: Macmillan Brown Library MB118-13001

concert, Angelo's manager absconded with all his money. To earn his living and to fund the rest of the singers, Notariello had little option but to teach Italian in Christchurch. A friend of Viola's suggested she should have Italian lessons from him, so the couple met and, says her daughter Antonietta, 'it was definitely love at first sight.' Terence mulls over the days when his aunt had all those suitors: 'She had ample choice, yet she chose this man

Viola being sketched at Holmbank, Fendalton c 1900.
Ref: Macmillan Brown Library MB1991-1-6785

who was a different sort of person altogether. He wasn't one of the tall, dark, handsome types at all.'[571] In around 1924, the couple got engaged but they never told John. Neither did she tell Millicent. By 1926 Angelo had made enough money to pay for the entire group of stranded Italian singers to return home, and he left for

England to sing in concerts booked for him. When John died in 1935, Viola's eleven-year wait was over. She went to England and married Angelo in Bournemouth in 1936.[572]

At that time it was not uncommon for the eldest daughter to not marry but remain with the parents to care for them in their old age, but it is a sad reflection that John, a man who could be so passionate about his interests and his own marriage, could not bring himself to understand the intensity of someone else's emotions, especially those of his own daughters. He was difficult to look after. He was extremely stubborn and often dismissive of his own health. But living with him wasn't all control and discipline. Viola told her daughter Antonietta that there was a sweet and genial side to her father and that he enjoyed listening to Viola playing the piano to him in the evenings. In her introduction to his memoirs she comments in a very positive way: 'He helped very many people both financially and in other ways but never said anything about it… He was the most delightful, interesting and charming companion… He very patiently and cheerfully put up with all ills and disabilities… I counted myself fortunate in sharing those years with him.'[573]

John Macmillan Brown left a substantial legacy to the University of Canterbury, which was used to establish the Macmillan Brown Library in 1935 and the Macmillan Brown Centre for Pacific Studies in 1988. The nucleus of the library was the 15,000 books that John had at Holmbank. The current holdings consist of approximately 115,000 publications, four linear kilometres of documentary archives, 120,000 architectural drawings and over 100,000 photographs.[574] The New Zealand and Pacific section of the Macmillan Brown Library contains eighteenth and early nineteenth century literature covering the arrival of Europeans in New Zealand and the South Pacific and many works from nineteenth and early twentieth century Pacific anthropology.[575]

Macmillan Brown Library today, University of Canterbury, Christchurch

In her interview with Bruce Harding about her celebrated grandfather's legacy, Antonietta commented 'I think my grandfather would be absolutely thrilled to know that it was being continued in such a vivid way… I've been very interested to see how his vision has developed.'[576]

In the early 1980s, Max Broadbent visited Millicent, primarily to talk to her about the creation of the centre that would later be named the Macmillan Brown Centre for Pacific Studies. Millicent was now about ninety. They had lunch together at Patricia and Don Lawson's house in Brighton. Max recalls 'I had been placed beside her because of my connection with her father's bequest to the university. After one or two attempts to engage her on the library and her father, I began to realise she was not anxious to pursue these topics. After a short pause she said to me "I think I have finally forgiven my father," so I dropped the subject, which I am sure she intended.' [577] Max Broadbent has frequently thought about that remark and makes an assessment of Millicent's complicated relationship with her father, and of her inherent honesty:

> I felt that a woman who kept everyone at a cool distance was deliberately giving me an insight into something deeply personal. Her remark was made as though she were giving as accurate an account of her conscience as she could, about something that really mattered. She had transformed what I was approaching as a cultural and historical concern of objective public interest, [the setting up of the Macmillan Brown Centre] into a personal and moral issue. She had made me conscious of the depth of the difficulty in the relationship [with her father]. Considering her great age and how long it was since he had died, I felt she had shown me how profound was her moral struggle to be just to him as a human being whom she felt had not treated her well. Her simple remark and the way she said it conveyed to me that a family relationship matters more than a great public benefaction, that forgiveness is important and that it can be hard, that it may take over half a very long lifetime to reach. That impressed me.[578]

Max Broadbent's insightful analysis reflects the character of the woman that emerges from her memoirs, whose innate honesty almost always manages to surmount her personal prejudices. Perhaps this partly stemmed from her Scottish Presbyterian upbringing instilling in her a strong sense of right and wrong.[579] Max also recollects a more light-hearted moment at that same lunch, when:

> Don Lawson produced some very good raspberry jam he had made that morning using plenty of fresh raspberries. Urged to try some, Millicent took an appraising bite of a liberally jammed scone. Eventually, awarding about seven out of ten she carefully said 'Mmm It does taste faintly of raspberries.' I don't think she was trying to be funny. I recall a strong face, firm jaw, thin lips, with a cool blue stare and very white, completely white, hair. That is how I remember her appearance. She was

then very old. She spoke with the distinctly Anglicised voice that was once common among the rich in New Zealand, people who had come to maturity before the Great Depression. Very clearly articulated. Her son the poet was a great talker with a very arresting voice, too. I think there was a strong family resemblance – Brown, Millicent and the poet.[580]

John also left Millicent and Viola reasonably substantial inheritances, although they were in the form of annuities of a fixed £400 per year. It is to his credit that he made that bequest to Millicent as well as to Viola, bearing in mind his original strong disapproval of her marriage to Archie. And Millicent acknowledges that he also left them 'that intangible legacy, things of the mind, which are more important.'[581] The sisters were 'looked after' till the end of their lives. The legacy made a significant difference to Millicent and Archie's way of life, and it was probably John's money that funded Archie and Millicent's two-year trip around Europe in 1937 and enabled Terence and James to go to Quaker schools both in England and in New Zealand.

The couple would otherwise have been in financial strife along with most others during the late 1920s and 1930s when the Great Depression affected Brighton as much as elsewhere in the country. The dole queues lengthened, and men, some of whom had previously been white-collar workers, were labouring on the roads with not even enough money for boots. Millicent told David Young from NZ Listener 'In Brighton they brought out all the unemployed, who had mainly been clerks, and they had to work at making the roads and digging the ditches – hard manual labour. Their shoes gave out; they always had wet feet, unsuitable clothing and a perfectly inadequate dole.'[582] Mark and Sandy Baxter, Archie's two married brothers, received the married man's payment of 30 shillings a week. Millicent, ever aware of the locals' dislike of accepting any help from conscientious objectors, wasn't open about what help she gave and passed on blankets and clothing through an intermediary.[583]

One day, thirteen-year-old Terence came home saying he had been thrashed by the schoolteacher at Brighton School for making mistakes in his arithmetic examinations[584] but, according to Frank McKay, the now handsome teenager had been having a relationship with a sixteen-year-old schoolgirl.[585] Of course, 'a relationship' in those days usually had a very different connotation from today. Both the teacher and Terence were in a 'bad state of nervous upset' as Millicent puts it. Archie said 'You won't go back,' and had it out with the teacher but never revealed to Millicent what was said. They removed Terence from the Brighton School and sent him to the Quaker School in Wanganui,[586] St John's Hill School. James remained in Brighton.[587] Despite having Quaker friends such as the Oestreichers, Millicent and Archie never joined the Quaker movement, but they supported the Quaker view of liberalism, social action and most of all, pacifism.

The following year, 1935, they sold some assets, let out their home in Brighton and moved to Wanganui to be closer to Terence and to enrol James at the same

Quaker school. They rented a house and bought a Chevrolet, 'the Chev', to replace the old Ford. Millicent loved the scenery in the Wanganui district with its scarlet gum trees flowering in abundance, and nearby Kai Iwi grew to be a favourite spot to gather driftwood to avoid having to buy coal. It was at this time that Archie's cardiac problems manifested themselves. He became ill, having become chilled on the ferry returning from a business trip to the South Island. Millicent relates that

> When the pains first came on in the night, Archie kept on saying 'I took the money; I couldn't help it. They made me.' He was in a state of great excitement. I grasped that he meant the money from the military authorities. He had told me he had accepted it unwillingly, but he had never spoken of it again. (The money, so much per day for the two years he was supposed to have served, had to be accepted before he could get his discharge. He felt he had been forced to accept it and was quite bitter about it.) I was very alarmed, but managed after a long while to calm him down.[588]

Although the cardiograph showed no serious damage, their doctor was concerned. Archie was a chronic worrier and subject to deep bouts of despondency,[589] and Millicent later confided to Michael King that Archie was always frightened of becoming insane.[590] This is hardly surprising, bearing in mind how his war experiences had affected him and the fact that the army had declared him insane nine years earlier. Perhaps Archie was never really convinced this had been done to save his life and suspected that the diagnosis had some truth in it.

At the beginning of 1937, Millicent and Archie decided to tour abroad and, typically, she shouldered the burden of packing up and selling the Wanganui house, protecting her Archie from the upset of the move. Terence, already a man alert to the needs of others, lent a hand, and Millicent found him a great help: 'He was only 14 but he worked like a grown man: scrubbed floors, cleaned windows… he was absolutely tottering with having done too much.' As they crossed the Tasman in the Wanganella, Millicent suffered her usual seasickness, as did Archie and the boys. At Pompeii, a guide 'took Archie off to see the brothel with a phallic symbol over the door. After all, why not? It was just to show an historic fact. But the girls [whom they had met on the boat] created uproar. They wouldn't now; they would probably go to look themselves.'[591] Reading between the lines, I suspect Millicent wished she'd had a look herself. Millicent regularly thought laterally and was often willing to reject mainstream expectations and morality.

When they reached London they saw a lot of Viola. Her marriage with Angelo was proving to be an extremely happy one despite Millicent's predictions. Viola recalls Millicent's warning: 'Millicent, knowing nothing of my engagement for I had told nobody whatever about it, said "you must never marry because it's very unlikely that two sisters should have ideally happy marriages, and mine is." I proved her wrong!'[592]

At Viola's suggestion, Terence and James were sent to board at Sibford School near Banbury in Oxfordshire, a coeducational Quaker school close to the county borders of Warwickshire, Northamptonshire and Buckinghamshire with magnificent views across the Cotswold countryside. Terence was fifteen and James, eleven. The school was run along austere lines with unheated dormitories and dry bread and cocoa for supper before bed. Worship on Sundays at the nearby Quaker meeting house was held in silence, broken occasionally when someone felt moved to speak.[593]

Meanwhile, Millicent and Archie rented a home in Salisbury in Wiltshire for several months. One day they took the bus to Bulford where the Sling military camp had been and where Archie had been imprisoned and persecuted before being sent to the front. The visit was cathartic for Archie, and Millicent felt it helped with his recovery by freeing something that had been frozen deep inside him.[594] The result of that revisit was that Archie started to write his memoir, We will not cease. The timing was right also; it was 1937, and Archie's worldview of pacifism and concerns about a possible second war with Germany were enough to push him into the painful task of writing the book. Again, Archie was making a stand. He wanted to remind people of the sin of war: 'war is evil. It is murder and I object to murder and to people being forced into doing it.'[595] But he wanted also to record, to document and to expose. In the field of pacifism, he was an absolutist and in writing the book he wanted to argue the case for non-violent resistance.

Terence told Paul Millar in 1995 that it was Archie who first thought of writing the book, but he needed Millicent's encouragement to put his idea into action. 'Many men wouldn't achieve anything if they didn't have a wife behind them saying "You can do that." This happened to my father when he wrote his book... He got the idea himself of writing it, but once he started, it was quite a thing to take on trying to remember what went on earlier, and he had to re-live it again which he didn't want to do.'[596] Millicent was a strong character with a lucid intellect and sharp political mind, and since meeting Archie she had become as involved in pacifism as he was. It would not be surprising that she wanted the world to know his story. Don Lawson says 'Millicent was Archie's mouthpiece really. She was the one who confronted authority and power. Now Archie did, quintessentially, the ultimate facing of power, but expressed that in a quite different verbal manner. She was completely focused on what was in her head, what the political issue was, or what the intellectual issue was. And all the peripheral organisations were totally sort of ignored really, or out of the equation.'[597]

Millicent says Archie dictated his recollections to her because she wrote more quickly.[598] She laboriously wrote down the information in longhand, entering her firm, bold handwriting in exercise books that still lie in the Hocken Library among a feast of material about this now famous family. In their Salisbury house and while out on walks, Millicent prised out of her husband the gruelling fact: 'It was painful and, in many ways, healing, for it brought to the surface things that were buried deep down in pain and suffering... It was hard to get him to give his feelings. I would say "You are giving me only the bare bones. You must give me more than that." And Archie would say, "Surely if I give them the facts, people can use their imaginations." '[599] Ironically, when Millicent was writing her memoirs forty years later, Christine Cole Catley was forever asking Millicent for more of her feelings.[600]

Like many survivors of the war, Archie found it hard to relive the barbaric treatment he had experienced, and from time to time he would turn to sixteen-year-old Terence when he felt that Millicent was asking too much of him: 'She used to get at him a lot, and he used to talk to me sometimes. We'd go for a walk and he'd say, "You know, I'm having an awful time just now, she's at me all the time about it." He was almost at the end of his tether. As soon as he told her anything, it was "Well, what happened next?" ' Until this time, Terence was virtually unaware of his father's past. James's son, John Baxter, talked of Millicent's recollections of this time in a radio interview with Chris Laidlaw: 'After my father died I became quite close to Millicent and she had talked to me about Archie writing the book, or dictating it to her, and she found it was just a flat recitation of the facts, so Gran found that quite annoying. She wanted a bit of colour in the story.' John also found his grandmother could herself be quite dispassionate: 'She had a detachment where you could discuss the most appalling things or the most beautiful things with her, but always with a detachment – which Archie didn't have; Archie was a very passionate man.'[601]

It is worth taking a look here at who exactly wrote 'We will not cease' which has become an iconic text in New Zealand. There has been some scepticism about whether Archie exclusively wrote it, whether a relatively uneducated man could write such an articulate book, or if Millicent originated some of the text herself. After all, she was a Cambridge graduate and Archie a farmer, educated only to the age of twelve. Did Millicent record his words faithfully, or did she shape the text in her own way? Certainly the text does occasionally seem to have a 'Millicent voice': systematic, attending to detail. However, to Katherine Baxter, Archie and Millicent's granddaughter

> It's a finer piece of writing than Gran could have produced on her own... and she was so much younger herself then and probably a lot more open to be influenced by what he wanted to say, so probably more committed to being faithful to what he wanted to say. On the other hand she couldn't have written it down without making the sentences grammatically perfect, whereas he might not have done that. Also, she would have been motivated politically to get the story out because her politics were a lot more active than his.[602]

But Terence tends to think the writing of the book was collaborative:

> I think they probably worked together on it and she might write down, write it in a certain way you see and a certain wording, and ask him what he thought about that and he'd say, "Oh well that's alright, but it's not quite right, I'd rather have it slightly different this way," and they'd come to some sort of decision on it. Because I don't think that she actually sort of wrote the book, but she certainly had a fair bit to do with writing it, and mainly with forcing him almost to remember what happened or what was going on…[603]

'We will not cease' is populated with convincing characters and detailed, lengthy dialogue, particularly between Archie and army personnel on the Waitemata, at Sling Camp and at the front. Is it possible that he could remember all those conversations in such detail two decades after the event? Almost definitely not. Those conversations must have been reconstructed and surely by Archie. The blow-by-blow events would have been prompted by his statement of his experiences that he had written for Harry Holland's book Armageddon or Calvary immediately after he returned home in 1918 when his memory was fresh. We know that Millicent didn't influence that work; it would be another 18 years before he met her. So in 1937, with a copy of that statement, Archie already had to hand the skeleton of We will not cease. The writing styles of the three examples we have of his prose writing: the statement for Holland, 'We will not cease' and Archie's unpublished novel[604], are similar; which suggests that Archie was essentially the sole author.

In his book, Calls to Arms: New Zealand Society and Commitment to the Great War, Steven Loveridge thinks it little matters who did the actual writing of We will not cease: 'Aside from the astonishing nature of the events recorded, the success of the text owes much to its narration and the imparted impression of Baxter's strength of character against hostile circumstances. Although the accuracy of the dialogue must be considered…the account, whether reflecting the reality or the retelling, remarkably illustrates the confrontation between objector and the tropes established around soldiers and shirkers.'[605]

Whether there was one author or two, Millicent's rigorous perseverance and Archie's good memory brought about the finished version of We will not cease, covering Archie's experiences of twenty-two months in the army, with almost no mention of his personal life before or after those times. The text is usually eloquent and the book is a memorable and exceptional narrative that shows a very singular individual. In many parts, it is so gut-wrenching that it has a profound effect on anyone who reads it; indeed, there are still members of the Baxter family who have not found it possible to finish the whole book. Archie's niece, Donald's daughter Diane Dore, even in her 60s, still finds it too emotionally difficult: 'I found reading the book that the names were all faces to me. They were all family which I knew and I just couldn't cope with that.'[606]

Certainly the title was Archie's idea. Millicent discussed it with Christine Cole Catley, who was responsible for its third edition in 2003: 'He selected it. He was very fond of Blake's poems. He loved poetry.' The title is of course derived from William Blake's poem, And Did Those Feet in Ancient Time, '…Bring me my chariot of fire! / I will not cease from mental fight…'[607] Blake's poem was inspired by the apocryphal story of Jesus establishing a New Jerusalem: a Christian's metaphor for heaven.[608] Perhaps the title suggests Archie's unswerving quest for his 'heaven', a world without war. His decision to change the words from I will not cease to 'We will not cease' takes the emphasis away from himself, placing him in the role of one pacifist among many, one conscientious objector among The Fourteen. The title is certainly apt; Archie's mental fight for pacifism never did cease.

While writing the book in England, Archie and Millicent continued to be very active in pacifism, and James and Terence became involved simply because they were taken everywhere with their parents when they weren't at school in Sibford. The family sailed to Esbjerg in Denmark then took the train to Copenhagen for Archie to address the War Resisters' International Conference. There they mixed with the English aristocracy. Millicent was distinctly unimpressed with the English class snobbery they were met with:

> …in the carriage were Lord Ponsonby and Canon Morris. Dick Shepherd had mentioned we were from New Zealand. The whole way they did not speak a word to us… that the taboo against colonials, which I knew was very strong, would have operated in a pacifist group seemed dreadful to us. English upper-class snobbery is particularly unreasoning. In the 1930s there was extreme anti-colonialism in England. Canadians were regarded as Americans and accepted, but New Zealanders were confused with Australians who were regarded as brash and uncouth.[609]

Terence and James were the only children at the conference, and at the hotel they ran pencils down the grooved bannister and kept racing up the down escalator.[610] After the conference, the family continued their beloved pastime of travelling, this time in Germany, Austria and France. In her memoirs Millicent tells of a bicycle accident while they were staying in Serrières on the banks of the Rhone that left Terence, then aged fifteen, with an injured back and broken arm.[611] He would suffer from back trouble for the rest of his life. Terence had clearly inherited his parents' stoicism and was never one to make a fuss, preferring, unlike his brother, to remain in the background. Also at Serrières, James, now fourteen, was dabbling with the opposite sex, but only in his already unsettled mind. His biographer William Oliver identifies Millicent as 'the awakener of sexual awareness' in James,[612] quoting from his poem At Serrieres, 'The new guitar of sex I kept on twanging / Inside the iron virgin / of the little smelly dyke, or that Easter Sunday / Through a chink in the bedclothes, watching my mother dressing / The heavy thighs, the black bush of hair.'[613] Also his sex education advanced a little when he saw one of the senior boys 'making the two-backed beast'[614] with the school beauty in long grass. Terence, more handsome and sociable, had far more success with girls at school than James did.[615]

Back in England, Millicent and Archie returned the boys to Sibford School where James was highly thought of as having the makings of a poet. His parents' pacifism was rubbing off on him and he wrote a poem, The Curse of War, set against the background of the Spanish Civil War which was raging at the time. There is no mention in Millicent's memoirs concerning the Baxters' take on the big issues of the day. What did they make of the rise of Fascism, the civil war in Spain, assertions that communism could create a just and peaceful social order, etc.? We do know that she felt shocked as each and every war took place; in 1980 she told David Young of the NZ Listener 'All those thousands of young men who died in the first war and the second war – horrible, horrible, horrible.'[616]

Leaving the boys behind this time, Archie and Millicent took off for France then Belgium, revisiting places where Archie had been sent and imprisoned. Later, they spent several months in Scotland visiting the sites of their ancestors, and the boys travelled up from Sibford to join them. It was delightful to be travelling as a family again. Being in the land of their ancestors and the land of Robbie Burns, Archie and James's cherished poet, was very rewarding for them: 'Jim has written "Scotland was my spiritual home", and I think we all felt that,'[617] Millicent writes. She was particularly fascinated by connections in the Glencoe region between the McColls and other families such as the Stewarts and the Campbells.

Millicent took her raft of exercise books containing Archie's story to a typist in London and started the search for a publisher. They took many rejections before it was accepted; English publishers seemed to have little interest in a tale from a remote colony that few had heard of. Millicent records that the colonial taboo was evident. Michael Joseph Ltd had written dismissively 'Who would be interested in the experiences of a New Zealand farmer?'[618] 'We will not cease' was finally published in London in 1939 by Victor Gollancz Ltd,[619] a major British book publishing house specialising in the publication of high quality literature, nonfiction and popular fiction. Gollancz made Archie alter all the names in the manuscript except those of The Fourteen objectors and, according to Millicent, Gollancz regretted his decision to publish the book: 'He was a Jew, and pro-war because of what was happening in Germany to the Jews. He did publish the book, but I believe he wanted to squash it, as he sent review copies only to Reynolds News and to the New Statesman and Nation. I don't blame Gollancz. It was just unfortunate for the book.'[620] But with or without Gollancz's influence and prejudices, fate prevailed. Most of the unsold copies were destroyed in the Blitz in 1941 – war demolished the anti-war message. Few copies had managed to reach New Zealand before World War Two started, so little was known of it in Archie's own country until its second printing, by Caxton Press thirty years later in 1968. This second publication carried a foreword by Archie, and the book soon became a well-known pacifist text. Further reprints occurred in 1980 and 1983 by Christine Cole Catley's publishing firm Cape Catley Ltd; in 1980 by Eddie Tern Press in Oregon USA; in 1995 by Penguin Books (NZ) Ltd and in 2003 by Cape Catley a third time with an additional foreword by Michael King.

In March 1939, the editor of the New Statesman, Kingsley Martin, wrote a full-page review headlined Crucifixion. In this he states that Archie's endurance was 'all the more remarkable because he was not, in the conventional sense of the term, a religious man. He was not buoyed up by hopes of heaven; his martyrdom was a private and lonely affair... It will shock people who think that the use of torture as a political weapon is confined to the Fascist Powers.'[621] Martin's comment on Archie's lack of rancour would be echoed throughout all future reviews. It is one of the most startling aspects of the book; Archie's forgiveness of his torturers seems without limit, and surely this is the sign of a warm and loving man who could 'forgive thy enemies.' But Martin may not be altogether correct in saying Archie was not religious. He was spiritual, and while he followed no specific religion, he believed in God. He attended church on occasions, but as he wrote early on in the book 'I belonged to no organized Church and did not base my beliefs on the teaching of any sect. To me, Christianity is based on the Commandment "Thou shalt love thy neighbour as thyself." I do not profess to be able to live up to this ideal, but one can at least go so far along the road as to try to treat other people as one would wish to be treated by them, and war cuts this position at its very roots.[622]

Looking at reviews of 'We will not cease' in republications, Michael King in his foreword to the 2003 edition praises the work as a classic:

> 'We will not cease' has become a classic of anti-war literature because of the understated and affecting eloquence of its prose; and because, miraculously it would seem, it is devoid of rancour... he retained no bitterness... His determination neither to cease nor to rest while the Christian ideal of peace remained unrealised, reflected in the words of Blake used for the book's title, was matched by a determination to forgive those who, in Archie's charitable view, knew not what they did... It is this conjunction of activism and humanity, of force and grace, combined with a poet's preference for simplicity of language, that makes this book a great one.[623]

In 2004 David Hill reviewed the 2003 publication of the book along with The Memoirs of Millicent Baxter, starting with a note of gratitude to Christine Cole Catley 'for eschewing the schlock of the new by returning these two old-time New Zealand writers to print.' For him Archie's memoir really hit home: 'The character of the guy still blazes through: bolshie, gravely courteous, prolix, enduring... He had the same moral fervour as Millicent. He could forgive nearly every individual and hardly any institution. You could speculate that, with parents of such intellectual ardour and ferocious moral integrity, James K Baxter was bound to have a voice.'[624]

From the first edition of 'We will not cease' seventy-five years ago, to the present day, the book has had significant impact, not just on New Zealand history and literature, but also on politics and social change. The book remains shockingly topical and significant as a reminder of the inhumanity that war creates, as demonstrated by the well-known psychological experiment at conducted at Stanford University in the 1970s. Volunteer students were chosen at random to be guards or prisoners in a prison situation. In less than a week the "guards" behaviour became inhumane and they severely abused the "prisoners" psychologically. Video footage from this experiment showed behaviour that closely paralleled abusive behaviour videoed at U.S. run prisons in Abu Ghraib in 2003 and more recently in Guantánamo Bay. The conclusion from the experiment was that inhumane behaviour is fostered in persons who are given authority to discipline another whom higher authorities have labelled 'bad'. Rather than the individuals – such as Sergeant Booth in Archie's story – it is the situation that is the cause of brutality. Booth and Baxter were in such a situation. War is one of those situations where man's inhumanity to man is drawn to the surface.

With the centenary of the start of World War I in 2014, we recognise the 'heroism of our lads that fought for our freedom'. But a great many people now have sympathy and respect for pacifists and conscientious objectors, and pacifism is now growing as a movement etc. Archie Baxter has not been in vain. 'We will not cease' lives on as the quintessential pacifist narrative. In the last five years or so the book has had a higher profile than ever: on Anzac Day 2009 at Downstage Theatre, Wellington, there was a reading of a play by Michael Galvin. The play, War Hero, was about Archie and the other objectors in The Fourteen. While Archie might be uncomfortable being called a hero, hero he undoubtedly was. In 2012, David Hill published his book for young adults, My Brother's War, basing a main character on Archie Baxter. Martin Tolich, Associate Professor in Sociology at the University of Otago, has, for several years, been running a course: The conscientious self: Enriching Sociological Social Psychology 101. We Will Not Cease' (sic) is a main text for this course.[625] Tolich sees Archie's endurance of Field Punishment No 1 as described in 'We will not cease' as being topical today, saying 'water boarding is today's equivalent.'[626] He states, 'this single text provides my students with the opportunity to apply the entire course themes – moral career, lifelong socialisation, identity enhancement, stigma management, impression management, and emotion management – to a novel data-set.'[627] In 2014, the television film 'Field Punishment No 1' was released. In addition to all of this, Dunedin's well-known composer, John Drummond, has composed an opera called 'War Hero,' due to be shown in 1917, the centenary of Archie's compulsion into the army.

Archie Baxter would be astonished.

CHAPTER 10
The Conchie Son

Late in 1938, with the political situation in Europe becoming more ominous, the Baxter family made the decision to return to New Zealand. War was looming and Millicent was worried about leaving her sister in England. They travelled on the Rangitiki,[628] tourist class, 'so-called, really third', corrects Millicent. The New Zealand election took place while they were on board, and Archie and Millicent were relieved to see the Labour Party had been voted in again. The entire voyage was now down to thirty-five days, so they were back home in Brighton in time for Christmas.[629]

Terence and James were now fifteen and eleven respectively and their trip overseas, something almost unknown to other young New Zealanders, was behind them. They were now facing big changes in their lives. By now the brothers were developing their own distinctive personalities and Millicent reflects on the difference between them: 'Terence is an introvert, as Archie was. Jim was an extrovert like me. When they were children, Terence was the moody, dreaming one; Jim was open and direct, although it may be difficult to believe this from some of the anguished poems he wrote in later years.'[630] Terence started work as a welder in the foundry at the agricultural implements factory, Reid and Gray Ltd, in the Dunedin suburb of Burnside. It was the largest manufacturer of agricultural implements in the southern hemisphere.[631] In his spare time he was 'driven by this feeling to get out boating.'[632] He would sail his boat, Plucky, in the waters around Taieri Mouth, with its notorious sand bar, and sometimes in the safer regions of Otago Harbour. Plucky had been a lifeboat to a tug of the same name which had been built in Dumbarton, Scotland in 1880 but had plied the Otago waters for some years.[633] Out in the open air and on the water, Terence was doing what he liked best, and at times felt almost ethereal: 'I used to

Terence, Millicent, James and Archie. c 1938
Ref: Hocken Library MS-975-230 S15-596

get out there sailing about midnight or one o'clock in the morning and, if the moon was up, it was a strange sort of feeling. You felt you were going faster and you also felt you weren't even on the water. You were floating almost above the water, the same type of feeling as you get if you get up Central Otago – if you get out on a deserted sort of place, a sort of feeling of being lifted off the ground.'[634] He was often in dangerous waters and Archie, a natural worrier, didn't like his son going out to sea.

Along with everyone else, life for the Baxters in Brighton would soon be in upheaval. Days after Germany's invasion of Poland, New Zealand's prime minister, Michael Joseph Savage, declared war on Germany on 5 September 1939, only 20 years after World War One – the war to end all wars. Savage died just over six months later in March 1940, and Peter Fraser succeeded him as prime minister. At this time in New Zealand, pacifists were small in number, particularly in Brighton. The League of Nations and the No More War Movement that Archie and Millicent strove to strengthen, were barely surviving.[635] The landslide victory of the Labour Government in the election of 1935 had raised the hopes of the country's peace-lovers that Peter Fraser and other government ministers who had been jailed for their anti-war views in World War One would be faithful to the cause. This was not to be. As with the previous war, recruitment for World War Two declined after the first flush of enthusiasm, and Fraser reversed his own previously heartfelt view. In July 1940, conscription was re-introduced.[636] Fraser failed to acknowledge inconsistencies in his action. He believed that each war required a different response judged on its merits and its nature and determined that New Zealand should participate in this war to defeat the threat of fascism.

He took the view that World War Two was a different and decent war, and in his eyes nobody had a right to opt out and get away with it easily.[637]

The Baxters felt betrayed by the Labour ministers they had trusted and even befriended. In Millicent's eyes, they were 'no longer pacifist, or even anti-militarist... It was a very bitter period for those who had thought that the Labour Party in power would preserve some of their idealism. For the whole period of the war and for some time afterwards I recorded an invalid vote.'[638] The government could now trawl their net for every man between nineteen and forty-five. Although conscription was run on a ballot system, the young and single were more likely to be called up than older married men and others were exempt if they worked in essential industries. Māori, war veterans, invalids and those in hospital or prison were also exempt.[639] Any others who refused enlistment faced

Terence about 18 years-old, shortly before he was imprisoned
Ref: Hocken Library MS-975-232 S15-596

detention. In May 1941 Terence was nineteen. He and other members of the wider Baxter family were eligible for conscription. A month later, Terence was called up for territorial service. He immediately appealed on conscientious grounds. Since September 1940, the Armed Forces Appeal Boards had been authorised to consider conscience appeals on individual merits rather than on membership of any particular faction championing pacifism. Theoretically, this should have been in the Baxters' favour as they didn't belong to any religious group. The family also thought that Terence's Quaker education, together with the fact that he was part of a famous pacifist family, would work in his favour. But it seems to have worked the other way and that there was a prejudice against him.[640]

Millicent reflects on how the boys' upbringing affected their decision to become pacifists: 'We never made a conscious effort to instil our own convictions in our sons, but they couldn't help but pick up the influence towards peace. It was part of our life and it no doubt flowed through the house where the children were brought up.'[641] So Terence's action might appear almost instinctive. But was it? Lenore Baxter, in an undated letter to Frank McKay, says

> It could be said that he didn't have a choice – or that it was Hobson's choice – as it was choosing to be rejected by society or rejected by his family, as it would have been a great blow to his much beloved father if he had not taken a stand. I am not saying that the choice was not his, nor that he did not sincerely believe in the principles he stood for. I just feel that it was much harder for him to be incarcerated than it was for some…His freedom and his independence were integral to his personality.[642]

Terence could have appealed on medical grounds because of the scoliosis in his spine caused by the bicycle accident in France four years earlier, but to him that wouldn't have been a fair appeal. In his usual no-fuss, self-effacing manner he says '…many people have got curved spines. But it never stopped me from working. Just occasionally it drops me to the floor, but it always heals up.'[643] His employer at Reid and Gray had already offered to lodge an appeal on his behalf; the manager told him that he was a good worker and it wasn't necessary to declare himself a conscientious objector because as they were manufacturers of agricultural machinery they were an essential industry.[644] Despite the problems he knew it would cause him, Terence declined the offer, believing it important that he should be seen to make a stand. Lenore says, 'I think that's incredibly brave for a boy of nineteen. And he stuck by it, too. That was the only thing that he wouldn't do. He wouldn't wear a uniform.'[645] Terence was recommended for non-combatant service, which he wasn't prepared to accept, although he did consider welding work on boats designated as Otago Harbour minesweepers, but he was arrested before he had the chance to take up the work.[646] The Baxters were flabbergasted; both Terence and Millicent believed that a mistake had been made, that Terence had been confused with his cousin,

John Archibald Baxter (Terence was Terence John) whose case had been heard and turned down some months before.[647]

In December 1941, he was sentenced in court to a defaulters' camp for the duration of the war. Archie and Millicent were appalled; they felt strongly that Terence was being victimised because of his father's actions in World War One. Archie appeared in court as a witness, which he would also do for five of his nephews, but to no avail.[648] [649] Terence was the first person in Otago to be proceeded against in court and sentenced. He spent Christmas in Dunedin gaol, and he says in his usual understated way 'In a way you could say I spent one of the worst Christmases I've ever had.'[650] A pseudonymous supporter was shocked enough to write to the Otago Daily Times: 'On December 19 [Terence Baxter] was charged in court… He has spent the time since then in the Dunedin gaol. There is no definite information as to when he is going to be sent to camp. He is therefore undergoing a term of imprisonment to which he has not been sentenced. No objector in Otago other than this boy of 19 has received this treatment. I am, etc. British Justice.'[651]

Terence's decision to stand up for his beliefs, or perhaps more accurately for his parents' beliefs, was to cost him dearly. He took the news of the sentence very hard though he was aware how much harder it would have been if his family had been against his decision, as was the case with so many objectors. It is clear he had a keen sense of obligation to uphold his parents' principles: 'Having been brought up the way I was, I was inclined to lean towards the pacifist point of view and also I could feel my parents' concern if I moved towards the other way. Any friends I had were patriotic or inclined that way, including the men I worked with. It was very hard for me to take this step. My parents were very thankful that I went the way I did, even though they didn't tell me so there was a feeling of relief with them both.'[652] In later interviews with Terence[653], it's evident that he didn't have the unswerving conviction his father had; his personal pacifism was less concrete. But his comments echo the raw honesty of both his parents when he talks about killing someone:

> I'm not sure, but I think quite likely if I hadn't had a father like that, that I could have just joined the navy and thought not very much about it. But I think in general though, with my nature I don't reckon I'd have been able to kill somebody, straight out kill a man, just because if you don't kill him he'd shoot you. And I think if that had happened I'd have had that in my conscience for the rest of my life. I'd never live it down that I'd killed not just one man but more than one – especially if I'd had a machine gun. And of course you're not that closely associated with who you're killing, because they're out over a field a fair distance away usually. But man-to-man combat, I think my nature would have gone against that. I'm not very sure…

Lenore Baxter seems more sure of the strength of her husband's conviction: 'It was not just a matter of an individual not taking part in a war but it was necessary to make a positive protest against any war as a method of settling international disputes.'[654]

In any event, this reserved and solitary man, a teenager who loved the open air and messing about in boats, was confined for four years in prison and detention camps. Early in 1942, he was transported to the Strathmore base detention camp located on the volcanic plateau in central North Island, southeast of Rotorua. The camp suited its surroundings: stark and primitive, surrounded by a fence two and a half metres high with sixteen lines of barbed wire.[655] Terence was surprised to find how different the men's personalities were, despite their similar anti-war beliefs, and generally he found the camp staff fair:

> Most of the men that were over us were fairly alright, one or two might not have been too good. Some came along with the attitude that they were going to sort these fellows out, lay down the law and be hard on them, but after they'd got to know them out on the gangs, working the bush, they got to like them. They'd sit down in a hut at night together and then human beings are human beings. Things sort of changed.[656]

The treatment received by objectors during World War Two was indeed different from that dispensed during World War One. Army Field Punishment No 1 was no longer used, and no one was deported. Walter Nash, as Acting Prime Minister while Peter Fraser was abroad, pushed for a more humane punishment than that dealt to conscientious objectors in World War One. Back in August of 1941, he had announced that defaulters would be sent to specially constructed work camps.[657] That is not to say there was no brutality. Ian Hamilton provides an incensed and embittered account of his experiences as a conscientious objector in various prisons in his searing book Till Human Voices Wake us.[658]

Five men outside a hut at a detention camp for conscientious objectors, in the early 1940s

The civilian dissenter camps in World War Two were designed to be less comfortable than the army but not as punitive as gaol.[659] One of the worst aspects for the prisoners, and for different reasons for the prison administrators, was that the term of their confinement was an indefinite sentence – for the duration of the war. Leonard Greenberg, the Controller-General of defaulter detention camps, initially hoped that the camps could be run as cooperative communities, but the longer the detainees were in camp the more mutinous they became and the less the idea worked. Some went on strike and refused to work. Terence wasn't involved but remembers that the men who refused to work were put in huts in solitary confinement.[660] In the end, the protest broke down, but Greenberg was now disliked. Millicent had long arguments by letter with Greenberg over the matter of Terence's teeth. She had never let her boys eat sweets but, like his father before him, Terence developed a decayed tooth while in detention, and Millicent took up the fight on his behalf. Greenberg replied 'I've got enough trouble trying to look after these people without worrying about teeth.'[661] The ever-pragmatic Millicent didn't give in to that: 'A decayed tooth could be yanked out. That was all. But I managed to get dental treatment for him by never giving up and, I presume, treatment for others as well.' And she can't resist adding proudly 'Looking now over copies of the letters I sent and Greenberg's replies, I am rather impressed with my ability to put the case.'[662]

The mild-mannered Terence differed strongly from his father in his acceptance of what was happening to him as a result of his defiance. While they both appear to have felt no bitterness or rancour over their punishment, Archie refused every order that was given to him throughout the duration of his time in the army. But Terence had, and still has, the attitude that if you make your own bed you have to lie in it:

> Myself, I would never complain about it. If you go against the law of the land – I went against the way things were then – well I had to expect whatever happened. That's all there was about it. But there were some in the camp that reckoned that they were wrongly treated because of the way they thought. But I don't think that way – if you don't think the way other people think, that is what's going to happen to you… I didn't have any trouble myself at the camp because of the way I was. I was reasonably polite and accommodating, and I didn't have any problems at all that I can remember. It's the way you approach it – mind you there were some that would show their worst sides all the time, they were just that sort of man. That's the way they are.[663]

Strathmore camp soon became overcrowded as more objectors arrived, and Terence was transferred to a new camp ten kilometres east of Turangi on the Desert Road at the southern end of Lake Taupo. One of ten detention camps, it was named Hautu Detention Camp after a nearby prison farm.[664] When Terence arrived, the camp was still being made secure and barbed wire was being put on top of the fences.[665] Hautu was regarded as the 'bad boys camp' where there was strict discipline and harsh conditions.[666] Terence's relocation to Hautu was surprising as he considered himself to be among the mildest of detainees. He always had the niggling notion that he was victimised from the start because of Archie's stand in World War One. He felt keenly the unfairness that he hadn't been allowed to be transferred to the Conical Hill detention camp twenty-nine kilometres from Gore, closer to his home: '…they didn't put me down there, they didn't put anybody from local areas down there. They shoved us all over the place. I think it was done intentionally.'[667]

So while the Hautu camp proved to be a much more hospitable landscape than Strathmore, with native bush and a nearby stream, life there was nevertheless spartan. Each of the detainee huts was

> a prefabricated but solid military-style structure eight feet wide by ten feet long housing two men. They were arranged in straight rows, back-to-back, facing a communal "piss-tin" in the middle of the compound, as the ablution block was barred from use after lights out… Bedding comprised a straw paillasse, four or five army blankets (often thin and holey), one flax or straw pillow and two pillow cases. Inmates shivered at night during the winter months with frost… to minus 10°C occurring regularly… Electrician Jack Rogers rigged up a 40-watt lamp in a jam jar to keep warm in his Hautu bed while his companions gathered round river stones, placed them in the social hall fire to heat up then put them in sacks at the bottom of their beds.[668]

For Terence, the worst aspect of his incarceration was the lack of privacy. He was a loner and not comfortable with the company of people he didn't know: 'I was not very keen on being in camps and fitting in with other people. This is probably why I'm living by myself right now. Even now I tend to keep to myself. How on earth I ever managed to live through the camp, looking back on it, the way I am, it's a bit of a mystery to me, because you didn't have any privacy.'[669] One of the sonnets in James's Autumn Testament reflects Terence's loss of freedom during his sentence that must have seemed like an eternity: 'In the time when a Labour Government planted my brother / On the Hautu prison farm for five years / For walking in my father's footprint / And refusing to carry a gun.'[670] But Terence, unlike his father before him, had consented to work as soon as he got to Strathmore. At Hautu, the inmates were given a thousand acres of virgin Crown land to develop into economic farming units, and Terence laboured in gangs grubbing thistle, ragwort, fern and manuka sometimes reaching fifteen metres high.[671] At least the hard work relieved some of the drudgery and the prisoner's constant awareness of the indefinite sentence. Eventually, there was some attempt to relieve the monotony of life there with activities provided by a vegetable garden, enactment of plays and a library. 'Any books that were in the camp were read and re-read…we'd always be looking for new literature in the camp. There was a certain amount of time for reading – we'd be shut down at night fairly quickly.'[672]

James would send Terence books, usually about sailing and the sea. In one of his letters to another inmate Noel Ginn, he finishes, 'Will send 'Cook's Voyages' up for Terry when I can. Two copies here – one my mother wants to keep has my grandfather's notes in it…Best wishes and love to Terry and you. Jim.'[673] It was in Hautu camp that Terence had met Noel, the poet who played a significant role in James's life and writing. Ginn and James corresponded regularly between 1942 and 1945, when Noel was a 'conchie' and James was in Dunedin at King's High School, and later when at the University of Otago. Noel was a poet and Christian Pacifist much influenced by the well-known Ormond Burton, the decorated soldier turned pacifist, who later with Archibald Barrington formed the Christian Pacifist Society.[674] Noel was one of the 'bad boys' who, as a religious conscientious objector in Strathmore, had refused to work. At Strathmore, someone had pointed Terence out to him, as the son of Archie Baxter – a man whom Noel regarded as a saint. However, until Hautu, there had been no contact between them. He was keen to find out more about Terence and one Saturday afternoon during 'free time,' they met:

> 'We' on the lawn were mainly five or so Wanganui pacifist Methos [Methodists]. Terry, dark, mysteriously rather aloof figure, was washing clothes and sheets in the stream…he did his washing in a clumsy unused way. Having rinsed the sheets & hand-wrung them he picked up the other washing & came up the bank when he tripped on the upper bank & scattered his load in trodden muddy ground. He uttered a curse and we on the upper bank laughed good-naturedly & he acknowledged us briefly with a serious grin on the way to a scowl and went doggedly back to rinse the washing over again. Suddenly I felt sorry for him and went down the bank to help him out. I was used to washing clothes and so was pleased at this chance to get to know him.[675]

The two young men were very different characters, Noel an extrovert, and Terence introverted with a 'stolid fatalism'. But over time, a friendship ensued. Noel discovered that 'behind Terence's dour southerner's mask was a good sense of humour and a keen intellect – he had read many classic novels – although Terence insisted that he didn't follow after his Macmillan Brown relatives and had no interest in scholarship.'[676] Noel seems to get to the core of this complex man, 'He was – there's a word called 'harmless' – and it doesn't just mean not hurting anybody. It was in thought as well which is a very strong virtue – he had that, and because of that he never made enemies as it were, because there was no criticism in him. He would always defend the down-and-out in some way, or the unpleasant character.[677] In the course of their friendship, Terence noticed Noel reading and writing poetry

Noel Ginn
Ref: Hocken Library E5589/15A

146

and told him that his younger brother also had a passion for writing poetry and suggested that the two might write to each other.[678] The long period of correspondence would play a significant role in James's life during the crucial period at King's High School and then at the University of Otago.

Because of an injury, Noel was eventually returned to Strathmore camp, which saddened both him and Terence, but they were able to break the rules of correspondence being forbidden between inmates by sending books to one another with short letters inserted down the spine: 'They were written in invisible ink i.e. strong sugar solution – on scorching the paper before a candle flame the burnt sugar script could be seen. I know some inmates used urine for this purpose. This was great fun.'[679] If this sounds like boys in boarding school, it is not far from the truth; both young men were still in their 20s, Terence only 21. Any relief from the confinement and boredom was welcomed. Terence remembers that occasionally the work gangs would sneak off out of sight of the supervisor down to the river to catch trout by hand then cook them over a fire.[680]

Finally both Terence and Noel were shifted to a new camp at Whitanui, close to Shannon between Palmerston North and Levin, but life there was no better at all. James wrote 'they put my brother behind barbed wire, to be eaten alive…by the devil of boredom, weeding flax in a bog at Shannon.'[681] Terence passed his spare time by constructing models, the first of which was a small scale replica of his treasured Plucky. His pièce de résistance was his construction of a steam engine based on a scale replica model of a Great Western railway engine he had seen at Sibford School in England: '…there was practically nothing in camp to build it out of. Somehow or another I got a few pieces together, a bit of galvanised pipe to make the two cylinders. It was a lot of effort to get them evenly round inside. Made pistons for it, bent the crankshaft out of something which was reasonably thick, which took a bit of doing. In the end I made a boiler and got things going.'[682] Unlike many men in the camp, Terence didn't spend a lot of time writing letters; one of the few he wrote to James finished by saying 'Well Jum, I think I'll close now. Let the other people in the house know that you have heard from me.'[683]

Despite their pride in Terence becoming an objector, the 'other people in the house' had been very disturbed right from the start about Terence's detention. Millicent writes

> The whole thing was a terrible blow to Archie. He developed a carbuncle on the back of his neck. For the first week it had to be bathed with hot water every two hours, day and night, the pain was so bad; but it gradually grew better, and a peculiar grey cone came out of the hole and afterwards it improved. The hollow remained in the back of his neck until he died. He said he felt it was a just retribution for the feelings of rage that rose up inside him.[684]

147

Millicent makes little mention of Terence's absence. The long incarceration of her first child must have been as painful to her as it was to Archie, yet she barely mentions it. We get used to her silence in her memoirs of what is really important to her. Terence's internment had increased the already intense prejudice in Brighton against the Baxters. Millicent remembers a man coming to the house at Bedford Parade declaring himself to be a conscientious objector and wanting Archie to advise him as to what he should do: 'Archie was suspicious… and wouldn't commit himself in any way. The man, after trying hard to get him to say something definite, finally went away in the still-waiting taxi. Later, Archie used to see him quite often amongst the detectives in court when he went in to give evidence on behalf of some objector.'[685] The Baxters were fast becoming known throughout the country as pacifists. On Sundays they often had a houseful of pacifists and conscientious objectors.[686] The Brighton inhabitants became even more hostile which in turn brought out hostility in Millicent, something that she later deeply regretted.

In 1941, following the introduction of conscription, the Armed Forces Appeal Boards began hearing the cases of conscientious objectors, and Millicent and Archie attended a great many of the local hearings.[687] They were also heavily involved in helping objectors in their appeals. Some men who had their appeals turned down didn't continue with their resolve of dissension, but Millicent was sympathetic: 'One couldn't possibly blame them. Their families and the girls they were engaged to were often opposed to their views, which made things very difficult for them.' She felt the board members were in no way fit to pass judgement on the difficult and complicated cases of conscience: 'The inarticulate were turned down immediately, and so often the inarticulate were obviously sincere.'[688] In New Zealand, of the 3000 appeals against conscription on conscience grounds, only 600 were allowed.[689]

Archie went to Wellington several times to help establish the rights of pacifists to express their views, and Millicent saw MPs and ministers, attempting to ensure reasonable conditions for Terence and other detained objectors and arguing the objectors' case.[690] On one occasion in 1943, Millicent went to Parliament with a friend, whose son was also an objector, to see the Minister of Justice about the revision of objectors' sentences. Millicent asked to see the Honourable Walter Nash, Minister of Finance, and they were ushered into his office even though he was busy preparing to speak on the budget that night: 'Mr Nash said "When I heard the name I simply had to meet you. Will you believe me, Mrs Baxter, when I tell you I didn't know your son was in detention camp until I heard it in a letter I have just received from Lincoln Efford?" I believed him.'[691] On a later occasion when he was in Dunedin, Nash gave Millicent an anthology of poetry. 'Over the years we read and re-read it aloud to the boys until it fell to pieces.'[692] Then Millicent adds, bluntly admitting her lack of love of poetry, '[Archie] loved poems. I did not. The only ones I ever cared for were [in that anthology] from Walter Nash.'[693]

During the years Terence was in captivity, Millicent would regularly send him food parcels, a cake on his birthdays and any medication he needed.[694] But the Baxters weren't free to go and see him whenever they wanted. Visits to dissenters' camps were discouraged by the camp administrators and long distance travel became very difficult with the Japanese entry into the war in December 1941 as this resulted in stricter petrol rationing which lasted until the end of the war. Terence had only two family visits in all the years he was in detention. One was when Archie visited him in Hautu detention camp, travelling with their pacifist friend Alice Huband who was visiting her husband, a conscientious objector in Hautu prison. Terence remembers that it was an enormous effort for him to make the journey; he didn't travel well, particularly by sea, and the passage was rough across Cook Strait to Wellington.[695]

Millicent also made only one visit, in late August 1944 with eighteen year-old James, when Terence was in the camp at Shannon. She had booked rooms at Shannon and intended having a good night's sleep in order to appear at her best when she visited the son she hadn't seen for three years. But to her chagrin she had to share her room with the mother of another objector who spent most of the night telling Millicent her life history: 'I suppose it didn't really matter what I looked like, and it probably did her a lot of good to get it off her chest.' Characteristically, Millicent mentions no details of the visit nor the emotional effect it had on her. She simply says 'I wondered if visiting the men in detention was really a good idea. It definitely wasn't for husbands and wives. It upset them badly. And yet, not to visit them would seem like neglect.'[696] Towards the end of the war, the policy of strict confinement was relaxed and the detainees were allowed some visits home. Terence was allowed only one trip, four all-too-short days in early February 1944.[697] The family found him much changed, and James felt his brother was permanently scarred mentally.[698]

Throughout Terence's confinement Millicent had been politically active, keeping up a stream of letters to the government members relating to the treatment of conscientious objectors. She was a member of the Fellowship of Conscientious Objectors, which continued throughout the war to May 1946 when the very last defaulter was released.[699] In 1945 she produced a raft of correspondence with another leading member, Lucy Gibson, a prominent Labour Party antimilitarist.[700] They wrote in support of the five defaulters in Auckland's Mt Eden Prison who went on hunger strikes fighting for the abandonment of government policy to hold genuine conscientious objectors indefinitely.[701]

Finally, with the German surrender in May 1945 and the Japanese surrender three months later in August, the Labour Government in New Zealand was anxious to close down the detention camps as soon as possible. In January 1946, Terence, then later Noel Ginn, was released from the Shannon camp, but for the ensuing eight months they were forced into various labouring jobs by the government.[702] First, however, the two men were allowed to go to Brighton for the Christmas fortnight of 1945-46. It was the second of only three occasions that Noel met James, despite the hundreds of letters and poems that passed between them by mail. He was much affected by this visit and his brief immersion into Baxter family life: 'It was a period of disarray and confusion. The air was thick with the names of dispersed friends and acquaintances, much news, always change. Jim was part of this ferment, but his disorientation was from a different base. There was exhilaration as we talked of poetry, of life and world affairs, there was much humour also.'[703] In 1994, Noel gave a very perceptive account of the family to Paul Millar:

> Millicent was easy to get to know, she was so coherent and very positive – a delightful character: she was always being appalled, or horrified, or distressed, or concerned, and she would raise her eyes right up so that the whites only were showing – she had this wonderful gesture – wonderful characteristic. And she was a very, very charitable person, but she would go to battle quite readily – she was quite a formidable person.
>
> The father, Archie – he was a dear – one loved him. He had gentleness and a strong beautiful face, many attest to that. And it was of course his wonderful book 'We will not cease' that drew me further into the pacifist thought streams of the day. He always wanted one of his sons to be a poet – that was his deepest wish. I've read quite a lot of his own poems of course – they're quite good really, they're not intellectual exercises, they're more wisdom pieces. Simple. Inspired by simple experiences, much in the formal ballad or four-line stanza.
>
> Terence, I would think, was overwhelmed by the success of his family as personalities. He loved his father, and his father of course had come up to his highest understanding of what a good man should be. And the earthy side of his mother and father, he very much appreciated them in all their phases. Jim of course, although he was three [sic] years younger, overshadowed him. The grandmother was a very brilliant woman – his grandfather a professor – and [Terence] had no attainment in anything and he rather felt a ring-in as it were in the family. He was well liked by people generally – very modest and he had a little sense of humour that was very endearing.[704]

When Terence returned to the North Island, having had a taste of freedom for the first time in four years, he was dismayed that the man-powering scheme would further delay him returning home for good, but accepted his fate with his usual tolerance:

> I was in the camps for a fair few years, and of course it wasn't all over when the war was finished because we weren't going to be allowed out – which was fair enough as they saw it – until the last soldier had returned home from overseas. Even after we were let out of the camp, we were still under supervision. When

we were man-powered you couldn't choose what you wanted to work at – it was like I was almost back in camp again, not absolutely locked in, but still in the same vicinity doing the same sort of work. Later on I was man-powered into a freezing works in Wellington, which was not the sort of place I would choose to work in. I don't like the type of place. The smell of the place gets right into your skin, right into your pores, you could tell a person that worked in the freezing works.[705]

But there were compensations. The Gear Meat Works was in Petone, on the northern shore of Wellington Harbour, and Terence seized the opportunity of taking up his beloved pastime of sailing: 'I just couldn't resist it. There was that beautiful harbour sitting out ahead of me. I couldn't resist getting a yacht... I sailed to Days Bay, Somes Island and Ward Island... I got into a bit of trouble and caught a storm – some others were drowned and I was out in the water for a long time.'[706] Millicent has a slightly less restrained version of the story, but of course only slightly: 'He was capsized. He clung to the overturned boat for some time but because it was so cold he abandoned it and swam in, three-quarters of a mile.' Then she adds pragmatically 'He was put in a hot bath when he landed.'[707] Terence wrote to James around this time revealing that he had felt bitter at times during his imprisonment: 'You can't believe how pleased I am to be living a real life again. The joy of being free still remains. I'm just losing the coldness towards people and the bitterness that I've felt towards my fellow men in the last few years... I'm just writing to let you know that life is worth living once more. Thank Christ I'm free!'[708]

But when Terence and Noel were finally released for good later in the year, they both experienced great difficulty adjusting to life after being detainees for nearly five years. Noel explains:

> It was a major emotional event leaving detention, the worst feature of which had been the indeterminate nature of its duration. Now the sentence was over, the necessary strong emotional associations & attachments were rudely broken – the glorious day of liberation proved a mirage – all was grey, spent & without hope – the savage destruction of lives as well as nations had bitten into our awareness – made more poignant when we met returned men who often said we were right. I, for one, was not sure. I will never be convinced that we were all that right. My friendship with T. and Jim would now be in suspension, we had to go our ways.[709]

They did. There is no doubt that both detention and the influence of his family caused Terence to withdraw into himself after his release, and Noel vouches for this: 'The theory that the overshadowing by his father (his heroism & strength

151

during WW1 & later in the persecuting community) together with the brilliance of his mother & brother, created in Terence a humbling and diminished self-image, seems reasonable to me.'[710] Terence, always rather a loner, feels that as a result of his incarceration, his ability to relate to other people was affected even more: 'In some sort of way or another it's had its effect, it's done some sort of thing to me… the way I look on life and other people. I don't mix in with people unless I've had a couple of drinks, not get drunk, but just enough to break the ice and be a bit more friendly.'[711]

Terence John Baxter age 24, shortly after his release from detention camp
Ref: Hocken Brown Library S04-333

Terence resumed sailing his beloved Plucky and eventually returned to Reid and Gray in Dunedin, who had kept their promise to keep his job as welder open for him. He later worked there as a liaison officer between the management and the workers. James was delighted to have his older brother back home and two years later felt the damage of imprisonment was beginning to fade:

'though he has his ups and downs, he is a normal citizen again. I have grown very fond of him in the past two years.'[712] But Terence felt the years apart had caused a gap between himself and James: 'when he was going through university, I was out of his way. Even after I came out of camp, I had to stay up there for a while. So all that was sort of a hole in our life during the time that we were together and after that he went his own way and I got friendly with my group in town…'[713]

Frank McKay, who spent a good deal of time interviewing Millicent, has much to say on this period in Terence's life. He notes that Terence was always successful with girls: he was very good-looking, a good dancer, sexually attractive, romantic and elusive,[714] but:

Terence sailing his beloved boatboat Plucky
(Family collection)

The effect of imprisonment on Terence was profound. From having been outgoing and sociable, a person who related easily to others – much more than his brother, in fact – he had become moody and withdrawn. He seemed to have lost faith in society. In the family, of course, he was regarded as a man of the same mould as his father. Archie was proud of his son's good looks and strength of character. And he knew better than anyone the cost of refusing to conform. Terence's relationships with his peers were affected…and there had also been displacement in the home. His brother was now older and Terence noticed the time he spent discussing poetry with their father. The subject was clearly of passionate interest to both of them. He felt excluded and later confessed to a certain amount of jealousy. He decided to yield his brother's chosen territory, though it interested him once. More and more it became alien to him as he was driven to develop his own skills in making and doing.[715]

Then a new player comes into the story, 23-year-old Lenore Bond, who was studying at the University of Otago. During the university break of the summer of 1945 – 46, Lenore went to work at Trevose, a guest-house in Brighton around the corner from the Baxters. There she met Elsie Gill. Lenore felt herself to be a stupid, flippant, mad person in those days and was surprised when Elsie wanted to introduce her to Millicent Baxter. Despite the age difference, Lenore and Millicent got on well and through Millicent, Lenore got to know James. Knowing that Lenore wrote copious letters to the 'boys' who were away at war – she preferred that to knitting socks – James persuaded her to write to his brother Terence, still under sentence, commandeered in Wellington. This she did, and they struck up a correspondence. When Terence was finally released, they went out together a few times a week and saw each other intermittently for the next couple of years. Lenore belonged to a radical group of politically active students and she tried without success to get Terence interested. Nevertheless, the relationship blossomed and history repeated itself – Terence, quiet, thoughtful and non-academic like his father, had fallen for an outgoing intellectual like his mother.

On 22 August 1947 the couple got married in the South Dunedin Baptist Church. The family was thrilled with the match and Lenore was accepted into the Baxter household as one of them. They settled in a house in Caversham, Dunedin. In 1948, Kenneth was born and Millicent and Archie were delighted to have a grandchild. Young Kenneth would stay with them at Bedford Parade, and Lenore remembers Millicent taking him into bed with her in the morning and reading her diaries to him, which Lenore says 'he put up with. He apparently enjoyed it. He absolutely adored his grandfather as everybody else did of course.' Three more children were born: Alan Francis, in 1950, who lived for just ten days; Katherine

153

Millicent, in 1951 and Helen, in 1954. Lenore and Millicent would sit by the fire when Lenore's children were small and talk for hours.[716] Her daughter Katherine remembers those times very well:

> Every Sunday afternoon we went out there. We'd turn up and there'd be lunch, then Dad would go somewhere with Granddad, and they'd go out in the garden and do things. And Mum and Gran would talk for three hours non-stop – every week. Now you cannot be a good friend without doing that. And they were giving each other books. They were always arguing. Mum was always Devil's advocate in a way, because she's not a Scot. She used to take the English side. And Gran was always arguing for the Scots. And they would redo battles from history. They would talk about religion. They didn't agree with everything on that, they didn't agree with each other on lots of things, but they did agree on the literature, and they would read all the same novels...[717]

Diane Dore, Donald Baxter's daughter, was born the same year as Kenneth, and she remembers Millicent more like a grandmother than an aunt:

> She wouldn't sit down and talk small talk but she was always interested to talk to you if you asked any questions about anything. She would always explain what she knew about it. But she was a very approachable person, like she wasn't scary like another of my aunts...But she wouldn't stand any nonsense. She asked you to do something and expect you to do it, but not in a bossy sort of way. She would just nicely ask you to do something or to stop doing something if you were doing something you shouldn't have been doing.[718]

In the early Sixties, the difference in background and outlook began to tell on Terence and Lenore's marriage, and when Kenneth had just started at university, they split up. Terence, predictably, takes his fair share of the blame in the break-up: 'I'm inclined to be independent and avoid socialising, which is probably one of the reasons my marriage broke down. There's always two sides to a broken marriage.'[719] Lenore moved to Timaru with the girls and then settled in Wellington. Later she developed her own secretarial business. Terence worked until the Seventies at the Hillside Railway Workshops of Reid and Gray, which played a major role in the construction of locomotives and freight wagons for New Zealand's railway system.[720] He was eventually made redundant. Also in the Seventies, after many years of solace gained by sailing in and around Brighton waters, he sold Plucky to someone who had good use for the old tug lifeboat. The new owner intended to renovate her, in time: 'I still see her outside his garage, carefully covered in a tarpaulin,' says Terence. 'He'll get round to it one day.'[721]

At the time of writing, Terence had recently left his family home in Caversham. He was over ninety-two when he fell and hurt his back badly and is now in a retirement home in Dunedin's North East Valley, five kilometres from where his mother lived in Kinsman Street. On his wall, facing his bed, is a picture of him sailing his beloved Plucky. He is still a fiercely independent man. He still has a rich, unwavering, well-spoken voice, though not quite as Anglicised as his mother. The way English is spoken is important to him. He thinks often of his time in dissenters camps in World War Two: 'I think all my life since then, I've had a half sort of fear of being imprisoned or locked in so that I can't get out – so much so that if I see a moth on the window now, I have to let him out. I like to see it fly away free. I feel that very strongly'[722] Until his early nineties he swam ten to twelve lengths in the physiotherapy pool and took a walk every morning. He tended his vegetables in his garden and found that he slept better if he didn't go to bed until three in the morning! He biked almost every day to get his shopping, though his uncertain balance sometimes worried him; he was fearful he might fall off into a line of traffic. Reading was difficult and when he has a bit of sewing to do, he threaded the needle by guesswork and he wrote letters by feel.

Today his eyes, the same clear, strong blue as his mother's, fail him at times. But he is bright and lucid. He is still a gentleman.

CHAPTER 11
The Poet Son

While Terence was enduring prison for years, life for James couldn't have been more different. It was a period of constant change and tortuous adolescence. Initially, when the family arrived back from overseas, he went back to Brighton School for the last few weeks of 1938. Although he progressed well academically at Brighton School, he was never happy there, nor popular. His parents' unconventional philosophies, his own unusual background of education in Wanganui and abroad plus his own natural rebelliousness meant he stood out from his schoolmates, something children often find difficult. This deracination James felt so keenly, affected him for some time. He reflects in his Notes on the Education of a New Zealand Poet how much of an outsider he felt, and how he found poetry a consolation:

> I think the gap between myself and other people was increased considerably by the fact that I was born in New Zealand, and grew up there until I was nine, and then attended an English boarding school for a couple of years, and came back to New Zealand at thirteen, in the first flush of puberty, quite out of touch with my childhood companions and uncertain whether I was an Englishman or a New Zealander. This experience too, though very painful, was beneficial; for I fell into the habit of poem-writing with a vengeance and counted it a poor week when I had not written four or five pieces of verse. [723]

In his autobiographical novel, The Man on the Horse, James writes, 'Objectively I remember my childhood as a happy time. My health was good. There were plenty of things to do. My parents, my schoolteachers and my companions treated me well enough…Yet a sense of grief has attached itself to my early life, like a tapeworm in the stomach of a polar bear… it may determine the rather gloomy tone of my verse.'[724] He writes in that revealing poem 'A Family Photograph, 1939' of the agonies of pubescence that had started to engulf him: 'I, in my fuggy room at the top of the stairs, / A thirteen-year-old schizophrene / Write poems, wish to die.'[725] Then the happier side of his nature would emerge and life would be fine again. Perhaps that can be typical of many teenagers, but in James the tendency towards depression never left him.

He returned to the Friends' School at Wanganui for a year then when he was fourteen he started at King's High School in South Dunedin. After a number of small private schools, he was now faced with the bustle and confusion of a large state school. He was habitually late for the bus, often stopping to sit on a bench to do the homework he should have done the night before. James ignored Millicent's orders to dress smartly and wore his baggy shorts below his knees with his unbuttoned shirt hanging out, elbows sticking through holes in his jersey and socks around his ankles if he was wearing any. He was often barefoot, even in the coldest of winters.[726] Millicent's neglect of housekeeping extended to irregularity of meals, or even non-existence of meals – possibly because she had taken a trip to the library in Dunedin for her weekly feast of books – and she often neglected to give him lunch to take to school. If he had the money, he would buy a pie or fish and chips after school.

Sex, or at least thinking about it, was beginning to become an obsession that would never leave him. His good friend Bob Craigie remembers him always talking about sex on the bus and coming out with outrageously coarse expressions. Apart from thinking and talking about sex, James seemed oblivious to most things except poetry. As his hatred of academia grew, his marks, apart from English, dropped to merely adequate.[727]

In anybody's eyes, James's and Terence's parents were quite radical and at complete odds with most of the Brighton population. As James grew older, he wrote of the great 'difference between my own socialist-pacifist family and the semi-militarist activities of the people about us, which gave me a sense... of a gap between myself and other people.' This sense of difference taught him 'to distrust mass opinion and create his own ideas.'[728] James would write several

James, Archie and Millicent, taken around 1939
Ref: Hocken Library MS-975-230 S15-596

poems focussing on his family. Aged fifteen, he wrote in a gushing Romantic idiom, a poem 'To My Mother', ' ...Oh friend and mother in one form combined / To thee I owe the pleasures of the mind.../ And I know thy loving kindness cast / A sheen of beauty o'er my babyhood: / To thee my love, to thee my gratitude.'[729] But he matures unrecognisably in that more credible poem, A Family Photograph 1939, describing a domestic scene at Bedford Parade of the family: Archie happy in his garden, Millicent in her chaotic kitchen, and the ubiquitous newspapers:

157

…My father in his gumboots
Is up a ladder plucking down
…passion fruit for home made wine.
My mother in the kitchen sunshine
Tightens her dressing gown,
Chops up carrots, onions, leeks,
For thick hot winter soup. No broom or duster
Will shift the English papers piled on chairs
And left for weeks.[730]

Millicent was miffed at that poem: 'In everything [James] wrote, to and of his father, he is admiring and loving. I, on the other hand, come off badly, mostly as a bad housekeeper. Well, I was, and am, but it's hard to have to go down to posterity in that character. Besides, I was an excellent cook, which he doesn't mention.' She goes on to comment on another of James's poems Mother and Son written in 1966: 'Blowflies dive-bomb the sitting-room / Table, this dry spring morning, / In my mother's house.' She retorts 'Well of course there are blowflies if you live surrounded by greenery! But I dealt with them.'[731] And it seems James inherited his mother's ability to talk a great deal. Millicent told Michael King 'He would talk and talk, a compulsive talker – well I am a bit myself – and he would pursue me into the kitchen when I was making cakes or making the dinner and I would forget to put in the baking powder and he just talked and talked and talked and he always brought us round to his point of view.'[732]

James was fifteen when Terence began his detention. Being conscripted was a constant dread of his. He had a fear of pain and knew he wouldn't be able to go through what Archie had endured. He was always worried that Terence might suffer the same fate as their father and was horrified at the thought of him experiencing pain or torture. King's High School had a cadet corps: 'Every boy we train is a nail in Hitler's coffin' was the cry.[733] Archie applied to the Rector to exempt James from cadet training and Dudley Chisholm agreed without question, but while there was no antagonism from the staff, James began to suffer from taunts and physical bullying from fellow pupils. Millicent told Bruce Harding in 1982 that 'he had a rough time from his schoolfellows – he never told us anything about it; his elder brother told us. And it did strike me that perhaps it's not fair to put a boy of thirteen[734] in such a position. It wouldn't have been his decision; it was ours. And later on he became a pacifist. There was another boy at King's whose parents were pacifists but he covered up and got exempted through health – but James would never do that.'[735] She clearly agonises over this; two years later in her memoirs she brings up the same question:

Should one ask a boy early in his teens to go through unpleasantness and often persecution for a cause which at that

158

age cannot really be his own? Probably, in the end, it is best. But plenty of people have [later] made excellent pacifists who, at school, went in enthusiastically for cadet training –Stephen Hobhouse[736] for one; and in New Zealand Harry Urquhart[737] and Paul Oestreicher and probably many others whose cases I do not know. It remains with me an unsettled question.'[738]

Terence was even more concerned about James; he not only had his father's reputation to contend with but also a defaulter brother who was locked up.[739] On cadet-training days James would stand out by wearing civvies amongst a sea of khaki uniforms, and boys would mock him with cries of 'Conchie! Conchie!'[740] Millicent remembers James being reasonably unaffected by the experience of being dumped in a rubbish tin for his anti-militarist views.[741] The beatings and the jibes were hard to take but James saw a positive side: 'These experiences were in the long run very valuable, for they taught me to distrust mass opinion and sort out my own ideas; but at the same time they were distinctly painful. I could compare them perhaps with the experiences of a Jewish boy growing up in an anti-Semitic neighbourhood. They created a gap in which the poems were able to grow'.[742] Between 1942 and 1946 he drafted some 600 poems. While the cadets practiced with unloaded rifles, James weeded flowerpots. 'It might have been pleasanter [to be a cadet but] on the other hand,

James Keir Baxter age 18
Ref: Hocken Library E1073:25 S15-599

it would have been one more mental jail which I'd have had to climb out of later in life. I could see that the boys I knew became less themselves the more they became members of the corps. Their faces became wooden and their language monotonous.'[743] So while Terence weeded flax in Shannon, his friends fought and died in the war. And while James weeded pots in Dunedin, his peers were training to fight and die in the same war.

Opinions in Brighton had not altered since the last war; during the whole of World War Two, James and his parents experienced increasingly vehement prejudice against their pacifist views from many of the locals, and their activities were viewed with suspicion. When Japan entered the war, they were even accused of spying; up in James's 'fuggy room' they couldn't even put on the light at night because the excessively patriotic neighbours thought they were signalling to Japanese submarines.[744]

At the end of 1943, James managed to matriculate and even he was thrilled. He was top in English and an excited Millicent recalls the milkman giving them a bottle of cream to celebrate the occasion.[745] The obvious pathway was to go to university, but James had grave doubts. With his hatred for academia, he questioned its validity, particularly in the light of his father having done so well without any secondary education. But James finally made his decision and went to Otago University in March 1944. Millicent was thrilled but it did mean she and Archie had to help with his fees. James reduced spending by cycling the nineteen kilometre journey every day. He plunged into literary life and entered for the Macmillan Brown prize for poetry, with the topic of convoys. His was a very pacifist poem, much of it about bitterness, hatred, and the futility of war. What would John Macmillan Brown have thought of that? James was off on a splendid start at university and everybody was talking about him as a poet. The long grey overcoat that would become renowned made its appearance, and his charm was beginning to work. But his new-found freedom from home and school led him to drink heavily; as he says himself, his 'incipient alcoholism' took wings. His favourite waterhole became The Bowling Green Hotel on the corner of Cumberland and Frederick Streets, just around the corner from where his great-grandparents Helen and George Connon had lived eighty years earlier. But he continued to attain high marks and to enjoy the university experience. He was also becoming very interested in religion although he called himself an agnostic. Millicent in her usual bold manner had warned him to keep away from the girls at university who might want to sleep with him, but for James, no such luck, 'No Otago girl ever tried to rape me. For many long months I searched hard for such a siren, without success. Those iceberg virgins never melted.' [746]

It was around this time that he met Lenore Bond, who later married Terence. She was also at university but she was five years older than him. He would come to Trevose, the guest-house around the corner from the Baxters, and show off in front of all the girls who were working there. In January 2010, Lenore, a frail but very alert eighty-eight-year-old relives the memory:

> I just couldn't get over how beautiful he was; he had the most beautiful complexion, it was like a girl's, and he blushed which of course annoyed him very much. But he had a fair skin, blonde hair, very blue eyes, and the most gorgeous smile. And, of course, the girls weren't smitten by him, but they were rather fascinated because he did things like telling everybody's fortune. And, of course, all this while holding your hand. So after that, when I went up with Elsie to visit Millicent, I quite often saw him...Yes well I think the thing about Jum that most people don't realise was that apart from being slightly mad, he did have a brilliant intellect.[747]

All the time Lenore was talking about James in this interview, her eyes were so animated and alight with the memory of him that one couldn't help wondering if she had been just a little in love with the younger brother. Sadly the question couldn't be asked; she died of cancer just a few days later.

It was in the winter break that James and Millicent travelled to the North Island and visited Terence in the Whitanui camp at Shannon. On the way back to Dunedin, they stopped at Christchurch for three days. James had been writing poetry since he was seven and Archie had declared it was time his poetry was published. So Millicent took James to Caxton Press. Lawrence Baigent was an exempted conscientious objector and was running the business in the absence of Denis Glover, who was serving in the Navy.[748] Lawrence Baigent remembers the incident well when this 'dumpy little woman' marched up to his desk and presented him with a bundle of James's poems, while the poet in question 'just stood there, gazing rather vacantly around him, didn't utter a word and followed his mother out the door.'[749] Millicent writes in her memoirs of the incident: 'Baigent obviously, and quite reasonably, regarded me as the usual doting mother, looking on her son's scribbles as worthy of publication. I didn't mind. I knew Archie was a good judge.'[750] Baigent went home and, with little enthusiasm, started reading the poems: 'I was completely bowled over by them. Next morning Jim himself came along. I said we'd be delighted to publish a volume.'[751] Caxton Press published his collection of poems, Beyond the Palisade: Poems / by James K. Baxter [752] early in 1945 and it was a great success. James' career as a poet had begun.

James maintained that Aphrodite, Bacchus and the Holy Spirit were his tutors during his first year at university,[753] though Aphrodite seemed not to be on his side. Noticeably, he doesn't mention Apollo the God of knowledge and poetry. During this time, James expected to be called up for service, and had prepared an appeal on conscientious grounds. Although his name didn't appear on the ballot, he did send in a letter to the Appeal Board giving his family's history of pacifism and his views on war: 'During a trip to Europe in 1937 and 1938 I had opportunity to observe people of various nationalities, including Germans. My experiences reinforced my belief that the difference between nationalities are slight and that War in any circumstances is not more justifiable than any other form of murder... My conscientious objections are both religious and humanitarian.'[754] He went on to explain that he was brought up to regard all wars as futile and immoral, but declared that despite his father's history and attitude 'I have arrived at my present attitude in the main by independent thinking.'[755]

Early in 1945 James decided to leave university to give himself more elbow room to get on with living and writing: 'the truth is that I have no wish to be an intellectual...I am frightened at the closing up of minds I see, and recognise the same symptoms in myself.'[756] Much more frightening was the prospect of telling his mother. Like her father before her, Millicent had plans for her child to go to Oxford or Cambridge and in James's case to become a lecturer in English Literature. The prospect of confrontation clearly made a deep impression on him and he fictionalises the experience in his novel Horse, when he plucks up courage to tell his mother he is leaving university:

> He paused at the door of his mother's bedroom…He stiffened his muscles and edged the door open. His mother put down the paper and gave him a searching, anxious look over her glasses. The room had a dry smell of sun-baked books and talcum powder. As he drew near the bed, she lifted her face to be kissed, a face whose power lay in its capacity to be hurt, framed in grey hair and a pink nylon bed-jacket. His stomach sank like a stone in a bog. Horse and his mother loved each other. The misunderstanding between them, more profound than any communication, stretched right back to the cotton wool and enemas and forsekin-clipping doctors of a Karitane nursing home. Bending over the pillow he received the sacramental kiss, dry and cool and faintly sweet as apples kept in a loft. The danger of collapse into a dutiful son was now at its greatest. He retreated to the end of the bed and gripped the U-shaped barricade in both hands…
>
> 'Mother I've decided not to go back to Varsity next year.'…[757]

There then ensues a tirade from Horse's mother about letting his education go down the drain, how he must stop drinking and how he must work harder: 'Her cheeks were flushed and her eyes were burning. This was the climax he was fearing. If he began to argue, he would be lost. On open ground her cavalry would cut his forces to smithereens…"I am sorry Mother…I'm not going back to Varsity. I'll get a job instead." ' He leaves her and walks across the paddock to the river 'shaking all over. He burst into tears and gripped the huge smooth bole of the tree as if it were a human body.'[758]

This account seems not very fictional at all and could well be a not very exaggerated version of what really did happen when he told Millicent of his intention to leave university. But does that grief under the tree stem from the confrontation with the real James's mother, a feeling of failure at university or the despair that seems to accompany him for so much of his life? James's love for his mother always had an element of apprehension. Given the sensitivity of the content, Horse wasn't published until 1985, the year after Millicent died – had she read it, she surely would have been horrified that she had had such an effect on him.

James got his first job in March 1945 at the iron foundry at Green Island. It was with hard-drinking men and he kept pace with them, and more. Six months later he moved to a far healthier environment: sheep drafting and top-dressing at Wanaka Station in Central Otago, a place he could drink no alcohol. He began to lose some of his hectic adolescence and began managing some detachment from his parents.[759] He also felt less reliance on women. He wrote frankly and tellingly to his mother: 'Though I'm quite capable of infatuations, I think I could do without

women. Excepting you and one or two others, they do not attract me as persons...' [760]
But this would prove to be simply one of his oscillations in and out of his obsession
with alcohol and sex which would continue for most of his life. In November, he
returned home to Brighton where he took up heavy drinking again, often causing
clashes with Millicent when he didn't return home at night.[761] In an unpublished
poem that he dedicates to her, he writes 'I that was nearer thee / than the leaf is to
the tree / the stone to the bedded stream / walk upright and alone.'[762] He found his
father more understanding, but Archie tended to keep himself out of the arguments
between mother and son.

By now the war had ended. In the aftermath of the war, the German food
situation was dire; prevailing ration levels that ranged from 840-1400 calories were
less than half of their British counterparts.[763] Millicent's friend Mrs Oestreicher set
up a relief organisation called Dunediner Hilfswerk - Dunedin Aid, and with a great
deal of help from Millicent sent out 8000 - 10000 food parcels to her homeland,
Germany, something that today we would call refugee aid. The two women became
close friends; they were both 'outcasts' and their relationship was greatly aided by
Millicent being able to speak German. Mrs Oestreicher's husband Paul was their
family doctor who also became a very good friend. The Oestreichers' experience
of prejudice in New Zealand at that time was typical of many German immigrants.
He was a paediatric specialist, a patriotic German who had served as an officer
in the German army in World War I. While Mrs Oestreicher was not Jewish, her
husband was and though a Christian, he had Jewish parents. They experienced the
persecution of the Jewish race under Hitler's regime and by the time Kristallnacht,
the wave of violent anti-Jewish pogroms which took place on November 9 and
10, 1938, the Oestreichers knew they had to leave. Most countries closed their
doors, but they and their eight year-old son, also named Paul, were accepted into
New Zealand in 1939. Dr Oestreicher's medical qualifications weren't recognised
in New Zealand so the family went to Dunedin so he could undertake another three
years of clinical studies at the University of Otago medical school. Their son Paul,
five years younger than James, remembers being the object of attention and ridicule
at Musselburgh School where children would chase him around the playground
calling him a Hun and a Jew:

> Dunedin was a very monocultural society. The only non-
> indigenous children I was aware of were Chinese children[764] . . .
> some of whom were my friends. They were outsiders too, but in
> my family's case it was even more extreme. We were a family
> hunted out of Germany – expelled. But we arrived with German
> passports and within two months we were legally termed enemy
> aliens. Aliens in New Zealand were allowed to remain in the
> community, but there were restrictions. We were not allowed
> to leave the town without police permission and we were not
> allowed to possess a camera or a shortwave radio. There was an

alien officer at the Dunedin police station whose job it was to
keep an eye on us and to check my parents and others.'[765]

Being uprooted and replanted affected the family tremendously, and their ways of
coping were quite different. While Paul senior loved the medical profession and
his work – he had graduated again and established a general practice in Dunedin
– he always felt an outsider and a stranger. Mrs Oestreicher came from a peasant
family who loved country life. She loved her music, her garden and her friends. She
embraced life in New Zealand.[766] Having Millicent as a close friend must have been
very precious to her.

After the war, young Paul had become a regimental sergeant-major in the cadets
at King's High School, but by the time he left in 1949 he had become a pacifist.[767]
He had been profoundly affected and influenced by Archie's recently published We

James and Archie, probably in the mid-1940s

will not cease.[768] As a boy
he was often sent to stay
with the Baxters at
weekends and remembers
the household being
extremely stimulating,
with Millicent as the
talker and Archie as 'a
very quiet character who
sat smoking a pipe. Their
house was total chaos –
Millicent was no
housekeeper, but they
were lovely people and
that's what mattered and, of course, you couldn't help but be influenced by people
of that kind.'[769] Sixty or so years later, Paul Oestreicher gave a speech to University
of Otago graduands on 23 May 2009, dedicating it to Archie Baxter, a man he
describes as 'an outstanding New Zealander of huge moral and spiritual courage. I
talk about the duty of the citizen not just to go with the flow but to have a conscience
and to say no to certain things. In Christian terms I call it holy disobedience. In
other words, there are times when it is our duty to disobey, when it is our duty to be
critical of power for the sake of humanity.'[770]

Although James was a pacifist, he had little time to put his views into any
sort of action. Once he was back on his home territory he revelled in bars, getting
thoroughly drunk. For food he would drink copious amounts of milk, sometimes
with some eggs thrown in, sometimes drinking the milk left by the milkman outside
houses. This period coincides with one where he was receiving accolades for
Beyond the Palisade and everyone wanted to be seen with him. But he also had
an on-going problem about sex and sexuality. Terence, now back from dissenters'
camp, had so much more sex appeal than James did and had no trouble at all in

attracting girls. While they found James fascinating, they were more attracted by his intellect and conversation than by anything physical. He had a brief homosexual affair with a lecturer at the university and admitted to other homosexual episodes in his life, something he never really came to terms with.[771]

James was still officially living at home although he often crashed on friends' sofas at various flats in Dunedin. There were constant arguments with Millicent over his behaviour, but he even had battles with his adored father, and this worried him.[772] While he had always placed Archie in a loving, favourable, heroic light he wrote 'To my Father' at this time in which that relationship was becoming more stressful:

> There is a feud between us. I have loved you
> More than my own good, because you stand
> For country pride and gentleness, engraved
> In forehead lines, veins swollen on the hand;
> Also, behind slow speech and quiet eye
> The rock of passionate integrity...
> Finding no fault in you, I have been tempted
> To stay your child. But that which broke
> (Nature) the naval cord, has not yet exempted
> Even your light and sympathetic yoke.
> It is in me your true mettle shows;
> Nor can we thus be friends till we are foes.[773]

The hero worship he had for his father added to James's inner anguish. He knew that he could never have endured the suffering his father had been subjected to, nor could he live up to the innate goodness Archie possessed.

In 1995, Dr Janet Wilson of the University of Waikato examined the three autobiographies of the family: Archie's We will not cease, Millicent's Memoirs of Millicent Baxter and James's Horse, in an attempt to evaluate how the family dynamics contributed to James's makeup. She has this to say about James's relationship with his parents:

> While the father figure is always benevolent in Baxter's verse, there is no sign that [Archie] any more than the women to whom [James] looked for salvation, could have redeemed him from the alienation caused by misunderstanding with his mother. Archie's empathy with his son's intuitive poetic nature did not extend to intervening in this problematic relationship. Furthermore, while his own charisma undoubtedly extended beyond the domestic circle, his son's hero worship might also, paradoxically, have served to distance him. His very mystical powers which impressed James's imagination as saintliness, put

him in touch with pain and suffering but couldn't provide the answers to the problems they evoked.[774]

While Wilson agrees that Archie did little to intervene in the arguments between James and his mother, she takes a very tough line with Millicent and her parenting, and sees her as an alienating mother:

> [Millicent's] lack of self-reflexivity in matters to do with James is remarkable: at no point does she question whether she and Archie were suitable parents for someone so tormented and talented as their son. Nor does she contemplate the likely possibility that the ingredients of their successful union – they were diametrically opposed, yet complementary characters – meant that there was little room, psychologically, within which a child as bright and as sexually curious as James could develop. But Baxter was born into this marriage of emotional exclusiveness, a seemingly monolithic institution where he was forced early on to negotiate his self-identity. His failure to achieve relatedness with his mother, to discover a sense of autonomy other than momentarily through his art, probably contributed to his obsessive urges, his alcoholism, his intense piety, his search for an alternative society, and the compulsion to write as a release. Millicent would have seen the symptoms of this malaise in both his work and his life, but characteristically her Memoirs, far from responding to it, constitute a defence of her position which reinforces the very conflict between them, which caused it, and existed from the time he was born.[775]

Wilson, as I understand her, suggests that Millicent and Archie were opposites. Together they took up the entire spectrum of personal identity, which left James nothing with which to forge an identity that was distinctly his own. What could he do to be different and equal? James finally did manage to achieve a self-identity separate from his parents through his poetry, his work with the disadvantaged and the setting up of the commune at Jerusalem. But for much of his life, the struggle for identity and, possibly, to overcome feelings of inferiority to both his parents caused him psychological stress. He had less in common with Millicent than he did with Archie and he came to reject her background, particularly the academic aspect of it, and any effects that background manifested in her.

A large amount has been written about the origins of the complex nature of James's personality and behavior, and little should be added significantly to that, but Wilson's argument about Millicent's parenting cannot go completely uncontested. Wilson finds fault with Millicent's reluctance to acknowledge her and Archie's role in James's psychological turmoils. Presumably, she means a major role. That

Millicent was aware that her attitudes and parenting affected her sons is not in doubt. She certainly struggled when James took up the pacifist stance at school, knowing it was the effect of having such singular, pacifist parents.

But when it was suggested to her that conflict between James and herself was primarily of her own making, she defended herself, and understandably. Of course Millicent's attitudes left an impression on James as he matured, but how much it was the cause of James's psychological difficulties as an adult cannot be known least of all by herself, emotionally tied up in the relationship.

Wilson talks of James being born into this marriage of 'emotional exclusiveness.' Millicent and Archie were certainly bound up in one another, and perhaps neither parent had room to see much of the inner turmoil of James. Christine Cole Catley also had some evidence for this. During one of their frequent recorded chats together, Christine was discussing Millicent's passion for Archie and their ideal marriage, and quoted the adage 'the children of lovers are orphans':

> Millicent said nothing but she looked straight at me with those piercing blue eyes with absolute recognition. And realisation dawned. Had she shown enough love to her children, had she kept too much for Archie? I'm quite sure too from reading Jim's poetry and from talking to Millicent, that she was so in love with Archie that there wasn't quite enough love over for the sons. And because of that – this is my reading of the situation – a lot of Jim's great poetry came out of that.[776]

While Christine's theory is very possible there is another way of looking at Millicent's reaction. Perhaps she was thinking about *herself* being the orphan of *her* parents; that she felt shut out from her parents, on the perimeter of their lives. Certainly she didn't have an over-abundance of genuine love shown to her when she was a child; her parents and nurses were so busy with their own lives.

And Millicent and Archie certainly were bound up in their pacifist cause. Archie probably could never escape from these obligations and once Millicent had allied herself to his cause, neither could she. But I don't believe that James – or Terence – faced difficulties in establishing identities and a sense of self-worth because they were "orphans". More likely, burden of expectations was the cause, and this extended well beyond Millicent and Archie. James certainly felt the burden to excel academically: his famous academic grandfather Macmillan Brown staring down at him with expectations, his dead grandmother imposing her scholarly will on him from her grave and his mother with her Cambridge education all added to that load; something Millicent surely must have recognised having experienced similar pressure from her parents.

If Millicent's dominant personality and academically demanding expectations were a primary cause of James's problems it is unlikely she would be able to initiate discussion of the issues with James as that would be more of the same: a dominating controlling mother telling her son what's best for his life.

She could have shown greater acceptance for James as an adult: not let him know she found his poems coarse, not comment on his clothes or buy him a new coat, although these are natural comments for any mother to make. Approval from Millicent may well have eased his ability to acquire psychological independence and to develop a feeling of self-worth. But Millicent can only be considered negligent if James's behaviour and mental turmoil were in fact caused to a considerable extent by his need to establish an identity separate from her, and that Millicent believed this. I am not sure she did. And I like to think that Millicent eventually wholeheartedly accepted and appreciated James.

He shouldn't have had to have gone to that extent to finally get her approval, but if that is what spurred his creativity and passions, thank God he did. If his striving for identity and self-worth was a battle against Millicent, we are the beneficiaries, for his poetry came from the cradle of this personal anguish. If we hold Millicent to account for James's personal anguish we must credit her for giving us New Zealand's most acclaimed poet. But this is attributing too much; while Millicent undoubtedly had a major role in moulding the boy who became James K Baxter, Archie's contribution was no less. Archie was famous, a Jesus figure who endured torture for his beliefs, one who stood up for peace and who shared with James his love of poetry. James became famous, a Jesus figure, a spokesman for peace, and a poet.

Whatever Wilson thinks, there is no doubt that both James and Terence received love, care and attention as well as a good education, from both parents. Granddaughter, Katherine Baxter, feels that Millicent loved both her sons very much. With particular regard to James she says 'I don't know how much she understood his poetry but she was immensely proud of him, immensely – probably more so than Granddad even, in a strange kind of way. I think she adored Jum, she really did.'[777] Millicent was sometimes upset by James's poetry when it included his frank descriptions of her, and there is that telling line in Horse – which thankfully she never read – when Horse approaches his mother to tell her he is leaving university: 'she lifted her face to be kissed, a face whose power lay in its capacity to be hurt…'[778] And she was often hurt by James, but it is very likely that Millicent knew nothing of that power and therefore never used it.

Certainly she was irritated by the way James frequently mythologised his life in his writing; she tells us crossly that 'In his teens Jim read romantic books… all about the sensitive artist having an unhappy childhood, with an insensible, stultifying family. Jim had to be the stranger in his family. What nonsense!… He admitted, when he was mature, that he had had a happy childhood – which was hard for him, because happy families destroy poets. He had to have an interesting tragic background, his own mythology.'[779] She felt that poets feel they have to exaggerate and that they don't have to distinguish between fiction and fact. She even went as far as to say in an interview with Radio New Zealand that James was completely unreliable in his statements about nearly everything.[780]

At the end of 1947 James moved to Christchurch, ostensibly to make a fresh start at a new university career at the University of Canterbury but also to re-establish his independence from his parents and to be close to friends including Lawrence Baigent, Denis Glover, Charles Brasch, Rex Fairburn, Bill Pearson, Colin McCahon, Allen Curnow and others in literary and artistic groups. Many of them met at Caxton Press in Victoria Street and often ended up in the Gladstone or the Albion, hotels nearby. It was a fascinating time to be a poet in Christchurch, and James, the 'marvellous boy' of New Zealand poetry, was welcomed with very open arms. There was also a cluster of artists he sometimes mixed with, many of whom belonged to 'the Group' that James's aunt Viola had helped found some ten years before. The Group now included Rita Angus, Colin McCahon, Olivia Spencer Bower, Leo Benseman, Evelyn Page, Doris Lusk and Bill Sutton.[781] Viola's celebrated friend Ngaio Marsh was in her prime when James was at the university, although he found her a little daunting; McKay maintains 'strong women still threw him off balance. They reminded him too much of his mother.'[782]

James also went to Christchurch to visit Greta Christeller[783], a Jungian psychotherapist with a particular interest in the creative mind.[784] His sessions did not solve many of James's problems but he felt she gave him self-confidence and a better sense of responsibility. He began reading Jung and incorporating Jungian symbolism into his poetry.[785]

But there was yet another motivation for James to go to Christchurch; someone who turned out to be probably the most significant person, after his parents, in his life – Jacqueline Sturm. Jacquie, as she was known to everyone, was a young Māori woman who was a medical student at Otago University where they first met. She was born in 1927 at Opunake in Taranaki and raised by Ethel Sturm and Bert Sturm when her mother died within weeks of her birth. She began writing poetry at the age of eleven, and then, in her late teens, decided to train as a doctor.[786] In 1946, she enrolled at the University of Otago in Dunedin to study medicine.[787] Jacquie was the only Māori woman on campus, and she felt distinctly conspicuous. Later, she changed from medicine to anthropology and moved to the University of Canterbury in late 1947. James had met Jacquie at Otago University, and his to move to Christchurch was, in part, because of her.[788]

The pair saw a lot of each other and Jacquie got to know James's literary and artistic friends but felt much more comfortable on the outer ring of that out-going group.[789] While Jacquie worked on her anthropology assignments at university, James was drinking heavily at the local pubs. Denis Glover, whose poetry James revered, maintained he was an alcoholic before he moved to Christchurch says 'There he was, this cherubic, innocent-faced, baby boy from Otago. He'd say "Let's go and have a drink."…He was totally addicted to alcohol. He found strong drink liberated him from all the toilsome world around him and enable him to carry on with his real vocation of writing.'[790] Both Millicent and Terence felt that Glover with his heavy-drinking had a bad influence on James.[791] Money spent on alcohol and visits to his psychotherapist meant he had little left over. He took a variety of jobs to make ends meet but he and Jacquie never had enough money, and when they ran out of it, they simply didn't eat. Sometimes James thought of suicide. But 1948 saw the publication of James's second collection of poetry, Blow, Wind of Fruitfulness,[792] and it was received as enthusiastically as Beyond the Palisade.

As an adolescent, James had doubted the existence of a God but now he turned to a search for a religious faith. Unbeknown to Jacquie he started looking into Catholicism, but was baptised as an Anglican in November 1948.[793] He wrote to his parents saying that he now felt he had come to terms with them, that some umbilical cord had been broken and that he could see them clearly for the first time without mistrust and feelings of insecurity. In the same letter he talked of the mythology of his childhood: 'I'm inclined to think, too, that I had a singularly pleasant upbringing; probably if anything, you and Daddy were too easy on me – I must have been rather irritating at times.'[794] An understatement perhaps.

During this period, Millicent and Archie went to Christchurch to stay with their pacifist friends, the Milligans, then to the West Coast to stay with Elsie and Jim Gill. Lawrence Kirwan, with whom Archie had shared Army Field Punishment No 1 many times, was living in Hokitika. Archie decided not to call on his old friend, as Kirwan had earlier made it clear to two of Archie's brothers that he wanted to forget his anti-militarist past and didn't want to know or meet the Baxters.[795] Not all 'conchies' felt comfortable about their actions, or lack of action, during the war. The last survivor of The Fourteen, Garth Ballantyne, died in 1984. He had never married, and lived a Spartan lifestyle perhaps, as has been speculated, in atonement for his earlier stand as a conscientious objector.[796]

Late in 1948 James proposed marriage to Jacquie and she accepted. There was strong disapproval from both sets of parents. When Jacquie's mother first met Jim, she exclaimed 'You should look after him, he looks like an unmade bed!'[797] Ethel and Bert Sturm had hoped for someone much better for their daughter, who was by now very highly regarded at the university. They even persuaded her professor to offer James a job as a writer in Antarctica. Archie and Millicent also were dismayed at the prospect of the couple marrying. Liberal though they were, they were aware of the racial prejudice that existed in New Zealand at the time, and were very worried at the prospect of James marrying a Māori.[798] Again there is a parallel here with her own marriage, but there is no mention of her concern in her memoirs.

Despite their parents' attitudes, on 9 December 1948 James donned his suit and married Jacquie in St John's Cathedral, Napier. He was twenty-two; she was twenty-one. 'I was a gloomy drunk / You were a troubled woman. Nobody would have given tuppence for our chances...'[799] They moved from Christchurch to Wellington. They were expecting a baby and they struggled to exist on James's wages from work at the Ngauranga abbatoir. James gave up drinking. Their daughter Hilary was born on 18 June 1949 and baptised Anglican. The renowned artist Colin McCahon was Godfather.[800] James wrote to his parents: 'She seems so fragile and small that I am afraid to touch her. It is a great privilege to have a child to look after.'[801] Money was a constant problem for them but although Archie and Millicent offered to provide finance for them to buy a house, James would have none of it. Instead he accepted a loan for a year's rent on the house. The following year the three of them moved to Messines Road in the heart of middle-class Karori.

All went well until Jacquie had a miscarriage and began to have ill health. With the turmoil involved in living with James, the progress on her university studies had been erratic, but she was an excellent student and continued with her BA degree. James started drinking again. He took a temporary job as a postman in March 1950, and although Wellington's infamous wind and that winter's rain annoyed him, he took the opportunity of composing poetry, savouring every phrase of the poem he was currently creating, while he walked. He wasn't the best postman, and it didn't take long for the His Majesty's Service to release him. However, the previous year he had resumed studies at Victoria University and found himself doing well in Literature. In February 1951 he enrolled at Wellington Teacher's College to train as a primary school teacher.[802] He was very aware that he drank too much but felt that although it was destroying him, it released from him his best poetry, and that if he gave up alcohol, he might lose his gift.[803] Was the drinking part of the writing or the writing part of the drinking?

Then, May 1951 brought a pivotal event for James's career as a poet. He presented Recent Trends in New Zealand Poetry,[804] at the New Zealand Writers' Conference at Canterbury University. He must have felt the illustrious ghosts of his grandfather and grandmother, Helen and John Macmillan Brown within those hallowed halls. It was a brilliant lecture, and 'the almost magical nature of his performance', was acclaimed as a huge success.[805] It proved to be the fulcrum that began James's career as a performer as well as a poet. William Oliver maintains 'His voice was among his most commanding characteristics. The unusually long and pure vowels were perhaps derived from his mother's patrician speech; the drooping cadences were wholly his own.'[806]

On 29 October 1952 his son John McColl was born. By this time, Jacquie had done a great deal better at university than James. She had completed her BA, and was now undertaking an MA in Philosophy, which when gained, made her the first Māori woman to do so. Yet another parallel and yet another lofty academic for James to feel threatened by. All his life, James kept up a regular correspondence by letter with his parents, and Millicent and Archie frequently visited them. Summer holidays alternated between the Baxters in Brighton and the Sturms in Napier. Millicent and Archie had been continuing their work for pacifism and enjoying their less stressful life in Brighton. Early in 1952 Millicent, now sixty-four and Archie, seventy-one, took another trip overseas, this time with their pacifist friends, Alice Huband and Rita Warburton. In England they stayed with Viola, Angelo and their two daughters Antonietta and Felicity, none of whom they'd seen for fourteen years. After a few weeks of touring England, they went to Switzerland where Millicent showed Archie her old childhood haunts. After tours to other European countries, they returned to Britain for another visit to Scotland and in late November 1952, left for New Zealand in time for the christening of James and Jacquie's baby. It was an Anglican christening but James was doubting that Anglicanism was right for him.

Millicent and Archie returned to their house in Brighton. Millicent developed her passion for alpine plants during her European travels, an interest she first acquired all those years ago when visiting there with her parents. Archie dug three new beds in the garden for her. Her memoirs are littered with detailed descriptions of plants. She and Archie sometimes joined their old friends Elsie and Jim Gill at a house they had at Blackstone Hill near St Bathins in Central Otago. There, they spent many days tramping in the hills and mountains in search of plants. Archie was rarely fit enough to join them on the steeper walks but did so whenever he could. Otherwise, he and Jim would often give the women a lift in 'the Chev' and then go fishing.[807] On one of these trips Archie found a plant in a rock crevice that they took back to grow in their garden. After experts examined the specimen it was found to be a new Gingidium and was named after the Baxters - Gingidium enysii var baxterii. 'The baxterii is right because it was Archie who found it' says Millicent. [808]

In Millicent's memoirs there is no further mention of her great, probably best friend, Elsie Gill, possibly because she wouldn't want to comment on such an emotional time for her, but also because there was a cloud over Elsie's death in 1982, aged seventy-seven. Elsie had suffered from depression after her husband died and four years after, took all her tablets and died five days later in hospital. Millicent was distraught. Don Lawson, Elsie's son-in-law, knew how close the two women had been – he viewed Millicent as a much more pragmatic sort of intellectual thinker and Elsie more of a dreamer and a serious depressive.[809]

In about 1956 Archie wrote his novel (unpublished) about the pioneering days in the Brighton district. That same year, Millicent, now aged sixty-eight, joined the Dunedin Naturalists' Field Club that undertook trips to areas of natural interest and beauty. Archie joined a year later and together they went on the Club's annual excursions. Millicent tells Christine Cole Catley in 1979

> We used only to pay 50c subscription, for about 100 years, that is all. It was changed last year to $1. We pay extra for bus trips. We have quite a lot of young members and married members and they have children but we can't take children on the trips. Birds and rocks are also identified. There is an annual excursion which last 8 to 10 days; the first trip was to Murchison – a train to Christchurch, then a bus over the Lewis Pass to Murchison where we hired a bus and made expeditions in the neighbourhood. We always all try to stay in the same hotel. We meet after dinner every night and hold an identification parade. We examine all our specimens and if we haven't identified them then almost certainly someone will. They are put down the book for that expedition as having been found, then the specimens are collected in polythene bags and two drops of water put in – too

much water rots the plant. We take them home and bring them to the meeting the following day. Afterwards we plant them in our own gardens.[810]

Millicent was a member of the Field Club for the rest of her life, eventually becoming its president. She organised the annual week-long field excursions until 1975 when she was eighty-seven; 'No doubt I ought to have withdrawn before, but I enjoyed it and didn't'.[811] She took a host of photographs of the alpine plants she came across, and had an advantage over others in the Field Club for the names of the plants with her knowledge of Latin.[812] She would put the specimens she'd collected into a supermarket bag and take them to the Botany Department at the university to ask for expert opinions as to whether she had correctly named them.[813] As with so many people who met her, Millicent was a force to be reckoned with amongst the new and particularly young members of the club. Asking her once for the name of a plant was fine, asking her about the same plant again and you would get a metaphorical rap across the knuckles. Toni Wilson, still a member of the club, remembers 'You were expected to have made a little diagram, you should have sketched it, you should have gone away and you should have looked it up. That's how she operated. She was very passionate about these plants, they were precious to her. When she created her own alpine garden at Brighton, it would not have been easy; she would have to have got exactly the right soil, the right texture of gravels etc.'[814] No wonder children were never allowed near her prized alpine garden. Millicent shared her passion in her letters with her friend Jean Bertram and one letter illustrates how she got her blood up when challenged on her pet subject:

> I am no longer knowledgeable about identifying alpines or exotics. Memory for names – especially botanic ones – has almost entirely left me and I am blind in one eye – cataract – so that I can no longer identify plants in the wild... But there's one thing I refuse to give way to Allen on, and that is I refuse to accept the mountain beech cliffortioides as a variety of the black beech Solandri. Chromosomes be hanged! The pattern of the leaves on the stem is unique. In a hundred years' time – if there are still human beings on this earth, which I doubt – a botanist will come along and take my view just as he will sweep Gingidium baxterii which was called after me by Dr Dawson, [wasn't that Archie's find?] back under Anisotome aromatica where it rightly belongs![815]

In those years, even though World War Two had been over fifteen years, prejudice against pacifists was still strong. Margaret, Maggie Baxter's daughter, worked in the late 1950s as a nurse in Parkside Hospital, Dunedin, when she was about twenty and she remembers:

I was nursing this elderly lady. I was her best friend and she wouldn't let anyone else look after her or bath her or wash anything... So I went on duty this particular morning and I went in and said 'Good morning', and she just looked at me and said 'Don't come any further. Don't come near me.' And I said 'Oh what's happened, what have I done?' She said 'I've just found out who you are and who your relations are... You're a relative of all those Baxters from Brighton. I don't want you in my room!'[816]

Pacifism had spread widely among the Baxter family in the generations since Archie and his brothers took their stand. In the 1960s Terence and Lenore had made it clear they wouldn't forbid their son Kenneth undertaking compulsory military training when it came to the Vietnam War. Kenneth, without interference from his parents, came to the decision not to accept the ballot.[817] Lenore herself had very strong pacifist views:

Anybody who's studied the history of Europe and the Middle East, even since the First World War, will see that what's going on there today has been caused by us, just as much as it's been caused by them. And it's because we want their oil and we want their territory...War doesn't ever cure anything. There's just no point in trying to squash it from the top. You've got to work it out from the bottom. That's what they found in Vietnam, wasn't it? You can't impose democracy on anybody. It must grow from the roots up.[818]

John Baxter, James and Jacquie's son, has his own personal brand of pacifism today: 'The damage to individual lives, social infrastructures, economies and cultures by modern warfare is incalculable. In the end, people have to talk to sort out their differences; why not before things get violent rather than after? The waste otherwise is appalling and benefits a tiny elite minority only.' He has been a pacifist since he attended those early protests with his father in the 1960s: 'As part of the compulsory military training process, I registered as a conscientious objector at secondary school. I have always supported the anti-war and peace movements by participation in demonstrations and petitions etc. I am an active supporter/writer for Amnesty International.'[819]

Some of the present Baxter family wouldn't call themselves pacifists but have a passionate belief in peace and peaceful protest and support the United Nations having peacekeeping forces in war zones. Donald's daughter Diane would still never dream of going to an Anzac Parade because, as the daughter of a pacifist, she was never allowed to do so by her father when she a child.[820] She recognizes the lack of logic in this but still cannot do it. She doesn't consider herself to be a pacifist because, if necessary, she would fight to protect her children and family. She also remembers how the family pacifism affected her brother to such an extent it brought about his suicide – the threat of having to ever join the army worried him to the point of him taking his own life.[821] Her cousin Barry, grandson of Archie's brother Mark, has suffered from depression all his life, which he attributes to his abandonment as a child caused by his father being imprisoned as a dissenter in World War Two. Nevertheless, he himself registered as a conscientious objector when he was eighteen, in 1960:

> I missed out on the ballot and that was the best day of my life. I never questioned pacifism – I was brought up by a pacifist and was surrounded by a whole family of pacifists; I never dreamt of thinking anything else. Over the years I have thought about this subject of pacifism constantly…and have arrived at the following philosophy. In the event of our country being the aggressor and attacking another country, I would stand unconditionally as a conscientious objector and stand against any such action. In the event of our country being attacked, I wouldn't necessarily become a sworn soldier, but I would protect my family and fellow man with the ferocity of any wild animal protecting its young ... [822]

Going back to James and Wellington at the end of 1952, he left Victoria Teachers' College and the following year attended university full-time on a full salary. That year he still did little university work but saw the publication of The Fallen House,[823] his third major collection of poetry and his most accomplished publication to date. Many of the poems stem from his childhood and adolescent experiences and there is a poem each for Archie, Jacquie and little Hilary. A look at 'To My Father' reveals the unbreakable affinity James always felt for Archie but also of the constant striving necessary to achieve freedom from his father, and the freedom from war:

> I shall compare you to the bended bow,
> Myself the arrow launched upon the hollow
> Resounding air. And I must go
> In time, my friend, to where you cannot follow…
> We have one aim: to set men free
> From fear and custom and the incessant war
> Of self with self and city against city–
> So they may know the peace that they were born for…[824]

His poetry was flourishing but his personal life was collapsing. He was always trying so hard but always failing at university, as a father, as a husband, and at his battle with alcoholism. He also had a dependence on Benzedrine and a constant

The Baxter Family - Archie, Millicent, Jacquie, Lenore, James, Terence, Katherine, Helen, John, Kenneth and Hilary. Taken in the mid 1950s

need to bludge on his friends. Things improved a little when in February 1954 he was appointed Assistant Master at Epuni School in Lower Hutt. While working here he wrote poetry specifically for the children. A collection was eventually published posthumously in The Tree House and Other Poems for Children[825] in 1974, and Frank McKay maintains it was 'without doubt the finest volume of children's poetry produced in this country.'[826] As James became more and more interested then committed to the Catholic church, he became close friends with Pat Lawlor, a Wellington poet and a

Catholic publicist.[827] Lawlor kept a diary about their meetings. He saw him in April 'dejected, remorseful and repentant' and told him he was 'not an alcoholic, but a victim of his own self-dramatisation and pride. He agreed with me.'[828] In 1955 his poetry recitals and another book, The Fire and the Anvil: Notes on Modern Poetry[829], were well received, but despite this James wrote a letter to Millicent and Archie which reveals a great deal about this complex, tortured man:

Jacquie, Millicent, Lenore, Archie, Terence, Hilary, John, Katherine, Helen, and Kenneth Baxter at Christmas 1960

> I do not easily find peace
> of mind and some such peace is necessary to build work and marriage securely. It comes, I think, of having 2 minds – the one careful, considerate and awake to necessary obligations; the other egotistical, erratic and much at the mercy of feelings. Love in marriage I know is pretty central; but it seems to be the product of many things including one's own perseverance...
> The ready-made schemes – to drink only tea; to work to a set routine – are about as useful as firm resolves to control one's temper. I think I will always have on my hands more than I can conveniently deal with. A clearer vision and a lack of egotism

are what I need most, more than money, artistic reputation, or a first-class job…To want to be a good man is one thing; to want to be a good poet is another. I hope they are not incompatible, for if so I may well not make the grade.[830]

It is difficult to assess whether this letter contains the 'self-dramatisation and pride' that Pat Lawlor talks of, or if James is genuinely opening up his heart to the two of the people who matter most to him in his life. It's also hard to gauge how Archie, Millicent and even Terence would have viewed the James in this letter; all three were so much more stable and grounded, less tormented and fragile and much less 'egotistical, erratic and…at the mercy of feelings.' Archie was the most in tune with James but who knows if his insight would have been able to help his son. Archie was a great listener, not a great talker. And James had many listeners in his life.

By this time James, Jacquie, Hilary and John moved into a place of their own on the edge of the Otari-Wilton Bush. Life was beginning to look good again and the prospects even better with James's degree almost finished and Jacquie having started writing poetry. But in December, writing and publishing poetry, teaching, attending university part-time and copious drinking affected James's health and he was told he had trouble with his heart.[831] His conscience was also suffering – his wife and two children often got none of his pay when it was spent instead on alcohol, and relationships with women and sometimes men. Overcome with guilt as he was, and try as he might, it seems he was unable to do change these habits.

The family still made visits to Millicent and Archie and, in strong contrast to his chaotic life, there is a delightful photograph of James and the Baxter family indicating none of the adversity that any had suffered or was suffering. It was likely taken in the summer of 1954/55. It shows Millicent, Archie, their two sons and daughters-in law and their five grandchildren, including Terence and Lenore's daughter Helen who had been born in 1954. It is a sunny day in Brighton, probably in Millicent and Archie's garden

While he was still teaching at Epuni School, James joined Alcoholics Anonymous, swiftly becoming an ardent convert. He spent hours helping fellow alcoholics and counselling other marginalized people: prisoners, down-and-outs – the underdogs. Jacquie as a wife and mother also found the process extremely tough; instead of James bringing drunken friends back to the house, he now brought recovering alcoholics with all their problems.[832]

Things improved a little when James's great aunt Hetty, the sister of Millicent's mother Helen, died and left James a large legacy. James and Jacquie bought a house in Ngaio. Jacquie became active in Māori affairs, particularly through the Māori Welfare League and the Ngati Poneke Young Māori Club, set up in Wellington in 1937 to keep young people off the streets and arouse their interest in Māori culture. It was one of the first Māori performing arts clubs in Aotearoa.[833] She was also publishing articles and book reviews, particularly in the Māori magazine Te Au Hou. James took little interest in that side of her life;[834] he was too busy leading his own. At long last he graduated BA in May 1956. He resigned from Epuni School and became sub-editor for the Department of Education's School Publication's Branch, producing primary-school bulletins for children from nine to thirteen. At last things seemed to be falling into place for James and the family. He loved his children and all that seemed to be missing was his lack of certainty regarding his religious beliefs; he had been oscillating between Anglicism and Catholicism for some time. On 17 September 1957, Pat Lawlor wrote in his diary: 'Great News! Jim comes in radiant; he has lit his candle at our Lady's altar [at St Mary of the Angels Church in Boulcott Street], went straight over to the presbytery and arranged for instruction into the Faith from Father McHardy... James and I marked the great occasion by going out and having a cup of coffee.'[835]

But Jacquie knew none of this. When James finally told her he was about to become a Catholic she was hurt and offended that he could take such a huge step in

his life without even talking to her about it. It proved to be the final straw in the many heartaches and problems the marriage had already gone through. They separated in October 1957 and James, living in various flats, would come and see the children at weekends, while she took the train into town to work, and their trains would cross.[836] He was received into the Catholic Church early in January 1958 and according to Pat Lawlor, the literary world was agog.[837]

James, Jacquie, Hilary and John Baxter in Wellington, taken in the late 1950s

Jacquie and James were still separated when he got the offer of a UNESCO Fellowship to visit Japan and India, but Jacquie bravely agreed to meet him in India with the children. For the last fifteen years James hadn't thought much about pacifism, but in Japan he was appalled to see first-hand the effects the war had had: 'It offends me that these were the people on whom the bombs were dropped in Hiroshima and Nagasaki... the most spectacular results of Western technology they have so far seen have been the giant bulldozer and the atom bomb. We will only win their confidence by learning to understand their ways of thought – not to change it or exploit it, but in order to meet them more than half-way with respect and even love.'[838]

He met Jacquie, Hilary and John in Bombay (Mumbai). With their reunion, Jacquie and James agreed to find ways around their religious differences – Jacquie had no intention of becoming a Catholic – and to build a new relationship in India, away from friends and confused relatives. They took a small house in New Delhi where the family stayed while James travelled by train to Bombay, Madras and Calcutta. He despaired at the suffering of the many beggars and gave away so much money he often had none left for his own food.[839] This, plus the lack of hygiene, damaged his health and by the time he left India he was a sick man.

Back in their house in Ngaio at the end of 1960, the couple found their time in India had brought them closer together. Jacquie had also been helping poor people in India in practical ways. James was appreciated her much more and realised he had much to learn from her. Their time there had been a significant experience for James and it perpetuated his loathing of the modern western world, its inequality and selfishness. In 1961 Once Over Howrah Bridge was published by Oxford University Press in London.[840] Paul Millar in his article, James K. Baxter's Indian Poems, includes a 'foreword' by Jacquie:

> I myself am quite convinced that India was a sort of crossroads, and Jim, being the kind of person he was, had no choice but to turn in the direction of a new and then unknown destination– Jerusalem. I'm not now just referring to a particular spot on the map. The immediate and obvious effect on him as a writer produced Howrah Bridge, but this of course was only the tip of the ice-berg. And this is what India did to Jim the man. I mean ordinary man. It didn't shake him to his foundations…but from his foundations. And it took nearly 10 years to find himself again in a new relation to God and man.[841]

But Jerusalem was some way off. By the end of 1960 work was going well and while James still hadn't beaten his alcoholism he was drinking less. Pat Lawlor writes: 'There is a luminous quality in his face. It is always there, even when he was drinking but now it is spiritualised. He told me he goes to Communion every day except the odd occasions when he feels he must go to Confession instead!'[842] James resigned from the School Publications Branch in mid-March 1963 and became a postman again, this time on the permanent staff of the New Zealand Post Office, Wellington. It was the work he liked the best; he had time to think, compose poems and even pray.[843] Jacquie's mother died that year and with a realisation of what his own parents meant to him, he wrote to Archie and Millicent: 'I know I have often wounded you in my struggle to become whatever I intended to be. I regret this. You are my dear ones.'[844] Jacquie by now was having some considerable success with her own writing and poetry and when, years later, C.K. Stead included 'For All the Saints' in New Zealand Short Stories, 1966, she became the first Māori writer selected for a New Zealand anthology.[845]

During the early 1960s, political protests had reached an all-time high. James went to many of these protests against war, racial discrimination, civil rights, nuclear armament and particularly the National Government's foreign policy. He also protested in 1965 against the decision that New Zealand should dispatch soldiers to the Vietnam war.[846] He wrote a number of polemical poems in protest against this war, published them as broadsheets and distributed them at protests.

He spoke at a large rally in front of parliament buildings, presenting himself as 'a Catholic, a poet and a worker.'[847] His protests weren't based on politics, they were entirely on humanitarian and pacifist grounds, and in his own way he was emulating his father and brother by taking a defiant and public stand against war.

In the early 1960s James was delighted to learn that his parents were considering becoming Catholics. It started with Archie being admitted to the Mater Hospital in Dunedin (now the Mercy Hospital) in the mid-60s for a small eye operation. One day he asked to see the hospital chaplain. Father Sellar, a thirty year-old Roman Catholic priest who had been ordained about six years before, met Archie's request. He is obviously a very insightful and perceptive person who has strong memories of meeting and instructing Archie and Millicent. He wrote his impressions of them both:

> On that first meeting [in Mater Hospital] after a very comfortable and enjoyable hour in conversation, during which time I learned that he was the father of James K Baxter, he asked if I would visit him at his home in Brighton to continue our conversation. I readily agreed because I found him such a delightful and engaging person. So, a week later I drove out to his little wooden cottage. Typically, he was at the front gate ready to welcome me, then took me inside to meet Millicent. From that moment I was always somewhat in awe of her. Here was Professor Macmillan Brown's daughter, and I became acutely aware that I couldn't keep up with her when she discussed books. In all the time I knew her she was always Mrs Baxter to me, and she would always refer to me, with a distinct note of formality, as Father Sellar.[848]

For months, the three of them enjoyed their weekly meetings very much. Sellar felt a strong rapport with Archie: 'I always felt closer to him than to Millicent. To me he was a genuine mystic because he had this effortless sense of oneness with nature, with other people, with his God, and within himself, with all converging effortlessly into one.' Sellar rethought his description of Archie as a mystic a week or so later: 'On reflection, I think that Archie could be better described as a contemplative rather than a mystic because mysticism can give the impression of someone who lives in a different world of esoteric thought, sometimes quite disconnected from reality.'[849] Archie seldom spoke directly about his war-time experiences as a conscientious objector, though he did give Sellar his only copy of We will not cease, making him promise solemnly that he would return it. 'Reading about what he experienced, especially Field Punishment No.1, I made a point of staying alert to see if there were still some simmering resentment about the injustices and indignities he was put through. Never did I find the slightest resentment or unresolved anger over these events. I could only conclude that he was one of those rare people who bore no grudges because he had completely forgiven his torturers.'[850]

In conversations with Millicent, Sellar found:

> She explored questions back to their ultimate causes with clarity
> of thought that displayed the trained mind. She was never a cosy
> maternal figure, yet I detected a deep and passionate esteem for
> all who were significant to her... I am pondering the question
> about Archie being in Millicent's shadow. The answer is I don't
> think so. Archie was his own man, and I believe that is something
> Millicent treasured...He was introverted in the richest sense,
> because without this reliance on his inner convictions and the
> truth of himself, he could never have survived all the torture
> and vilification he received after his return from World War I
> and throughout subsequent years. His quiet conviction was so
> important to Millicent, and she so valued it.[851]

Archie finally told Sellar that he would like to explore Catholicism but felt that Millicent didn't share his interest. It seems, however, that Millicent had been thinking exactly the same way. It's interesting that this had previously happened with James and Jacquie: one not confiding in the other about their interest in becoming a Catholic. It had happened also between Viola and Millicent when Viola had become a Catholic in England some time before she told her sister, even though they wrote to each other very regularly.[852] Archie's brother Donald's daughter Diane Dore says that despite Archie and her father being very close, her father had no idea that Archie had become a Catholic – until Archie's funeral.[853] It seems for some people there are certain subjects like religion that are so very personal that they do not share their thoughts even, or perhaps particularly, with those who are closest to them. Perhaps the secrecy was not so very surprising; a Scottish Presbyterian becoming an Anglican or a Catholic could have been considered almost traitorous and could well have caused ructions. What is surprising is that they changed their religious beliefs.

Sellar then undertook the necessary period of instruction preparatory to receiving baptism and admission into the Church. He talked with them each week about Catholic beliefs and the teaching of the Church, just as James had been taught seven years before. For Archie 'there was no "changing gear" as he moved from his garden to having a chat, to spending time reading St Francis of Assisi in a reflective way. For him it was all one.'[854] For Millicent, it was more difficult. It didn't sit well with her logical mind, and she wondered if she would ever be able to become Catholic.[855] She told Michael King that 'Archie could rise to heights I couldn't, and in some ways he was mystic – I'm not – and therefore I couldn't meet him on it... for instance, receiving Holy Communion meant a tremendous amount to him... Jum had all those things very strongly and I suppose he was nearer to his father in those things than I was... he and my sister were explaining all sorts of things you see, trying to make it easier for me.'[856]

James was hugely enthusiastic about his parents joining his faith and wrote every day to Millicent to help her through the process.[857] Several months later the couple finally felt ready to be received into the Catholic Church. Sellar was very happy about this but for Millicent and Archie there was one serious obstacle to overcome: could they remain pacifists and at the same time become Catholics? Sellar prepared himself with the answer that in about the second or third centuries, some of the Church fathers wrote about Christians being excluded from military service. The following, however, week Millicent and Archie welcomed him with the news that they had found the answer themselves: Pope John XXIII had made a statement before he died in which he urged the world to abandon war and work for peace.[858] [859]

They now had all the reassurance they needed and Archie and Millicent's baptism and reception into the Catholic Church took place on 3 July 1965 at St Peter Chanel Church in Green Island. Archie was eighty-four at the time, she was seventy-seven and remembers that before they went to the church, Archie prepared to plant a rose bush sent to them by Elsie Gill. He was carrying a spade in one hand and the bush in the other when he tripped over and bruised his face. Millicent 'fixed it up as well as I could with my make-up but it still showed. However, he said the Bishop gave him a wonderful smile, and all was well.' The pair took on new baptismal names: Archie took on 'Francis' after St Francis of Assisi, the loving and gentle saint who had always inspired him, and Millicent took the name 'John', after her adored Pope John XXIII.[860] Sellar vividly remembers re-meeting James – he had met him on several previous occasions:

> James once described me as, "My parents' kind of priest," and I doubt that this was a compliment... I was wanting to make sense of the struggles and questions of ordinary people as I had experienced them, particularly in the slums of Glasgow and the East End of London. I felt that Jum never understood my questions. On one occasion he told me, "You need to get your hands into the shit, right up to the armpits." He didn't know that as prison chaplain and in several other settings, his wish that I would work in the muck, right up to the armpits, would come about. Perhaps at this time he was struggling with the question of how he would do this. Would he set up a drug rehabilitation place in Auckland; would he become something of a recluse at Jerusalem with his followers seeking his guidance; how could he best become a prophet, alerting the young to the traps of modern living?[861] [862]

And James would do all of these things.

After his parents' baptisms, James returned to Wellington, back to being a postie. The most important poems from the period formed Pig Island Letters,[863] written in September and October 1963 and published in 1966 by Oxford University Press.[864] It was widely acclaimed and James felt he would never write as well again.[865] Finally he tired of 'pounding the Wellington streets on a postman's round' and applied for and gained the 1966 Robert Burns Fellowship in Creative Writing at his alma mater, the University of Otago in Dunedin. It was a victorious homecoming for the man who had left twenty years before as failed academic and a notorious young drunk. He was now a (slightly more) responsible adult with a wife and two children, a dried-out alcoholic, a Catholic and a poet recognised to be one of the greatest in the land. The prodigal son had returned.

Plaque to James K. Baxter, in The Writers' Walk in the Octagon in Dunedin - alongside other luminaries such as Janet Frame and his drinking mate Denis Glover
(taken by Torsten Sohrmann in 2015)

His family in Brighton was delighted. Jacquie got on well with her in-laws and Hilary and John now had grandparents down the road in Brighton and cousins to play with at weekends. They moved into a university house in Dunedin's Cumberland Street. James's output of poems was prodigious and the university happily agreed to his request to extend his Burns Fellowship for a further year. He continued his protests against war in Vietnam, and the homosexuality laws. He was a powerful and popular speaker, and his pacifist family connections added clout to his quietly impassioned, though often bawdy, pleas at the microphone, frequently placed at the base of the Robbie Burns statue in the Octagon. He always had a desire to shock, but it was usually mixed with a serious message, frequently about a hatred of war.

In early 1968, the Burns Fellowship had ceased and the Catholic Education Office offered him a position to teach English to upper forms in Catholic schools and to write some articles in The Tablet. His office was a dim and cold room in the basement of the Moran Building in the Octagon, and it was here he became great friends with Frances Mulrennan and Shirley McLeod. Frances worked with Mary Hussey in the Catholic Centre Library upstairs and Shirley ran the Catholic Centre Shop at street level. There was a chapel there with a daily midday Mass and James would often meet with the three women. Shirley remembers his unquenchable ability to talk: 'I used to go and have coffee with him when I had an assistant and you literally couldn't get a word in. I didn't want to, but I don't think he was even aware of a reaction. He just had to have a face to talk to. And he was absolutely – so was Mrs Baxter – a compulsive talker.' Many people attest to this. James was known to talk incessantly when he would stay the night at a friend's house then wake up in the morning and immediately continue with the same conversation.[866]

Once she had become a Catholic, Millicent also became a regular visitor to the Catholic Library, usually every Monday, and also befriended Shirley and Frances. She loved biographies on a wide variety of people including members of the British royal family and Oscar Wilde. Frances says that 'If she'd been reading for instance a biography of Queen Caroline, you'd get it from go to whoa…I would just sit there mesmerised by enchantment of the sheer weight of words and detail. She spoke very clearly and also with great clarity about it. She said what she wanted to say and her voice was very agreeable, that crisp clear voice. But she talked, she was relentless! It seems that Millicent's flow of words never really let up, and if someone were around to listen she, like James, would simply talk of what she was thinking about at the time. And of course Millicent would meet James at the Catholic Centre; Shirley would make them from the Zip water heater in the sacristy and these two insatiable raconteurs would sit over coffee and the talking 'contest' would begin. Nonetheless, if the argument got too passionate, it would eventually be James who would defer to his mother. But although Millicent had this ability to daunt people with her 'cool, blue stare' she was never antagonistic. Shirley adds 'I think Mrs Baxter was too self-confident to be assertive; it's insecurity that makes people assertive or aggressive.' Shirley also remembers going to see James and Jacquie at the house they rented in Highgate, 'and Janet Frame was there and they were sitting on a couch, and Janet Frame with her aureole of hair and just smiling, not saying anything. But I was aware of who she was.'[867]

By1968 Archie was suffering from angina and very poor circulation. He was now eighty-seven. He had such frequent angina attacks they would carry brandy around with them as medication.[868] He was considerably involved in the re-publication of 'We will not cease' that year by Caxton Press, and it received very good reviews. Archie had written a foreword for this edition and it is clear that his anti-war feelings hadn't diminished one jot. His commentary is no longer restricted to the First World War and reads as a text very pertinent to today:

> This book contains the record of my fight to the utmost against the power of the military machine during the First World War. At that time to be a pacifist was to be in a distinct minority. But today– as war, which was always atrocious, becomes more obviously atrocious and anti-human– to be a pacifist is to be spokesman even of a confused majority who have begun to see that, whatever, the national issue may be, all wars are deeply atrocious and no war can be called just. Though methods of warfare have changed, the military machine remains essentially the same; and the record of my battle against that machine, on behalf of my fellow-humans, is therefore relevant to this time also.
>
> A greater barbarism than any the human race had known in the past has risen among the nations. In the First World War

multitudes of conscript soldiers were buried alive in the mud of France. Villages were also annihilated. But the greatest numbers of casualties were among the conscript troops. In the Second World War the wholesale slaughter of civilians, by high explosives, by firebombing, and finally by atomic weapons, became a matter of course. Reports from the present Vietnam War indicate that eighty per cent of the casualties are occurring among civilians. War has at last become wholly indiscriminate… We make war chiefly on civilians and respect for human life seems to have become a thing of the past. To accept this situation would be to accept the devil's philosophy… Though methods of warfare have changed, the military machine remains essentially the same; and the record of my own battle against that machine, on behalf of my fellow-humans, is therefore relevant to this time also…

I [do not] have any feeling of hostility towards the officers whose duty it was to do me harm. They, unlike the soldiers, had become part of the military machine, and had submerged themselves in it; and it was the military machine I was opposing, not them as persons.

This remarkable man could still look back on the brutality inflicted on him and show not an iota of animosity against anyone except the perpetrators of war. Remembering that Stanford University experiment and the observation that war has the capacity to change a normally good, honest man into a one capable of gross inhumanity, it is extraordinary how Archie could perceive that and see those individuals who treated him inhumanely as victims rather than perpetrators and able to forgive them. He must have been a deep, rational and intelligent thinker to do that.

Archie and Millicent derived great enjoyment from having James and the family nearby for the three years they were down from the North Island. Archie still gardened, looked after the chickens and grew a profusion of vegetables. He had also developed an interest in geology; the age of rocks and their identification fascinated him. [869] He tended the flower garden and a small vegetable patch up to his final days. In the last years of his life he was unable to go to Mass, arthritis made walking too difficult and he couldn't kneel. A priest brought Holy Communion to Archie every now and then, and that meant a great deal to him.[870]

The divorce between Terence and Lenore upset Archie very much, but Millicent felt they were much happier apart. Despite her Catholicism, she writes with a modern conviction: 'Divorce is regrettable, but there are so many unfortunate domestic experiences. Very often, I believe, these come about because the partners have married too young. But, of course, as young marriages have their dangers, older ones have the problems of childbirth and of adjusting to each other after a different, independent life. The essential thing is to have a flexible mind.'[871]

James and Jacquie had been getting on very well in the years they had been in Dunedin. They had never been so comfortably off, and being back in his home territory James was able to write more poetry based on places that were integral to his early life. Although they were experiencing the usual trials of having adolescent children, life with a secure income was a welcome change. Nevertheless, James felt ensnared in marriage and domesticity. Our diarist Pat Lawlor visited him in Dunedin in February 1968 and wrote in the diary:

> Emotional strain, overwork and sex obsession (mind only) have drawn that almost beautiful face of his into tragic lines; the eyes huge, with queer yellowing at the corners; long wiry hair standing upright; still the bent, lumbering walk. Over two cups of coffee we talked for an hour and I discovered two Baxters, warning them that they had to meet and not be kept apart. Jim is the most discussed man in religious and literary circles today. Too many young people (and young priests) think he is almost a god. Every article he writes for the Tablet, such being the fruits of his religious and emotional upheavals, pours from his pen in a clear and uncanny light.[872]

James at Jerusalem - early 1970s

Despite his success and fame, James was exhausted and feeling himself to be a failure as a husband, and was fast losing touch with his seventeen and nineteen-year-old children. He wanted to practice what he preached in his poetry and began to mix with young people, particularly drifters who were losing their way in life. He would spend hours with them in a wine shop on the corner of Great King Street and Howe Street, sharing their problems and helping them when they had the shakes or the DTs.[873] But his personal life was worsening again. The contract with the Catholic Education Office was nearing its end and there was no job on the horizon to replace it. About the end of March 1968, having prayed to God for a solution to his difficulties, he woke the next morning to what he called a vision – a voice or some other sort of spiritual communication – calling him to Jerusalem on the Wanganui River, and he resolved to follow that calling. He delayed his departure from Dunedin because Hilary was pregnant. In September, aged twenty, she had her baby and called her Stephanie.[874] James felt that going to Jerusalem might solve his marital problems, that a temporary break from Jacquie might finally lead to reconciliation. McKay quotes him as saying 'To stay with the present pattern would mean we would gradually rot apart and not be joined again… she who is likely to be taken from me by the process of life on the Pakeha side of the fence will be restored to me on the Maori side… James K. Baxter must die. He has served his purpose; but this no longer seems to be God's purpose.'[875] So at the end of the year or very early in 1969, James departed from his wife, two children and granddaughter for the next and final stage of his life.

James reached Jerusalem, or Hiruharama, in February 1969, as Hemi – the Māori version of his name, having taken off his shoes and socks and walked barefoot the hundred and twenty kilometre journey from Wanganui. He established himself in the Nuns' Cottage belonging to the Sisters of Compassion, the only home-grown Catholic order in New Zealand. [876] His only company was the bespectacled stare of the founder Sister Suzanne Aubert from her portrait on the kitchen wall. He now dressed in his new and often filthy garb of long hair and beard, bare feet and a worn-out suit – appearing like a cross between Jesus and Fagin. When Millicent asked him why he dressed as he did when he had perfectly good clothes in the wardrobe in Wellington to wear, he replied that if he had short hair and neat suit he would appear as a do-gooder and be of no use at all: 'I have to be like the people I'm working with.' Millicent saw the sense in his answer. 'Trying to work from above people is no use whatever.'[877] It did try her patience when he gave away a coat that she gave him: 'she felt this was a bit much, that she'd saved up and got a nice coat for him and then he gave it away straight away!'[878]

With the help of local Māori at the pā, the reluctant assistance of the mission Sisters and an elderly resident pastor, Father Te Awhitu, the commune grew. It was aimed at what James called 'nga raukore': the abandoned, the disillusioned, the castoffs, 'the trees who have had their leaves and branches stripped away,'[879] but Tim Shadbolt described it less romantically: 'It wasn't a commune. It was simply a rural crashpad, a place where anyone could stay when the city smashed their souls and their brains.'[880] James's poetic inspiration continued to flourish and he during that year he published his famous Jerusalem Sonnets: Poems for Colin Durning,[881] along with Jerusalem Day Book,[882] now recognised to be some of his finest poetry.

There has been criticism that James deserted his family during the years he spent in Jerusalem, that he only thought about himself and the commune. This is not true; he maintained contact with the family as much as he felt he could and visited them often. The contact with Millicent and Archie during the years he spent in Jerusalem was through a regular flow of letters. In August 1970, James heard that Archie was very ill and dying, so he left Jerusalem and went straight to Dunedin's Mater Hospital. The previous month, Archie's health had deteriorated considerably. Before his eyes began to fail, he spent a lot of time reading his book We will not cease. 'I don't know why', says Millicent, 'I thought it wasn't good for him but didn't speak of it, and he never did.' Millicent believes he contracted influenza. A fortnight later he deteriorated and was admitted to the Mater Hospital. While Millicent was out of the room getting ready to go with him, Archie said to his nephew's wife, Marguerite, who had come to help 'There's something I want to tell you. I am tremendously fond of my wife.'[883] Archie's great-nephew Barry Baxter was a full-time ambulance officer in Dunedin at the time and remembers very well taking Archie to hospital: 'Archie was not to be carried and proceeded to walk to the ambulance with Millicent taking his arm... he said he would walk, and walk he did – with dignity. He was a strong and gentle man and it was a privilege to assist.[884]

Archie Baxter c 1960s
(By kind permission of Diane Dore)

Eventually the doctor telephoned Millicent to say Archie had pneumonia and should have the Last Rites. James arrived the next day. For the final two nights he and his mother stayed in the hospital, taking it in turns to sit up with Archie. Terence maintains that his father who lived for peace didn't die in a peaceful way: 'Every now and again his eyes would start stirring and he would start watching this thing out ahead of him and trying to fight the thing off, whatever it was, something completely out of this world. I don't believe in devils, but it was something like a devil... he was not exactly terrified of it, but in a fighting mood to try to see the thing away...'[885]

On the last night, he had been given morphia and seemed quiet and asleep, and the nurses persuaded Millicent to go to bed. At six the next morning, on Monday 10 August, Millicent was told that Archie had died ten minutes earlier, never having recovered consciousness. He was not far off eighty-nine. Millicent writes 'I had prayed that he would go first because he had become dependent on me, and the thought of leaving him alone in the world was horrible. Well, my prayer was answered.'[886]

Both sons of course were very supportive and in the midst of his own grief, James organised the funeral, had his mother buy cards for replies to condolences and informed everyone of the death of this much-loved and well-known man. At the Requiem Mass in St Mary's Church, Kaikorai, Dunedin, he read the lesson 'in his beautiful voice', and Father Sellar gave the eulogy.[887] Sellar remembers particularly making a point of speaking about Archie's conscientious objection because it was so central to his life and to Millicent: 'I had made a very strong link between Archie's deep conviction about the value of life and of people, and how this was lived out in his pacifist convictions, even to the point of experiencing Field Punishment No.1. To me this connection was profoundly significant...'[888]

There was a large gathering of family and friends at the graveside in Green Island Cemetery.[889]

Millicent's silence over Archie's death speaks volumes. What she does record is that she didn't grieve for Archie in the usual way. By that she probably means that she didn't cry – that wasn't Millicent's way. She adds 'I felt him in me, and was always able to speak to him in my mind. Also I knew I hadn't much longer to live, and would join him.'[890] She actually had another sixteen years before she got her wish to be with Archie. She does talk about her marriage, and marriage generally; she even starts her memoirs with the words, 'When I was ninety someone asked me what I would do if I were sixty years younger and I said at once, "I'd marry my husband again."'…In this book I should like to show that it is possible to have an ideal marriage.' She says she would have married earlier if she had met someone who attracted her enough but then she would never have known Archie and may never have known what a blissful marriage was like.[891] Later in the book she says:

> I think one of the most necessary ingredients of a happy marriage is to share the same sense of humour. Private jokes, known only to husband and wife, ridiculous nicknames, absurd situations – though they sound trivial – do make for a lasting unity of spirit. And that is one of the things one misses when one's partner dies. One doesn't find it again on earth. I believe also that monogamy is essential for the perfect marriage. If it's a good marriage, money – everything – is shared, perfectly naturally.[892]

In one of her interviews with Christine Cole Catley she goes into more detail:

> In a perfect marriage, one is a friend as well as a lover. Archie and I were absolutely attuned despite the differences in our background. If I had met Archie when I was in my 20s I wouldn't have married because I was too solidly imbedded in convention. I don't think it would have been possible for me to have moved out of my academic life. There is a tide and a time. I agree that it is quite a good thing to live together to see if you really are compatible and very often you are not. Although I am a Catholic and some Catholics wouldn't approve, I do feel it isn't a sin to try to discover whether you are the right people.[893]

Millicent arranged for a headstone for Archie's grave. To make it fit, the stonemason had to abbreviate Archie's name, Archibald McColl Learmond Baxter, to Archibald McC.L. Baxter, but Millicent specifically asked for R.I.P. to be inscribed in full, 'Requiescat in Pace': 'I spelt it carefully for him. He didn't know any Latin and pronounced pace to rhyme with race. But then, rather extraordinary, I found that he had put Requiescant, the plural, so that it will do for both of us. When I told Jim he called it a good mistake.'[894] And she had her wish; when she died, she was buried next to her beloved husband sharing a joint headstone.[895] [896]

After the funeral James returned to Jerusalem. He decided to allow the press to visit and the effect was instantaneous: the tiny village was flooded with young hippies, some genuine who would stay on, but a host of sticky-beakers came to see the show at weekends and university holidays.[897] The little commune overflowed and a couple of derelict cottages were rescued from the blackberries and christened 'Bag's End' and 'Top House.' There are differences in opinion on how many women James slept with and how many, if any, children, if any, he fathered. Weighing up the various opinions, the answer seems likely to be 'some' in both cases. Millicent wryly gives her opinion: 'I knew that plenty of people looked on him as a dreadful character; once someone said that the young people in his community at Jerusalem were all his illegitimate children, though how he could have had so many I don't know.'[898] Certainly love in its highest sense was at the core of the commune. No-one was turned away. The greater someone's need: the more they were welcomed.

But the commune completely lacked order and its first phase ended in September 1971. James returned to Wellington to be closer to his family. Nevertheless, his heart was in Jerusalem and in February 1972 he returned to a smaller, more cohesive group. He continued to write poetry there and his last collection of poems, Autumn Testament,[899] was published that year. He constantly questioned life's values and wondered who had suffered most; he for his failures or his father for his convictions: 'Father, is it easier to fight / The military machine, or the maggots of one's own heart.'[900]

In July he went to Dunedin to take part with his poetry in Impulse '72 and in the Town Hall he looked like a prophet as he stood on the stage in front of nearly 5000 people.[901] He stayed with Millicent who reminisces in her book: 'He seemed to be in excellent health and to have gained a serenity and a very spiritual outlook on life…He was so gentle and serene, filled with peace and love and compassion for everyone, even for the policemen who had behaved badly to people he loved.'[902] Perhaps James had arrived at a state of psychological independence, that he had at last reached the point where he believed he was OK and no longer at the mercy of his mother's and everyone else's judgement.

But Millicent was wrong about James's health. In the next three months he grew thin and friends felt the life had gone out of him. He realised he could no longer look after the community. His poor diet over the years, his personal torments, his endless travel around the country and, above all, the dozens of people who demanded his physical and mental resources had squeezed him dry.[903] He went to Auckland and based himself in a commune in Mount Eden, visiting a retired psychiatrist every day for several weeks over an obsession with his relationship with Millicent, feeling that she hadn't loved him enough.[904] Thankfully McKay's book telling us that was not published until six years after Millicent's death; she would have been distraught to have learned that. James's son John also believes that his father had lost his faith.[905] [906] Oliver maintains '[James] felt betrayed, at least at times... he felt acute discouragement; once he said he had given everything and received nothing back. He made demands, sometimes imperiously, upon the generosity and patience of his friends, and both gave and took offence. But that was nothing new; he had always been a bit of a nuisance.'[907]

On 16 October, James stayed for three days in Puhoi, forty-eight kilometres north of Auckland, with his friends Michael and Dene Illingworth. During that time he wrote in large, clear printing on one of their walls what is probably the last poem he ever wrote, 'A Pair of Sandals':

> A pair of sandals, old black pants
> And leather coat – I must go, my friends,
> Into the dark, the cold, the first beginning
> Where the ribs of the ancestor are the rafters
> Of a meeting house – windows broken
> And the floor white with bird dung – in there
> The ghosts gather who will instruct me
> And when the river fog rises Te ra rite tonu te Atua –
> The sun who is like the Lord
> Will warm my bones, and his arrows
> Will pierce to the centre of the shapeless clay of the mind.
>
> Hemi.

Paul Millar maintains that the poem is much more than a simple leave taking, 'Baxter, the empty meeting house, has been gutted by his commune's failure. Spiritually and emotionally he has become a hollow man, an empty meeting house.'[908]

On Friday, the night 20 October, he took a journey he had made often to Paremoremo prison to talk with his friends, the inmates. On the Sunday he complained of stomach and chest pains but told the doctor in Glenfield Road that he was too busy to have the recommended full check-up. He then had a violent heart attack outside but managed to stagger across the road and knock on the door of the house at No 544.[909] Vonney and Bruce Allan let in this wild, ragged man; he looked familiar. James, true to style, talked and talked to these complete strangers about his day then, more falteringly with deepening regret, about his wife and children and the sadness at being apart from them, and his intentions to go to Wellington soon. He ceased talking only when the pain in his chest and arms got too severe.[910] He died in a house of strangers on the night of Sunday 22 October 1972, aged forty-six.

When Terence came to tell Millicent that James had died the night before it must have been a huge shock, having seen James just three months before, healthy and seemingly happy. But while we have no idea of her inner reaction, externally Millicent appears to be remarkably accepting of her youngest son dying so prematurely in advance of herself: 'I believe Jim died when his time had come. When I learned of his death I was able to accept it. I was filled with his serenity, and was serene too.'[911]

The news sped around the country. 'No death I have ever known has so swept a country in a huge wave of grief', wrote playwright Bruce Mason,[912] such was James K. Baxter's fame – or infamy. Millicent flew up to Wellington with Terence, and Kellar Fowler, the son of Archie's sister Maggie, drove them to Wanganui and Jerusalem. Jacquie flew with Hilary and John and met James's great friend Colin Durning at Auckland airport, and they all drove together in a van with the body to Jerusalem, getting lost on the way in the mists from the Wanganui River.[913] By the time they arrived at Jerusalem a crowd of 800 had gathered. The full Māori tangi, a rare honour for a Pākehā, was arranged by the elders of Ngāti Hau, the commune members, and James's old friend, Father Te Awhitu, the first Catholic Maori priest. People came from all over the country: friends and followers of his poetry both Māori and Pākehā. They came on foot, by bicycle, in old bangers, in large cars along that gravel road from Wanganui to Jerusalem, the road that James had journeyed so often. They came from all over the country, a cross-section of New Zealand: 'poets, novelists, clergymen, nuns, social workers, academics, civil servants, activists, old friends and new... came to pay their last respects to Hemi... Bare feet and high heels sank into the sodden turf.'[914]

Terence, Millicent, John and Jacquie Baxter at James's funeral 1972

The service was held at a makeshift altar facing the lower marae. In the afternoon, a flurry of priests led the huge ragged procession of people behind the coffin. With several changes of pallbearers, Terence among them, it was carried up the steep hill that overlooked the marae and was lowered into the ground close to Top House, the centre of James's community. People climbed trees for a view over the masses of heads around the gravesite. Music was played, laments sung and a haka was performed – releasing a huge torrent of emotion. The myriad of photographs taken by the press show the emotional strain of the faces of the family trudging up the steep hill behind the coffin. Katherine Baxter, twenty-one at the time, well remembers her grandmother at the funeral:

At some point in the proceedings, it was my job to hold her arm as we trooped up the hill to the graveside...And all these young women kept coming up and, because they all knew that she was Jum's mother, they were kissing her on the cheek.

And I remember her saying to me, when somebody gave her a particularly affectionate embrace…"Oh goodness me. Am I supposed to know her?" She got more and more English, the more they did it. She said, "Do I know that young woman?" And then it carried on and, in order to keep her own end up, she was making remote jokes and she was saying things like, "Oh goodness, all this trouble. They've come up all this way up the river, and to bring the hearse up the river. What a lot of trouble! What if I just die now, and then you can use the same hearse to take me back again." It was her way of inserting a little bit of herself into some proceedings.[915]

It was also, no doubt, a method of concealing her real emotions.

One photograph shows Terence, Jacquie, Millicent, John and Hilary, by the graveside, their heads bowed. Terence's receding hair contrasts with John's long curly hair, parted in the middle, flowing down his shoulders. John towers over his diminutive grandmother as he puts his arm around her. Millicent has her big black hat pulled down over the top of her sad old resolute face. She has a plaster showing beneath her sensible stockings,

Millicent, John and Jacquie Baxter at James's funeral

and she grasps that huge handbag and I wouldn't be surprised if Archie's letter was still inside. It's raining and someone, probably John, has draped a waterproof jacket around her shoulders. She was eighty-four.

Millicent writes that 'Jacquie sat, hour after hour, by the open coffin, receiving hundreds who came, and being embraced. It was a very trying ordeal for her. All around me people were sobbing... It was moving to see the hundreds of young people, Pākehā and Māori, showing their grief for the loss of a friend.' Then she adds, as though she has astonished herself, 'and I found myself weeping too.[916] When writing and speaking about the funeral of her own son, Millicent gives us a rare look at her emotions. In her interview with Bruce Harding she admits that she was 'so upset by the vast numbers of young people weeping – it was a terrible experience. I don't cry but it was just a physical thing coming up like that, all those people Māori and white, it was a terrific testimony, just hundreds and hundreds.'[917]

A year later a boulder from the Wanganui River inscribed Hemi / James Keir

Baxter / i whanau 1926 / i mate 1972 was placed on the grave which was unveiled by his little five year-old granddaughter Stephanie. James had offered an alternative inscription: 'He was too much trouble by his own absurdity.'[918] This charismatic man who loved to shock, who stage-managed his life and who disarmed everyone by admitting all his faults had constantly mythologised his life. He mythologised his mother into a tyrannising figure and his father into a man of perfection. During his life he had suffered ceaseless guilt, assuaged by many visits to the confessional only to commit the same sins the next day or week. His renunciations alcohol and sex ran much the same course. Religion became a passion then an anguishing compulsion to help the helpless. His other obsession was a desire to be noticed. James was brilliant, charming, warm and compassionate with many conflicting personas. Now, perhaps he has found peace.

After James's death the Jerusalem commune continued until its closure in late 1975. Under Greg Chalmers' steady leadership, the bi-cultural life between Pākehā and the Pā improved and led towards something closer to James's dream of a regenerative partnership between the two. Today the average residential population of the Jerusalem village is about thirty. The grave is rarely visited now; only the few determined seekers push their way up an overgrown pathway past the house James once lived in to the white-painted headstone. There is an air of abandonment strangely unfitting for a man whose name was once on the lips of most of the population of New Zealand. But unlike his grave, this selfish, selfless, defiant man is not forgotten. He was a teenage prodigy who burst onto the poetry scene in the mid-1940s and would remain in the spotlight until his death. He remains an iconic figure as New Zealand's home-grown, counter-culture champion, a reputation that has not lessened very much at all since his death. His poetry is still studied in schools and universities, and to many he remains the definitive New Zealand poet. Jacquie would tell a journalist for the Listener 'When you study Baxter you realise how many technical skills the man had. The best of Baxter is the best we have had. It wasn't all ideas in the night. There was a lot of hard slog.'[919]

One of James's greatest friends, Father John Weir, vowed on the day of James's funeral – he was supposed to deliver the panygeric that day but was too traumatised by James's death he couldn't do it – that he would one day publish both his poems and his prose. He managed the former in 1980, but the prose had to wait forty-two years until August 2015. Weir says that there are over 700 items, many of which could have been books in their own right. 'when he's writing at his strongest, I am not aware of any writer in the English language in the past 100 years who has written plain English with his power.[920]

But I give his mother the last word – many words of course – on her son: 'I don't consider that Jim was eccentric... He was always doing things I wished he wouldn't do, but I do believe he was led by overwhelming compassion, that feeling which overwhelmed other considerations, and was stronger than anything. I think that, as with Archie, it was the strongest element in his character.'[921] Surprisingly, in many ways she approved of the commune at Jerusalem: 'He became a sort of cult.

They even preserve his shirts. I don't believe in relics. I had a shirt of his which was given to him by an abbot up in the North Island and it is now wrapped round the pipes to prevent them from freezing... But Jerusalem didn't continue. It's faded out now. It was a pity. In spite of Jim's desire that it shouldn't have a leader, it had to have a leader, there is no question about that.'[922]

And lastly in that interview with Bruce Harding:

> James did a great deal for prisoners and it used to exhaust him utterly and he looked upon the prisoners as his friends; I think it was marvellous. He was a marvellous man really... He loved his father greatly, and he always loved him, and me he loved no doubt, but I thought it was hard that although I am a shocking housekeeper; housekeeping is nothing to me; I don't housekeep, I simply don't, and I'm not now but I was an excellent cook, and he doesn't mention it! Which is very unfair.[923]

And she was still wild about those blowflies.

CHAPTER 12
I am Myself

Millicent Baxter was a resilient woman. Two years before, she had lost her husband and now, her youngest son. As with Archie's death, Millicent sought and found much to sustain her after James's death: 'I knew Jim had been serene when he died. When I needed to, I spoke to him in my mind. A schoolboy wrote to me about Jim: "I am sorry for you but I am more sorry for many young people who have lost a stay in their life," and I wrote back saying "You are quite right, they need sympathy much more than I do."'[924] When Archie died in 1970, Millicent decided the Brighton house and garden were too large, and James arranged for an old school friend, Alan Coutts, to buy the house. Millicent moved into a small single-storey house at 10 Kinsman Street in the Kaikorai Valley, Dunedin. It was a very modest house in a modest street. This woman, who once lived in a very large house with servants, was always filled with humility. She tells us little about the house, just an abrupt 'Since 1970, when Archie died, I have lived alone in this house. The spouting needed renewal, but Terence fixed that.'[925] It was a radical change for her being separated from Archie and James, who had taken up so much of her head and heart and energy. As Max Broadbent says, 'It cannot have been easy being married to a secular saint and watching her son grow into our greatest lyric poet, with a taste for life as a mendicant guru. They both cast long shadows. They were mesmeric in New Zealand society and must have been "irresistible up-close and personal" to Millicent as the wife of one and the mother of the other.'[926]

In the last ten years of Archie's life he and Millicent had seen great social changes in New Zealand: capital punishment was abolished, troops were sent to Malaysia and later to Vietnam, the New Zealand Māori Council was established, the labour force reached one million, decimal currency was introduced and the National Government was elected four times in a row. The New Zealand Rugby Union refused to send a whites-only team to South Africa and the voting age was reduced to twenty. New Zealand was beginning to sever the strong cultural and economic ties with Britain. The Vietnam War generated questions about foreign policy links with the United States, and nuclear testing in the Pacific by France prompted anti-nuclear protests. During that decade, and until she died, Millicent wrote feverishly to the editor of the Otago Daily Times about a wide variety of local and international issues that were angering her such as the hydrogen bomb tests in the Marshall Islands in 1954,[927] the bid to raise the level of Fiordland's

Lake Manapouri to provide hydro-electricity for an aluminium smelter[928] and the British Government's condoning of torture of Irish prisoners in 1972.[929] If she had lived another year, she would have been aghast at the bombing by French government agents of the Greenpeace ship, Rainbow Warrior, in Auckland harbour; the ship was due to lead a fleet of vessels to Mururoa Atoll to protest against French nuclear testing in the South Pacific. But she would have delighted that the Labour Government under David Lange's leadership decided that New Zealand should be nuclear-free and focus its armed forces towards international peacekeeping and regional security. She would have been delighted twenty years later when Prime Minister Helen Clark declared 'We can take pride... in being nuclear free and in having the strength and independence not to send our young people off to fight in unjust wars.'[930]

A year after Archie died, Millicent aged eighty-three made what proved to be her last trip to Europe, this time by plane. She stayed with Viola whom she hadn't seen for nineteen years. The two sisters had always been close and had corresponded every week since Viola had left New Zealand in 1936 to marry Angelo. Millicent told her grandson Kenneth that going through modern airports was all new to her, so ever the pragmatist, if she heard a Kiwi accent she would tap these people on the shoulder and say 'can I go through after you and just keep an eye and make sure I do things right?'[931] The two sisters spent a month together touring Italy before returning to London. A fortnight later Millicent was off again, this time flying to Dusseldorf then on to Paris where she stayed on her own, using the German and French she had learned seventy years before. She had always had a great respect for Oscar Wilde so she visited the cemetery of Père Lachaise to see his grave. Back in England, she spent a day in Colchester with James's old friend Noel Ginn and finally returned to New Zealand before Christmas.[932]

Millicent and friend in Europe 1973.
(By kind permission of Antonietta Baldacchino)

With the support of Terence and good friends, she kept up her interests with the Canterbury Alpine Garden Society and particularly the Naturalists' Field Club, continuing to take the annual trips in the South Island. She celebrated her ninety-third birthday, on 8 January 1983, on a nine-day camp with the club.[933] Her everyday life in Dunedin without Archie began to take on a routine. Terence would visit at least once a week. Books and reading remained a passion all her life and she was in the library at Moray Place two or three times a week, always returning home with several books. Mary Ronnie, city librarian at the Dunedin Public Library at the time[934] remembers her going there frequently from the days after the war through to the 1980s:

> We loved it when people came from out of town, and being a non-resident they had to pay to come, so they all wanted books so badly; they were coming in for a real purpose. We were sort of awestruck by Millicent Baxter. She was so highly intelligent; she knew exactly what she wanted. She always wanted something of real merit, never a romance or anything. She was looking for a series of things that she knew about. We knew her first of all as the daughter of Macmillan Brown who was famous throughout the country as a prominent academic and, secondly, as Archibald Baxter's wife and we knew of him with great respect... She would always be formally dressed as people were in those days when they ventured into town.[935]

And yes – every Friday, dressed in matching dress, coat and gloves, Millicent would go into town by taxi to the very elegant Savoy Hotel in Princes Street for a morning or afternoon tea of cucumber sandwiches and cake from exquisite cake-stands. The image conjures up a scene from a Hollywood movie. This is where she would entertain her relatives or friends throughout her time at Kinsman Street.[936] There is no doubt about the influence she had on people. The well-known businessman, Howard Paterson, is one example. Millicent was able to cope living alone – no doubt ignoring the books and papers and blowflies – but she did occasionally have help to tame the overgrown garden. Two young Dunedin students, Richard Hatherly and Howard Paterson, both aged about eighteen, looked after Millicent's garden in the early 1970s before James died. It seems she took a shine particularly to Howard. Richard Hatherly recalls:

> Howard Paterson and I, while running a gardening service in the university holidays in 1971–72, received a letter from Mrs Baxter of Brighton, asking that we cut her knee-high lawns and take away her collection of rubbish. We drove to her house, a modest and old-fashioned worker's cottage on the inland side of the road, where a delightful old lady, Millicent as it transpired, gave us a cup of tea and a scone, a good talking to about her inability to provoke any meaningful work from her son James who was up the Whanganui River, and the contract. Howard was an enormously productive worker, went like a madman, but on this and subsequent site visits, I would do most of the work as Howard and Millicent sat and talked over tea brewed on her coal range, provoking the 18-year-old Howard into realms of

thought he would have been unlikely to have cause to consider in the normal course of his day.

While Millicent was very interested in this extraordinary young man, Howard was fascinated by Millicent and what she had to say, and she imbued in him a great interest, among other things, in religion in general and Catholicism in particular and the associated philosophies. While the work was limited by her somewhat impecunious circumstances, they continued to maintain her property and an unlikely but very real and sincere friendship evolved, which continued until Millicent's passing. Subsequently, as a direct result of their association and friendship, Howard studied gained a BA from the University of Otago, with a double major in Phenomenology of Religion and Philosophy (Ethics).

There is no doubt that Millicent Baxter's friendship with Howard shaped the direction of his subsequent studies and influenced the way he lived his life and the manner in which he conducted his business affairs.[937] Howard Paterson became a prominent South Island businessman and was considered to be one of the wealthiest.[938]

In May 1972, Millicent went up to Wellington and stayed with her now ex-daughter-in-law, Lenore Baxter. She took the opportunity to visit the Defence Department, where she was able to see sections of Archie's file. According to her memoirs, these were records which had had all references to Archie's punishments removed for fear his famous poet, pacifist and counter-culture son James used them in a campaign against compulsory military training in the 1960s.[939] [940] She discovered many mistakes in the thirty-one sheets closely written on both sides, but it was the report from the Boulogne hospital that gave her the greatest shock, 'The New Zealand military authorities were pressing to have Archie back. They were going to try him for desertion in face of the enemy, and for that the sentence would be death'[941] If this is correct, then it is probably true that the Medical Board who declared Archie 'insane' did so to save his life.[942]

Like her husband, Millicent displays no bitterness towards Archie's persecutors, only impatience with some seemingly genuine mistakes in the records. Shirley McLeod and Frances Mulrennan speak about how Millicent was greatly affected by the visit: 'I remember she came into the [Catholic] shop and, for once, she betrayed some real emotion. She was very upset and cried. She had great trouble getting to the records. She wanted to see what had happened and how it was recorded. She succeeded in the end and I think it distressed her greatly because it was so unjust.' Frances adds 'She had this weight of hating the people who'd done those things to Archie, she said it was on her like a weight. And she said she used to ask God to take it away from her because it was so terrible to live with, that weight… And, she said to me one day in Mass, it was simply taken from her because she'd asked to be relieved, that she'd prayed for that.' To which Shirley comments 'Strange for such an intelligent, educated, sophisticated woman. It was almost a child-like faith wasn't it?'[943]

Something that exasperated Millicent was constantly being acknowledged as an add-on to her mother, father, husband and son. She says at the start of her memoirs, 'Before I married I was often referred to as the daughter of Professor John Macmillan Brown, one of the founding professors of Canterbury University College, or the daughter of Helen Connon, the first woman graduate with honours in the British Empire. In more recent years I have found myself known as the mother of James K. Baxter. I am myself, but I remain Mrs Archie Baxter.'[944] On a Field Club outing to the West Coast in January 1973, Millicent went to the Catholic church at Hari Hari, to ask the priest to say a Mass for Lawrence Kirwan who had just died. When she gave her name he said, 'You are no relation, I suppose, of James K Baxter?' She replied resignedly, 'I am his mother.' The whole atmosphere changed. The priest rushed out to tell the news to those of his parishioners who were still there. A car pulled up and a woman offered her a lift. When Millicent got in the woman said, 'I am privileged to give you a lift.' 'Why? asked Millicent. 'Because you are the mother of James K. Baxter.'[945] Millicent told Michael King, 'One gets rather tired of being just an appendage to a famous person instead of in one's own right.'[946]

But she had had to get used to attending functions acknowledging those more celebrated people. Later that year she was one of the celebrities at the Canterbury University Centenary celebrations, and of course she was invited as the daughter of one of the founders. The Memoirs of John Macmillan Brown was published a year later – Viola, Millicent and James had contributed introductory sections. John had been unable to complete his memoirs before he died. The highlight of the celebrations was the banquet, 'a magnificent affair which took a very long time, interspersed as it was by speeches... I was interviewed by The Press, and the photograph, about twelve had to be taken, was not too frightful. Most of them usually are.'[947] She was very well used to being captured on film or tape. One photographer who photographed her ten years later in 1983 in an attempt to include her in the acclaimed A Day in the Life of New Zealand in 1983[948] was Paul Donovan, a film professional in Dunedin. He had the idea of photographing the mother of James K Baxter ('There it goes again!' we can hear Millicent cry). He had heard a radio broadcast with her the year before which had increased his fascination for her, but he underestimated the vigour, intelligence and constant conversation of this tiny ninety-five year-old:

> I decided on the day how was I going to handle this dear little old lady. How was I going to light her in this dim little house she lived in. And I decided I wasn't going to use flash because it wouldn't give the look you were after and be too intimidating, so the focus is soft, because she was moving as she was talking. But not only that, I was in awe of her; it was me that felt intimidated...
>
> She basically initiated a lot of the conversation – and a lot of

it was too highbrow for me to be able to a) keep up with and b) engage in that level of conversation while trying to photograph her. I don't think she stopped talking, and she came out with something along the lines of, "I really don't go along with what the British did in India!" And this just came out of left field. And I was trying to take photos – all I could do was really kind of small talk, whereas this woman basically needed a fellow intellectual there to be able to have a real debate… She was delightful. As I left the house, she followed me up to the gate, and I photographed her getting something out of her letterbox and opening it. As so often happens with photography, I might spend hours in the house with her with all the lights under the sun and then you get outside to say goodbye and suddenly something spontaneous happens that makes for a beautiful photo.[949]

In that photograph she peers short-sightedly into the camera, the letter in her hand. Grey hairs sprout from her chin, clipped short with her nail scissors. She wears a summer dress and no hat!

Millicent aged 90 in her lounge at Kinsman Street, Dunedin
(Taken by Paul Donovan in 1978)

But back in 1978 Millicent was ninety, still sprightly and alert. She put this down to coming from strong stock and remaining active. She had a touch of arthritis and angina and these days she had to hibernate in the winter because the cold Dunedin winds bothered her. But come summer, she would be out and about again.[950] She still was active in the Naturalists Field Club, United Nations Association of New Zealand, Amnesty International, Catholic organisations concerned with peace and justice, Patron of Voice of Women, and still writing furiously to the newspapers. She was never really lonely. People regularly came to see her to gather information about her husband or son for a thesis, a book or an article. 'I know they're hurrying down to talk to me now, before I die. But I don't mind. I can probably give them first-hand facts they probably couldn't get from anywhere else.' She looked back on times when she was young and said 'Life for the middle-classes was lovely when I was a girl. We were all content with our own personal lot and didn't seem aware or worried about too many other people.'[951] How her life changed so absolutely once she met Archie.

At the urging of Frances Mulrennan and Mary Hussey, Millicent started writing her own memoirs in the late 1970s. In fact she dedicated her book to these two women. Frances says the memoirs were written quickly, 'she had a job to do and she resolutely did it – with characteristic diligence.' [952] She would go to the Dunedin Library with sheaves of notes, and every Monday she'd go to the Catholic library. One day Mary Hussey, who was shy and reserved, said when Millicent left one Monday "I almost go numb" when Millicent has had one of her talking sessions. Frances explains: 'She could be overwhelming in her beautifully articulated way. She almost didn't need you in the conversation; not that she didn't listen to you but she just didn't really need you, even as a sounding board. It was a sort of self absorption and yet the conversation wasn't about her but about the subject in hand.' [953]

On Fridays Millicent would take a break from writing with a cup of tea at the Savoy Hotel. She didn't find the writing process particularly easy:

> I am now older than my father when he was writing his memoirs, and I am up against the same thing as he was, the blurring of memory with regard to the middle years. I am aware of it – I don't think he was. The memory of one's childhood is clear-cut and correct. Later, so many things come crowding in upon one that it is difficult to place them in their correct sequence. Certain outstanding events remain forever clear, and help is needed in the correct placing of other less important events.[954]

She went on frequent drives with Michael King while he prised out of her more intimate thoughts and views than she would manage to write herself. It was Michael King who suggested that Millicent should contact Christine Cole Catley as a prospective publisher. Christine tells of one occasion when Millicent stayed with her in the Marlborough Sounds: 'I can see her now standing very tall and every sinew decisive and she said, "Dear, the book you should be [re]publishing is Archie's!" ' In those days Cole Catley Ltd was a very new and small publishing firm so when Christine hesitated, Millicent declared decisively that she would advance her the money. 'No question whether I'd like to or not!' continues Christine 'So I published Archie's book first and of course it was received very well indeed, so enough money came in very early on for me to repay Millicent and have a bit over for other books.' Christine really appreciated Millicent's sense of fun. 'I remember there were four of us sitting around this very table which I had in the Marlborough Sounds… Millicent was ninety, my husband Doug seventy, me, fifty and Marguerite Gee, Maurice's wife, was thirty. Four generations! And we had a marvellous evening!'[955] And the proof is there on the tapes – a series of whoops of laughter comes from Millicent.

Shortly after Millicent started writing her memoirs she met peace activist Jim Albertini, from Hawaii. The meeting was arranged by eighteen-year-old Cecily McNeill, who was working as a volunteer for the Catholic Church's Evangelisation, Justice and Development wing in Dunedin and was co-ordinating the programme for Jim's visit.

> It was like watching this amazing meeting of minds. He was probably in his late thirties, and she was ninety-one or something, and she totally ignored me, totally. I was like a fly on the wall. I sat on the couch and the two of them chatted away and then, after an hour or so, it was deemed to be time to close the interview – and she fixed her beady eye on me and she said, 'And you, you must come and see me.' And I was thoroughly intrigued by this, so I went. I thought, 'Gosh, what an opportunity.' I'd been totally fascinated by her, and the thing I liked about her was her consideration of ideas that came up. Her response was never automatic. It was always considered, and I just loved it. And also her knowledge of peace activities and I was quite new in this area of work, evangelisation, justice and development. And so I thought, "I've got heaps to learn from her,' and so I went to see her several times…
>
> She would sit in a chair, a bucket chair the arms of which were as high as the back, and very square. And opposite her was a pencil sketch of Archie on the wall, drawn by the notable artist and family friend, Theo Schoon. Around her on the floor were books and papers and newspapers and letters. She wasn't interested in housework. She didn't think that it rated in terms of brain-power, so she was very untidy. And the kitchen was hilarious because she had all her spices out on the kitchen table, like an acre of them, and all those little Gregg's boxes, and

Empire I think used to make those little packets of spice, and she'd have them all out on the table.[956]

Cecily started taking Millicent to Mass at Holy Name Parish Church in Great King Street, North Dunedin. After Mass, they would have breakfast at Cecily's flat in Stuart Street:

> It was a big old rambling house which was full of holes and very draughty and horrible. But she would come in, and she would have Molenberg bread toasted, and she would have 'mu-es-li' – she enunciated every syllable – 'mu-es-li.' I was a bit in awe of her. I was very careful not to say anything out of turn because she was so intense. There was no possibility of small talk. I never tried any humour with her...I have very warm feelings about her, yes. I found her very lovely.[957]

Around that time Millicent suspected she had cancer and of course she approached the whole matter in her usual rational way, 'I discovered lumps in my breasts... Hummmph – cancer at my age! So I supposed that I would die of cancer. I rather

Millicent Baxter about 1980 outside her house at Kinsman Street, Dunedin (taken by Cecily McNeill)

hoped I was going to die of heart. I told Terence and we consulted over it and the next day I went to the doctor and he said it was mastitis... I was immensely relieved, I must say. It was quite late in life to develop mastitis. I was 91. It wasn't painful, just lumpy.'[958]

Viola last visited New Zealand in 1980. The sisters spent a few weeks travelling through Lawrence, Te Anau, Milford Sound and Doubtful Sound, with Viola painting the dramatic scenery. Millicent and Viola recorded two long sessions with Radio NZ for the programme Looking Back, talking about their lives, family and beliefs. The timbre of their voices and their accents are identical. Though nearly ten years younger than her sister, Viola wasn't as well as Millicent, who at this time was 92. When they farewelled one another at Dunedin station, Millicent felt it would be the last time she would see Viola, and sadly she was right; Viola died a year later from a heart condition.[959]

In October of that year, the eighth anniversary of James' death, Millicent went to Wellington to attend the launching of her son's Collected Poems, edited by John

Weir.[960] The book is 600 pages long. 'It was a remarkable occasion', writes Millicent. 'Jacquie and her family were very good to me. She has become the daughter I never had, my friend.'[961] [962]Viola once remarked that while Millicent made friends easily, she doesn't convey this in her writing, to which Millicent comments abruptly 'Well, I am a talker, not a writer.'[963] While she was in Wellington, she worked with Christine Cole Catley 'to try to get these memoirs in order and make them as requested, less impersonal, but I do not write easily of my feelings.'[964]

Towards the end of her book Millicent reflects on Archie. 'He was free of rancour towards anyone. "They were caught up in the military machine and were not to be blamed," he said. Archie was completely compassionate. He would help anyone, any time. Jim's compassion came from him.'[965] 'We will not cease' was again published in 1980, through Cape Catley, and once more it was well received. The editor and former broadcaster Geoff Walker, who would shortly become publishing director of Penguin New Zealand, said

> For me, personally, it is one of the most important books ever published in this country. I first read it in my late teens, at a very formative stage, and it made an enormous impression on me. It had a quite definite influence on my attitudes to war and politics. As a youngster I knew deep inside that things were wrong with the world, and I'd read a lot of material from overseas, but here was a good honest New Zealander saying the kinds of things I just knew were true, and paying a real kind of penalty. It all had a huge effect on me.[966]

'Perhaps my own greatest wish' continues Millicent, 'is that Archie's voice, what it stands for, should go on being heard. People, among them Tim Shadbolt, Jim's friend, have asked about making plays and films from the book. The television producer, Tony Isaac, has said he intends making a dramatised documentary of 'We will not cease' in 1982. I hope I am around to see it.'[967] She was around in 1982, but it would be another thirty-two years before a film was made about her husband. On 9 April 2014, the first screening of Lippy Pictures television film Field Punishment No 1[968] was shown to members of parliament at the 'Beehive' in Wellington. It is a searing film and had a strong emotional effect on everyone. Archie Baxter's granddaughter, Katherine Baxter, at an interview shortly after said

> It seemed like an extraordinary thing for my grandfather to stand up in a conflict like that and say this isn't the way to solve things. It was amazingly insane, really. But now we think maybe it's not such an impossible thing after all, maybe we could get to the point where we can manage without conflict. We're not there yet, but it's not an impossible dream anymore...There's going to be a lot of World War One stories coming out soon, and

if we want to understand our history then we need to look at the full picture. There's no doubt that conflict had a huge impact on us as a nation.

For us as a family, it affected our entire lives… we know our grandfather and he was a very wise person, and almost in a Maori sense like a kaumatua in the family, and he had a very strong influence on our family culture. We admired him, and we saw him as someone who stood for his principles.[969]

The film was screened on TVNZ channel One on 22 April 2014 and it has now been screened internationally. Archie Baxter's story is beginning to be known around the world. As the producers, Donna Malane and Paula Boock, say about the film, it doesn't in any way lessen the respect and honour afforded to those men who died fighting in that war, but what is does do is honour those men who did everything they could do to stop the war.[970]

Millicent would be very pleased.

In the last few pages of her book, Millicent tells us that she lives peacefully in Kinsman Street with Terence coming each Sunday to do her gardening, to eat the dinners she cooks him and to talk and read with her. She ends her memoirs philosophising about her life and how she would like to see the world shaped:

> Jim said once, 'I would like to change the emotional climate of this country, make it one per cent warmer before I die.' I think perhaps that is what we all must strive for, and first to have a change of heart in ourselves.
>
> My life has been very full, and it has been lived through a time of complete change in the life-style, habits and attitudes of mankind. Whether this change will ultimately be for the good of the human race lies in the hands of the oncoming generations. May they take the right road.
>
> At my age I don't mind, now, what people think of me. It used to be so important when I was younger – I did worry. Now it is acceptance of myself. [971]

She perceived herself as a non-conformist and felt that she had changed radically since she was a young woman under the influence of her father. 'If I feel things are right I shall do them no matter what they are. People are just as much conformists as they ever were. Young people are conformists in their dirty untidy clothes – they are conformists completely, just as much as we were. All that permissiveness – that's conformism just the same.[972] She finishes with some advice for us all – which probably sums up the whole of her memoirs: 'Accept yourself as you are, and do your best. That is so simple and obvious – but all the important things are obvious and simple.'[973]

Her memoirs were painstakingly typed out by Josephine Baker, the grand-daughter of Justice Alpers who had been a colleague of Millicent's father and were published by Cape Catley in 1981. On the cover, designed by her grandson John, are unpretentious head-and-shoulder photographs of Archie, Millicent, Terence and James. The huge life of that tiny indomitable woman occupies just a small slim volume. The book is a rather dry, blow-by-blow account of the nine decades of Millicent's life. In places, it is an impersonal travelogue. Very different from Archie's We will not cease. The quintessential Millicent rarely appears; it's all about the people around her. But perhaps all autobiographies are a little this way. In undated and unsigned notes for a television interview reviewing the book is the following:

> A memoir need not be concerned with great events [hence Millicent's omission in commenting on the wars?] provided the memoirist has an enquiring mind, an eye for detail, the ability to select from and synthesise disparate fragments of experience, and an openness which invites the reader to become involved in the events of another person's life... [Millicent Baxter's] book is not merely a catalogue of memoirs. It is an account of three loves. The first is her love of learning, which was reinforced by overseas study and travel and frequent excursions into the New Zealand high-country. In her memoirs she wears her historical, genealogical, linguistic and botanical learning as comfortably as a pair of old gardening-gloves. The second is for her family and, above all, for her husband – a love which outlasts death. The third is for truth and justice, embodied in particular in her pacifist convictions. In her memoirs she is concerned for accuracy of reporting and is therefore an eye-witness rather than an interpreter of events. Although she <u>does</u> describe her reactions the reader wishes that she would have allowed herself to step even further forward into the light.[974]

The family was disappointed in the book; they had hoped to find the real essence of their mother, aunt, grandmother and strongly felt that they did not. Katherine Baxter once heard an interview with Christine Cole Catley, who said that she always advised her writers when they're writing their autobiographies or memoirs, to write in a way that won't embarrass the family. Katherine felt this was the worst piece of advice, because they wanted to find the whole Millicent, her real personality – and if it meant embarrassing the family, then so be it. Millicent, already extremely reticent in expressing her emotions, clearly paid heed to Cole Catley's guidance. Paradoxically, she would relate certain things but when Christine started to write them down, Millicent would often say, 'Oh no, dear I know I said it, but it wouldn't do in a book.'[975] It is also clear when listening to the tapes of interviews between the two women that Christine omitted many of the more candid and personal feelings that Millicent did express, anything that would appear 'unseemly' that would risk upsetting relatives or friends. The result is a factual and restrained memoir which has been my bible in writing this work.

At the launching of the memoirs, in April 1981, Millicent, now aged ninety-four, stood up and said firmly 'I know people will read my book to see what I say about James K., to see him from another angle. Well I loved my son, I was proud of his brilliance, but I don't want to be swamped by him. All my life I have been swamped by famous relatives, but I urge you to read this book as my autobiography.'[976] As usual, her apparent confidence and almost pompous air belies her real feelings; she confessed to her friend Jean Bertram who helped Christine Cole Catley on the compilation of the memoirs that she was actually very worried about the launch, in fact dreading it.[977]

It was in her letters to Jean Bertram that her language revealed how she truly felt about her friend, and from anyone else it might have sounded gushing; while still addressing her as Mrs Bertram of course, she starts in one letter 'You are indeed a noble and wonderful friend,' and ends, 'Many, many thanks again, you lovely friend, yours ever, Millicent Baxter.'[978] She thoroughly enjoyed many of the interviews she gave that year with various newspapers and magazines, and wrote to Jean Bertram: 'I have been interviewed for the Women's Weekly by a charming girl with the right attitudes. Two and a half hours of pure enjoyment.'[979] All these letters are written in very readable, strong handwriting, though she confesses: 'I must apologies for my handwriting. My arthritic fingers can no longer depress the keys of the typewriter.'[980]

In 2003, the memoirs were published again by Cape Catley together with the seventh printing of We will not cease. David Hill reviewed both books in an article in The Listener, Mr and Mrs Baxter: 'Excuse me, but here is a personal message. Nobly done, Christine Cole Catley, for getting so many first-time New Zealand authors into print, keeping so many several-time New Zealand writers in print, and eschewing the schlock of the new by returning these two old-time New Zealand writers to print.' Reviewing Millicent's memoirs he starts off disliking her with her privileged background, but clearly admires her by the end: 'She can write prose as scoured as driftwood... So polite. So grammatical. So absolute.' It was thirty years since Hill had read We will not cease, 'This time, it's the tenacity and tenuousness of human decency that struck me. That, plus the absence of any happy ending, and the martial ferocity of civilians back home.' He finishes with 'You could speculate that, with parents of such intellectual ardour and ferocious moral integrity, James K Baxter was bound to have a voice.'[981] In the last few years of her life, Millicent was still a member of all those organisations concerned with justice and freedom and peace, still battling in what she saw as the fight between the spirit of evil and the spirit of love and tirelessly striving to teach people the necessity of world reconciliation.[982] 'Usually I write about four letters a month to political prisoners on behalf of Amnesty International... When I write to the president and to the Minister of Education of Benin, I use flowery wording such as I remember in letters my mother occasionally received: "Kindly agree, dear sir, to the expression of my distinguished sentiments." I believe my mother would have smiled. She was such a wise woman, ahead of her time. Archie's experiences accustomed me to horror. I am able to read details of terrible tortures in Amnesty International literature.'[981] Despite the prospect of nuclear war in the world, she drew solace from the fact that she had seen the peace movement and tolerance of pacifism grow immeasurably in her lifetime.[984]

She was always a staunch pacifist, and a believer in compassion:

> Compassion means suffering with, and Archie suffered so very much with the young men slaughtered around him. When Jim was sixteen – he was steeped in Archie – he wrote a poem called Song of the Sea-Nymphs at the Death of Icarus. It ends, 'Lament ye for young Icarus / Lament again! / For he is youth / Forever living and forever slain.' And slaughtered for what? Nothing. And war goes on and on. Violence of any kind breeds violence. Wars breed other wars. You cannot bring good out of evil, which is what violence is.[985]

Jim Neilan, the parish priest in Kaikorai at the time, used to visit her in Kinsman Street once a week and, if it were a Friday, take communion to her. 'She was always very appreciative of that. She really felt this was a closer contact with God.' Her housekeeping habits hadn't changed: 'you sort of had to push your way through this room, through piles of letters and manuscripts and everything, but if you asked her to get something, she'd know where it was. She used to come to Mass on Sundays; she'd walk up that steep hill, always perfectly dressed with her hat on, up Taieri Road – in her late 80s – and she would read a lesson at the Masses on the Sunday in that beautiful voice.'[986]

In practical terms, she spent most of her time trying to keep warm in the Dunedin winters in her little house in Kinsman Street. In one of her many letters to her friend Jean Bertram, she writes in her firm but nearly 93-year-old hand: 'With the rise in electricity costs – I must stay warm in order to keep alive – I am economising by not buying books. We are having the most appalling weather: damp, horrible mist for the last four days. All the people with arthritis, and there are many, find it atrocious. I am too old to migrate elsewhere so will just have to hang it out till the Lord chooses to remove me.'[987]

As ever she was always humble, even self-effacing. In 1981 she wrote to Noel Ginn and reminisced about their day together in Colchester and their conversations about eastern religions:

I am a simple-minded person and the simple Christian faith
satisfies me, although I know I am not a good example of it.
But one has to do the best one can with the faulty human nature
one has been given…I have had a long and very happy life and
I am close to the end of it and I don't dread it. Perhaps that is
arrogant but I think it is trust in the mercy of God. I hope I live
long enough to see the production of the documentary about
my husband's book 'We Will Not Cease'. They are seriously
enthusiastic about it and I think it has a message for the young.
The future of the world is in their hands. I hope they will take
the right path.[988]

Millicent Baxter lived at Kinsman Street very happily for a total of thirteen years
until early July 1983. Leaving the house one day to go to a lecture, to her immense
irritation, she tripped getting into a taxi and broke her hip. Even though she certainly
didn't look or act her ninety-five years, she was of course very old. She was taken to
Mater Hospital – Later named Mercy Hospital – where Archie had ended his days
fourteen years before.[989] Frances Mulrennan went straight to see her and Millicent
immediately reeled off a list of telephone numbers of tradesmen, such as her grocer,
because she wouldn't be needing them anymore. 'She was so matter-of-fact that
part of her life was ended – without any regret or recrimination or "isn't this bad
luck!"…she had perfect clarity, perfect memory with no hesitation.'[990]

She came through the operation of having a pin put in her hip joint with flying
colours, but the broken hip proved to be the beginning of the end. Dementia began
to set in. Frances continues: 'She had often said, "I've asked God not to take my
mind," but the interesting thing is, in a way her mind was taken, but she didn't
know it.'[991] Terence says, 'I took that a bit hard in a way…her brain just going
absolutely into another world altogether. You couldn't get any sense out of her at
all. She got all sorts of fantasy theories.'[992] His son Kenneth remembers a tinge of
jealousy appearing with her dementia, about her sister Viola having all those young
men in sports cars coming up the drive to her father's house coming to see her.[993]
But apparently her senility made little difference to her personality, and during the
weeks she was in hospital she held court among a constant stream of visitors. About
a year after her accident she died – on Tuesday 3 July 1984.

Three days later a Requiem Mass was held for Millicent at St Mary's Church,
Taieri Road.[994] Jim La Rooy, a pacifist who had emigrated from Holland to New
Zealand after World War Two, helped carry the coffin into the church the night
before the Mass. His story illustrates how little Millicent was known in her own
right:

A friend had told me about Archibald Baxter and 'We will not
cease' and I was so fascinated with that book that I gave it to my
son. And I've given it to certain other people – among others,

to the United States ambassador to New Zealand, Moseley Braun…

No, I didn't meet Millicent. I only knew of her, and I admired her from afar so to speak. [He had previously heard Millicent speak at a General Amnesty International meeting]. So when the death notice came into the paper, my son was by then 15, I said "you will come with me because we are going to honour a woman who is very important to us and to New Zealand and to all."… It was a coldish, dark, beautiful winter's night. I said, "We'll go to the rosary to honour her because it will be a big funeral but there's not so many people at the rosary," So I walked in with my son and we were early and I was on my knees when someone tapped me on the shoulder and said, "Would you please help us to bring the body into the church," I was so saddened that here, the wife of Archibald, and the mother of James, that there weren't people jamming the gate to bring her in.'[995] [996]

The funeral itself the next day had a large attendance of family and friends. Father Flaherty took the Requiem Mass,[997] with a piper piping in the mourners.[998] Millicent

Millicent and Archie's gravestone at Green Island Cemetry, Dunedin
(taken by Penny Griffith in 2011)

was buried in Green Island Cemetery alongside her treasured Archie beneath the gravestone engraved Requiescant In Pace. She had her wish, and there was room for her details beneath his:

Archibald Mc.C.L. Baxter
Died 10th August 1970
Aged 88 years
Also loved wife
Millicent Amiel
Died 3rd July 1984
Aged 96 years
Requiescant In Pace

If you continue from Block II Plot 161[999] seventeen kilometres along Brighton Road, you come to Kuri Bush where Archie and Millicent spent the happiest decade of their lives. The southerlies still try to blow down the remains of their two-storey barn where the two of them milked the cows, where Terence chased the mice from his father's precious sacks of oats, and where Millicent lit the kerosene lamp for Archie to hold James to look up at the stars.

BIBLIOGRAPHY

Books:

Baker, Paul. King and Country Call: New Zealanders, Conscription and the Great War. Auckland: Auckland University Press, 1988.

Baxter, Archibald. We will not cease: Autobiography of a Conscientious Objector. London: Gollancz, 1939.

Baxter, Archibald. We will not cease. Christchurch: Caxton Press, 1968.

Baxter, Archibald. We will not cease. Auckland: Cape Catley, 2003.

Baxter, James K. "A Death Song for Mr Mouldybroke." The Collected Poems of James K. Baxter. Edited by J.E. Weir. Wellington: Oxford University Press 1979: 411

Baxter, James K. Beyond the Palisade: Poems by James K. Baxter. Christchurch: Caxton Press, 1944.

Baxter, James K. Blow, Wind of Fruitfulness: James K. Baxter. Christchurch: Caxton Press, 1948.

Baxter, James K. Recent Trends in New Zealand Poetry. Christchurch: Caxton Press, 1951.

Baxter, James K. The Fallen House: Poems by James K. Baxter. Christchurch: Caxton Press, 1953.

Baxter, James K. "Lament for Barney Flanagan, Licencee of the Hesperus Hotel", and "The King and the Clown". The Spike Wellington: Victoria University College Students' Association, 1954

Baxter, James K. The Fire and the Anvil: Notes on Modern Poetry. Wellington: New Zealand University Press, 1955.

Baxter, James K. Howrah Bridge and Other Poems. London: Oxford University Press, 1961.

Baxter, James K. Pig Island Letters. Oxford: Oxford University Press, 1966.

Baxter, James K. The Man on the Horse. Dunedin: University of Otago Press, 1967.

Baxter, James K. Jerusalem Sonnets: Poems for Colin Durning. Dunedin: University of Otago Press, 1970.

Baxter, James K. Jerusalem Daybook. Wellington: Price Milburn, 1971.

Baxter, James K. Autumn Testament. Wellington: Oxford University Press, 1972.

Baxter, James K. The Tree House and Other Poems for Children – James K. Baxter. Wellington: Price Milburn, 1974.

Baxter, James K. "To My Father." The Collected Poems of James K. Baxter. Edited by J.E.Weir. Wellington: Oxford University Press, 1979: 65

Baxter, James K. Horse. Auckland: Oxford University Press, 1985.

Baxter, Millicent. The Memoirs of Millicent Baxter. Whatamongo Bay, N.Z.: Cape Catley,1981.

Belich, James. Making Peoples: A History of the New Zealanders: From Polynesian Settlement to the End of the Nineteenth Century. Auckland: Allen Lane/Penguin, 1996.

Belich, James. Paradise Reforged: A History of the New Zealanders from the 1880s to the Year 2000. Auckland: Allan Lane/Penguin, 2001.

Blake, William. Preface to "Milton: A Poem." The Poetical Works of William Blake, edited by John Sampson. London, New York: Oxford University Press, 1908.

Brasch, Charles. Indirections : A Memoir, 1909– 1947. Wellington: Oxford University Press, 1980.

Caughey, Angela. Pioneer Families: The Settlers of Nineteenth Century New Zealand. Auckland: David Bateman Ltd, 1994.

Day, Kelvin, ed. Contested Ground :The Taranaki Wars, 1860– 1881, Te Whenua I Tohea. Wellington: Huia, 2010.

Donaldson, W."Oliphant, Carolina, Lady Nairne (1766–1845)." New Oxford Dictionary of National Biography. Oxford: Oxford University Press., 2004.

Eldred-Grigg, Stevan. A New History of Canterbury. Dunedin: John McIndoe, 1982.

Gardner, W.J., Beardsley, E.T., and Carter, T.E. A History of the University of Canterbury. Christchurch: Caxton Press, 1973.

Grant, David. Out in the Cold: Pacifists and Conscientious Objectors in New Zealand During World War II. Auckland: Reed Methuen, 1986.

Grant, David. Field Punishment No. 1: Archibald Baxter, Mark Briggs & New Zealand's Anti-Militarist Tradition. Wellington: Steele Roberts Publishers, 2008.

Grossman, Edith Searle. The Life of Helen Macmillan Brown. Christchurch, Wellington, Dunedin and Melbourne: Whitcombe and Tombs Ltd, 1905.

Gustafson, Barry. Labour's Path to Political Independence: Origins and Establishment of the New Zealand Labour Party, 1900– 19. Auckland: Auckland University Press, 1980.

Hedges, Chris. What Every Person Should Know About War. New York: Free Press (A Division of Simon & Schuster Inc.) 2003.

Hight, J. and Candy, A. A Short History of the Canterbury College (University of New Zealand): with a register of graduates and Associates of the College. Edited by Mrs K. Evans. Auckland : Whitcombe and Tombs, 1927.

Hill, David. My Brother's War. Auckland: Puffin Books, 2012.

Holland, Harry. E. Armageddon or Calvary: The Conscientious Objectors of New Zealand and the Process of Their Conversion. Brooklyn, N.Z: H.E. Holland, 1919.

King, Michael. Wrestling with the Angel: A Life of Janet Frame. Auckland: Viking, 2000.

Lawlor, Pat. The Two Baxters: Diary Notes by Pat Lawlor. Wellington: Millward Press, 1979.

Looser, Frieda. Fendall's Legacy: a History of Fendalton and North-West Christchurch. Christchurch: Canterbury University Press, 2002.

Lovell-Smith, Margaret. Easily the Best: the Life of Helen Connon, 1857– 1903. Christchurch: Canterbury University Press, 2004.

Loveridge, Steven. Calls to Arms: New Zealand Society and Commitment to the Great War. Wellington: Victoria University Press, 2014.

Lawry, Walter. We Said No to War! Dunedin: Wordspinners Unlimited, 1994.

Macmillan Brown, John. The Memoirs of John Macmillan Brown. Christchurch: Whitcombe and Tombs, 1974.

Marsh, Ngaio. Black Beech and Honeydew: an Autobiography of Ngaio Marsh. Auckland: William Collins Publishers Ltd, 1981.

McKay, Frank. The Life of James K. Baxter. Auckand: Oxford University Press, 1990.

Millar, Paul. Ka Mate Ka Ora: a New Zealand Journal of Poetry and Poetics. New Zealand Electronic Poetry Centre, March 2007.

Millar, Paul. Ed Spark to a Waiting Fuse: James K. Baxter's Correspondence with Noel Ginn, 1942– 46. Introduced by Paul Millar. Wellington: Victoria University Press, 2001.

Millar, Paul. "'The Rent Due for a Skull': James K. Baxter and the Legacy of Parihaka." Te Miringa Hohaia. Edited by Gregory O'brien and Lara Strongman. Parihaka: The Art of Passive Resistance (Wellington: City Gallery; Wellington: Victoria University Press; Parihaka: Parihaka Pa Trustees, 2001

Newton, John. The Double Rainbow: James K. Baxter, Ngāti Hau and the Jerusalem Commune. Wellington: Victoria University Press, 2009.

O'Brien, Gregory and Strongman, Lara, eds. Parihaka : The Art of Passive Resistance. Wellington: Victoria University Press, 2001.

Oliver, William, H. James K. Baxter: A Portrait. Christchurch: Whitcoulls Ltd, 1983.

Olssen, Erik. The History of Otago. Dunedin: John McIndoe Ltd, 1984.

Peddie, Barbara. Christchurch Girls' High School, 1877– 1977. Christchurch: Pegasus Press, 1977.

Pugsley, Christopher. On the Fringe of Hell: New Zealanders and Military Discipline in the First World War. Auckland: Hodder and Stoughton, 1991.

Rice, G. W. Christchurch Changing. Christchurch: Canterbury University Press, 1999.

Scott, Dick. The Parihaka Story. Auckland: Southern Cross Books, 1954.

Bibliography

Scott, Dick. Ask That Mountain: the Story of Parihaka. Auckland: Reed/Southern Cross, 1975.
Shelton, McGregor Malcolm. A Day in the Life of New Zealand: Friday, March 18th, 1983. Auckland: J.M. McGregor, 1983.
Strange, Glyn. The Arts Centre of Christchurch: Then and Now. Christchurch: Clerestory Press, 1994.
Truby King, F. Feeding and Care of Baby. London: Macmillan and Co., 1913.
Tullberg, Rita McWilliams. "Strachey, (Joan) Pernel (1876–1951)", Oxford Dictionary of National Biography. Oxford: Oxford University Press, 2004.
Weir,J .E. Ed. The Collected Poems of James K. Baxter. Wellington : Oxford University Press, 1979.
Yska, R. Truth: The Rise and Fall of the People's Paper. Nelson: Craig Potton Publishing, 2010.

Journals and Periodicals

Broughton, W. S. "Vonney Allan's Account of James Baxter's Death" Bauer Media. Auckland 2015,Journal of New Zealand Literature (1995): n13, 285– 290.
Millar, Paul. "Jacquie Baxter/J.C. Sturm (1927-2009)." Ka Mate Ka Ora: A New Zealand Journal of Poetry and Poetics. Issue 9, (March, 2010).
Millar, Paul. "James K. Baxter's Indian Poems." Ka Mate Ka Ora: A New Zealand Journal of Poetry and Poetics. Issue 3, (March, 2007).
O'Connor, Peter. S. "The Awkward Ones: Dealing with Conscience, 1916– 1918." New Zealand Journal of History. 8, No. 2 (1974).
Wilson, Janet, "Archie, Millicent and James: The Baxter Autobiographies." Journal of New Zealand Literature .No.13 (1995): 47– 64.

Theses:

Cumming, Belinda C. "Parents, Siblings and Pacifism: The Baxter Family and Others (World War One and World War Two)". University of Otago, 2007.
Hall, F.J. "The Greater Game: Sport and Society in Christchurch during the First World War, 1914– 18", Thesis, University of Canterbury, 1989.
Hutching, Megan. "Turn Back This Tide of Barbarism – New Zealand Women Who Were Opposed to War, 1896– 1919", M. A.Thesis, University of Auckland, 1990.
Loveridge, Steven. "'Soldiers and Shirkers": An Analysis of the Dominant Ideas of Service and Conscientious Objection in New Zealand during the Great War", Thesis, University of Waikato, 2009.

Archival Sources

Baxter, Archibald. Unpublished novel. Hocken Library. Ms 975/195.
Baxter, Donald, Letter from Donald Baxter, Waikeria Reformatory, /9/1918, Letters from Donald Baxter, Ms-0975/206, Baxter Family: Papers (Arc-0351), Hocken Library, Dunedin.
Baxter, Donald. Letter from Donald Baxter, Waikeria Reformatory, 15 December 1918, Letters from Baxter, Donald Ms-0975/205, Baxter Family: Papers (Arc-0351), Hocken Library, Dunedin.
Baxter, Donald. Poem by Donald Baxter, 26 July 1917; Letters from Donald Baxter. Ms-0975/205, Baxter Family: Papers (Arc-0351), Hocken Library Dunedin.
Baxter, James K. First Years Remembered: Kuri Bush. Unpublished Poem. Hocken Library, Dunedin Ms 704/17.
Baxter, James K. Letter to Lawrence Baigent. 24 February 1945.
Baxter, James K. Letter to Millicent Baxter. 15 October 1945.
Baxter, James K. Letters to Baigent; Letter to Archibald and Millicent Baxter, 1948; Letter to Archibald and Millicent Baxter, October 1948; Letter to Archibald and Millicent Baxter, 11 April 1954; Letter to Archibald and Millicent Baxter, 25 August 1963. Hocken Ms 976/183.
Baxter, James K. To My Mother. Hocken Library, Dunedin, Ms704/4: 184.
Baxter, Lenore. Letter to Frank Mckay. 7 July 1985. VUW Library, Wellington. Ms Mckay 10/7/32.
Baxter, Millicent. Letter to Noel Ginn, 18 June 1981. Papers (Arc-0401), Hocken Collections, Dunedin.
Baxter, Millicent. Letter to Jean Bertam. 17 November 1981. Papers of James and Jean Bertram,

215

Bibliography

Alexander Turnbull Library, Wellington, Wellington, 93-103-13.

Baxter, Millicent. Letter to Jean Bertam. 9 May 1981. Papers of James and Jean Bertram, Alexander Turnbull Library, Wellington, 93-103-13.

Baxter, Millicent. Letter to Jean Bertam. 6 June 1981. Papers of James and Jean Bertram, Alexander Turnbull Library, Wellington, 93-103-13.

Baxter, Millicent. Letter to Jean Bertam. 10 March 1981. Papers of James and Jean Bertram, Alexander Turnbull Library, Wellington, 93-103-13.

Baxter, Millicent. Letter to Jean Bertam. 6 October 1980. Papers of James and Jean Bertram, Alexander Turnbull Library, Wellington, 93-103-13.

Baxter, Millicent. Letter to Jean Bertam. 29 September 1980. Papers of James and Jean Bertram, Alexander Turnbull Library, Wellington, 93-103-13.

Connon, Maria. Letter to Helen Connon, 1 July 1898. Mb 118, Macmillan Brown Papers, A2 Correspondence 1908-09, Macmillan Brown Library, Christchurch.

Edger, Kate. Letter to Professor Brown, 3 March 1884. Macmillan Brown Library, Christchurch. MB 118, Macmillan Brown Papers, A1 Correspondence 1880–85.

Gibson, Lucy. Correspondence with Millicent Baxter 1945. Alexander Turnbull Library, Wellington, 91-142-03.

Ginn, Noel. Letter to Frank Mckay. 13 January 1983. VUW Library, Ms Mckay Item 10/4/17.

Ginn, Noel. Letter to Paul Millar. January 1995.

Ginn, Noel. Letter to Paul Millar. April 1995.

Hargreave, Margaret. Letter to Frank Mckay. 18 February 1944. VUW Library, Ms Mckay 10/5/36.

Kuri Bush School History File. Hocken Library, Dunedin. Ag-294-49/124, 1962.

Macmillan Brown, John. Letter to Haast, 23 April, 1886. Ms-Papers-0037-035, Haast Family Papers, Alexander Turnbull Library.

Macmillan Brown, Helen. Letter to John Macmillan Brown. 17 June 1899. MB118, Macmillan Brown Papers, A3 Correspondence, 1900.

Radio New Zealand Review of the Memoirs of Millicent Baxter. Alexander Turnbull Library, Wellington, 93-103-13.

Skinner, Philippa. Letter to Anotonietta Baldacchino. 15 July 1983.

New Zealand Defence Force Personnel records:

Baxter, Alexander. Archives New Zealand. Aabk 18805 W5520 0012621.

Archives New Zealand.

Baxter, Archibald Mccoll Larmond (Sic). Archives New Zealand. Aabk 18805 W5520 0012624.

Baxter, Donald. Archives New Zealand. Aabk 18805 W5520 0012630.

Baxter, Hugh. Archives New Zealand. Aabk 18805 W5520 0012653.

Baxter, John. Archives New Zealand. Aabk 18805 W5520 0012666.

Baxter William. Archives New Zealand. Aabk 18805 W5520 001269.

Statutes:

Statutes of New Zealand: No.8, Military Service Act, 1916, Section 35

Interviews:

Cole Catley, Christine. Recorded Interview with Millicent Baxter.

Cass 1, Side 1, March 1979: Hocken Library Ms-3099/013

Cass 2, side 1, 1979: Hocken Library Ms-3099/013

Cass 3, Side 1, March 1979: Hocken Library Ms-3099/013

Cumming, Belinda. Interview with Terence Baxter. 18 August 2007.

Griffith, Penny. Interview with Antonietta Baldacchino. 6 June 2010.

Griffith, Penny. Interview with Cecily McNeil. 17 August 2010.

Griffith, Penny. Interview with Christine Cole Catley. 2 September 2009.

Griffith, Penny. Interview with Clarice Holland, Jack Holland and Diane Dore. 23 January 2010.
Griffith, Penny. Interview with Diane Dore.21 January 2010, 21 May 2010, 10 April 2014. May 2010.
Griffith, Penny. Interview with Don Lawson. 17 August 2010.
Griffith, Penny. Interview with Frances Mulrennan and Shirley McLeod. 20 May 2010.
Griffith, Penny. Interview with George McIntosh. 22 January 2010.
Griffith, Penny. Interview with John Baxter and Colin Durning. 3 August 2010.
Griffith, Penny. Interview with Jim La Rooy. Dunedin, 22 February 2011.
Griffith, Penny. Interview with Jim Neilan. 16 November 2010.
Griffith, Penny. Interview with Katherine Baxter.18 April 2010, 28 May 2011, 4 August 2013, 4 July 2011, 8 December 2009.
Griffith, Penny. Interview with Lawrence Jones. 4 May 2008.
Griffith, Penny, Interview with Lawrence Jones and Diane Dore. 22 May 2010.
Griffith, Penny. Interview with Lenore and Katherine Baxter. 2 May 2010.
Griffith, Penny. Interview with Margaret Gibson. Auckland: 3 September 2010.
Griffith, Penny. Interview with Mary Ronnie. 23 February 2011.
Griffith, Penny. Interview with Max Broadbent. 12 May 2008, 9 June 2008.
Griffith, Penny. Interview with Paul and Beatrice Donovan. 28 January 2010.
Griffith, Penny. Interview with Paul Oestreicher. 19 May 2010.
Griffith, Penny. Interview with Pamela Gordon. 24 February 2011.
Griffith, Penny. Interview with Ray Grover, Army Historian. 23 July 2013.
Griffith, Penny. Interview with Ray Edwards. 26 January 2010.
Griffith, Penny. Interview with Rosamund Mccreadie and Diane Dore. 23 February 2010.
Griffith, Penny. Interview with Sally Page. 24 October 2014.
Griffith, Penny. Interview with Terence Baxter and Kenneth Baxter. 9 January 2010, 3 February 2010.
Griffith, Penny. Interview with Terence Baxter. 19 August 2013, 24 December 2013,
Griffith, Penny. Interview with Toni Wilson. 1 February 2010.
Griffith, Penny. Interview with Wynn Geeves. 12 January 2010.
Griffith, Penny. Personal Communication with Michael Kelly. 29 July 2013.
Griffith, Penny. Telephone Interview with Frances Mulrenan 25 September 2011.
Harding, Bruce. Interview with Antonietta Baldacchino. 20 November 2001.
Harding, Bruce. Interview with Millicent Baxter. 8 April 1982.
King, Michael. Interview with Millicent Baxter. October 1978. Tape transcript, Christine Cole Catley. Hocken Library MS-3099/014.
McKay, Frank. Conversation with Terence Baxter. 8 July 1984.
McKay, Frank. Interview with Canon Paul Oestreicher. April 1987.
McKay, Frank. Interview with Terence Baxter. 8 July 1984. Baxter Box One: Transcripts of Interviews No.L-20, Beaglehole Room, University of Victoria, Wellington. 1984.
Millar, Paul. Interview with Terence Baxter. 11 December 1995.
Millar, Paul. Interview with Noel Ginn. August 1994.

Correspondence: to Penny Griffith:

Baldacchino, Antonietta. Email to Penny Griffith. January 2013.
Baxter, Barry. Emails to Penny Griffith. March– April 2014.
Baxter, John. Letter to Penny Griffith. 9 December 2013.
Baxter, Katherine. Email to Penny Griffith. 31 March 2014.
Baxter, Terence. Letter to Penny Griffith. 28 April 2010,12 April 2012.
Best, Haydie. Gillions Funeral Services email to Penny Griffith. 21 March, 2014.
Broadbent, Max. Email to Penny Griffith. 13 May, 2008.
Christchurch City Libraries email to Penny Griffith. 15 October 2014.
Dore, Diane. Email to Penny Griffith. 7 August 2013, 9 December 2013.
Durney, Jill. Email to Penny Griffith. 28 January 2013.
Hatherly, Richard. Email to Penny Griffith. 13 April 2014.
Lovell-Smith, Margaret. Email to Penny Griffith. 29 October 2014.

Bibliography

Neilan, Jim. Email to Penny Griffith.18 March 2014.
Sellar, Stuart. Email to Penny Griffith. 5 November 2010, 28 October 2010.
Walker, Geoff. Email to Penny Griffith. 27 November 2014

Newspaper and Magazine Articles:

Baxter, Millicent. "Northern Ireland"Otago Daily Times. 7 March 1972: 18.
Baxter, Millicent. "The H-Bomb"Otago Daily Times. 14 April 1954: 4.
Baxter, Millicent. "Manapouri" Otago Daily Times, 24 November, 1969: 8.
Broom, Nicola. "Doing Her Own Thing – at 93" Otago Daily Times. 1 May 1981.
Gates, Charlie. "Partial Christ Church Cathedral Demolition". The Press. 28 October, 2011.
Gibb, John. "Lest We Forget: Memorial to City's 2500 Dead". Otago Daily Times. 25 April 2008.
Goodwin, Eileen. "Pacifists Also Deserving of Recognition". Otago Daily Times. 30 December 2013.,
K. "Her Own Voice." The Press. 2012.
Hess, Dale. "The Story of Stephen Hobhouse." The Australian Friend (June, 2003).
Hill, David. "Mr & Mrs Baxter N.Z." New Zealand Listener. 24 January, 2004.
Killick, David. "No Ordinary Cottage" The Press. 28 June 2000.
Larsen, Ken. "Wartime Hell of an Otago Conscientious Objector" New Zealand Herald. 27 February 2004.
Little, Paul. An Interview with J. Weir about "James K. Baxter: Complete Prose." North & South: Notes and Queries. Issue 353, August 2015: 97
Rabbit, Lindsay. "Jim, Jacquie and Baxter". New Zealand Listener. 7 June 2000.
Rudd, Allison. "Oestreicher: Disciple of Universal Compassion" Otago Daily Times. 23 May 2009.
Seear, Annette. "A Pacifist Who Came into Her Own" The Evening Star. 4 February 1978.
Young, David. "A Poet for a Son". New Zealand Listener. 25 October 1980.
"Baxter Case: the Conscientious Objector". Otago Daily Times. 24 October 1918.
"Forcibly Deported Conscientious Objectors" Maoriland Worker. 25 July 1917.
"Marriage" The Lyttelton Times. 10 December 1886.
"National Council of Women: Peace and Arbitration" Otago Daily Times. 11 May 1900.
"Veteran New Zealand Peace Campaigner Dies" Otago Daily Times. 4 July 1984.

Film and Radio Sources

Field Punishment No 1. Film produced by Donna Malane & Paula Boock, 2014.
Morrison, Bruce. Director The Road to Jerusalem. Produced by William Grieve. 1998.
Laidlaw, Chris. "Ideas – a Pack of Hoons – Conscientious Objectors in New Zealand History." Sunday Report with Chris Laidlaw. Radio New Zealand, 2009.
McNeish, James. Intimate Strangers: James McNeish Interviews Viola Notariello. Radio N.Z. 18 September 1980.
Anon. "Interview with Millicent Baxter" Looking Back. Radio New Zealand. 24 January 1981. http://collections.soundarchives.co.nz/search.do?view=detail&id=135578&db=object.

Electronic Resources

"1939 PM Declares NZ's Support for Britain." New Zealand History Online. Ministry for Culture and Heritage. http://www.nzhistory.net.nz/pm-declares-new-zealands-support-for-britain-in-famous-radio-broadcast
"50 Years Ago: The Pope Received the Balzan Prize." International Balzan Prize Foundation News http://www.balzan.org/en/news/news-detail/50-years-ago-the-pope-received-the-balzan-prize
"60 Beautiful Hillside Sections." The Christchurch Press. http://paperspast.natlib.govt.nz/cgi-bin/paperspast?a=d&d=CHP19081014.2.71.7
"And Did Those Feet in Ancient Time." https://www.princeton.edu/~achaney/tmve/wiki100k/docs/And_did_those_feet_in_ancient_time.html
"Army and Air Force (Annual) Bill." Hansard 24 April 1923 http://hansard.millbanksystems.com/

Bibliography

lords/1923/apr/24/army-and-air-force-annual-bill

Beaglehole, Diana. "Whanganui Region : a Troubled Decade – the 1860s." Te Ara – The Encyclopedia of New Zealand. Updated 16 November 2012 http://www.teara.govt.nz/en/photograph/19031/moutoa-battle-memorial-1860s.

Blankschaen, Bill. "Faith Walkers at Patheos : Nelson Mandela's Legacy in South Africa: A Unique Perspective." http://www.patheos.com/blogs/faithwalkers/2013/12/nelson-mandelas-legacy-in-south-africa-a-unique-perspective/

Bohan, Edmund. "Page, Sarah." Te Ara – the Encyclopedia of New Zealand: Dictionary of New Zealand Biography. http://www.teara.govt.nz/en/biographies/3p1/page-sarah

Brookes, Barbara. "King, Frederic Truby." Te Ara – the Encyclopedia of New Zealand: Dictionary of New Zealand Biography. http://www.teara.govt.nz/en/biographies/2k8/king-frederic-truby

"Burton, Ormond Edward." Te Ara – the Encyclopedia of New Zealand: Dictionary of New Zealand Biography. http://www.teara.govt.nz/en/biographies/5b53/burton-ormond-edward

"Cambridge Mathematical Tripos." http://en.wikipedia.org/wiki/Cambridge_Mathematical_Tripos.

Cairns, Lois. "Provincial Chambers Repair Bill $70m." http://www.stuff.co.nz/the-press/news/christchurch-earthquake-2011/10101635/Provincial-chambers-repair-bill-70m

"Canon Paul Oestreicher Speaks in Wellington." Peace Movement Aotearoa. http://www.converge.org.nz/pma/pauloes.htm

"Christchurch City Libraries." Early Christchurch: a Brief History http://christchurchcitylibraries.com/heritage/earlychristchurch/earlychristchurch.asp

Clayworth, Peter. "Prisons: Developing a National Prison System, 1880–1949." Te Ara – the Encyclopedia of New Zealand. http://www.TeAra.govt.nz/en/photograph/36765/mt-cook-prison-1896

Cooper, Annabel. "Baxter, Millicent Amiel." Te Ara – the Encyclopedia of New Zealand: Dictionary of New Zealand Biography. http://www.teara.govt.nz/en/biographies/3b20/baxter-millicent-amiel

Cowan, James. "Professor J. Macmillan Brown, a Great Teacher, Writer and Traveller." Famous New Zealanders. No.24 http://nzetc.victoria.ac.nz/tm/scholarly/tei-Gov09_12Rail-t1-body-d5.html

"Cruel Punishment for Those Who Would Not Fight : Interview with Katherine Baxter." Sunday Star Times.20 April 2014. http://www.stuff.co.nz/entertainment/tv-radio/9954000/Cruel-punishment-for-those-who-would-not-fight

"Dame Ngaio Marsh's Home" http://www.ngaio-marsh.org.nz

Davis, Bryan R. "Page, Robert Owen," Te Ara – the Encyclopedia of New Zealand: Dictionary of New Zealand Biography. http://www.teara.govt.nz/en/biographies/5p4/page-robert-owen

Derby, M. "Conscription, Conscientious Objection and Pacifism." Te Ara – the Encyclopedia of New Zealand. http://www.teara.govt.nz/en/conscription-conscientious-objection-and-pacifism/3

"Dunedin City Council Bush Tracks - Ross Creek Reservoir." http://www.dunedin.govt.nz/facilities/walking-tracks/bush-walk.

"Dunedin City Council Cemeteries Search." http://www.dunedin.govt.nz/facilities/cemeteries/cemeteries_search?recordid=72353&type=Burial

"Engineering Sources at the Hocken Collections: Reid and Gray Limited." http://www.otago.ac.nz/library/pdf/Engineering_Guide.pdf

"HMNZT New Zealand Transport Ships – Flotilla Australia." http://www.flotilla-australia.com/hmnzt.htm#29

"Flogging & Field Punishment No.1." http://www.historicalfirearms.info/post/75095899088/flogging-field-punishment-no1-the-british-army.

Foster, Bernard John. "Brown, Charles Edmund Bevan." Te Ara – the Encyclopedia of New Zealand. http://www.teara.govt.nz/en/1966/brown-charles-edmund-bevan.

"Efford, Lincoln Arthur Winstone." Dictionary of New Zealand Biography: Te Ara – the Encyclopedia of New Zealand. http://www.teara.govt.nz/en/biographies/5e1/efford-lincoln-arthur-winstone

"Field Punishment No.1." Televison Showcase N.Z. on Air. http://www.nzonair.govt.nz/television/showcase/field-punishment-no1/

"Fraser, Peter." Dictionary of New Zealand Biography: Te Ara – the Encyclopedia of New Zealand. http://www.teara.govt.nz/en/biographies/4f22/fraser-peter

Grant, David. "Baxter, Archibald McColl Learmond, 1881– 1970." http://www.dnzb.govt.nz/DNZB/alt_essayBody.asp?essayID=3B19.

Bibliography

Grant, David. "Mark Briggs," Dictionary of New Zealand Biography. Te Ara – the Encyclopedia of New Zealand. http://www.teara.govt.nz/en/biographies/3b48/briggs-mark

Grimshaw, P.A. "Women's Suffrage Movement." Te Ara – the Encyclopaedia of New Zealand. http://www.teara.govt.nz/en/1966/womens-suffrage-movement/1

"King's High School." http://www.kingshigh.school.nz/about-us/.

"Hanmer Springs History." http://hanmersprings.co.nz/about/history.

Hankin, Cherry. "Brown, John Macmillan," Dictionary of New Zealand Biography: Te Ara – the Encyclopedia of New Zealand. http://www.teara.govt.nz/en/biographies/2b41/1.

Harris, Nancy. "Baughan, Blanche Edith (1870–1958)." Te Ara – the Encyclopedia of New Zealand: Dictionary of New Zealand Biography. http://www.teara.govt.nz/en/biographies/3b17/baughan-blanche-edith

"Harry Holland." New Zealand History Online. Ministry for Culture and Heritage, http://www.nzhistory.net.nz/people/harry-holland.

"History of Jerusalem." Sisters of Compassion website. http://www.compassion.org.nz/jerusalem/history-of-jerusalem/.

"History of the Macmillan Brown Library, University of Canterbury." http://www.libr.canterbury.ac.nz/mb/mbhist.shtml

"History of Mater Misericordiae Hospital." http://www.mercyhospital.org.nz/about-us/mercy-hospital/history

"History of the National Party." http://www.national.org.nz/about/history.aspx.

Hughes, Beryl. "Edger, Kate Milligan." Te Ara – the Encyclopedia of New Zealand: Dictionary of New Zealand Biography. http://www.teara.govt.nz/en/biographies/2e3/edger-kate-milligan.

Hutching, Megan. "Bain, Wilhelmina Sherriff 1848– 1944," Te Ara – the Encyclopedia of New Zealand: Dictionary of New Zealand Biography. http://www.dnzb.govt.nz/dnzb/.

Jones, Lawrence. "Mythology of Place: Homage to James K Baxter." http://www.lloydgodman.net/baxter/Intros/JamesK.html

"In Dissent: Second World War at Home." New Zealand History Online. Ministry for Culture and Heritage, http://www.nzhistory.net.nz/war/second-world-war-at-home/in-dissent

"Influenza Epidemic." New Zealand Disasters. http://christchurchcitylibraries.com/Kids/NZDisasters/InfluenzaEpidemic.asp

"International Relations - Changing Foreign Ties." http://www.tepapa.govt.nz/WhatsOn/exhibitions/SliceofHeaven/Exhibition/InternationalRelations/Pages/Changingforeignties.aspx

James K. Baxter and the Jerusalem Commune." Te Ara – the Encyclopedia of New Zealand. http://www.teara.govt.nz/en/communes-and-communities/page-2.Keane, Chris. "Terence Macswiney." Irish Volunteers Commemorative Organisation. http://irishvolunteers.org/2012/05/terence-macswiney/

Lambert, Ron. "The Invasion of Parihaka," Te Ara – the Encyclopedia of New Zealand. http://www.teara.govt.nz/en/photograph/25325/the-invasion-of-parihaka

"Legends and Traditions of the Great War." The Great War Society. http://www.worldwar1.com/heritage/hfcorner.htm.

"Lost Christchurch – Strange & Co. Building." http://lostchristchurch.org.nz/strange-co-building-corner-of-lichfield-and-high-streets

Lochhead, Ian. J. "Seager, Samuel Hurst." Te Ara – the Encyclopedia of New Zealand: Dictionary of New Zealand Biography. http://www.teara.govt.nz/en/biographies/3s8/seager-samuel-hurst.

McClure, Margaret. "Auckland Region – Population." Te Ara – the Encyclopedia of New Zealand. http://www.teara.govt.nz/en/auckland-region/page-5

"Māori Dictionary." http://www.maoridictionary.co.nz/search?idiom=&phrase=&proverb=&loan=&keywords=Matatea&search=

Millen, Julia. "Libraries – Library Associations and Librarians." Te Ara – the Encyclopedia of New Zealand, http://www.TeAra.govt.nz/en/photograph/41646/mary-ronnie-national-librarian-1978

"Mountfort, Benjamin Woolfield," Dictionary of New Zealand Biography: Te Ara – the Encyclopedia of New Zealand. http://www.teara.govt.nz/en/biographies/1m57/mountfort-benjamin-woolfield

"New Zealand and the Second World War." New Zealand History Online. Ministry for Culture and Heritage, http://www.nzhistory.net.nz/war/new-zealand-and-the-second-world-war

"New Zealand History – Lady Liverpool Great War Story." Ministry for Culture and Heritage. http://

Bibliography

www.nzhistory.net.nz/media/video/lady-liverpool-great-war-story

"Newnham College, University of Cambridge." http://www.newn.cam.ac.uk/about-newnham/college-history

Norton, John. "Baxter's Breakdown. 29 June 1918." http://paperspast.natlib.govt.nz/cgi-bin/paperspast?a=d&d=NZTR19180629.2.48

Ogilvie, Gordon. "Glover, Denis James Matthews." Dictionary of New Zealand Biography: Te Ara – the Encyclopedia of New Zealand. Phillips, Jock. "'History of Immigration – British Immigration and the New Zealand Company," Te Ara – the Encyclopedia of New Zealand. <http://www.TeAra.govt.nz/en/history-of-immigration/3>

"Quakers: the Religious Society of Friends." Religions. BBC http://www.bbc.co.uk/religion/religions/christianity/subdivisions/quakers_1.shtml

"Rangitiki, Rangitata & Rangitane". http://www.derbysulzers.com/shiprangitki.html

"Red Feds and Prussianism." An address by Professor John Macmillan Brown. The Christchurch Press. 13 April 1917.
http://paperspast.natlib.govt.nz/cgi-bin/paperspast?a=d&cl=search&d=CHP19170413.2.36&srpos=1&e=-------10-CHP-1----2RED+FEDS+AND+PRUSSIANISM--

"South African War 1899-1902." New Zealand History. Ministry for Culture and Heritage, http://www.nzhistory.net.nz/war/saw-introduction.

"Sister Sue Cosgrove DOLC." http://www.maristmessenger.co.nz/2013/02/01/sr-sue-cosgrove-dolc/.

Stafford, Jane. "Marsh, Edith Ngaio." Dictionary of New Zealand Biography: Te Ara – the Encyclopedia of New Zealand. Updated 13-Nov-2013. http://www.teara.govt.nz/en/biographies/4m42/marsh-edith-ngaio.

"Street History: The Terrace." The Wellingtonian.
http://www.stuff.co.nz/dominion-post/news/local-papers/the-wellingtonian/7223556/Street-history-The-Terrace

"The Barclays in South Canterbury, N.Z." http://www.rootsweb.ancestry.com/~nzlscant/barclay.htm

"The Caxton Press: History." http://www.caxton.co.nz/history.html

"The Defence Act, 1909" Encyclopaedia of New Zealand. Edited by A. H. Mclintock.. Originally Published in 1966. Te Ara – the Encyclopedia of New Zealand. http://www.TeAra.govt.nz/en/1966/compulsory-military-training/2

"The Group 1927– 1977." http://christchurchartgallery.org.nz/media/uploads/2010_06/Survey_16.pdf

"The History of Parihaka." http://www.parihaka.com/About.aspx.

"The Home Front: Pacifism." Volume 1, Chapter 5. The New Zealand Electronic Text Centre, http://nzetc.victoria.ac.nz/tm/scholarly/tei-WH2-1Hom-c5.html

"Launching of the Lady Egidia." The Ships List http://freepages.genealogy.rootsweb.ancestry.com/~ourstuff/LadyEgidia1861.htm

"The Musket Wars." New Zealand History Online. Ministry for Culture and Heritage http://www.nzhistory.net.nz/war/new-zealands-19th-century-wars/the-musket-wars.

"The National Council of Women: Women and the Vote." New Zealand History Online. Ministry for Culture and Heritage http://www.nzhistory.net.nz/politics/womens-suffrage/national-council-of-women.

"The New Zealand Wars: A History of the Maori Campaigns and the Pioneering Period: Volume 2: The Hauhau Wars, (1864-72):The Taranaki Frontier and the Expedition to Parihaka." The New Zealand Electronic Text Centre.

"The Passchendaele Offensive." NZ History Online. Ministry for Culture and Heritage. http://www.nzhistory.net.nz/war/new-zealanders-in-belgium/passchendaele
http://nzetc.victoria.ac.nz/tm/scholarly/tei-Cow02NewZ-c43-2.html

Pool, Ian & Rosemary Du Plessis. "Families: a history – Colonial families: 1840–1879". Te Ara - the Encyclopedia of New Zealand. Updated 13 July 2012. http://www.teara.govt.nz/en/families-a-history/page-2

"The Quaker Peace Testimony." http://www.quaker.org/minnfm/peace/

"The Quotations Page." http://www.quotationspage.com/quote/27169.html

"The Second World War at Home – Ballot Boys." Ministry for Culture and Heritage. http://www.nzhistory.net.nz/war/second-world-war-at-home/war-work

Bibliography

"Remembering Peacemakers on Anzac Day." http://lestweforget.org.nz/about/

Roberts, Heather. "Grossmann, Edith Searle." Te Ara – the Encyclopedia of New Zealand: Dictionary of New Zealand Biography. http://www.teara.govt.nz/en/biographies/2g22/grossmann-edith-searle

"The Reserve Bank and New Zealand's Economic History: Colonial Economy 1840–1890: the 'Long Depression'." http://www.rbnz.govt.nz/research_and_publications/fact_sheets_and_guides/3072801.pdf

Shoebridge, Tim. "James K. Baxter." New Zealand History Online. Ministry for Culture and Heritage. http://www.nzhistory.net.nz/people/james-k-baxter

Smith, Brian J. "Dendy, Arthur (1865–1925)." Australian Dictionary of Biography, National Centre of Biography, Australian National University, http://adb.anu.edu.au/biography/dendy-arthur-5951

"Socialist Objection: Conscientious Objection in the First World War." NZ History Online. Ministry for Culture and Heritage. http://www.nzhistory.net.nz/war/first-world-war/conscientious-objection/socialist-objection

"The Story of Suzanne Aubert." The Sisters of Compassion website http://www.compassion.org.nz/suzanne-aubert/the-story-of-suzanne-aubert/

"The Vietnam War: New Zealand and the Vietnam War." Ministry for Culture and Heritage, http://www.nzhistory.net.nz/war/vietnam-war

"The Waitemata Wobbler". New Zealand WWI Troopship magazine. Auckland War Memorial Museum. http://webapi.aucklandmuseum.com/media/presto/av/b0653fcfa50f337b50078aeef14a4419a76994b7/original.pdf

"Troopships:Waitemata – Date of Departure 24 July 1917." http://muse.aucklandmuseum.com/databases/general/SearchResults.aspx?dataset=Cenotaph&c_embarkingtransport_search=%22hmnzt+89%22&c_embarkingtransport_logic=or&Page=133

"University of Canterbury: Chronology." http://www.canterbury.ac.nz/theuni/backgrnd/chronology.shtml

"University of Canterbury: History." http://www.canterbury.ac.nz/theuni/backgrnd/history.shtml

"The War Effort of New Zealand." NZETC, http://www.nzetc.org/tm/scholarly/tei-WH1-Effo-t1-front-d6.htm

Ward, Tony. "The Parihaka Project." http://www.tonywardedu.com/images/critical_practice/parihaka-project-1.pdf.

Wells, K. "The Australian Gold Rush." http://australia.gov.au/about-australia/australian-story/austn-gold-rush

"Wilfred Owen." http://www.warpoetry.co.uk/Owena.html

"William Stafford (1914 - 1993)." http://www.poetrymountain.com/classics/williamstafford.html

"Ypres in the Great War of 1914-1918." http://www.greatwar.co.uk/ypres-salient/town-ieper-history-1418.htm.

http://www.teara.govt.nz/en/biographies/4g11/glover-denis-james-matthews

Weir, John. "The Spirituality of James K. Baxter." http://www.catholicworker.org.nz/cg/CG63-TheSpiritualityOfJamesKBaxter.html

ENDNOTES

CHAPTER 1 - The College Idol and the God Professor

1 To be more accurate, she was the first woman to gain honours (in 1877) in a university examination that was intended to be equivalent to that taken by men for a degree. Annie would have to wait another 43 years before she had her degree conferred and spent all her life at the university, meeting her death on one of Oxford's cobbled streets on her bicycle, aged 81.

2 Most people refer to the book as 'We Will Not Cease'. 'We will not cease' is the correct title.

3 "The Quotations Page" http://www.quotationspage.com/quote/27169.html.

4 "The Quaker Peace Testimony." http://www.quaker.org/minnfm/peace/.

5 Baxter, James. K. "Pig Island Letters 8" in Collected Poems of James K. Baxter, edited by J.E. Weir. Wellington N.Z.: Oxford University Press, 1979, 281.

6 "William Stafford (1914 - 1993)."http://www.poetrymountain.com/classics/williamstafford.html.

7 Frank McKay, The Life of James K. Baxter (Auckland: Oxford University Press, 1990), 14. Note: Much of the biographical material on the family background is drawn from this book.

8 Frank McKay, The Life of James K. Baxter (Auckland: Oxford University Press, 1990), 14. Note: Much of the biographical material on the family background is drawn from this book.

9 Millicent Baxter, The Memoirs of Millicent Baxter (Whatamongo Bay, N.Z.: Cape Catley, 1981), 13.

10 Bruce Harding, Interview with Millicent Baxter, 8 April 1982.

11 Lovell-Smith, Easily the Best:The life of Helen Connon, 1857–1903, 11.

12 Edith Searle was an ardent feminist with rather puritanical views. She became head girl at Christchurch Girls' High School when Helen Macmillan Brown was principal and Helen persuaded her to go to Canterbury College. She graduated B.A. in 1884 and received an M.A. with first-class honours in 1885. She married Joseph Grossmann in 1890, but Joseph was imprisoned for fraud in 1898, and Edith lived in England and Europe for 10 years working as a free-lance journalist. She also wrote several novels. Ref: Heather Roberts, "Edith Searle Grossmann," in Dictionary of New Zealand Biography: Te Ara — the Encyclopedia of New Zealand. http://www.teara.govt.nz/en/biographies/2g22/Grossmann-edith-searle.

13 Edith Searle Grossmann, Life of Helen Macmillan Brown (Christchurch, Wellington, Dunedin and Melbourne: Whitcombe and Tombs Ltd, 1905), 22.

14 Millicent Baxter, The Memoirs of Millicent Baxter, 12.

15 Lovell-Smith, Easily the Best:The life of Helen Connon, 1857–1903, 12.

16 Lady Nairne was Carolina Baroness Nairne, née Oliphant, who under a pseudonym composed Jacobite songs among which were Charlie is my Darling, Will Ye no Come Back Again and The Hundred Pipers — which is likely to have been sung by the Baxter brothers. She loved the poetry of her contemporary, Robbie Burns, so if the family legend regarding Helen Hart's parentage is true, Lady Nairne shared this passion with her great, great, grandson Archie and his son James.

17 Lovell-Smith, Easily the Best: The life of Helen Connon, 1857–1903,12.

18 Ibid., 13.

19 Ibid., 13.

20 Grossmann, Life of Helen Macmillan Brown, 10.

21 Lovell-Smith, Easily the Best:The life of Helen Connon, 1857–1903, 16.

22 Grossmann, Life of Helen Macmillan Brown, 10.

23 Lovell-Smith, Easily the Best:The life of Helen Connon, 1857–1903,14.

24 Ibid.,16.

25 Note: Hokitika is the setting for Eleanor Catton's book The Luminaries, winner of the 2013 Man Booker Prize. Catton, a New Zealander, is the youngest author (at age 28) ever to win the award.

26 Lovell-Smith, Easily the Best:The life of Helen Connon, 1857–1903, 17–18.

27 Ibid., 17.

28 Ibid., 20–21.

29 Grossmann, Life of Helen Macmillan Brown, 14.

30 Ibid.

31 Lovell-Smith, Easily the Best:The life of Helen Connon,1857–1903, 21.

32 It is possible that there was another child, Peter. The death certificates of Helen's parents indicated that there was a seventh child, a son. There is a grave of a four-year-old child, Peter Connon, buried in Hokitika in 1868, but his death certificate reveals no information to confirm the connection to our Connon family. Ref: Lovell-Smith, Easily the Best:The life of Helen Connon, 1857–1903, 21

33 "Early Christchurch: a brief history — Christchurch City Libraries." http://christchurchcitylibraries.com/heritage/earlychristchurch/earlychristchurch.asp.

34 Ibid.

35 Frieda Looser, Fendall's Legacy: a History of Fendalton and North-West Christchurch (Christchurch: Canterbury University Press, 2002), 7.

36 "Mountfort, Benjamin Woolfield," Dictionary of New Zealand Biography. Te Ara — the Encyclopedia of New Zealand. http://www.teara.govt.nz/en/biographies/1m57/mountfort-benjamin-woolfield.

37 John Macmillan Brown, The Memoirs of John Macmillan Brown (Christchurch: Whitcombe and Tombs, 1974), 4.

38 Ibid., 7.

39 W.J. Gardner, E.T. Beardsley, and T.E. Carter, A History of the University of Canterbury (Christchurch: Caxton Press, 1973), 88.

40 Cherry Hankin, "Brown, John Macmillan," Te Ara — the Encyclopedia of New Zealand: Dictionary of New Zealand Biography. http://www.teara.govt.nz/en/biographies/2b41/1.

41 Gardner et al., A History of the University of Canterbury, 87–89.

42 Macmillan Brown, The Memoirs of John Macmillan Brown, introduction James K. Baxter, xxxv.

43 Grossmann, Life of Helen Macmillan Brown, 18.

44 Gardner et al,, A History of the University of Canterbury, 89–90.

45 Hankin, "Brown, John Macmillan"

46 Ibid.

47 Millicent Baxter, The Memoirs of Millicent Baxter, 11.

48 Lovell-Smith maintains Helen and John started using the name Macmillan Brown when they married in 1886. Ref: Lovell-Smith, Easily the Best:The life of Helen Connon,1857–1903, 8.

49 Gardner et al., A History of the University of Canterbury, 83.

50 Lovell-Smith, Easily the Best:The life of Helen Connon,1857–1903, 26.

51 Grossmann, Life of Helen Macmillan Brown, 9.

52 Lovell-Smith, Easily the Best:The life of Helen Connon,1857–1903, 29.

53 Grossmann, Life of Helen Macmillan Brown, 8. Cited by Lovell-Smith, Easily the Best, 28.

54 Lovell-Smith, Easily the Best:The life of Helen Connon,1857–1903, 28.

55 Looser, Fendall's Legacy, 124.

56 Ibid., 30.

57 Barbara Peddie, Christchurch Girls' High School, 1877-1977, (Christchurch: Pegasus Press, 1977), 28.

58 Grossmann, Life of Helen Macmillan Brown, 43.

59 Lovell-Smith, Easily the Best:The life of Helen Connon,1857–1903, 43.

60 Peddie, Christchurch Girls' High School, 30.

61 Lovell-Smith, Easily the Best:The life of Helen Connon,1857–1903, 31–32.

62 Grossmann, Life of Helen Macmillan Brown, 25.

63 Ibid.

64 Lovell-Smith, Easily the Best:The life of Helen Connon,1857–1903, 25.

65 Beryl Hughes, "Edger, Kate Milligan," Te Ara — the Encyclopedia of New Zealand: Dictionary of New Zealand Biography. http://www.teara.govt.nz/en/biographies/2e3/edger-kate-milligan. Te Ara - the Encyclopedia of New Zealand, http://www.teara.govt.nz/en/biographies/2e3/edger-kate-milligan.

66 Grossmann, Life of Helen Macmillan Brown, 27.

67 Lovell-Smith, Easily the Best:The life of Helen Connon,1857–1903, 33–34.

68 Ibid.,19.

69 The Canterbury Provincial Council buildings, on the corner of Armagh and Durham Sts are widely acknowledged as New Zealand's most outstanding example of high Victorian gothic revival architecture, but the buildings were badly damaged in the February 2011 earthquake. The Christchurch City Council is determined to see the buildings restored, at a cost of up to $70m. Ref: Cairns, Lois. "Provincial chambers repair bill $70m." http://www.stuff.co.nz/the-press/news/christchurch-earthquake-2011/10101635/Provincial-chambers-repair-bill-70m.

70 Angela Caughey, Pioneer Families: The Settlers of Nineteenth-Century New Zealand (Auckland: David Bateman Ltd., 1994), 190.

71 Grossmann, Life of Helen Macmillan Brown, 24.

72 Ibid.

73 Lovell-Smith, Easily the Best:The life of Helen Connon,1857–1903, 47–48.

74 "Canterbury College — Girls' High School." The Press, 17 January 1883, 3. http://paperspast.natlib.govt.nz/cgi-bin/paperspast?a=d&d=CHP18830117.2.28.2.

75 Peddie, Christchurch Girls'High School, 40.

76 Lovell-Smith, Easily the Best:The life of Helen Connon,1857–1903, 49.

77 Peddie, Christchurch Girls' High School, 44.

78 Ibid., 34.

79 Lovell-Smith, Easily the Best:The life of Helen Connon,1857–1903, 45.

80 Up to 1910 the street numbers within the four avenues of Christchurch ran from East Belt (Fitzgerald Avenue) to Hagley Park. After all the boroughs amalgamated in 1910, the numbering was changed to run the other way. So 80 Lichfield St became 177 Lichfield St. Ref: Email from Christchurch City Libraries, 15 October 2014. This possibly ties in with the fact that in 1880 to 1881 George was listed as a builder in Barbadoes Street, between Lichfield and Tuam Streets since that land might well have included 177 Lichfield Street. Ref: Lovell-Smith, Easily the Best:The life of Helen Connon,1857–1903, 25.

81 Grossmann must be wrong in stating it was 81 Lichfield Street. Ref: Grossmann, Life of Helen Macmillan Brown, 48. Wise's New Zealand Directories for 1885—1886 records: Connon, Miss Helen, teacher [living at] 80 Lichfield Street.

82 Lovell-Smith, Easily the Best:The life of Helen Connon,1857–1903, 55.

83 Hankin, "Brown, John Macmillan."

84 Charles Brasch, Indirections: A Memoir, 1909-1947 (Wellington: Oxford University Press, 1980), 119.

85 Millicent Baxter, The Memoirs of Millicent Baxter, 30.

86 Ibid., 141.

87 Years later Bickerton had a long dispute with the university authorities who finally dismissed him in 1902, seven years after John resigned. Ref: G. W. Rice, Christchurch Changing (Christchurch: Canterbury University Press, 1999), 55.

88 McKay, The Life of James K. Baxter, 16.

89 Macmillan Brown, The Memoirs of John Macmillan Brown, 180.

90 Ibid.

91 Grossmann, Life of Helen Macmillan Brown, 24.

92 Millicent Baxter, The Memoirs of Millicent Baxter, 16.

93 Macmillan Brown, The Memoirs of John Macmillan Brown, 180.

94 Gardner et al., A History of the University of Canterbury, 30.

Endnotes

95 "J.M. Brown to My Dear Haast." MS-Papers-0037-035, Haast Family Papers, Alexander Turnbull Library. 23 April, 1886. Quoted by: Lovell-Smith, Margaret. (2004). Easily the Best:The life of Helen Connon,1857–1903, 57

96 Macmillan Brown, The Memoirs of John Macmillan Brown, introduction Millicent Baxter, xv.

97 Grossmann, Life of Helen Macmillan Brown, 27.

98 Lovell-Smith, Easily the Best:The life of Helen Connon,1857–1903, 40.

99 Cole Catley, recorded Interview with Millicent Baxter. Cass 2 side 1. (Hocken Library Ms-3099/013), March 1979.

100 Cole Catley, recorded Interview with Millicent Baxter. Cass 2 side 1. (Hocken Library Ms-3099/013), March 1979.

101 Canterbury College became Canterbury University College in 1933 and in 1957 became the University of Canterbury. By 1975 it had completed its move to a purpose-built 76 hectare site in the suburb of Ilam, 7km from the old city site, and the buildings at the old town site were given to the people of Christchurch as an arts centre (they were severely damaged in the February 2011 earthquake, but at the time of writing they are being restored). In 1991, women graduates outnumbered men for the first time in the University's 118 years. There are now about 15,000 students. Ref: "University of Canterbury: Chronology. "http://www.canterbury.ac.nz/theuni/backgrnd/chronology.shtml. And: "University of Canterbury: History." http://www.canterbury.ac.nz/theuni/backgrnd/history.shtml.

102 Lovell-Smith, Easily the Best:The life of Helen Connon,1857–1903, 60.

103 Looser, Fendall's Legacy, 24.

104 Macmillan Brown, The Memoirs of John Macmillan Brown, 182.

105 Looser, Fendall's Legacy, 61–62.

106 Macmillan Brown, The Memoirs of John Macmillan Brown, 181.

107 Ibid.

108 Macmillan Brown, The Memoirs of John Macmillan Brown, introduction Millicent Baxter, xix.

109 Millicent Baxter, The Memoirs of Millicent Baxter, 16.

110 Macmillan Brown, The Memoirs of John Macmillan Brown, 182.

111 Grossmann, Life of Helen Macmillan Brown, 47–48.

112 Lovell-Smith, Easily the Best:The life of Helen Connon,1857–1903, 61.

113 Grossmann, Life of Helen Macmillan Brown, 47.

114 Millicent Baxter, The Memoirs of Millicent Baxter, 16–17.

115 Macmillan Brown, The Memoirs of John Macmillan Brown, 182.

116 Harding, Interview with Millicent Baxter, 8 April 1882

117 Macmillan Brown, The Memoirs of John Macmillan Brown, 182.

118 Ibid., 183.

119 Ibid., 33–34.

Chapter 2 - A Solitary Childhood

120 Macmillan Brown, The Memoirs of John Macmillan Brown, introduction Millicent Baxter, xviii–xviv.

121 James Belich, Making Peoples: A History of the New Zealanders: From Polynesian Settlement to the End of the Nineteenth Century (Auckland: Allen Lane/Penguin, 1996), 450.

122 James Belich, Paradise Reforged: A History of the New Zealanders From the 1880s to the Year 2000 (Auckland: Allan Lane; Penguin, 2001), 174.

123 2007. "The Reserve Bank and New Zealand's economic history: Colonial economy 1840–1890; The 'long depression.'" http://www.rbnz.govt.nz/research_and_publications/fact_sheets_and_guides/3072801.pdf.

124 By 1901 Auckland was drawing ahead of all other regions and has remained ahead ever since. Ref: McClure, Margaret. 2012. "Auckland region – Population." Te Ara — the Encyclopedia of New Zealand. http://www.teara.govt.nz/en/auckland-region/page-5.

125 Belich, Paradise Reforged: A History of the New Zealanders From the 1880s to the Year 2000, 19–20.

126 Grossmann, Life of Helen Macmillan Brown, 48.

127   Millicent Baxter, The Memoirs of Millicent Baxter, 16.

128   Macmillan Brown, The Memoirs of John Macmillan Brown, 186.

129   In the early morning of 1 September 1888, an earthquake with an estimated magnitude of 7.0 – 7.3 struck North Canterbury about 100 kms north-west of Christchurch. Felt from New Plymouth to Invercargill, the quake caused damage to buildings over a wide area, including Christchurch. The top eight metres of the stone spire of Christ Church Cathedral collapsed, partly because of the sway of the heavy iron cross secured to its top. (http: / / www.teara.govt.nz / en / historic-earthquakes / 4). Note: In the February 2011 earthquake, Christ Church Cathedral again suffered severe structural damage, including the complete collapse of its steeple. On 9 November 2011, the cathedral was deconsecrated so demolition work could be carried out to make it safe. Ref: Gates, Charlie. 2011. "Partial Christ Church Cathedral demolition" The Press, 28 October 2011. http://www.stuff.co.nz/the-press/news/christchurch-earthquake-2011/5866482/Partial-Christ-Church-Cathedral-demolition.

130   Macmillan Brown, The Memoirs of John Macmillan Brown, 186.

131   Lovell-Smith, Easily the Best:The life of Helen Connon,1857–1903, 63.

132   A merchandising and furniture store housed in a magnificent four storey building, built in 1900, on the corner of Lichfield and High Streets. The building replaced a row of old dilapidated weatherboard shops dating back to the early days of Christchurch. Ref: "Lost Christchurch - Strange & Co. Building." http://lostchristchurch.org.nz/strange-co-building-corner-of-lichfield-and-high-streets.

133   Lovell-Smith, Easily the Best:The life of Helen Connon,1857–1903, 63.

134   Ibid., 65–66.

135   Millicent Baxter, The Memoirs of Millicent Baxter, 17

136   Ibid.

137   Millicent Baxter, The Memoirs of Millicent Baxter, 16–17.

138   Ibid., 24.

139   Macmillan Brown, The Memoirs of John Macmillan Brown, xvi.

140   Millicent Baxter, The Memoirs of Millicent Baxter, 18.

141   Grossmann, Life of Helen Macmillan Brown, 31.

142   Millicent Baxter, The Memoirs of Millicent Baxter, 18–19.

143   Caughey, Pioneer Families: The Settlers of Nineteenth-Century New Zealand, 191.

144   Segregated nude bathing was the order of the day in those early years at the Hanmer Springs pools. An item of male or female clothing (skirt or trousers) was hoisted up a pole to indicate the gender of people permitted in the pool at any particular time. Ref: "Hanmer Springs History." http://hanmersprings.co.nz/about/history.

145   Millicent Baxter, The Memoirs of Millicent Baxter, 17–18.

146   Ibid., 24.

147   Macmillan Brown, The Memoirs of John Macmillan Brown, 186.

148   It is possible that he might have confused the date with the miscarriage that Millicent refers to later. Ref: Lovell-Smith, Easily the Best: The life of Helen Connon,1857–1903, 68.

149   Millicent Baxter, The Memoirs of Millicent Baxter, 13.

150   P.A. Grimshaw, "Women's Suffrage Movement" Te Ara — the Encyclopaedia of New Zealand. http: / / www.teara.govt.nz / en / 1966 / womens-suffrage-movement / 1.

151   Gardner et al., A History of the University of Canterbury, 106.of the University of Canterbury, 106.

152   Lovell-Smith, Easily the Best: The life of Helen Connon,1857–1903, 71.

153   Macmillan Brown, The Memoirs of John Macmillan Brown, 188.

154   Ibid., introduction by Millicent Baxter, xvi.

155   Peddie, Christchurch Girls'High School, 48.

156   Lovell-Smith, Easily the Best, 91.

157   bid., 69.

158   Millicent Baxter, The Memoirs of Millicent Baxter, 20.

159   Ibid., 25.

160   Hankin, "Brown, John Macmillan."

161   Millicent Baxter, The Memoirs of Millicent Baxter, 18.

162   Ibid., 19.

163   Brian J. Smith, 1981, "Dendy, Arthur (1865–1925)." Australian Dictionary of Biography, National Centre of Biography, Australian National University. http://adb.anu.edu.au/biography/dendy-arthur-5951.
164   Millicent Baxter, The Memoirs of Millicent Baxter, 19.
165   Rice, Christchurch Changing, 59.
166   Lovell-Smith, Easily the Best: The life of Helen Connon 1857–1903, 77–78.
167   Macmillan Brown, The Memoirs of John Macmillan Brown, Millicent Baxter's Introduction, xix
168   Millicent Baxter, The Memoirs of Millicent Baxter, 21.
169   Macmillan Brown, The Memoirs of John Macmillan Brown, introduction Millicent Baxter, xvii
170   Ibid.
171   Millicent Baxter, The Memoirs of Millicent Baxter, 23.
172   Ibid.
173   Ibid., 23.
174   Macmillan Brown, The Memoirs of John Macmillan Brown, 194.
175   Ibid., introduction by Viola Helen Notariello, xxvi.
176   Lovell-Smith, Easily the Best: The life of Helen Connon,1857–1903, 84.
177   Caughey, Pioneer Families: The Settlers of Nineteenth-Century New Zealand, 192
178   Cole Catley, Recorded interview with Millicent Baxter. Cass 2 Side 1 (Hocken Library MS-3099/013), March 1979.
179   "Māori Dictionary." http://www.maoridictionary.co.nz/search?idiom=&phrase=&proverb=&loan=&keywords=Matatea&search=.
180   Lovell-Smith, Easily the Best: The life of Helen Connon,1857–1903, 84.
181   David Killick, "No Ordinary Cottage." The Press, 28 June 2000.
182   Ian. J. Lochhead, "Seager, Samuel Hurst." Te Ara — the Encyclopedia of New Zealand: Dictionary of New Zealand Biography.   http://www.teara.govt.nz/en/biographies/3s8/seager-samuel-hurst.
183   Lovell-Smith, Easily the Best: The life of Helen Connon,1857–1903, 84–85.
184   bid., 24–25.
185   The house is still there today, at what is now 2 Whisby Road and is a listed Grade 1 heritage building. Ref: Lovell-Smith, Email to Penny Griffith, 29 October 2014.
186   This and a later work Limanora, a science utopian fantasy, were published under the pseudonym Godfrey Sweven in America in 1901 and 1903. Ref: Hankin, "Brown, John Macmillan."
187   Lovell-Smith, Easily the Best, 87.
188   Letter from Helen to Macmillan Brown, 17 June, 1899. Cited by Lovell-Smith, Easily the Best, 88.
189   Lovell-Smith, Easily the Best: The life of Helen Connon,1857–1903, 89.
190   Ibid., 99
191   Millicent Baxter, The Memoirs of Millicent Baxter, 26.
192   Macmillan Brown, The Memoirs of John Macmillan Brown, 197.
193   Ibid.
194   Millicent Baxter, The Memoirs of Millicent Baxter, 27.
195   Ibid., 99
196   Lovell-Smith, Easily the Best: The life of Helen Connon,1857–1903, 101.
197   Millicent Baxter, The Memoirs of Millicent Baxter, 27.
198   Caughey, Pioneer Families: The Settlers of Nineteenth-Century New Zealand, 102.
199   Millicent Baxter, The Memoirs of Millicent Baxter, 27.
200   Ibid.
201   Caughey, Pioneer Families: The Settlers of Nineteenth-Century New Zealand, 191.
202   Lovell-Smith, Easily the Best: The life of Helen Connon,1857–1903, 110.
203   Millicent Baxter, The Memoirs of Millicent Baxter, 28.
204   Macmillan Brown, The Memoirs of John Macmillan Brown, introduction Millicent Baxter, xxii.
205   Cole Catley, Recorded Interview with Millicent Baxter. Cass 1 Side 1 (Hocken Library Ms-3099/013), March 1979.
206   Millicent Baxter, The Memoirs of Millicent Baxter, 29.

207 Ibid.

208 Grossmann, Life of Helen Macmillan Brown, 22–23.

209 Ibid.

210 Millicent Baxter, The Memoirs of Millicent Baxter, 29.

211 Lovell-Smith, Easily the Best: The life of Helen Connon,1857–1903, 114.

212 Glyn Strange, The Arts Centre of Christchurch - Then and Now, (Christchurch: Clerestory Press, 1994), 29.

213 Peddie, Christchurch Girls'High School, 65.

214 Macmillan Brown, The Memoirs of John Macmillan Brown, introduction Millicent Baxter, xvii.

215 Macmillan Brown, The Memoirs of John Macmillan Brown, 214.

Chapter 3 - Getting an Education

216 Cole Catley, Recorded Interview with Millicent Baxter. Cass 2 Side 1 (Hocken Library Ms-3099/013), March 1979.

217 Millicent Baxter, The Memoirs of Millicent Baxter, 30.

218 McKay, The Life of James K. Baxter, 17–18.

219 Ibid.

220 Macmillan Brown, The Memoirs of John Macmillan Brown, 214.

221 Ibid.

222 Cole Catley, Recorded Interview with Millicent Baxter. Cass 1 side 1 (Hocken Library Ms-3099/013), March 1979.

223 Penny Griffith, Interview with George McIntosh, 22 January 2010.

224 Millicent Baxter, The Memoirs of Millicent Baxter, 30.

225 Ibid., 30–31.

226 Ibid., 31.

227 Ibid.

228 Ibid., 31–32.

229 Ibid., 31.

230 Ibid., 33.

231 Ibid., 35–36.

232 Rita McWilliams Tullberg, Strachey, (Joan) Pernel (1876–1951). Oxford Dictionary of National Biography, (Oxford: Oxford University Press, 2004).
 Millicent Baxter, The Memoirs of Millicent Baxter, 36–37.

233 McKay, The Life of James K. Baxter, 18.

234 Ibid., 18.

235 Cole Catley, Recorded Interview with Millicent Baxter. Cass 2 Side 1 (Hocken Library Ms-3099/013), March 1979.

236 Millicent Baxter, The Memoirs of Millicent Baxter, 40.

237 Ibid., 47.

238 Ibid., 80.

239 Ibid., 39.

240 Ibid., 41.

241 Ibid., 42.

242 A first attempt to secure titles for women's degrees were rebuffed in 1887 and 1897. Undergraduates demonstrating against the granting of these titles to women caused hundreds of pounds worth of damage in the market square. During World War One the women tried once more to gain inclusion, this time asking not only for the titles of degrees but also for the privileges and involvement in university government that possession of degrees proper would bring. In Oxford this was secured in 1920, but in Cambridge the women were defeated again, in 1921, having to settle for the titles – the much-joked-about 'BA tit' – but not the substance of degrees. This time, the male undergraduates celebrating victory over the women used a handcart as a battering ram to destroy the lower half of the bronze gates at Newnham College bearing a memorial to Anne Jemima Clough who was an early English suffragist and a promoter of higher education for women. Finally in 1948, the women were

admitted to full membership of the University but even then the university still retained powers to limit their numbers. Ref: "Newnham College, University of Cambridge." http: //www.newn.cam.ac.uk/about-newnham/college-history.

243   As the principal of Newnham College, Joan Pernel Strachey took a leading part in the unsuccessful Girton–Newnham campaign in 1921 to win degrees and membership for women at Cambridge University. Ref: Tullberg, Strachey, (Joan) Pernel.

244   Millicent Baxter, The Memoirs of Millicent Baxter, 42.

245   Ibid.

246   Ibid., 40–45.

247   Ibid., 45.

248   Ibid., 47.

249   The house still stands within its substantial gardens and is 35 Macmillan Avenue. The name of the avenue was a coincidence; it was not named after John.

250   14 October 1908. "60 Beautiful Hillside Sections." The Press. http://paperspast.natlib.govt.nz/cgi-bin/paperspast?a=d&d=CHP19081014.2.71.7.

251   Hankin, "Brown, John Macmillan."

252   Griffith. Interview with Terence Baxter and his son Kenneth Baxter, 3 February 2010.

253   Millicent Baxter, The Memoirs of Millicent Baxter, 48.

254   McKay, The Life of James K. Baxter, 19.

255   Millicent Baxter, The Memoirs of Millicent Baxter, 48.

256   McKay, The Life of James K. Baxter, 31.

257   Paul Millar, Interview with Terence Baxter, 11 December 1995.

258   Millicent Baxter, The Memoirs of Millicent Baxter, 48.

259   Ibid.

260   Rice, Christchurch Changing, 74.

261   Ibid., 79.

262   Arthur Rhodes had established the first New Zealand branch of the Red Cross Society in Christchurch in 1915. Ref: Rice, Christchurch Changing, 79.

263   Millicent Baxter, The Memoirs of Millicent Baxter, 49.

264   "NZ History: Lady Liverpool Great War Story" Ministry for Culture and Heritage, http://www.nzhistory.net.nz/media/video/lady-liverpool-great-war-story.

265   Millicent Baxter, The Memoirs of Millicent Baxter, 49.

Chapter 4 - The Leap to Pacifism

266   John Norton, "Baxter's Breakdown. 29 June 1918." http://paperspast.natlib.govt.nz/cgi- bin/paperspast?a=d&d=NZTR19180629.2.48.

267   Millicent Baxter, The Memoirs of Millicent Baxter, 51.

268   "Veteran New Zealand Peace Campaigner Dies." Otago Daily Times, 4 July 1984.

269   Redmar Yska, Truth: The Rise and Fall of the People's Paper (Nelson: Craig Potton Publishing, 2010), 62.

270   Paul Baker, King and Country Call: New Zealanders, Conscription and the Great War (Auckland: Auckland University Press, 1988), 197.

271   Ian Hamilton, Till Human Voices Wake Us, (Auckland: I Hamilton,1953), 19.

272   Harris, Nancy. "Baughan, Blanche Edith (1870–1958)" Dictionary of New Zealand Biography: Te Ara — the Encyclopedia of New Zealand. http://www.teara.govt.nz/en/biographies/3b17/baughan-blanche-edith.

273   Baker, King and Country Call: New Zealanders, Conscription and the Great War, 196.

274   Millicent Baxter, The Memoirs of Millicent Baxter, 84.

275   Millicent Baxter, The Memoirs of Millicent Baxter, 51–52.

276   John Macmillan Brown, Professor, "Red Feds and Prussianism" An address to the Overseas Club, April 1917, reported in The Press, 13 April 1917. http://paperspast.natlib.govt.nz/cgi-bin/paperspast?a=d&d=CHP19170413.2.36.

277   M. Derby, "Conscription, Conscientious Objection and Pacifism: Pacifism." Te Ara — the

Encyclopedia of New Zealand, http: / / www.teara.govt.nz / en / conscription-conscientious-objection-and-pacifism / 3.

278   Dick Scott, Ask That Mountain: The Story of Parihaka (Auckland: Reed/Southern Cross, 1975), 113–114.

279   Megan Hutching, "Turn Back This Tide of Barbarism: New Zealand Women Who Were Opposed to War:1896—1919." (Thesis M.A. History, University of Auckland, 1990), 9.

280   McKay, The Life of James K. Baxter, 7.

281   "The Defence Act of 1909," from an Encyclopaedia of New Zealand, Edited by A. H. Mclintock, Originally Published in 1966. In Te Ara — the Encyclopedia of New Zealand (2009). http: / / www. TeAra.govt.nz / en / 1966 / compulsory-military-training / 2.

282   Hutching, "Turn Back this Tide of Barbarism", 67.

283   The Defence Act 1909 from an Encyclopaedia of New Zealand, Edited by A. H. Mclintock, Originally Published in 1966. in Te Ara – the Encyclopedia of New Zealand (2009). http: / / www. TeAra.govt.nz / en / 1966 / compulsory-military-training / 2.

284   Baker, King and Country Call: New Zealanders, Conscription and the Great War, 15.

285   David Grant, Field Punishment No. 1: Archibald Baxter, Mark Briggs & New Zealand anti-militarist tradition (Wellington: Steele Roberts Publishers, 2008), 15.

286   Harry E. Holland, Armageddon or Calvary: The Conscientious Objectors of New Zealand and "The Process of Their Conversion" (Brooklyn, N.Z: H.E. Holland, 1919), 7.

287   McKay, The Life of James K. Baxter, 8.

288   Baker, King and Country Call: New Zealanders, Conscription and the Great War, 73.

289   Belich, Paradise Reforged: A History of the New Zealanders From the 1880s to the Year 2000, 95.

235   Cole Catley, Recorded Interview with Millicent Baxter. Cass 2 Side 1 (Hocken Library Ms-3099/013), March 1979.

236   Millicent Baxter, The Memoirs of Millicent Baxter, 40.

237   Ibid., 47.

238   Ibid., 80.

239   Ibid., 39.

240   Ibid., 41.

241   Ibid., 42.

242   A first attempt to secure titles for women's degrees were rebuffed in 1887 and 1897. Undergraduates demonstrating against the granting of these titles to women caused hundreds of pounds worth of damage in the market square. During World War One the women tried once more to gain inclusion, this time asking not only for the titles of degrees but also for the privileges and involvement in university government that possession of degrees proper would bring. In Oxford this was secured in 1920, but in Cambridge the women were defeated again, in 1921, having to settle for the titles – the much-joked-about 'BA tit' – but not the substance of degrees. This time, the male undergraduates celebrating victory over the women used a handcart as a battering ram to destroy the lower half of the bronze gates at Newnham College bearing a memorial to Anne Jemima Clough who was an early English suffragist and a promoter of higher education for women. Finally in 1948, the women were admitted to full membership of the University but even then the university still retained powers to limit their numbers. Ref: "Newnham College, University of Cambridge." http: //www.newn.cam.ac.uk/ about-newnham/college-history.

243   As the principal of Newnham College, Joan Pernel Strachey took a leading part in the unsuccessful Girton–Newnham campaign in 1921 to win degrees and membership for women at Cambridge University. Ref: Tullberg, Strachey, (Joan) Pernel.

244   Millicent Baxter, The Memoirs of Millicent Baxter, 42.

245   Ibid.

246   Ibid., 40–45.

247   Ibid., 45.

248   Ibid., 47.

249   The house still stands within its substantial gardens and is 35 Macmillan Avenue. The name of the avenue was a coincidence; it was not named after John.

250   14 October 1908. "60 Beautiful Hillside Sections." The Press. http://paperspast.natlib.govt.nz/cgi-bin/paperspast?a=d&d=CHP19081014.2.71.7.

251   Hankin, "Brown, John Macmillan."

252   Griffith. Interview with Terence Baxter and his son Kenneth Baxter, 3 February 2010.

253   Millicent Baxter, The Memoirs of Millicent Baxter, 48.

254   McKay, The Life of James K. Baxter, 19.

255   Millicent Baxter, The Memoirs of Millicent Baxter, 48.

256   McKay, The Life of James K. Baxter, 31.

257   Paul Millar, Interview with Terence Baxter, 11 December 1995.

258   Millicent Baxter, The Memoirs of Millicent Baxter, 48.

259   Ibid.

260   Rice, Christchurch Changing, 74.

261   Ibid., 79.

262   Arthur Rhodes had established the first New Zealand branch of the Red Cross Society in Christchurch in 1915. Ref: Rice, Christchurch Changing, 79.

263   Millicent Baxter, The Memoirs of Millicent Baxter, 49.

264   "NZ History: Lady Liverpool Great War Story" Ministry for Culture and Heritage, http://www.nzhistory.net.nz/media/video/lady-liverpool-great-war-story.

265   Millicent Baxter, The Memoirs of Millicent Baxter, 49.

266   John Norton, "Baxter's Breakdown. 29 June 1918." http://paperspast.natlib.govt.nz/cgi- bin/paperspast?a=d&d=NZTR19180629.2.48.

267   Millicent Baxter, The Memoirs of Millicent Baxter, 51.

268   "Veteran New Zealand Peace Campaigner Dies." Otago Daily Times, 4 July 1984.

269   Redmar Yska, Truth: The Rise and Fall of the People's Paper (Nelson: Craig Potton Publishing, 2010), 62.

270   Paul Baker, King and Country Call: New Zealanders, Conscription and the Great War (Auckland: Auckland University Press, 1988), 197.

271   Ian Hamilton, Till Human Voices Wake Us, (Auckland: I Hamilton,1953), 19.

272   Harris, Nancy. "Baughan, Blanche Edith (1870–1958)" Dictionary of New Zealand Biography: Te Ara — the Encyclopedia of New Zealand. http://www.teara.govt.nz/en/biographies/3b17/baughan-blanche-edith.

273   Baker, King and Country Call: New Zealanders, Conscription and the Great War, 196.

274   Millicent Baxter, The Memoirs of Millicent Baxter, 84.

275   Millicent Baxter, The Memoirs of Millicent Baxter, 51–52.

276   John Macmillan Brown, Professor, "Red Feds and Prussianism" An address to the Overseas Club, April 1917, reported in The Press, 13 April 1917. http://paperspast.natlib.govt.nz/cgi-bin/paperspast?a=d&d=CHP19170413.2.36.

277   M. Derby, "Conscription, Conscientious Objection and Pacifism: Pacifism." Te Ara — the Encyclopedia of New Zealand, http: / / www.teara.govt.nz / en / conscription-conscientious-objection-and-pacifism / 3.

278   Dick Scott, Ask That Mountain: The Story of Parihaka (Auckland: Reed/Southern Cross, 1975), 113–114.

279   Megan Hutching, "Turn Back This Tide of Barbarism: New Zealand Women Who Were Opposed to War:1896—1919." (Thesis M.A. History, University of Auckland, 1990), 9.

280   McKay, The Life of James K. Baxter, 7.

281   "The Defence Act of 1909," from an Encyclopaedia of New Zealand, Edited by A. H. Mclintock, Originally Published in 1966. In Te Ara — the Encyclopedia of New Zealand (2009). http: / / www.TeAra.govt.nz / en / 1966 / compulsory-military-training / 2.

282   Hutching, "Turn Back this Tide of Barbarism", 67.

283   The Defence Act 1909 from an Encyclopaedia of New Zealand, Edited by A. H. Mclintock, Originally Published in 1966. in Te Ara – the Encyclopedia of New Zealand (2009). http: / / www.TeAra.govt.nz / en / 1966 / compulsory-military-training / 2.

284   Baker, King and Country Call: New Zealanders, Conscription and the Great War, 15.

285   David Grant, Field Punishment No. 1: Archibald Baxter, Mark Briggs & New Zealand anti-

militarist tradition (Wellington: Steele Roberts Publishers, 2008), 15.

286   Harry E. Holland, Armageddon or Calvary: The Conscientious Objectors of New Zealand and "The Process of Their Conversion" (Brooklyn, N.Z: H.E. Holland, 1919), 7.

287   McKay, The Life of James K. Baxter, 8.

288   Baker, King and Country Call: New Zealanders, Conscription and the Great War, 73.

289   Belich, Paradise Reforged: A History of the New Zealanders From the 1880s to the Year 2000, 95.

290   Steven Loveridge, Calls to Arms: New Zealand Society and Commitment to the Great War, (Wellington: Victoria University Press, 2014), 26.

291   "Socialist Objection: Conscientious Objection in the First World War." NZ History Online, http://www.nzhistory.net.nz/war/first-world-war/conscientious-objection/socialist-objection.

292   Grant, Field Punishment No. 1: Archibald Baxter, Mark Briggs & New Zealand anti-militarist tradition, 17.

293   Baker, King and Country Call: New Zealanders, Conscription and the Great War, 23.

294   Ibid., 30.

295   Ibid., 170.

296   Millicent Baxter, The Memoirs of Millicent Baxter, 52.

297   Antonietta Baldacchino, Email to Penny Griffith, 21 Feb 2013.

298   Millicent Baxter, The Memoirs of Millicent Baxter, 52.

299   "Influenza Epidemic." New Zealand Disasters. 2013.

300   "Influenza Epidemic." http: / / christchurchcitylibraries.com / Kids / NZDisasters / InfluenzaEpidemic.asp.

301   Millicent Baxter, The Memoirs of Millicent Baxter, 54–55.

302   Ibid., 55.

303   Ibid., 55–56.

304   Griffith, Interview with Katherine Baxter, 18 April 2010.

305   Millicent Baxter, The Memoirs of Millicent Baxter, 56.

306   Ibid., 57.

307   Their son was a conscientious objector in World War Two, though not in the same camp as Terence.

308   Millicent Baxter, The Memoirs of Millicent Baxter, 57.

309   Ibid.

310   Brasch, Indirections: A Memoir, 1909-1947, 119.

Chapter 5 - The Rabbiter

311   Janet McKellar had married John Baxter in North Bute Church in 1847 and she was buried there.

312   2007. "The Ships List: Launching of the Lady Egidia." http://freepages.genealogy.rootsweb.ancestry.com/~ourstuff/LadyEgidia1861.htm..

313   McKay, The Life of James K. Baxter, 3.

314   Family legend holds that Margaret was the daughter of an English baronet, Mark Learmond, who married a commoner, Janet McIntosh, and was disinherited by his family – a story that is echoed a little in Millicent and Archie's marriage. Ref: McKay, The Life of James K. Baxter, 6.

315   Ian Pool & Rosemary Du Plessis. "Families: A History: Colonial Families: 1840–1879", Te Ara — the Encyclopedia of New Zealand. http://www.teara.govt.nz/en/families-a-history/page-2.

316   McKay, The Life of James K. Baxter, 4–5.

317   Millicent Baxter, The Memoirs of Millicent Baxter, 62.

318   McKay, The Life of James K. Baxter, 6.

319   Ibid., 5.

320   Griffith, Interview with Terence and his son Kenneth Baxter, 3 February 2010

321   James K. Baxter, "Winter Sea" in Collected Poems of James K. Baxter, 389—90.

322   McKay, The Life of James K. Baxter, 7.

323   Millicent Baxter, The Memoirs of Millicent Baxter, 63.

324   Kuri Bush School History File. Hocken Library, Dunedin. Ag-294-49 / 124. 1962.

325   Ibid.

326   McKay, The Life of James K. Baxter, 6.

327   Grant, Field Punishment No.1: Archibald Baxter, Mark Briggs & New Zealand anti-militarist tradition, 42.

328   It seems that Archie had more of a Scottish lilt to his accent than any of his brothers. Both Katherine Baxter and her mother Lenore (Terence's wife) think that living with Millicent possibly retained his slight Scottish accent, whereas the other brothers became more 'Kiwi' as they got older. Ref: Griffith, Interview with Lenore and Katherine Baxter, 2 May 2011.

329   Barclay was the son of a pioneer Presbyterian minister. Ref: "The Barclays in South Canterbury, N.Z." http://www.rootsweb.ancestry.com/~nzlscant/barclay.htm. He was a Liberal MP but a Fabian, an admirer of Karl Marx and thus a strong supporter of socialism. He was also a lecturer in constitutional history at Otago University. Ref: Gustafson, Barry, Labour's Path to Political Independence: Origins and Establishment of the New Zealand Labour Party, 1900–19. Auckland: Auckland University Press, 1980.

330   Alfred R. Barclay, "The Origin of Wealth: Being the Theory of Karl Marx in Simple Form." An address delivered by A.R. Barclay at Roslyn, Dunedin, Tuesday 11 April 1899.

331   Archibald Baxter, We will not cease. (Christchurch: Caxton Press, 1968), 10.

332   Much of the biographical material on Archie Baxter and his army experiences is drawn from his memoir We will not cease.

333   Archibald Baxter, We will not cease, 9.

334   Ibid.

335   Griffith, Interview with Terence Baxter and his son Kenneth Baxter, 3 February 2010.

336   Griffith, Interview with Kenneth Baxter, 8 December 2009.

337   Griffith, Interview with Katherine Baxter, 28 May 2011.

338   Archibald Baxter, We will not cease, 9.

339   "Socialist Objection: Conscientious Objection in the First World War." NZ History Online, http://www.nzhistory.net.nz/war/first-world-war/conscientious-objection/socialist-objection.

340   Archibald Baxter, We will not cease, 11.

341   Griffith, Interview with Paul Oestreicher, 19 May 2010.

342   Paul Oestreicher has a very interesting background of pacifism; many of his former years were spent in Brighton where he got to know the Baxters. He was recently a chaplain at the University of Sussex and has been the founding Chair of Amnesty International; Vice President of the Campaign for Nuclear Disarmament; and a lifetime worker for peace and social justice. Ref: 2008. "Peace Movement Aotearoa – Canon Paul Oestreicher speaks in Wellington." http://www.converge.org.nz/pma/pauloes.htm.

343   Statutes of New Zealand, No.8, Military Service Act, 1916, Section 35.

344   Belinda C. Cumming, "Parents, Siblings and Pacifism: The Baxter Family and Others (World War I and World War 2)", (Thesis, University of Otago, 2007), 27.

Chapter 6 - The Conchie's War against War

345   The date is uncertain; Archie states in 'We will not cease' that it was around the end of February. His army records state that he "enlisted" on 16 November 1916 and that his "commencement of duty" was on 1 March 1917. Ref: "New Zealand Defence Force Personnel Records. Preserved by Archives New Zealand. Record Title: Archibald McColl Larmond (sic) Baxter. Archives Reference: Aabk 18805 W5520 0012624."

346   McKay, The Life of James K. Baxter, 8.

347   Archibald Baxter, We will not cease, 14.

348   Ibid.12–21.

349   Ibid. 21.

350   Peter S. O'Connor, "The Awkward Ones: dealing with conscience, 1916-1918." New Zealand Journal of History 8 (2) (1974): 122.

351   The Terrace Gaol, built in 1854, held some of the region's most notorious criminals until it was

Endnotes

demolished in 1925. It was one of Wellington's first prisons. Ref: "Dominion Post: Street History: The Terrace." http://www.stuff.co.nz/dominion-post/news/local-papers/the-wellingtonian/7223556/Street-history-The-Terrace.

352 Mt Cook prison was closed in 1900 and the building became the Alexandra Barracks for local military forces. Parts of the prison were reopened as a penal facility in 1903. Ref: Penny Griffith, Personal communication with Michael Kelly, 29 July 2013.

353 Archibald Baxter, We will not cease, 53.

354 Baker, King and Country Call: New Zealanders, Conscription and the Great War, 179.

355 Field Punishment No 1 (2014) Film. Producers Donna Malane and Paula Boock.

356 Holland, Armageddon or Calvary: The Conscientious Objectors of New Zealand and "The Process of Their Conversion", 22.

357 Two days later, Ballantyne's brother took the letter to Labour member Harry Holland, himself an anti-conscriptionist who had been jailed several times for sedition. Holland acted swiftly enough to send, and be part of, a deputation to the Minister of Defence James Allen, two days later. The following day it was reported in the Maoriland Worker, widely considered the most important publication of the New Zealand labour movement (edited by Holland), that Allen had made an assurance that the men wouldn't be subject to persecution, and that the idea of sending them to n buildings and apparently if each hut were to have been placed end-to-end they would have extended for nearly ten kilometres. It comprised four main sections: Auckland, Wellington, Otago and Canterbury Lines. At the end of the war, when there were delays in demobilising troops, the New Zealand soldiers were put to work carving the shape of a huge Kiwi (the Bulford Kiwi) and 'NZ' in the chalk of the hillside overlooking the camp. The Kiwi's beak alone is 46 metres long. Sling Camp is gone now, but the Bulford kiwi is still there today. Bulford Camp remains as a British Army camp. Ref: "New Zealand at War: 1914—1918: Sling Camp at Bulford on the Salisbury Plain, Wiltshire." http://www.archives.presbyterian.org.nz/photogallery14/page2.html.

362 Archibald Baxter, We will not cease, 79.

363 Holland, Armageddon or Calvary: The Conscientious Objectors of New Zealand and "The Process of Their Conversion", 49.

364 Baker, King and Country Call: New Zealanders, Conscription and the Great War, 182.

365 Grant, Field Punishment No.1: Archibald Baxter, Mark Briggs & New Zealand anti-militarist tradition, 47.

366 Archibald Baxter, We will not cease, 95.

367 It was from the Étaples base that on 12 October 1917, six days after some of the 14 objectors were sent there, 845 New Zealand soldiers were killed and over 2855 were wounded or missing at Passchendalele, Belgium – the worst ever day-long disaster in New Zealand's post 1840 existence. Ref: 'The Passchendaele offensive" NZ History Online. Ministry for Culture and Heritage.

368 Harry Holland, when compiling his book, learned of a letter regarding Harland: 'He, like Garth [Ballantyne], eventually took up medical work, but signed nothing and accepted no pay, though often near starving. They offered him a suit of clothes in Lyttelton [when he was returned to New Zealand], but when he heard he had to sign for it he would have none of it." Ref: Holland, Armageddon or Calvary: The Conscientious Objectors of New Zealand and "The Process of Their Conversion",119. Tragically, Little was killed in September 1918 while aiding a wounded man. Ref: Christopher Pugsley, On the Fringe of Hell: New Zealanders and Military Discipline in the First World War. Auckland: Hodder and Stoughton, 1991, 230.
Jack Baxter was considerably weakened by illness before he submitted.
Ballantyne, Little and Sandy Baxter were three times threatened with the death penalty, court-martialed and subjected to five years' hard labour under appalling conditions in a military prison in Dunkirk, the sentence later being commuted by Godley to two years. The three of them held out until June but eventually submitted. Two days later Sandy Baxter was sent to England with rheumatic fever, contracted by exposure and hardship in the prison. Ref: Holland, Armageddon or Calvary: The Conscientious Objectors of New Zealand and "The Process of Their Conversion", statement by Garth Ballantyne, 104.

369 Baker, King and Country Call: New Zealanders, Conscription and the Great War, 296.

370 Pugsley, On the Fringe of Hell: New Zealanders and Military Discipline in the First World War,

96.

371 "Flogging & Field Punishment No.1." http://www.historicalfirearms.info/post/75095899088/
flogging-field-punishment-no1-the-british-army.

372 Archibald Baxter, We will not cease, 105–06.

373 Ibid.

374 Holland, Armageddon or Calvary: The Conscientious Objectors of New Zealand and "The
Process of Their Conversion", statement by Garth Ballantyne, 97–98.

375 Archibald Baxter, We will not cease, 111.

376 In 1917, of the 435 New Zealanders admitted to the New Zealand Division Field Punishment
Camp, 189 were on Field Punishment No 1. In 1918, the numbers reduced to 25. Contrary to popular
belief in Australia, Field Punishment was awarded by Australian Commanding Officers and by
Australian courts martial to the same degree as in the New Zealand Division. By 30 April 1918,
the Australian Corps Field Punishment Compound reported total admissions of 2504 men on Field
punishment (both No One and Two). Ref: Pugsley, On the Fringe of Hell: New Zealanders and Military
Discipline in the First World War, 100–01.

377 Pugsley also writes: 'In hindsight one can see that the New Zealand military police running the
[punishment] centres were a law unto themselves. They determined to break "incorrigibles" and they
ignored restrictions placed upon them…There were hard men in the New Division and these were hard
times, but the brutality practiced in the New Zealand Division Field Punishment Camps was a failure
in command.' Ref: Pugsley, On the Fringe of Hell: New Zealanders and Military Discipline in the First
World War,102.

378 Box respirators used a two-piece design: a mouthpiece connected via a hose to a box filter
containing granules of chemicals that neutralised the gas.

379 Archibald Baxter, We will not cease, 118

380 Ibid., 123.

381 Griffith, Interview with Ray Grover, former chief archivist of Archives New Zealand and
honorary archivist of the Army Museum, Waiouru, 23 July 2013.

382 Archibald Baxter, We will not cease, 125–26.

383 Ibid., 128–29.

384 Briggs was a Yorkshireman who at 20 emigrated to New Zealand in about 1904. Always a
believer in social justice, he joined the flax millers' trade union in Manawatu and became a supporter
of the radical 'Red Feds.' A small man with dimples and an angelic face, he was militant in his
approach for better working conditions for flax-millers. Early in 1917, he refused to be conscripted, as
a conscientious objector on socialist grounds. His appeal was denied and he was escorted to barracks
at Trentham Military Camp, following a similar path to Archie Baxter. He refused all further military
orders to drill and was court-martialed. He served the first seven weeks of 84 days of hard labour
in Mt Cook prison then was sent to the Terrace Gaol where he met and talked with Labour leader
Peter Fraser, who had been charged with sedition for opposing the Conscription Act and sentenced
to 12 months' imprisonment. Ref: David Grant, "Briggs, Mark," Te Ara — the Encyclopedia of New
Zealand: Dictionary of New Zealand Biography. http://www.teara.govt.nz/en/biographies/3b48/briggs-
mark.

Briggs became one of The Fourteen deported to Britain and had been kept in irons for the whole of his
four weeks at Sling Camp. For the last five days he was there he went on a hunger strike. He proved
to be even more vociferous in his anti-militarist views than Archie. When the colonel at Sling Camp
insisted on his calling him 'Sir', Briggs told him that if he ever had to choose between calling him
"Sir" and never speaking again, he would choose the latter. On being sent to Étaples and refusing to
parade, he was sentenced to 28 days Field Punishment No. 1 at the Oudredoum compound. General
Russell, commander of the New Zealand Division arrived at the compound, interviewed him and
listened to him with respect. He said 'You know Briggs, you are fighting for freedom; so am I. But I
use different methods from you.' This was an astonishing thing for Russell to say, having once declared
that conscientious objectors should be court-martialed and shot. Ref: Holland, Armageddon or Calvary:
The Conscientious Objectors of New Zealand and "The Process of Their Conversion", statement by
Mark Briggs, 65–66.

385 By mid-April Briggs was returned to Étaples. It was now considered that he was likely to remain

an objector to the end, and early in 1919 he was invalided back to New Zealand where he refused the soldier's wage that was offered to him. Mark Briggs had won his war and unlike Archie Baxter, suffered remarkably little, mentally or physically, considering the horrors he had undergone. A quiet, thoughtful teetotaler, Briggs was a staunch supporter of the New Zealand Labour Party and was appointed to the Legislative Council (the upper house of the General Assembly of New Zealand) in 1936. In 1940 he was the only member of parliament, of either House, to vote against the introduction of military conscription in the Second World War. He died in Palmerston North in 1965 at the age of 80, saddened by the growing materialism of New Zealand society. Ref: Ref: Grant, "Mark Briggs."

386   Archibald Baxter, We will not cease, 131.

387   Ironically, conscientious objectors were in high demand as stretcher-bearers and in this sense, more were needed in the army – conscientious objectors tended to be hard-working and courageous enough to fulfil the needs of that terrible job. Ref: Griffith, Interview with Ray Grover, 23 July 2013.

388   Archibald Baxter, We will not cease, 135.

389   Archibald Baxter, We will not cease, 137–38.

390   Ibid., 142–44.

391   Ibid., 146.

392   Ibid., 159.

393   Ibid., 148.

394vNew Zealand Defence Force Personnel Records. Archives New Zealand. Record Title: Archibald McColl Larmond (sic) Baxter. Archives Reference: Aabk 18805 W5520 0012624.

395   Archibald Baxter, We will not cease, 148.

396   Baker, King and Country Call: New Zealanders, Conscription and the Great War, 187.

397   New Zealand Defence Force Personnel Records. Preserved by Archives New Zealand. Record Title: Archibald McColl Larmond (sic) Baxter. Archives Reference: Aabk 18805 W5520 0012624.

398   Archibald Baxter, We will not cease, 154.

399   The Boulogne Base mental specialist was W.D. Chambers, who concluded his report with 'The offence was obviously not a rational attempt to desert and, in my opinion, he was insane and not responsible for his actions… This man is insane.' Ref: Baker, King and Country Call: New Zealanders, Conscription and the Great War, 187.

400   New Zealand Defence Force Personnel Records. Archives New Zealand. Record Title: Archibald McColl Larmond (sic) Baxter. Archives Reference: Aabk 18805 W5520 0012624.

401   In We will not cease, Archie says it was Bradmore Hospital. Ref: Archibald Baxter, We will not cease, 162.

402   New Zealand Defence Force Personnel Records. Archives New Zealand. Record Title: William Baxter Archives Reference: Aabk 18805 W5520 0012691.

403   Archibald Baxter, We will not cease, 177–178.

404   Ibid., 178–79.

405   Cumming, "Parents, Siblings and Pacifism", 18.

406   Baker, King and Country Call: New Zealanders, Conscription and the Great War, 198.

407   Archibald Baxter, We will not cease, 184.

408   "Baxter Case: the Conscientious Objector." Otago Daily Times. P.6, 24 October 1918

409   Harry E. Holland, Armageddon or Calvary: The Conscientious Objectors of New Zealand and "The Process of Their Conversion" (Brooklyn, N.Z: H.E. Holland, 1919).

410   In his statement to Harry Holland in Armageddon or Calvary, Archie says, 'I would like to say in this connection that with me it was not a matter of setting up my will against the public but of doing what I believed to be right and refusing to do what I believed to be wrong; I do not believe that all that was done to me and to other objectors was done by the will of the community.' Ref: Holland, Armageddon or Calvary: The Conscientious Objectors of New Zealand and "The Process of Their Conversion", statement by Archibald McC. L. Baxter, 87. Unfortunately this was only read by the handful of readers who bought the book, and the bulk of them would have been pacifists.

411   New Zealand Defence Force Personnel Records. Archives New Zealand. Record Title: Archibald McColl Larmond (sic) Baxter. Archives Reference: Aabk 18805 W5520 0012624.

412   Archibald Baxter, We will not cease, 185.

413   Donald Baxter, Letter from Donald Baxter from Waikeria Reformatory, September1918, Letters

from Donald Baxter, Ms-0975 / 206, Baxter Family: Papers (Arc-0351), Hocken Library Dunedin.

414   Millar, Interview with Terence Baxter, 11 December 1995.

415   Archibald Baxter, We will not cease, 187.

416   New Zealand Defence Force Personnel Records. Archives New Zealand. Record Title: Archibald McColl Larmond (sic) Baxter. Archives Reference: Aabk 18805 W5520 0012624.

417   Archibald Baxter, We will not cease, 188.

418   Penny Griffith, Personal communication with Jan Kelly 30 November 2010.

419   Archibald Baxter, We will not cease, 185.

Chapter 7 - The Princess and the Pauper

420   Grant, Field Punishment No.1: Archibald Baxter, Mark Briggs & New Zealand anti-militarist tradition, 100.

421   Holland, Armageddon or Calvary: The Conscientious Objectors of New Zealand and "The Process of Their Conversion",107.

422   The list contains the names of 2045 men, including 160 objectors who were in prison. Defaulters regained their civil rights in 1927. Ref: Baker, King and Country Call: New Zealanders, Conscription and the Great War, 209–210.

423   Millicent Baxter, The Memoirs of Millicent Baxter, 60

424   John Gibb, "Lest we forget: memorial to city's 2500 dead." Otago Daily Times, 25 April 2008 http://www.odt.co.nz/news/dunedin/4017/lest-we-forget-memorial-city039s-2500-dead.

425   Cumming, "Parents, Siblings and Pacifism", 19.

426   McKay, The Life of James K. Baxter, 10.

427   "Interview with Millicent Baxter" in Looking Back, Radio New Zealand, 24 January 1981. http://collections.soundarchives.co.nz/search.do?view=detail&id=135578&db=object.

428   Millicent Baxter, The Memoirs of Millicent Baxter, 57–58.

429   Ibid., 58.

430   McKay, The Life of James K. Baxter, 20.

431   Millicent Baxter, The Memoirs of Millicent Baxter, 58.

432   Ibid.

433   Ibid. 58–59.

434   Cole Catley, Recorded Interview with Millicent Baxter. Cass 2 Side 1 (Hocken Library Ms-3099/013), March 1979.

435   Millicent Baxter, The Memoirs of Millicent Baxter, 59.

436   Ibid.

437   Griffith. Interview with Max Broadbent, 12 May 2008.

438   Ibid.

439   Cole Catley, Recorded Interview with Millicent Baxter: Cass 3 Side 1 (Hocken Library Ms-3099/013), March 1979.

440   Millicent Baxter, The Memoirs of Millicent Baxter, 60.

441   Ibid.

442   Today the dam is one of very few 19th century dams still in use in New Zealand. Ref: Dunedin City Council Bush Tracks: Ross Creek Reservoir. http://www.dunedin.govt.nz/facilities/walking-tracks/bush-walk.

443   Ibid. 60–61.

444   Cole Catley, Recorded Interview with Millicent Baxter, Cass 1 Side 1 (Hocken Library Ms-3099/013), March 1979.

Chapter 8 - From Mansion to Shack

445   Millicent Baxter, The Memoirs of Millicent Baxter, 61.

446   Frank McKay, Interview with Terence Baxter, 8 July 1984, Baxter Box One: Transcripts of Interviews No.L—20, Beaglehole Room, University of Victoria, Wellington,1984.

447   Griffith, Interview with Christine Cole Catley, 2 September 2009.

448   Cole Catley, Recorded Interview with Millicent Baxter. Cass 2 Side 1 (Hocken Library Ms-3099/013), March 1979.

449   Ibid.

450   Millicent Baxter, The Memoirs of Millicent Baxter, 64.

451   Cole Catley, Recorded Interview with Millicent Baxter. Cass Side 1 (Hocken Library Ms-3099/013), March 1979.

452   The house has now been replaced by a brick house a little further along the road.

453   McKay, The Life of James K. Baxter, 21.

454   Millar, Interview with Terence Baxter, 11 December 1995. Cited in Millar, Spark to a Waiting Fuse: James K. Baxter's Correspondence with Noel Ginn, 1942-46 / Edited and Introduced by Paul Millar, Wellington: Victoria University Press, 2001, 47.

455   Griffith, Interview with Terence Baxter and his son Kenneth Baxter, 9 January 2010.

456   Millicent Baxter, The Memoirs of Millicent Baxter, 60–61

457   Griffith, Interview with Margaret Gibson, 3 September 2010.

458   Cole Catley, recorded interview with Millicent Baxter. Cass 2, Side 1 (Hocken Library Ms-3099/013), March 1979.

459   Griffith, Interview with Margaret Gibson, 3 September 2010.

460   Griffith, Interview with Kenneth Baxter, 8 December 2009.

461   Griffith, Interview with Terence and his son Kenneth Baxter, 3 February 2010.

462   Griffith, Interview with Kenneth Baxter, 8 December 2009.

463   Millicent Baxter, The Memoirs of Millicent Baxter, 64.

464   Ibid., 61.

465   Griffith, Interview with George McIntosh, 22 January 2010.

466   Millicent Baxter, The Memoirs of Millicent Baxter, 61.

467   Ibid., 62.

468   Ibid., 121.

469   Griffith, Interview with Terence Baxter and his son Kenneth Baxter, 3 February 2010.

470   Millicent Baxter, The Memoirs of Millicent Baxter, 65.

471   Cole Catley, Recorded Interview with Millicent Baxter. Cass 2 Side 1 (Hocken Library Ms-3099/013), March 1979.

472   Millicent Baxter, The Memoirs of Millicent Baxter, 65.

473   Ibid.

474   Cole Catley, Recorded Interview with Millicent Baxter. Cass 2 Side 1 (Hocken Library Ms-3099/013), March 1979.

475   Griffith, Interview with George McIntosh, 22 January 2010.

476   Millicent Baxter, The Memoirs of Millicent Baxter, 62.

477   Cole Catley, Recorded Interview with Millicent Baxter. Cass 2 Side 1 (Hocken Library Ms-3099/013), March 1979..

478   William H. Oliver, James K. Baxter: A Portrait (Christchurch, N.Z.: Whitcoulls Ltd, 1983), 7.

479   Griffith, Interview with Frances Mulrennan and Shirley McLeod, 20 May 2010.

480   Ibid.

481   Millicent Baxter, The Memoirs of Millicent Baxter, 61.

482   Griffith, Interview with George McIntosh, 22 January 2010.

483   Ibid.

484   Ibid.

485   Ibid. 63–64.

486   Cole Catley, Recorded Interview with Millicent Baxter. Cass 2 Side 1 (Hocken Library Ms-3099/013), March 1979.

487   Griffith, Interview with George McIntosh, 22 January 2010.

488   Millicent Baxter, The Memoirs of Millicent Baxter, 64.

489   Ibid.

490   Terence MacSwiney was a Commander in the Irish Republican Army. He was arrested by the British on charges of sedition and imprisoned in Brixton, England where he starved himself to death

after a 74-day hunger strike. His funeral in Cork was viewed by over 100,000 people. His hunger strike and death brought worldwide attention to Ireland's freedom struggle against the British Empire. Ref, Keane, Chris 2012. 'Irish Volunteers.org: Terence MacSwiney.' http://irishvolunteers.org/2012/05/terence-macswiney/.

491   Truby King, F. Feeding and Care of Baby. London: Macmillan and Co, 1913.

492   Sir Frederic Truby King was a New Zealand health reformer and Director of Child Welfare. He is best known as the founder of the Plunket Society in 1907 and his first book on mother care, Feeding and Care of Baby, 1913, became famous throughout the world. His methods were controversial, but his baby care method grew in popularity, finding favour at least until the 1950s. Truby King also became well-known as the controversial medical superintendent of Seacliff Lunatic Asylum, later Seacliffe Mental Hospital, a post he held from1889 for 30 years. Ref: Barbara Brookes, "King, Frederic Truby." http://www.teara.govt.nz/en/biographies/2k8/king-frederic-truby.

493   There is another connection with the Baxter family here. Janet Frame CBE, one of the country's most well-known writers, was perhaps Seacliffe Mental Hospital's most famous inmate. Janet was a close friend of James and Jacquie Baxter and had close contact with the wider Baxter family. Wilson Gordon, the father of Janet Frame's literary executive Pamela Gordon, was a pacifist during World War Two and was in dissenters' camp with Terence Baxter. Gordon married Janet Frame's sister June and was a very good friend of Archie's nephew Jack Baxter. Ref: Griffith, Interview with Pamela Gordon, 24 February 2011.

494   Millicent Baxter, The Memoirs of Millicent Baxter, 65–66.

495   Ibid., 66.

496   Ibid.

497   "Fraser, Peter." Dictionary of New Zealand Biography: Te Ara — the Encyclopedia of New Zealand. http://www.teara.govt.nz/en/biographies/4f22/fraser-peter.

498   James K. Baxter, "Notes on the Education of a New Zealand Poet" in The

499   Millicent Baxter, The Memoirs of Millicent Baxter, 66–67.

500   James's son, John Baxter, maintains his father spent the first six to twelve months in an iron lung: 'You've got to remember that my father was a late-life baby. Archie would have been in his early 40s and Millicent in her very late 30s, I think. And he was in an iron lung for, I think, the first six months of his life – if not a year.' Ref: Colin Durning, Interview with John Baxter, 3 August 2010.

501   McKay, The Life of James K. Baxter, 23.

502   Millicent Baxter, The Memoirs of Millicent Baxter, 66–67.

503   Cole Catley, Recorded Interview with Millicent Baxter. Cass 2 Side 1 (Hocken Library Ms-3099/013), March 1979.

504   McKay, The Life of James K. Baxter, 23.

505   Griffith, Interview with Terence Baxter and his son Kenneth Baxter, 9 January 2010.

506   John Weir, "The Spirituality of James K. Baxter." http://www.catholicworker.org.nz/cg/CG63-TheSpiritualityOfJamesKBaxter.html.

507   Cumming, "Parents, Siblings and Pacifism", 24

508   Terence Baxter, Letter to Penny Griffith, 12 April 2012.

509   Millar, Interview with Terence Baxter, 11 December 1995.

510   Terence Baxter, Letter to Penny Griffith, 12 April 2012.

511   Millicent Baxter, The Memoirs of Millicent Baxter, 75.

512   James K. Baxter, First Years Remembered: Kuri Bush. Unpublished Poem, Ms 704/17, Hocken Library.

513   James K. Baxter, The Man on the Horse (1967). Cited in Lawrence Jones, "Mythology of Place: Homage to James K Baxter." http://www.lloydgodman.net/baxter/Intros/JamesK.htm.

514   James K. Baxter, "Pig Island Letters" in Collected Poems of James K. Baxter, 277.

515   Millar, Interview with Terence Baxter, 11 December 1995.

516   James K. Baxter, The Man on the Horse, 91.

517   The school was closed in May 1935 Ref: Kuri Bush School History File. Hocken Library, Dunedin. Ag-294-49 / 124. 1962.

518   McKay, The Life of James K. Baxter, 22.

519   Millicent Baxter, The Memoirs of Millicent Baxter, 69.

Chapter 9 - Roving and Writing

520   McKay, The Life of James K. Baxter, 23.
521   James K. Baxter, "A Family Photograph 1939" in Collected Poems of James K. Baxter, 237.
522   Ref: Dore, Diane, Email to Penny Griffith, 7 August 2013.
523   Griffith, Interview with Rosamund McCreadie and Diane Dore, 23 February 2010.
524   Ibid.
525   Griffith, Interview with Diane Dore, 10 April 2014.
526   Millar, Interview with Terence Baxter, 11 December 1995.
527   Griffith, Interview with Lawrence Jones, 4 May 2008.
528   Patricia first married John McCreadie then Don Lawson.
529   Max Broadbent, Email to Penny Griffith, 13 May 2008.
530   Millicent Baxter, The Memoirs of Millicent Baxter, 72–73.
531   Griffith, Interview with Wynn Geeves, 12 January 2010.
532   Griffith, Interview with George McIntosh, 22 January 2010.
533   Griffith, Interview with Don Lawson, 17 August 2010.
534   Griffith, Interview with Kenneth Baxter, 8 December 2009.
535   Millicent Baxter, The Memoirs of Millicent Baxter, 111–112.
536   Ibid., 69
537   James K. Baxter, "The Mountains" Hocken Library MS 704 / 7:437, 102–4 Cited in Millar, Spark to a Waiting Fuse, 2001, 183
538   Millicent Baxter, The Memoirs of Millicent Baxter, 71
539   Ibid., 70.
540   Millar, Interview with Terence Baxter, 11 December 1995.
541   McKay, The Life of James K. Baxter, 25.
542   McKay, The Life of James K. Baxter, 25.
543   Ibid., 68.
544   McKay, The Life of James K. Baxter, 27.
545   Millicent Baxter, The Memoirs of Millicent Baxter, 68.
546   Millar, Interview with Terence Baxter, 11 December 1995.
547   James K. Baxter, 1967. The Man on the Horse, 130.
548   McKay, The Life of James K. Baxter, 25.
549   Ibid., 32.
550   Millicent Baxter, The Memoirs of Millicent Baxter, 74.
551   Ibid., 69.
552   Michael King, Interview with Millicent Baxter, October 1978. Tape transcript from Christine Cole Catley. Hocken Library (MS-3099/014).
553   Griffith, Interview with Terence Baxter and his son Kenneth Baxter, 9 January 2010.
554   Ibid.
555   Ibid.
556   McKay, The Life of James K. Baxter, 10.
557   Millicent Baxter, The Memoirs of Millicent Baxter, 134.
558   Millar, Interview with Terence Baxter, 11 December 1995.
559   Baxter, Lenore. Letter to Frank Mckay, 7 July 1985, VUW Library, Wellington. Ms Mckay 10 / 7 / 32. Cited in Millar, Spark to a Waiting Fuse, 49–50.
560   Millar, Interview with Terence Baxter, 11 December 1995.
561   Griffith, Interview with Kenneth Baxter, 8 December 2009.
562   Griffith, Interview with Don Lawson, 17 August 2010.
563   Griffith, Interview with Rosamund McCreadie and Diane Dore, 23 February 2010.
564   Griffith, Interview with Lawrence Jones, 4 May 2008.
565   Cole Catley, Recorded Interview with Millicent Baxter. Cass 2 Side 1 (Hocken Library Ms-3099/013), March 1979.
566   Griffith, Interview with Rosamund McCreadie and Diane Dore, 23 February 2010.

567   Ibid.
568   Macmillan Brown, The Memoirs of John Macmillan Brown, introduction James K. Baxter, xxxv.
569   Millicent Baxter, The Memoirs of Millicent Baxter, 75.
570   James McNeish, Intimate Strangers – James Mcneish Interviews Viola Notariello. Radio N.Z. (Concert Programme), 18 September 1980.
571   Millar, Interview with Terence Baxter, 11 December 1995.
572   Harding, Interview with Antonietta Baldacchino, 20 November 2001.
573   1921, the year Archie and Millicent married, John had gone with Viola to Fiji, Tonga and Samoa, and the next year he sailed to Easter Island on the deck of a Chilean training ship. He spent seven months there, but the lack of nutritious food and vegetables affected his robust health. Nevertheless he still continued travelling (to South America and China) and at home always did his hour's exercising first thing in the morning followed by an hour or two of gardening, all before breakfast. He continued his research in philology and Polynesian culture and every winter sailed to the warm weather of the Pacific Islands. In 1930, aged 85, he sailed for England with Viola. He bought a large, comfortable car, and father and daughter drove all over England, Wales and Scotland then all over the Continent. His energy was inexhaustible. Back in New Zealand he continued lecturing. Once on his way to the college he tripped on a stone in the dim lighting and cut his leg badly, but, unabashed, gave his lecture with blood dripping on to his shoe. His last trip was to Niue then he spent the last two or three years of his life entertaining and enjoying the warmth of the fireside with his daughter. He finally relented to having a nurse come on occasion, but she had to be 'attractive, not young and a woman of sound commonsense.' Ref: Macmillan Brown, The Memoirs of John Macmillan Brown, introduction Viola Helen Notariello, xxx -xxxiii).Viola Helen Notariello's Introduction, xxx -xxxiii).
574   Jill Durney, Email to Penny Griffith, 28 January 2013.
575   History of the Macmillan Brown Library, University of Canterbury. http://www.libr.canterbury.ac.nz/mb/mbhist.shtml.
576   Harding, Interview with Antonietta Baldacchino, 20 November 2001.
577   Broadbent, Email to Penny Griffith, 13 May 2008.
578   Ibid.
579   Harding, Interview with Antonietta Baldacchino, 20 November 2001.
580   Broadbent, Email to Penny Griffith, 13 May 2008.
581   Millicent Baxter, The Memoirs of Millicent Baxter, 75.
582   David Young, "A Poet for a Son", 25 October 1980. The New Zealand Listener.
583   Millicent Baxter, The Memoirs of Millicent Baxter, 76.
584   Ibid.
585   McKay, The Life of James K. Baxter, 33.
586   Wanganui has now been renamed Whanganui, but since it was known as Wanganui during the time covered by this book, I have retained that spelling.
587   Millicent Baxter, The Memoirs of Millicent Baxter, 76.
588   Ibid., 77.
589   McKay, The Life of James K. Baxter, 33.
590   King, Interview with Millicent Baxter.
591   Millicent Baxter, The Memoirs of Millicent Baxter, 79–80.
592   James McNeish, Intimate Strangers – James Mcneish Interviews Viola Notariello.
593   McKay, The Life of James K. Baxter, 35.
594   Millicent Baxter, The Memoirs of Millicent Baxter, 82.
595   Archibald Baxter, We will not cease, (1968), 88.
596   Millar, Interview with Terence Baxter, 11 December 1995.
597   Griffith, Interview with Don Lawson, 17 August 2010.
598   Millicent Baxter, The Memoirs of Millicent Baxter, 83
599   Ibid., 82.
600   Griffith, Interview with Christine Cole Catley, 2 September 2009.
601   Chris Laidlaw, "Ideas – a Pack of Hoons: Conscientious Objectors in New Zealand History." In Sunday Report with Chris Laidlaw, 2009.
602   Griffith, Interview with Lenore and Katherine Baxter, 2 May 2011.

603 Griffith, Interview with Terence and his son Kenneth Baxter, 9 January 2010.
604 The novel (in his handwriting) is about his Gaelic-speaking ancestors after their arrival in New Zealand from Scotland. Ref: Baxter, Archibald. Unpublished Novel. Hocken MS 975/195.
605   Loveridge, Calls to Arms: New Zealand Society and Commitment to the Great War, 167.
606 Griffith, Interview with Lawrence Jones and Diane Dore, 22 May 2010.
607 William Blake, Preface to Milton: A Poem. 1810.
608 "And did those feet in ancient time." https://www.princeton.edu/~achaney/tmve/wiki100k/docs/And_did_those_feet_in_ancient_time.html.
609 Millicent Baxter, The Memoirs of Millicent Baxter, 83.
610 McKay, The Life of James K. Baxter, 35
611 Millicent Baxter, The Memoirs of Millicent Baxter, 85.
612 Oliver, James K. Baxter: A Portrait, 28.
613 James. K. Baxter, "At Serrières", in Collected Poems of James K. Baxter, 250.
614 James. K. Baxter, "The Bad Young Man" in Collected Poems of James K. Baxter, 118.
615 McKay, The Life of James K. Baxter, 38
616 David Young, "A Poet for a Son." The New Zealand Listener, 25 October 1980.
617 Millicent Baxter, The Memoirs of Millicent Baxter, 97.
618 Ibid., 91.
619 Archibald Baxter, We will not cease: Autobiography of a Conscientious Objector, (London: Gollancz, 1939).
620 Millicent Baxter, The Memoirs of Millicent Baxter, 97.
621 Ibid.
622 Archibald Baxter, We will not cease, (1968), 11.
623vArchibald Baxter, We will not cease, (Auckland: Cape Catley, 2003), Foreword.
624 David Hill, "Mr & Mrs Baxter N.Z." The New Zealand Listener, 24 January 2004.
625 In 2004, a review was, M. The conscientious self: Enriching Sociological Social Psychology 101: Using the Anti-Torture Biography We Will Not Cease. Otago University social psychology course.
626 Ibid.
627 Martin Tolich, The Conscientious Self: Enriching Sociological Social Psychology 101: Using the Anti-Torture Biography We Will Not Cease. 2013.Otago University social psychology course. http://www.ipp.org.nz/NZS%20issues/Vol24No209/NZS2426.pdf.

Chapter 10 - The Conchie Son

628 For 10 years the Rangitiki had been working between the UK and New Zealand as an immigration ship for many starting a new life in New Zealand. On the return she would carry refrigerated meat and dairy products, and wool. Ref: http: / / w ww.derbysulzers.com / shiprangitiki.html
629 Millicent Baxter, The Memoirs of Millicent Baxter, 105.
630 Ibid., 143.
631 Engineering Sources at the Hocken Collections: Reid and Gray Limited. www.otago.ac.nz / library / pdf / Engineering_Guide.pdf.
632 Millar, Interview with Terence Baxter, 11 December 1995.
633 Millar, Spark to a Waiting Fuse, 45.
634 Griffith, Interview with Terence Baxter and his son Kenneth Baxter, 3 February 2010.
635 David Grant, Out in the Cold: Pacifists and Conscientious Objectors in New Zealand During World War 2, (Auckland: Reed Methuen, 1986), 41.
636 Fraser's opposition to conscription in World War I hadn't been absolute. Rather, he was among those who argued it shouldn't be introduced unless it was accompanied by the conscription of wealth through taxes. Ref: "Fraser, Peter." Dictionary of New Zealand Biography: Te Ara — the Encyclopedia of New Zealand. http://www.teara.govt.nz/en/biographies/4f22/fraser-peter.
637 Cumming, "Parents, Siblings and Pacifism", 27–28
638 Millicent Baxter, The Memoirs of Millicent Baxter, 108.
639 "The Second World War at home: Ballot Boys." http://www.nzhistory.net.nz/war/second-world-

war-at-home/war-work.

640   Millar, Spark to a Waiting Fuse, 42.

641vAnnette Seear, "A Pacifist Who Came Into Her Own." The Evening Star, 4 February 1978.

642   Lenore Baxter, letter to Frank McKay, undated, MS McKay 10/7/33. Cited in Millar, Spark to a Waiting Fuse, 34.

643   Millar, Interview with Terence Baxter, 11 December 1995.

644   Millar, Spark to a Waiting Fuse, 42.

645   Griffith, Interview with Lenore and Katherine Baxter, 2 May 2011.

646   Millar, Spark to a Waiting Fuse, 43.

647   Millicent Baxter, The Memoirs of Millicent Baxter, 107.

648   McKay, The Life of James K. Baxter, 55.

649   Archie's brother Mark's sons all came up and had their appeals disallowed, except for non-combatant service. They all, with the exception of Billy who was turned down on account of his health, were held in detention camps.
 Millar, Interview with Terence Baxter, 11 December 1995.

650   "The Treatment of Conscientious Objectors", letter, Otago Daily Times 27 Dec 1941, Cited in Millar, Spark to a Waiting Fuse, 44.

651   "The Treatment of Conscientious Objectors", letter, Otago Daily Times 27 Dec 1941, Cited in Millar, Spark to a Waiting Fuse, 44.

652   Terence Baxter, Letter to Penny Griffith, 28 April 2010.

653   Our conversations always took place in a café. Terence loves his cup of tea and cookies. He would never let me into his "untidy house".

654   Lenore Baxter, letter to Frank McKay, undated, MS McKay 10/7/33. Cited in Millar, Spark to a Waiting Fuse, 67.

655   Millar, Interview with Terence Baxter, 11 December 1995.

656   Millar, Interview with Terence Baxter, 11 December 1995.

657   Grant, Out in the Cold: Pacifists and Conscientious Objectors in New Zealand During World War 2, 143.

658   Ian Hamilton, Till Human Voices Wake Us, (Auckland: I Hamilton, 1953).

659   "Second World War at home: In dissent." New Zealand History Online. Ministry for Culture and Heritage. http://www.nzhistory.net.nz/war/second-world-war-at-home/in-dissent.

660   Millar, Interview with Terence Baxter, 11 December 1995.

661   Ibid.

662   Millicent Baxter, The Memoirs of Millicent Baxter, 109.

663   Griffith, Interview with Terence Baxter and his son Kenneth Baxter, 9 January 2010.

664   Millar, Interview with Terence Baxter, 11 December 1995.

665   Griffith, Telephone Interview with Terence Baxter, 19 August 2013.

666   Cumming, "Parents, Siblings and Pacifism", 30.

667   Millar, Spark to a Waiting Fuse, 97.

668   Grant, Out in the Cold: Pacifists and Conscientious Objectors in New Zealand During World War 2, 149–150.

669   Millar, Interview with Terence Baxter, 11 December 1995.

670   James K. Baxter, 'Sonnet Fourteen', Autumn Testament.

671   Grant, Out in the Cold: Pacifists and Conscientious Objectors in New Zealand During World War 2, 152–153.

672   Millar, Interview with Terence Baxter, 11 December 1995.

673   VUW Library, MS McKay 28/39. Cited in Millar, Spark to a Waiting Fuse, 346.

674   Burton had fought in World War I because he believed the destruction of Prussian militarism would mean a new age of peace and freedom through forgiveness and reconciliation under God. Disillusioned and horrified with the terms of the Treaty of Versailles, he became a resolute convert to Christian pacifism. Ref: 2013. "Burton, Ormond Edward." http://www.teara.govt.nz/en/biographies/5b53/burton-ormond-edward.

Burton very probably came across Archie Baxter in France around April 1918, just before he and his platoon joined with the New Zealand Division to try and halt the German breakthrough on the Somme.

Endnotes

Ref: Millar, Spark to a Waiting Fuse, 29. He noticed a group of conscientious objectors under guard: 'They had been brought from New Zealand and forced into the front lines by the military police. There was a considerable amount of sympathy shown to them by the soldiers for the harsh treatment they had had to endure because they had refused to join the military when conscription was introduced in New Zealand.' Ref: Ernest Crain, I Can do No Other: A Biography of The Reverend Ormond Burton (Auckland: Hodder and Stroughton, 1986), 43. Cited in Millar, Spark to a Waiting Fuse, 29.

675   Ginn, Noel. Letter to Paul Millar, January 1995. Cited in Millar, Spark to a Waiting Fuse, 90

676   Millar, Spark to a Waiting Fuse, 90.

677   Millar, Interview with Noel Ginn, 25 October 1994.

678   Millar, Interview with Terence Baxter, 11 December 1995.

679   Millar, Spark to a Waiting Fuse, 92.

680   Penny Griffith, Telephone Interview with Terence Baxter, 19 August 2013.

681vJames K. Baxter, "Conversations about Writing", New Zealand Monthly Review 60 September 1965. Cited in Millar, Spark to a Waiting Fuse, 92.

682   Millar, Interview with Terence Baxter, 11 December 1995.

683   Baxter, Terence, Letter to James K. Baxter, undated [c. 1942-43], MS Hocken 975/183.' Cited in Millar, Spark to a Waiting Fuse, 92.

684   Millicent Baxter, The Memoirs of Millicent Baxter, 108.

685   Ibid., 108–109.

686   McKay, The Life of James K. Baxter, 106.

687   Cooper, Annabel. 5 Jun 2013. "Baxter, Millicent Amiel." http://www.teara.govt.nz/en/biographies/3b20/baxter-millicent-amiel.

688   Millicent Baxter, The Memoirs of Millicent Baxter, 107.

689   "Second World War at home: In dissent." New Zealand History Online. Ministry for Culture and Heritage. http://www.nzhistory.net.nz/war/second-world-war-at-home/in-dissent.

690   Cooper, Annabel. "Baxter, Millicent Amiel." http://www.teara.govt.nz/en/biographies/3b20/baxter-millicent-amiel.http://www.teara.govt.nz/en/biographies/3b20/baxter-millicent-amiel.

691   Millicent Baxter, The Memoirs of Millicent Baxter, 109.

692   Ibid., 66.

693   Cole Catley, Recorded Interview with Millicent Baxter. Cass 2 Side 1 (Hocken Library Ms-3099/013), March 1979.

694   Ibid.

695   Millar, Interview with Terence Baxter, 11 December 1995.

696   Millicent Baxter, The Memoirs of Millicent Baxter, 111.

697   Millar, Interview with Terence Baxter, 11 December 1995.

698   Recounted in a letter from James K. Baxter's friend Margaret Hargreave to Frank McKay, VUW Library, MS McKay 10/5/36.

699   Grant, Out in the Cold: Pacifists and Conscientious Objectors in New Zealand During World War 2, 177.

700   Gibson, Lucy. Correspondence with Millicent Baxter 1945. Alexander Turnbull Library 91-142-03.

701   Grant, Out in the Cold: Pacifists and Conscientious Objectors in New Zealand During World War 2, 212.

702   Millar, Spark to a Waiting Fuse, 121.

703   Ginn, Noel. Letter to Frank McKay, 13 January 1983, VUW Library, MS McKay item 10/4/17. Cited in McKay, The Life of James K. Baxter, 91.

704   Millar, Interview with Noel Ginn, August 1994.

705   Millar, Interview with Terence Baxter, 11 December 1995

706   Ibid.

707   Millicent Baxter, The Memoirs of Millicent Baxter, 112–113.

708   Cumming, "Parents, Siblings and Pacifism", 32.

709   Ginn, Noel. Letter to Paul Millar, January 1995. Cited in Millar, Spark to a Waiting Fuse, 123

710   Ginn, Noel. Letter to Paul Millar, April 1995. Cited in Millar, Spark to a Waiting Fuse, 124

711   Millar, Interview with Terence Baxter, 11 December 1995. Cited in Millar, Spark to a Waiting

Fuse, 123.

712   Hargreave, Margaret Letter to Frank McKay 18 February 1944, VUW Library, MS McKay 10/5/36. Contains transcripts from letters of James K. Baxter in Margaret Hargreaves' possession. Cited in Millar, Spark to a Waiting Fuse, 125.

713   Millar, Interview with Terence Baxter, 11 December 1995. Cited in Millar, Spark to a Waiting Fuse, 126.

714   McKay, The Life of James K. Baxter, 94.

715   McKay, Conversation with Terence Baxter, 8 July 1984. Cited in The Life of James K. Baxter, 92.

716   Griffith, Interview with Lenore and Katherine Baxter, 2 May 2010.

717   Griffith, Interview with Katherine Baxter, 4 August 2013.

718   Griffith, Interview with Diane Dore, 21 January 2010.

719   Millar, Interview with Terence Baxter, 11 December 1995.

720   During World War Two, Hillside manufactured three-inch mortars as well as machined components for other weapons systems. It was the largest industrial complex in the southern half of the South Island, employing a maximum of nearly 1200 people in 1946. Ref: http://www.ipenz.org.nz/heritage/itemdetail.cfm?itemid=51

721   Griffith, Interview with Terence Baxter, 24 December 2013.

722   Griffith, Interview with Terence Baxter and his son Kenneth Baxter, 3 February 2010.

Chapter 11 - The Poet Son

723   James K. Baxter, The Man on the Horse, 124.

724   Ibid., 130.

725   James K. Baxter, "A Family Photograph 1939" in Collected Poems of James K. Baxter, 237.

726   McKay, The Life of James K. Baxter, 50.

727   Ibid., 51–53.

728   James K. Baxter, The Man on the Horse, 123.

729   James K. Baxter, "To my Mother" Hocken. MS704/4: 184. Cited in Millar, Spark to a Waiting Fuse, 48.

730   James K. Baxter, "A Family Photograph 1939" in Collected Poems of James K. Baxter, 237

731   Millicent Baxter, The Memoirs of Millicent Baxter, 111.

732   King, Interview with Millicent Baxter.

733   McKay, The Life of James K. Baxter, 54.

734   James was probably fourteen.

735   Harding, Interview with Millicent Baxter, 8 April 1982.

736   Initially a keen participant in cadets at Eton and the University Rifle Volunteers at Oxford, this English Quaker became a prominent peace activist and conscientious objector in WW 1. Ref: Hess, Dale. June 2003. "The Story of Stephen Hobhouse" Journal Of The Religious Society Of Friends (Quakers) In Australia.

737   Harry Urquhart, a Christian pacifist, was jailed for 11 months for sedition for writing a pamphlet challenging compulsory conscription then jailed again for refusing to be conscripted. Ref: "Remembering Peacemakers on Anzac Day." Lest We Forget.

738   Millicent Baxter, The Memoirs of Millicent Baxter, 106.

739   Terence Baxter, Letter to Penny Griffith, 28 April 2010.

740   McKay, The Life of James K. Baxter, 57.

741   Young, "A Poet for a Son".

742   James K. Baxter, The Man on the Horse, 137.

743   Ibid.

744   Ibid., 123

745   Millicent Baxter, The Memoirs of Millicent Baxter, 109.

746   McKay, The Life of James K. Baxter, 71. Cited in James K Baxter, The Spike: or Victoria University College Review, 1954 (Wellington: Victoria University College Students' Association, 1954).

747   Griffith, Interview with Lenore and Katherine Baxter, 2 May 2010.

748   Caxton Press had been set up in 1935 in Victoria Street by John Drew and the renowned New Zealand literary figure, Denis Glover. Ref: "The Caxton Press: History." http://www.caxton.co.nz/history.html.
Glover wasn't there when James and Millicent visited; during the Second World War Glover served with the Royal Navy. On D-Day, he earned the DSC. Glover and James would eventually become friends but Glover's drinking, financial mismanagement and erratic attendance became a major problem at Caxton, and in 1952 he was dismissed. Faults he admitted to include an unrepentantly monocultural and masculine view of society and of literature, an 'immodest enthusiasm for draught beer' and a tendency to shed 'printing presses, wives and books' as he went. Ref: Ogilvie, Gordon. "Glover, Denis James Matthews." Te Ara — the Encyclopedia of New Zealand: Dictionary of New Zealand Biography. http://www.teara.govt.nz/en/biographies/4g11/glover-denis-james-matthews.

749   Lawrence Baigent, Conversation with Frank McKay. Cited in McKay, The Life of James K. Baxter, 75–76.

750   Millicent Baxter, The Memoirs of Millicent Baxter, 110.

751   McKay, The Life of James K. Baxter, 75.

752v James K. Baxter, Beyond the Palisade : Poems by James K. Baxter, (Christchurch [N.Z.] Caxton Press, 1944).

753   McKay, The Life of James K. Baxter, 79.

754   Letter from James K. Baxter to the Armed Forces Appeal Board, MS-0975/212, Baxter Family Papers (HC). Cited in Cumming, "Parents, Siblings and Pacifism", 40.

755   Ibid., 40–41.

756   James K. Baxter, Letter to Lawrence Baigent, 24 February 1945. Cited in McKay, The Life of James K. Baxter, 79.

757   James K. Baxter, Horse (Auckland: Oxford University Press, 1985), 7–8

758   Ibid., 9–11.

759   McKay, The Life of James K. Baxter, 86–89.

760   James. K. Baxter, Letter to Millicent Baxter, 15 October 1945. Cited in McKay, The Life of James K. Baxter, 88.

761   McKay, The Life of James K. Baxter, 92.

762   James K. Baxter, "Sunday: Chingford Park." Found amongst Baxter's letters to Baigent. Cited in McKay, The Life of James K. Baxter, 93.

763   Richard D Wiggers, "The United States and the Refusal to Feed German Civilians after World War I1." In Vardy, Steven Bela; Tooley, T. Hunt. Ethnic Cleansing in Twentieth-Century. http://forum.axishistory.com/viewtopic.php?t=138574.

764   Descendants of the Chinese miners who came to New Zealand for the gold rush in the 1860s.

765   "Canon Paul Oestreicher speaks in Wellington." 2008. Peace Movement Aotearoa http://www.converge.org.nz/pma/pauloes.htm.

766   Ibid.

767   Frank McKay, Interview with Canon Paul Oestreicher, April 1987. Cited in McKay,

768   McKay, The Life of James K. Baxter, 91.

769   Griffith, Interview with Paul Oestreicher, 19 May 2010.

770   Allison Rudd, "Oestreicher: disciple of universal compassion." Otago Daily Times, Sat, 23 May 2009.

771   McKay, The Life of James K. Baxter, 94–95.

772   Ibid., 99.

773   James K. Baxter, 1979. To My Father: Collected Poems of James K. Baxter, 65.

774   Janet Wilson, "Archie, Millicent and James: The Baxter Autobiographies." Journal of New Zealand Literature No 13 (1995): 47–64.

775   Ibid., 50–51.

776   Griffith, Interview with Christine Cole Catley, 2 September 2009.

777   Griffith, Interview with Katherine Baxter, 4 August 2013.

778   James K. Baxter, Horse, 7.

779   Millicent Baxter, The Memoirs of Millicent Baxter, 143.

780   Interview with Millicent Baxter in Looking Back.
781   McKay, The Life of James K. Baxter, 100–101.
782   Ibid., 106.
783   McKay, The Life of James K. Baxter, 100.
784   Michael King, Wrestling with the Angel: A life of Janet Frame (Auckland: Viking, 2000), 86.
785   McKay, The Life of James K. Baxter, 100.
786   Paul Millar, "Jacquie Baxter/J.C. Sturm (1927-2009)," Ka Mate Ka Ora: A New Zealand Journal of Poetry and Poetics 9 (March 2010).
787   Lindsay Rabbit, "Jim, Jacquie and Baxter." The New Zealand Listener, 17 June, 2000.
788   Millar, "Jacquie Baxter/J.C. Sturm (1927-2009)."
789   Ibid.
790   McKay, Interview with Denis Glover, 1978. Cited in McKay, The Life of James K. Baxter, 103.
791   McKay, The Life of James K. Baxter, 104.
792   James K. Baxter, Blow, Wind of Fruitfulness: James K. Baxter (Christchurch, N.Z.: Caxton Press, 1948).
793   McKay, The Life of James K. Baxter, 110.
794   James K. Baxter, Letter to Archibald and Millicent Baxter, Undated 1948. Cited in McKay, The Life of James K. Baxter, 118.
795   Millicent Baxter, The Memoirs of Millicent Baxter, 113.
796   Baker, King and Country Call: New Zealanders, Conscription and the Great War, 190
797   Rabbit, Lindsay, "Jim, Jacquie and Baxter." Interview with Jacquie Sturm.
798   McKay, The Life of James K. Baxter, 115 – 116.
799   James K. Baxter, "Autumn Testament no.8" in Collected Poems of James K. Baxter, 539.
800   McKay, The Life of James K. Baxter, 121.
801   James K. Baxter, Letter to Archibald and Millicent Baxter, 30 June 1969. Cited in McKay, The Life of James K. Baxter, 121
802   McKay, The Life of James K. Baxter, 125.
803   Oliver, James K. Baxter: A Portrait, 58.
804   James K. Baxter, Recent Trends in New Zealand Poetry (Christchurch: Caxton Press, 1951).
805   William H. Oliver, Landfall 5, No 3, September 1951, 222.
806   Oliver, James K. Baxter: A Portrait, 60.
807   Griffith, Interview with Rosamund McCreadie and Diane Dore, 23 February 2010.
808   Millicent Baxter, The Memoirs of Millicent Baxter, 122.
809   Griffith, Interview with Don Lawson, 17 August 2010.
810   Cole Catley, Recorded Interview with Millicent Baxter. Cass 3 Side 1 (Hocken Library Ms-3099/013), March 1979.3 (Hocken Library Ms-3099/013). March 1979.
811   Millicent Baxter, The Memoirs of Millicent Baxter, 125.
812   Griffith, Interview with Terence Baxter and his son Kenneth Baxter, 3 February 2010.
813   Griffith, Interview with Kenneth Baxter, 8 December 2009.
814   Griffith, Interview with Toni Wilson, 1 February 2010.
815   Millicent Baxter, Letter to Jean Bertram, 6 October 1980. Papers of James and Jean Bertram. Alexander Turnbull Library 93-103-13.
816   Griffith, Interview with Margaret Gibson, 3 September 2010.
817   Cumming, "Parents, Siblings and Pacifism", 45–46.
818   Griffith, Interview with Lenore and Katherine Baxter, 2 May 2010.
819   Ibid.
820   Griffith, Interview with Diane Dore, 21 May 2010.
821   Diane Dore, Email to Penny Griffith, 9 December 2013.
822   Baxter, Barry. Emails to Penny Griffith, March–April 2014.
823   James K. Baxter, The Fallen House: Poems by James K. Baxter (Christchurch, N.Z.: Caxton Press, 1953).
824   James. K. Baxter, "To My Father" in The Fallen House, 14.
825   James K. Baxter, The Tree House and Other Poems for Children: James K. Baxter, (Wellington, N.Z: Price Milburn, 1974).

826   McKay, The Life of James K. Baxter, 139.

827   Writers' Profiles: "Lawlor, Pat." The New Zealand Book Council, http://www.bookcouncil.org.nz/Writers/Profiles/Lawlor,%20Pat.

828   Pat Lawlor, The Two Baxters: Diary Notes by Pat Lawlor (Wellington: Millward Press, 1979) , 13

829   James. K. Baxter, The Fire and the Anvil: Notes on Modern Poetry, (Wellington: New Zealand University Press, 1955).

830   McKay, The Life of James K. Baxter, 142.

831   Ibid., 144.

832   Oliver, James K. Baxter: A Portrait, 78.

833   Wellington Scoop "Ngati Poneke to celebrate 75 years of kapa haka." http://wellington.scoop.co.nz/?p=45308.

834   Oliver, James K. Baxter: A Portrait, 78.

835   Pat Lawlor, The Two Baxters: Diary Notes by Pat Lawlor, 17.

836   McKay, The Life of James K. Baxter, 158–59.

837   Pat Lawlor, The Two Baxters: Diary notes by Pat Lawlor, 18

838   McKay, The Life of James K. Baxter, 167.

839   James K. Baxter, "This Indian Morning" in Collected Poems of James K. Baxter. Cited in McKay, The Life of James K. Baxter, 98.

840   James K. Baxter, Howrah Bridge and Other Poems, (London: Oxford University Press, 1961).

841   Paul Millar, Ka Mate Ka Ora: a New Zealand Journal of Poetry and Poetics, (March 2007).

842   Pat Lawlor, The Two Baxters: Diary Notes by Pat Lawlor, 29.

843   McKay, The Life of James K. Baxter, 192.

844   James K. Baxter, Letter to Archibald and Millicent Baxter, 25 August, 1963. Hocken MS 976/183.

845   Millar, "Jacquie Baxter/J.C. Sturm".

846   Despite the protests, more than 3000 New Zealand military and civilian personnel served in Vietnam between 1963 and 1975. Ref: New Zealand History Online "The Vietnam War: New Zealand and the Vietnam War." Ministry for Culture and Heritage. http://www.nzhistory.net.nz/war/vietnam-war.

847   McKay, The Life of James K. Baxter, 206.

848   Stuart Sellar, Email to Penny Griffith, 28 October 2010.

849   Stuart Sellar, Email to Penny Griffith, 5 November 2010.

850   Stuart Sellar, Email to Penny Griffith, 28 October 2010.

851   Ibid.

852   Antonietta Baldacchino thinks that possibly both Viola and Millicent became Catholic because it was a kind of release from the Protestant strictness they were brought up with. Ref: Harding, Interview with Antonietta Baldacchino.
 Griffith, Interview with Diane Dore, May 2010.

853   Griffith, Interview with Diane Dore, May 2010.

854   Sellar, Email to Penny Griffith 5 November 2010.

855   Millicent Baxter, The Memoirs of Millicent Baxter, 126.

856   King, Interview with Millicent Baxter.

857   Millicent Baxter, The Memoirs of Millicent Baxter, 126.

858   Sellar, Email to Penny Griffith, 28 October 2010.

859   Pope John received the Balzan Prize for Peace, Humanity and Fraternity among Peoples the month before he died in 1963. Ref: 11 May, 2013. "International Balzan Prize Foundation: 50 Years ago: the Pope received the Balzan Prize." http://www.balzan.org/en/news/news-detail/50-years-ago-the-pope-received-the-balzan-prize.

860   Millicent told Christine Cole Catley she adored Pope John XXIII. Ref: Cole Catley, Recorded Interview with Millicent Baxter. Cass 2 Side 1 (Hocken Library Ms-3099/013), March 1979.

861   Sellar, Email to Penny Griffith, 28 October 2010.

862   Stuart Sellar would become Director of Catholic Social Services, Dunedin, then, in 1985,

Lecturer in Theology at the Holy Cross College, Mosgiel, and the University of Otago, for nine years. He did an M.A. at Fordham University, New York then in 1992 became Dean in the Faculty of Theology, University of Otago for two years. He completed his PhD then did part-time teaching at La Trobe University, Australian Catholic University and Melbourne College of Divinity. From 2005 he has been Lecturer in Theology at Good Shepherd Theological College in Auckland. Ref: Stuart Sellar, Letter to Penny Griffith, October 2010.

863   Pig Island is a vernacular term for New Zealand.

864   James K. Baxter, Pig Island Letters (Oxford: Oxford University Press, 1966).

865   McKay, The Life of James K. Baxter, 204.

866   Griffith, Interview with Frances Mulrennan and Shirley McLeod, 20 May 2010.

867   Ibid.

868   Millicent Baxter, The Memoirs of Millicent Baxter, 127.

869   Ibid., 124.

870   King, Interview with Millicent Baxter.

871   Millicent Baxter, The Memoirs of Millicent Baxter, 129.

872   Pat Lawlor, The Two Baxters: Diary Notes by Pat Lawlor, 44.

873   McKay, The Life of James K. Baxter, 236   .

874   Stephanie would later be brought up by Jacquie. She died tragically of a blood condition in September 2009 aged 41. Her mother, Hilary, died of cancer in November 2013, aged 64.

875   McKay, The Life of James K. Baxter, 237.

876   There had been a Catholic Māori Mission in Jerusalem (Hiruharama) since 1854 but this went into decline after the 1864 battle of Motua. It was rejuvenated by Suzanne Aubert, better known as Sister Mary Joseph – or Mother Aubert – in 1883.

877   Millicent Baxter, The Memoirs of Millicent Baxter, 134.

878   Harding, Interview with Antonietta Baldacchino, 20 November 2001.

879   James K. Baxter, Jerusalem Daybook, (Wellington: Price Milburn, 1971), 21. Cited in John Newton, The Double Rainbow: James K. Baxter, Ngāti Hau and the Jerusalem Commune (Wellington: Victoria University Press, 2009), 67

880   Tim Shadbolt, "Baxter's Commune", The First New Zealand Whole Earth Catalogue, (Wellington: Alister Taylor, 1972), 137.

881   James K. Baxter, Jerusalem Sonnets: Poems for Colin Durning, (Dunedin: University of Otago, 1970).

882   James K. Baxter, Jerusalem Daybook, (Wellington: Price Milburn, 1971).

883   Millicent Baxter, The Memoirs of Millicent Baxter, 128–130.

884   Barry Baxter, Emails to Penny Griffith March-April 2014.

885   Griffith, Interview with Terence Baxter and his son Kenneth Baxter, 3 February 2010.

886   Millicent Baxter, The Memoirs of Millicent Baxter, 130.

887   Ibid., 131.

888   Sellar, Email to Penny Griffith, 5 November 2010.

889   Barry Baxter, Emails to Penny Griffith, March—April 2014.

890   Millicent Baxter, The Memoirs of Millicent Baxter, 132.

891   Ibid., 11.

892   Millicent Baxter, The Memoirs of Millicent Baxter, 121.

893   Cole Catley, Recorded Interview with Millicent Baxter. Cass 3 Side 1(Hocken Library Ms-3099/013), March 1979.

894   Millicent Baxter, The Memoirs of Millicent Baxter, 132.

895   The Archibald Baxter Memorial Trust was launched in September 2014 to erect a memorial to New Zealand conscientious objectors – particularly to the 14 deported objectors – in Dunedin. The first in the country to honour conscientious objectors, it will be called the Archibald Baxter Memorial. Terence Baxter is the project's patron. Professor Kevin Clements of The National Centre for Peace and Conflict Studies, University of Otago, is its chair and one of the trustees. The remaining trustees are Richard Jackson, also at the Centre for Peace and Conflict Studies; Alan Jackson, the long-time follower of Archie Baxter and the original proposer of the project; Tony Eyre, freelance writer for The Otago Daily Times; Terence's daughter, Katherine Baxter; David Grant, the author of Field Punishment

No 1 and Out in the Cold, and myself. While there has been some dissention regarding the project, overall there has been a lot of support for the idea. The memorial is due to be opened in March/April 2017, 100 years after Archie was forced into the army.

896   About 35 years after Archie's death, there was some talk of Labour Prime Minister Helen Clark making an official government apology to the Baxter family for the treatment of Archie – and presumably the other conscientious objectors who had been subjected to Field Punishment No 1. This was discussed by some of the immediate Baxter family and they agreed that an apology would not be appropriate. No public statement was made and the idea was dropped. Katherine Baxter says there are two reasons for the rationale for not seeking an apology: in a democracy when a citizen or citizens protests or takes political action against a decision by the majority, they often break the law. It wouldn't seem appropriate to stand up in that way and then object to the consequences and ask for an apology. The point of protesting is to bear witness and provoke a response. In the case of Archie and the other WW1 conscientious objectors, it's likely the only apologies they might have accepted from the Government would have been an apology for engaging in the war and an apology to the thousands of New Zealanders who lost their lives. For Archie it was never about him; it was always about resisting the military machine on behalf of others. He would never have sought or accepted an apology to himself ahead of an apology to the nation, or at least to all those who suffered, one way or another, in that war. Ref: Katherine Baxter, Email to Penny Griffith, 3 Mar 2015.

897   Newton, The Double Rainbow, 65–66.

898   Millicent Baxter, The Memoirs of Millicent Baxter, 140.

899   James K. Baxter, Autumn Testament, (Wellington: Oxford University Press, 1972).

900   James K. Baxter, "Autumn Testament no. 14" in Collected Poems of James K. Baxter, 547. Cited in McKay, The Life of James K. Baxter, 274.

901   McKay, The Life of James K. Baxter, 281.

902   Ibid.

903   Millicent Baxter, The Memoirs of Millicent Baxter, 137–38.

904   McKay, The Life of James K. Baxter, 281.

905   The Road to Jerusalem. (1998) Film. Producer William Grieve

906   John Baxter had had some considerable influence on his father during the previous few years, especially in regard to an interest in Buddhism. Ref: Oliver, James K. Baxter: A Portrait, 145.

907   Oliver, James K. Baxter: A Portrait, 152

908   Paul Millar, and I. Sharp, "A Note on James K. Baxter's Late Poem 'a Pair of Sandals'". Best New Zealand Poems 2001. http://www.vuw.ac.nz/modernletters/bnzp/2001/baxternote.html.

909   McKay, The Life of James K. Baxter, 289.

910   W. S. Broughton, "Vonney Allan's Account of James Baxter's Death" Journal of New Zealand Literature, N.13 (1995): 285—290.

911   Millicent Baxter, The Memoirs of Millicent Baxter, 138.

912   Newton, The Double Rainbow, 170.

913   Ibid., 170–171.

914   Oliver, James K. Baxter: A Portrait, 155.

915   Griffith, Interview with Katherine Baxter, 4 August 2013.

916   Millicent Baxter, The Memoirs of Millicent Baxter, 138.

917   Harding, Interview with Millicent Baxter, 8 April 1982.

918   Oliver, James K. Baxter: A Portrait, 155.

919   Rabbit, "Jim, Jacquie and Baxter."

920   Paul Little, James K.Baxter: Complete Prose (Victoria University Press, Wellington, 2015) "Notes and Queries" North & South, August 2015.

921   Millicent Baxter, The Memoirs of Millicent Baxter, 144.

922   Cole Catley, Recorded Interview with Millicent Baxter. Cass 3 Side 1 (Hocken Library Ms-3099/013), March 1979.

923   Harding, Interview with Millicent Baxter, 8 April 1982.

Chapter 12   **I am Myself**

924   Harding, Interview with Millicent Baxter, 8 April 1982.

925   Ibid.

926   Broadbent, Email to Penny Griffith, 13 May 2008.

927   Millicent Baxter. 14 April, 1954. "The H-Bomb." Otago Daily Times, 4.

928   Millicent Baxter. 24 November 1969. "Manapouri." Otago Daily Times, 8.

929   Millicent Baxter. 7 March 1972. "Northern Ireland." Otago Daily Times, 18.

930   "International Relations – Changing foreign ties." Slice of Heaven exhibition http://www.tepapa.govt.nz/WhatsOn/exhibitions/SliceofHeaven/Exhibition/InternationalRelations/Pages/Changingforeignties.aspx.

931   Griffith, Interview with Terence Baxter and his son Kenneth Baxter, 3 February 2010.

932   Millicent Baxter, The Memoirs of Millicent Baxter, 135–137.

933   "Veteran New Zealand Peace Campaigner Dies." Otago Daily Times, 4 July 1984.

934   In 1976 Mary Ronnie became the National Librarian, the first woman national librarian in the world. Ref: Julia Millen, "Libraries: Library Associations and Librarians." Te Ara — the Encyclopedia of New Zealand, http://www.TeAra.govt.nz/en/photograph/41646/mary-ronnie-national-librarian-1978.

935   Griffith, Interview with Mary Ronnie, 23 February 2011.

936   Griffith, Interview with Margaret Gibson, 3 September 2010.

937   Richard Hatherly, Email to Penny Griffith, 13 April 2014.

938   Howard Paterson became a farmer and innovator. His wealth has been estimated at $120 million; colleagues credit him with a knack of latching on to new ideas before others realised there was an opportunity. Paterson focused on four main areas of business: property development, large scale corporate farming, tourism investment in New Zealand, Fiji and the United States, and biotechnology. He died in 2003 at the age of 50. Ref: "Obituary: Howard Paterson." NZ Herald, http://www.nzherald.co.nz/nz/news/article.cfm?c_id=1&objectid=3510994

939   Baker, King and Country Call: New Zealanders, Conscription and the Great War, 190.

940   Certainly there are references to Archie receiving Field Punishment No 1 in the Defence Force Personnel Records today. Ref: New Zealand Defence Force Personnel Records. Preserved by Archives New Zealand. Record Title: Archibald McColl (sic) Baxter. Archives Reference: Aabk 18805 W5520 0012624.

941   Millicent Baxter, The Memoirs of Millicent Baxter, 137.

942   Archie's army records make interesting and often disturbing reading. There are a number of errors: His middle name Leamond is spelt Larmond; his date of birth is stated as 3 December 1882; it should be 11 December 1881. His religion was Plymouth Brethren but the record states "no religion". Contrary to what Millicent stated, there are references to Archie receiving Field Punishment No 1 in the Defence Force Personnel Records today. There is an entry dated 24 April 1918 at No 8 Stationary Hospital giving evidence for the Medical Board. Towards the end it reports: Headache & sleeplessness and feeling of depression. Had been in Army one year – in France two months. Had been a prisoner all the time until he went to the Front under escort. States he did not deliberately leave his unit. States he has done no work at the Front. Taken out each day but refused to do anything and will continue to refuse to work in uniform. In hosp. takes no interest in newspapers & reads nothing. Considered that his views on the war amount to an obsession & that owing to the strain caused by his compulsion in being taken to the Front a definite attack of confusion occurred during which he committed the offence. Opinion of specialist at Boulogne Base – 'insane' not fit for trial or punishment. Finding: Board considers he was not responsible for his actions at the time of his offence. Rec. his trans to "D" Block, Netley. Ref: New Zealand Defence Force Personnel Records. Archives New Zealand. Record Title: Archibald McColl (sic) Baxter. Archives New Zealand Reference: Aabk 18805 W5520 0012624

943   Griffith, Interview with Frances Mulrennan and Shirley McLeod, 20 May 2010.

944   Millicent Baxter, The Memoirs of Millicent Baxter, 11.

945   Ibid.,139.

946   King, Interview with Millicent Baxter.

947   Millicent Baxter, The Memoirs of Millicent Baxter, 140.

948   Malcolm Shelton McGregor, A Day in the Life of New Zealand: Friday, March 18th, 1983, (Auckland, N.Z.: J.M. McGregor), 1983.

949   Griffith, Interview with Paul and Beatrice Donovan, 28 January 2010. His entry into A Day In

the Life of New Zealand was shortlisted.

950 Annette Seear, "A Pacifist Who Came into Her Own." The Evening Star, 4 February 1978.

951 Ibid.

952 Griffith, Penny. Telephone Interview with Frances Mulrenan 25 September 2011.

953 Ibid.

954 Griffith, Interview with Christine Cole Catley, 2 September 2009.

956 Griffith, Interview with Cecily McNeill, 17 August 2010.

957 Ibid.

958 Cole Catley, Recorded Interview with Millicent Baxter. Cass 1 Side 1 (Hocken Library Ms-3099/013), March 1979.

959 Harding, Interview with Millicent Baxter, 8 April 1982.

960 James K. Baxter, Collected Poems of James K. Baxter.

961 Millicent Baxter, The Memoirs of Millicent Baxter, 144

962 Jacquie Baxter died on 30 December 2009. Like Millicent Baxter, she has received very little recognition considering what she achieved and the selfless, often anguished life she led. It is therefore worthwhile including here what Paul Millar writes: 'After Baxter's death, Jacquie focused on her family. In 1970 she found work at the Wellington Public Library, a position she held for many years while also raising Hilary's daughter Stephanie. Her collected stories, ready for book publication since 1966, languished and she didn't write more for over a decade. It was at the Wellington Public Library that Witi Ihimaera came to know her, and in 1982, he and Don Long placed two of her stories in their anthology of Māori writing, Into the World of Light. The following year the women's publishing collective, Spiral, produced her stories as The House of the Talking Cat, with reviewers praising the collection and Ihimaera hailing her in a review as a 'pivotal presence in the Māori literary tradition'... In retirement Jacquie returned to her first love, poetry, and in 1996 Steele Roberts published her inaugural collection, Dedications, which earned the Honour Award for Poetry in the 1997 Montana New Zealand Book Awards. Postscripts followed in 2000, and a mixed selection of poetry and prose, The Glass House, in 2006. Jacquie's role as a pioneering Māori literary figure was recognised in 2003 when Victoria University made her an honorary Doctor of Literature. Her output may seem modest on paper, but it becomes substantial when set against the obstacles placed before her as a woman, wife and mother and, for many years, her family's primary earner. Although Jacquie Baxter never wanted to be a role model, she never shirked her responsibility as a voice for Māori people and a campaigner against racial inequality. Her life and writing are testament to a woman of great integrity and quiet courage who helped clear the path that younger writers have followed to greater success and recognition. Life delivered Jacquie a final cruel blow in 2009 when Stephanie, her much loved grand-daughter and primary caregiver, died suddenly in her early 40s of an infection. Weeks later Jacquie was dead also. She was farewelled in a memorable tangi at Orimupiko Marae in the presence of her mountain, Taranaki, and buried in her whanau's beautiful coastal urupa at the foot of her mother's grave. Te mate i te wahine he pakaru tekere waka, me e tukuna te kuru pounamu ngaro ai i te wao nui ā Tāne." Ref: Paul Millar, "Jacquie Baxter/J.C. Sturm (1927-2009)."

963 Millicent Baxter, The Memoirs of Millicent Baxter, 141.

964 Ibid., 144.

965 Ibid.,142.

966 Geoff Walker, Email to Penny Griffith, 27 November 2014.

967 Millicent Baxter, The Memoirs of Millicent Baxter, 142

968 Field Punishment No 1 (2014) Film. Producers Donna Malane and Paula Boock.

969 "Cruel punishment for those who would not fight — Interview with Katherine Baxter" 20 April 2014. Sunday Star Times. http://www.stuff.co.nz/entertainment/tv-radio/9954000/Cruel-punishment-for-those-who-would-not-fight.

970 "Field Punishment No.1" Televison Showcase. TVNZ NZ on Air. http://www.nzonair.govt.nz/television/showcase/field-punishment-no1/.

971 Millicent Baxter, The Memoirs of Millicent Baxter, 144.

972 Cole Catley, Recorded Interview with Millicent Baxter. Cass 2 Side 1 (Hocken Library Ms-3099/013), March 1979.

973 Millicent Baxter, The Memoirs of Millicent Baxter, 144.

974   Radio New Zealand Review of The Memoirs of Millicent Baxter.
Alexander Turnbull Library 93-103-13.

975   Lovell-Smith, Easily the Best: The life of Helen Connon,1857–1903, 57.

976   Nicola Broom, "Doing Her Own Thing – at 93." Otago Daily Times, 1 May 1981.

977   Millicent Baxter, Letter to Jean Bertram, 9 May 1981. Papers of James and Jean Bertram.
Alexander Turnbull Library 93-103-13.

978   Millicent Baxter, Letter to Jean Bertram, 9 May 1981. Papers of James and Jean Bertram.
Alexander Turnbull Library 93-103-13.

979   Millicent Baxter, Letter to Jean Bertram, 10 March 1981. Papers of James and Jean Bertram.
Alexander Turnbull Library 93-103-13.

980   Millicent Baxter, Letter to Jean Bertram, 29 September 1980. Papers of James and Jean Bertram.
Alexander Turnbull Library 93-103-13.

981   Hill, "Mr & Mrs Baxter".

982   Nicola Broom, "Doing Her Own Thing – at 93."

983   Millicent Baxter, The Memoirs of Millicent Baxter, 142.

984   Young, "A Poet for a Son."

985   Millicent Baxter, The Memoirs of Millicent Baxter, 142–143

986   Griffith, Interview with Jim Neilan, 16 November 2010.

987   Millicent Baxter, Letter to Jean Bertram 17 November 1981, Papers of James and Jean Bertram.
Alexander Turnbull Library 93-103-13.

988   Millicent Baxter, Letter to Noel Ginn, 18 June 1981.

989   Philippa Skinner, Letter to Anotonietta Baldacchino, 15 July 1983.

990   Griffith, Interview with Frances Mulrennan and Shirley McLeod, 20 May 2010.

991   Ibid.

992   Griffith, Interview with Terence Baxter and his son Kenneth Baxter, 3 February 2010.

993   Ibid.

994   Haydie Best (Gillions Funeral Services), Email to Penny Griffith, 21 March 2014.Gillions
Funeral Services), Email to Penny Griffith, 21 March 2014.

995   Griffith, Interview with Jim La Rooy, 22 February 2011.

996   When a practising Catholic dies, it is not uncommon to have a brief service the night preceding
the Requiem Mass; this often takes the form of reciting the Rosary. This gives people who can't come
the next day, the opportunity to pay their respects and meet family members. The body stays in the
church for the Requiem Mass the next morning. Often, official pallbearers are arranged only for the
funeral itself. Ref: Jim Neilan, Email to Penny Griffith, 18 March 2014.

997   Best, Email to Penny Griffith, 21 March 2014.

998   Katherine Baxter, Email to Penny Griffith, 31 March 2014.

999   "Dunedin City Council Cemeteries Search." http://www.dunedin.govt.nz/facilities/cemeteries/
cemeteries_search?recordid=72353&type=Burial.

INDEX

Index